A DEADLY ART

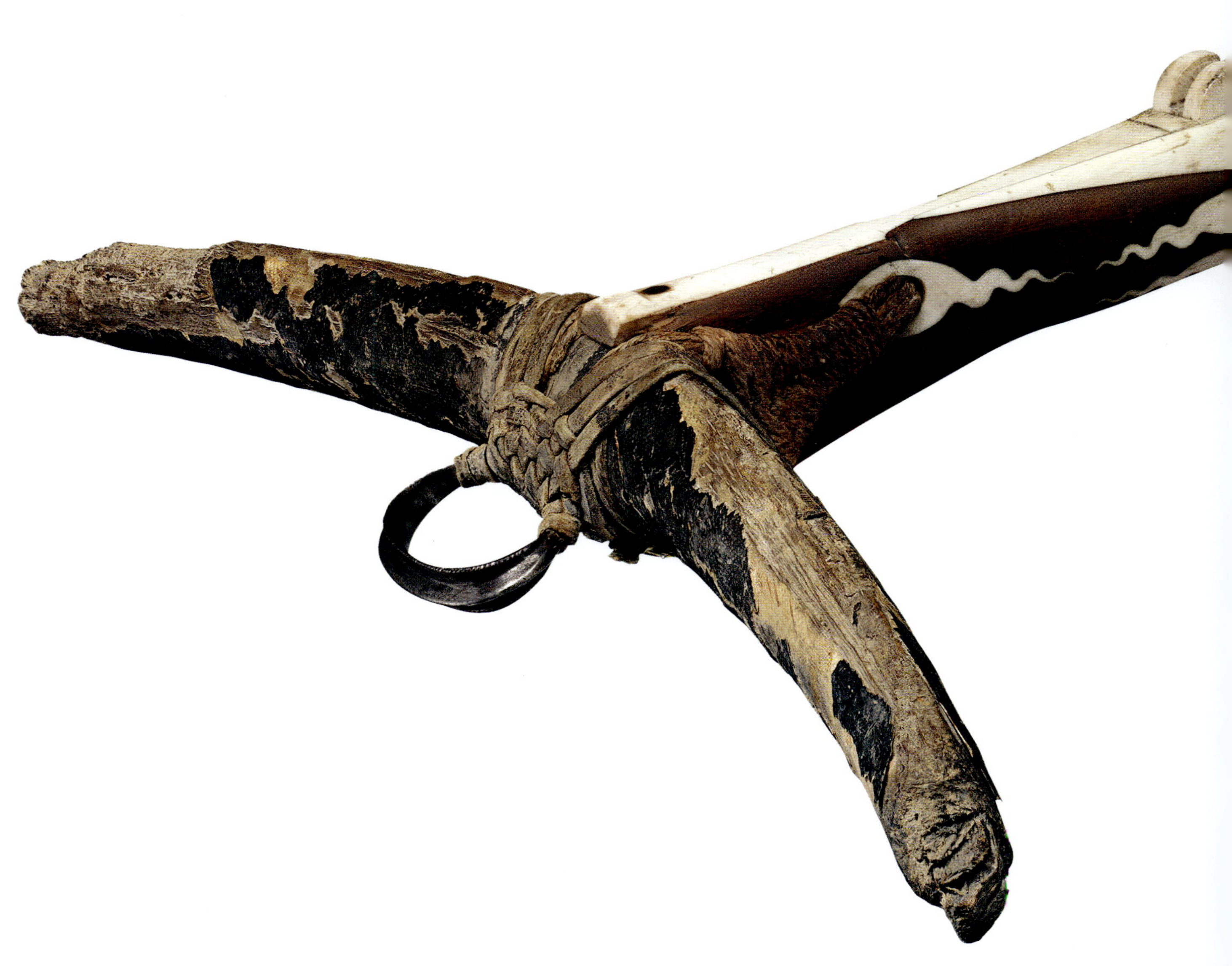

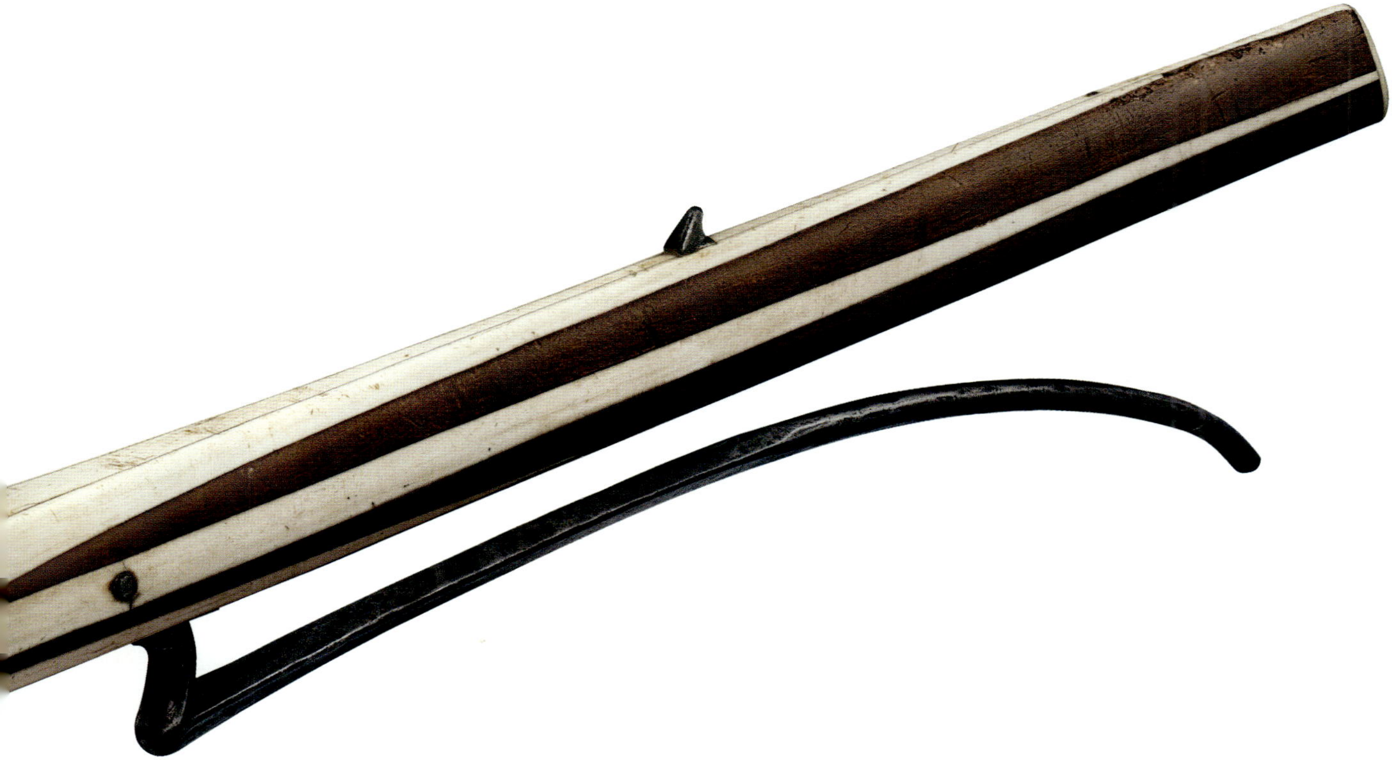

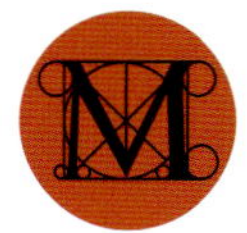

A DEADLY ART

EUROPEAN CROSSBOWS, 1250–1850

DIRK H. BREIDING

THE METROPOLITAN MUSEUM OF ART, NEW YORK

DISTRIBUTED BY YALE UNIVERSITY PRESS, NEW HAVEN AND LONDON

Contents

Director's Foreword

Among the Metropolitan's most beloved spaces are the galleries dedicated to arms and armor. The Museum's collection of fourteen thousand pieces, unrivaled in quality, depth, and diversity, encompasses objects from around the globe and across more than two millennia. Crossbows occupy a singular place in the history of weapons and their technology: they remained in use for more than two thousand years, and, until eclipsed by firepower, reigned as one of the dominant weapons throughout the world. Indeed, changes originally designed to increase the propulsive power of the simple bow evolved into the mechanisms that would define the operation of firearms.

European crossbows, with their projectiles and accessories, were also unique in that they were used—especially in the hunt and in competitions—by all social classes, and by women and children as well as men. For the original owners and subsequent collectors, decoration could be as important as function, and so the reader will find here opulent, artfully wrought exemplars embellished with precious woods, gold, staghorn, mother-of-pearl, and ivory. Presented in the pages that follow are the prized possessions of emperors, kings, and the highest nobility, side by side with more workaday models remarkable for the sophistication of their construction. More than mere artifacts, these weapons open a window onto their times, the craftsmen and artists who made them, and the people who used them.

It is fitting, in this period in which the centenary of the Metropolitan's Department of Arms and Armor is commemorated, to present this study of weapons once nearly universal throughout Europe. Dirk Breiding, former Assistant Curator in the department and now J. J. Medveckis Associate Curator of Arms and Armor at the Philadelphia Museum of Art, has brought his erudition to bear on this fascinating subject. We are grateful to The Carl Otto von Kienbusch Memorial Fund, the Grancsay Fund, STEGO Holding GmbH/STEGO, Inc., and Richard J. Gradkowski for their support of this publication.

Thomas P. Campbell
Director
The Metropolitan Museum of Art

Preface and Acknowledgments

The history of crossbows stretches back more than twenty-five hundred years and around the world. When considered as a technological device, and, indeed, as a physical object, the crossbow embodies a host of firsts and superlatives. Yet, while the bow, from which the crossbow derived, has traditionally been highly esteemed in many societies, the crossbow has rarely attained a comparable status or significance. Nor, by and large, has it borne the symbolic power with which the sword has been invested since ancient times. Historically, the crossbow was not a "noble" weapon, its use in warfare being difficult to reconcile with the principles of chivalry; in battle it was predominantly the weapon of the urban infantry and of mercenaries. (A close examination of pictorial sources and documents, however, reveals a rather more nuanced picture: in the hunt and in competitions, crossbows were shot by nobles and commoners alike, and women and children, too, enjoyed hunting and target shooting with them.) As weapons they would eventually be utterly eclipsed by firearms. The latter factor especially may go some way toward explaining why European crossbows (and related objects such as spanning devices, bolts, and quivers) have received relatively modest scholarly attention.

This general lack of interest has also led to several misconceptions about crossbows, the most prevalent of which are ubiquitous statements maintaining that the Church banned the use of crossbows and allowed its use only against non-Christians.[1] While it is true that the Second Lateran Council under Pope Innocent II (d. 1143) did issue a canon to that effect in 1139, the interpretation of the original Latin is debatable. Not only does the text mention crossbowmen as well as archers, but Pope Innocent at the time was involved in a lengthy conflict with King Roger II of Sicily (1095–1154) and he may have tried to use the Council as a propaganda tool for his own political ends. Part of the title of this book, *A Deadly Art*, is an allusion to this supposed first attempt to ban the crossbow. Deliberately chosen to draw attention to the inherent contradictions between politically motivated attempts of arms control and their modern (mis)interpretations, it also presents an interesting contrast to the historical realities of the crossbow's widespread use to the present day, its technological sophistication, and sometimes extraordinary degree of embellishment.

The Metropolitan Museum's Department of Arms and Armor possesses more than thirty European crossbows, three non-European examples, and several fragments; some twenty spanning devices; a quiver and two bolt boxes; and more than seventy bolts and bolt heads. It is the largest collection in North America, and the quality and historical and art historical significance of many of its objects place the Museum's holdings among the top collections of its kind.

Highlights of the collection include the earliest dated crossbows known (cats. 3, 4), a combination crossbow and wheel-lock gun (cat. 26), and three exceptionally large and elaborately decorated ceremonial projectile heads (cat. 47). Other noteworthy objects are archaeological finds (cat. 1), a richly embellished bolt box (cat. 49), a rare early seventeenth-century English crossbow weapon (cat. 9); and several seventeenth- and eighteenth-century examples from the court of the electors of Saxony (cats. 11–16). The majority of objects is published here for the first time. The present survey, uniting new research with previous studies, is intended as both a collection catalogue, describing the more important holdings in detail, and a concise introduction to the European facets of this intriguing subject. An initial essay provides an overview of the crossbow's origins, as well as its uses and history in Europe up to modern times. Of the six sections that follow, four examine groups of crossbows, one explores spanning devices—the sometimes ornately decorated mechanisms essential to the weapons' operation—and a final section studies examples of projectiles and crossbow accessories. The individual essays opening each of the sections present typological, art historical, and technological outlines of the selected objects.

On the occasion of this publication, a campaign of new photography was undertaken in order to present the most significant views and details of each object. In addition, a selection of crossbows was X-rayed, the wood of a few objects was carefully sampled, and all underwent visual examination by myself as well as by curatorial colleagues and conservators from the Metropolitan and other institutions. The present volume thus offers the most up-to-date physical descriptions of each object, including sometimes surprising new material identifications.

In conclusion, it is my pleasure to acknowledge the truly astonishing support of a large number of colleagues, friends, and family, both at home and abroad; I am only embarrassed that space considerations make it impossible to recognize each contribution fully.

First and foremost, I thank my friend Jens Sensfelder—one of the most knowledgeable people about all matters crossbow—who kindly reviewed most of the Museum's objects with me during a visit in 2011. He subsequently read a first draft of the catalogue entries and provided much additional information and several welcome corrections. I am extremely grateful to Werner Schmid, whose generous backing through STEGO Holding GmbH/STEGO, Inc., helped make this publication possible. I also wish to thank Richard Gradkowski for his support of this project.

At the Metropolitan Museum of Art I am indebted to my friends and former colleagues in the Department of Arms and Armor: Marilynn Doore, Stephen Bluto, Edward Hunter, and especially Hermes Knauer, as well as George Sferra, Jonathan Tavares (now at the Art Institute of Chicago), and Pierre Terjanian. Here, too, I must express my gratitude for all I have learned from Stuart Pyhrr and Donald La Rocca.

Numerous colleagues from other departments, both curatorial and in conservation, also contributed greatly to this publication: Susana Caldeira, Daniel Hausdorf, and Marijn Manuels; Yaëlle Biro; Carmen Bambach, Femke Speelberg, Freyda Spira, Nadine Orenstein, Perrin Stein, and Stijn Alsteens; Maryan Ainsworth and Andrea Bayer; Elena Carrara, Elizabeth Cleland, Daniëlle Kisluk-Grosheide, Erin Pick, Denny Stone, James Draper, Wolfram Koeppe, Marina

Kellen French Curator, Department of European Sculpture and Decorative Arts, and Luke Syson, Iris and B. Gerald Cantor Curator in Charge, Department of European Sculpture and Decorative Arts, as well as Ian Wardropper (now with The Frick Collection); Barbara Boehm, Christine Brennan, Helen Evans, Mary and Michael Jaharis Curator of Byzantine Art, Department of Medieval Art and the Cloisters, Melanie Holcomb, Nancy Wu, Peter Barnet, Charles Little, R. Theo Margelony, and Thomas Vinton; Dita Amory; Rebecca Capua, Valerie Faivre, and Marjorie Shelley; Adriana Rizzo and Marco Leona; Isabel Kim; Teresa Lai and Austin Fisher; Barbara File and James Moske; and the staff of the Thomas J. Watson Library.

I wish to express my appreciation to Peter Zeray, without whose extraordinary photography my writing about these unique objects would look incredibly dull. Likewise, for the indispensable putting it all together and making it shine, I am grateful to Alexandra Bonfante-Warren, Jude Calder, Crystal Dombrow, Jennifer Van Dalsen, Sally Van Devanter, Elizabeth Zechella, Peter Antony, Steve Chanin, Doug Malicki, Mark Polizzotti, and Michael Sittenfeld.

Outside the Metropolitan Museum, I gladly acknowledge the support of the following colleagues: Silke Ackermann, Carole Almond, Amelia Baldeón Iñigo, Anne Becker, Ines Bohn, Ellen Bosniak, Debra Breslin, Katherine Cuffari, Uta Deppe, Stephanie Déprouw, Louise Devoy, Madeleine Ding, Marta Dos Santos, Teresa Esteban, Sandra Faßbender, Michelle Fisher (née Jubin), Wendy Hodkinson, Yulia Igina, Heike F. Jass, Amanda Mikolic, Jane Neet, Christina Nielsen, Eva Oledzka, David Oliver, Alison Patterson, Sophie Picot-Bocquillon, Julia Poole, Robyn Radway, Lena Rangström, Joaneath Spicer, Katrin Tauscher, Annika Williams, as well as Raphaël Abrille, David Alexander, Paul Barton, Martin Baumeister, Christian Beaufort-Spontin, Horst-Dieter Beyerstedt, Adrian Boas, Franz A. Bornschlegel, David Caldwell, Tobias Capwell, Jens Ole Christensen, Francesco Civita, Carl Philip Graf Clam-Martinic, Jeremy Coote, Arthur Credland, Tom DelMar, Ian Eaves, Yuri Efimov, Franz Egger, Karl Graf zu Eltz, Godfrey Evans, Peter Finer, Stephen Fliegel, Jeffrey Forgeng, Andreas Frauendorfer, Gary Friedland, Claude Gaier, Alfred Geibig, Wolfgang Glüber, Manfred H. Grieb, Norbert Henritz, Daniel Hess, Stanislav Hrbatý, Michel Huynh, Geoffrey Jenkinson, Philippe Joris, K. Corey Keeble, David Kizirian, Gernot Klatte, Karl Knauer, Stefan Krause, Bengt Kylsberg, Eckhart Leisering, Sven Lueken, Stefan Mäder, Philippe Malgouyres, Jürg Meier, David Miller, Yuri Miller (†), Philippe Missillier, Hellmuth Möhring, Ralph Moffat, Alfred Moldovan, Christoph Nicht, Helmut Nickel, Vsevolod Obraztsov, Sergey Orlenko, Michael Otto, Angus Patterson, Matthias Pfaffenbichler, Steffen Poser, Michael Pourfar, Gerhard Quaas, Bernhard Freiherr von Rechenberg, William Reid, Olivier Renaudeau, Holger Richter, Anibal Rodriguez, Bernhard Roosens, Sergey Rymsha, Komei Sakai, Reinhard Sänger, Jörg Schärer, Holger Schuckelt, Lorenz Seelig, Matthias Senn, Nathaniel Silver, Robert Smith, Hugh Soar, Alvaro Soler del Campo, Graf Spiegelfeld, Chris Streek, Daniel Suter, Eric Vaule, Matthias Weiss, Romain Wenz, Peter Wiegand, Robert Woosnam-Savage, and Jerome Zwanger.

Finally, I dedicate this publication to the four most important people in my life: my parents, Ingrid, Jens, and Elisa, and my wife, Jasmine, in gratitude for their unfailing patience and encouragement: *mementote amamini*!

A DEADLY ART

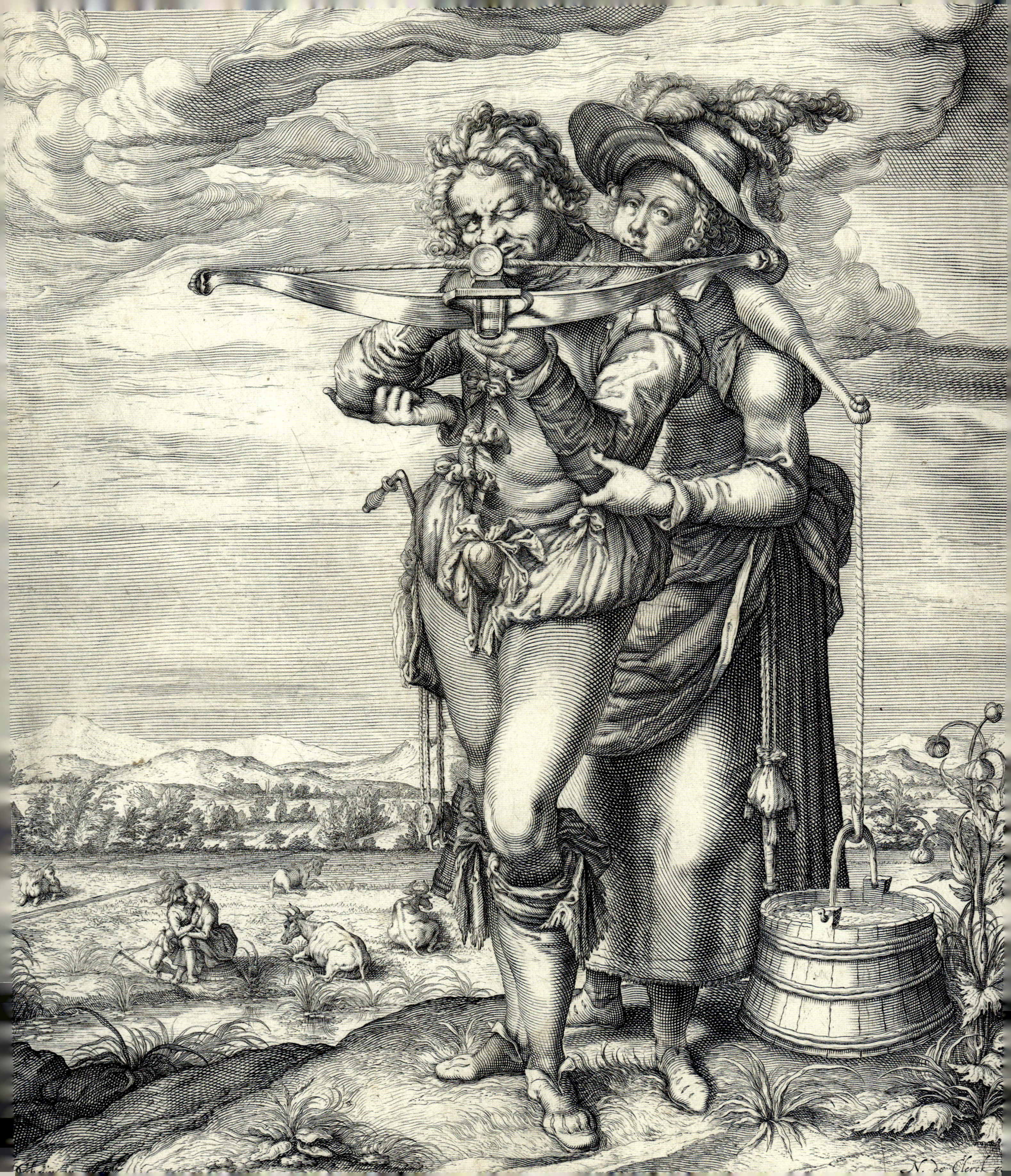
N. de Clerck.

European Crossbows:
An Introduction

crossbow consists of a bow mounted horizontally and at a right angle to the front, or fore-end, of a support, known as a tiller, or stock (fig. 2). The tiller is fitted with a catch or a lock that allows the bowstring to be retained in a "spanned," that is, drawn, position for any length of time. The history of the bow, or self-bow, of which the crossbow is a further development, has been traced back more than ten thousand years, but it is still uncertain when and where bows were first mounted to a support to form a crossbow. The earliest reliable documentary and archaeological evidence for its use comes from China, in the mid–first millennium B.C.; however, whether these Chinese weapons were introduced to Europe, or whether the European crossbows were an independent development, has still not been satisfactorily explained. In fact, except for two late Roman depictions from southern France, probably dating from the fourth or fifth century A.D., practically nothing is known about the construction, appearance, and use of European crossbows until the Middle Ages (the ninth to the twelfth century). During the past thousand years, however, the crossbow has at one time or another appeared on every continent around the world (including the seas around Antarctica), and until the mid-sixteenth century it remained one of the most powerful handheld weapons known to humankind.

In terms of practicality, the crossbow has often been compared to its ancestor, the self-bow, and occasionally to its successor, the firearm. For the greater part of the period under consideration, the three weapons differed comparatively little in their effective range and varied only somewhat in the initial power that their projectiles delivered at various distances. In terms of individual usage, a few general observations can be summarized. Self-bows are highly efficient weapons that can be produced cheaply, are light, and offer a relatively fast rate of discharge—an experienced archer could release about twelve arrows a minute. However, proficiency with this weapon required years of training with increasingly stronger bows, and the force of even the famed longbow is limited by the physical strength of the archer. The same limitation makes it difficult to take precise aim

Figure 1 Andries Stock (Netherlandish, 1572/82–after 1648), after Jacques de Gheyn II (Netherlandish, 1565–1629). *The Archer and the Milkmaid,* ca. 1610. Engraving, sheet 16 15/16 × 12 15/16 in. (41.4 x 32.8 cm). Published by Nicolaes de Clerck. The Metropolitan Museum of Art, New York, The Elisha Whittelsey Collection, The Elisha Whittelsey Fund, 1949 (49.95.1331)

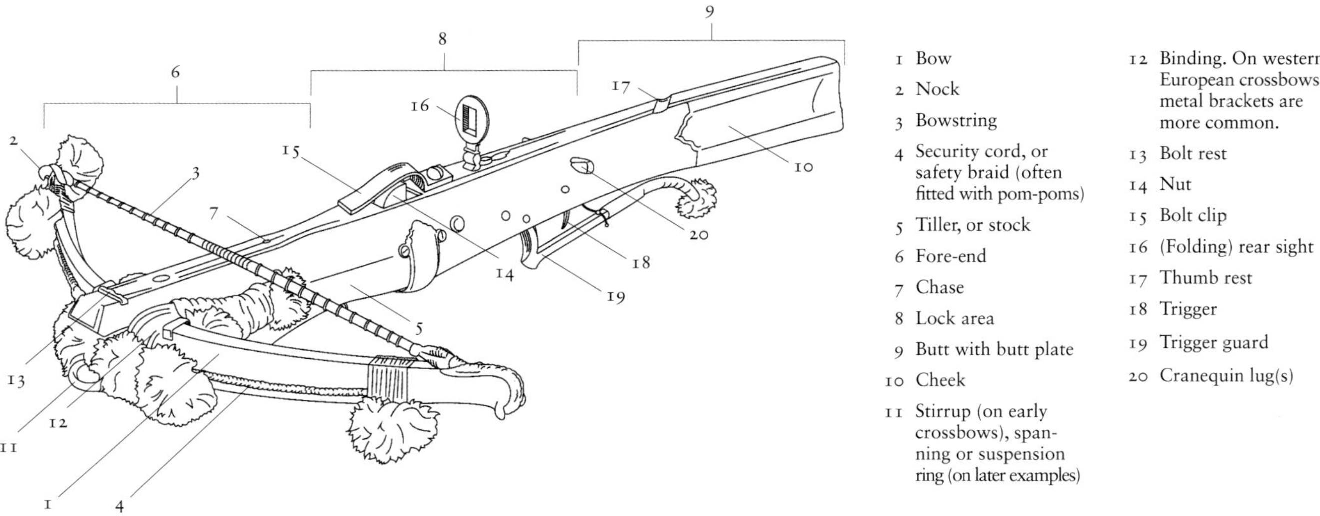

Figure 2 Diagram of crossbow

over an extended period of time; because of the considerable exertion required by the arm muscles that hold the bow spanned, those muscles will soon begin shaking and thus spoil the aim.

The crossbow, on the other hand, is more complex and heavier than a self-bow, and appears to have been more expensive, though still affordable to large parts of the populace. As a result the power of the bow did not remain limited by muscle strength for long: early crossbows could be spanned with both arms; beginning in the thirteenth century, semi-mechanical spanning aids were used; and, from the fifteenth century on, ever more powerful crossbows required increasingly complex mechanical spanning devices. Since the bowstring is retained in position not by the user's hand but by a catch or a lock, he or she can hold the spanned weapon without exertion, take aim for any length of time, and release a shot in a more controlled manner. Proficiency with a crossbow, therefore, may require practice but not specific physical capabilities that have to be built up through years of training: even an extremely powerful weapon can be spanned and shot by a person of average strength. The prices of these advantages are a slower rate of discharge—about one to four bolts a minute—and the need to alleviate through ever more complex internal-release mechanisms the greater strain that the stronger bows put on the lock and trigger.

The first firearms appeared almost simultaneously in parts of Europe as far apart as Italy and England during the 1320s. Commonly believed to have been crude and ineffective, these early guns were indeed of very simple construction, yet difficult to make, and expensive and cumbersome to use: gunpowder was costly to produce and to buy, and it took at least as long to prepare to fire a shot as to span a crossbow. Nevertheless, firearms were disseminated throughout the European continent within only a few decades after their first appearance. By the fifteenth century, advances in technology—including the appearance of more sophisticated ignition systems, inspired by crossbow release mechanisms—allowed guns to compete seriously with crossbows. Within two generations the latter were largely replaced on the battlefield—though not in the hunt or in competitions.

Documentary evidence indicates that crossbows were in use throughout Europe by the tenth and eleventh centuries, from Scotland and Scandinavia in the north to the Mediterranean shores in the south, although pictorial evidence remains exceedingly rare until the end of the twelfth century. The earliest sources—a handful of written references, stone carvings, manuscript illuminations, and frescoes—show that crossbows were employed both in war and for the hunt. By the twelfth and thirteenth centuries they also featured in competitions and other public entertainments, which, not unlike the medieval tournament, had probably evolved from military training exercises. In this context, the importance of the often-quoted "ban of the crossbow," issued by the Second Lateran Council in 1139, and of its later iterations has often been overstated: the Latin wording is ambiguous, and—as demonstrated here—none of these pronouncements had any lasting effect. On the contrary, during the thirteenth century and later, the crossbow steadily gained in efficiency and became increasingly popular, factors that contributed directly to the development of plate armor.

The crossbow never attained the social status of a knightly weapon, most likely because it was a long-range weapon, and fighting with it was not considered noble. Nevertheless, the military position of captain of crossbowmen was highly esteemed in Spain, France, and to some extent also in areas of Italy, while members of crossbow societies enjoyed considerable social status, especially in the Low Countries and Germany.

Crossbows in War

During the high Middle Ages and the early Renaissance, that is, roughly between the twelfth and fifteenth centuries, crossbows were held in high regard as efficient weapons of war. This is attested to by the large numbers kept in castle armories and city arsenals, and by the fact that they are often found among the possessions of male citizens, who were expected to purchase their own arms and armor in order to defend the city during times of conflict. In addition, city councils and the nobility alike frequently employed retainers and mercenaries armed with crossbows; these soldiers either provided their own equipment or were outfitted by their employers. Members of the nobility rarely carried crossbows on the battlefield, as they were generally not considered to be chivalric weapons—among the most famous exceptions was King Richard I of England, "the Lion-Hearted" (1157–1199); in a case of tragic irony, the king was himself mortally wounded by a crossbow bolt.

Crossbowmen fought on foot and on horseback. Depending on their function, these soldiers usually wore open-faced helmets and light armor for the torso (fig. 3), although some

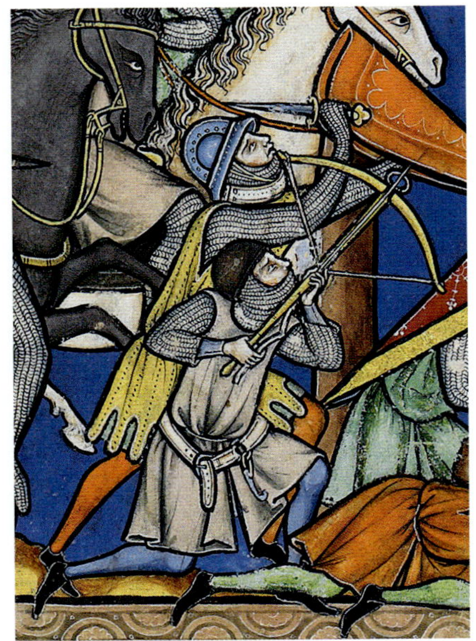

Figure 3 A crossbowman in battle, detail of an illumination depicting the conquest of Ai. French, ca. 1244–54. Mixed media on vellum, ca. 15⅜ × 11¹¹⁄₁₆ in. (39 × 30 cm). The Morgan Library and Museum, New York (M.638, fol. 10v); purchased by J. P. Morgan (1867–1943) in 1916

depictions also show them clad in full armor from head to toe. In addition to their main weapon—one or more crossbows and a supply of ten to sixty bolts—they often carried a sword and dagger. Most infantry crossbowmen were further protected by shields known as pavises. These were propped up on the ground, offering protection especially during the spanning and reloading process, when crossbowmen were most vulnerable. Made from a curved wooden core covered with rawhide or leather, a pavise might come in either of two sizes. The personal examples carried by individual soldiers were about waist-high. Most of these were relatively plain, usually painted only with the employer's heraldry (fig. 4), but the decoration of some central and eastern European examples could be quite exuberant (fig. 5). A substantially larger variety—as tall as or taller than a man—was much heavier and less mobile but offered considerable protection for small units of combatants (fig. 4).

Crossbows were ideally suited for sieges, where they were used by both sides for sharpshooting, to support or repel assaults, and for discharging incendiary projectiles against the besieged city or castle or the siege engines of the attacking forces. Especially in such circumstances large versions of the weapon were also employed: the "great crossbow" and its relative, the springald.[1] Both can be classified as small- and medium-size artillery, which were mounted on trestles or other frames or on carriages, and were operated by small crews. A springald, although similar in appearance to and often confused with a great crossbow, was not fitted with a large bow but instead propelled the same large and heavy projectiles by means of two torsion-operated arms (cat. 44d).

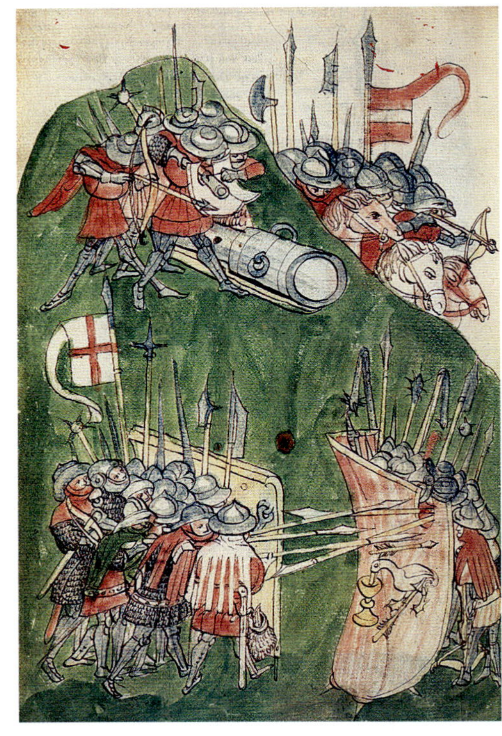

Figure 4 Attributed to Johannes Hartlieb (Austrian, ca. 1410–1468). Battle scene from the Hussite Wars. Illuminated page from a treatise on the art of warfare, ca. 1440. Watercolor on paper, folio ca. 12¹⁄₃₂ × 8³⁄₁₆ in. (30.5 × 20.7 cm). Österreichische Nationalbibliothek, Vienna (Cod. 3062, fol. 147v). Note the use of crossbows by soldiers on foot alongside firearms, as well as on horseback (in the background).

On the open battlefield, infantry crossbowmen were deployed against cavalry and infantry, and, just like other archers, shot in volleys. Especially in central Europe, they also fought from battle carts that were arranged to form a circular fortress (fig. 6). In addition, mounted crossbowmen often formed part of the light cavalry in order to engage an opponent's infantry or their own counterparts, and period artwork not infrequently depicts them as scouts.

For naval warfare, crossbowmen employed a combination of battlefield and siege tactics (volleys, sharpshooting, and the use of incendiary projectiles). It is often noted that the crossbow's slower rate of discharge placed its users at a disadvantage, compared with archers armed with self-bows. While this assessment is generally accurate—especially for crossbows that required mechanical spanning devices—considerable evidence suggests that this disadvantage was reduced when crossbowmen made use of two or more weapons each, as well as of stationary spanning devices, with the spare weapons being readied by attendants. On and off the battlefield, finally, the crossbow's versatility—it could be used by foot soldiers and cavalry, on the open battlefield and during sieges, in urban warfare and aboard ship—also made it an ideal weapon for bodyguards (fig. 7).

As weapons of war, crossbows were gradually replaced by firearms during the second half of the fifteenth century, and by the middle of the sixteenth century they had lost any military significance, except aboard ship, where their use is occasionally recorded until the seventeenth century.

The Hunt

The crossbow was also a popular hunting weapon. Both self-bows and crossbows are ideally suited for this activity, because they offer a near-silent discharge (unlike firearms, which produce flashes and smoke), while allowing the hunter to stay at a distance from dangerous or shy animals. However, the self-bow requires more room for operation and some movement immediately before the shot (lifting the bow and drawing back the bowstring), a limitation that does not apply to the crossbow, since it is easily held

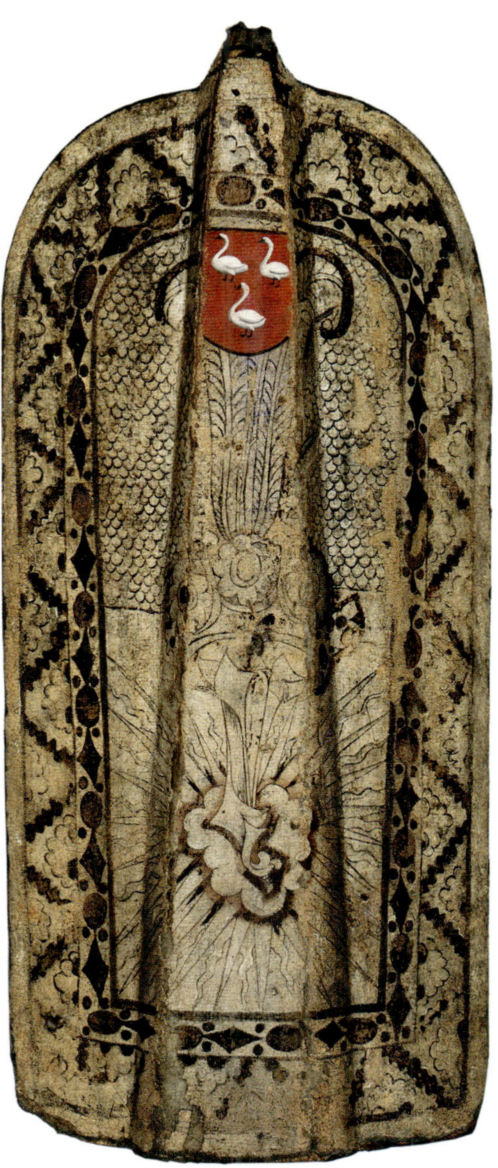

Figure 5 Infantry shield (pavise) decorated with the arms of Zwickau, Bohemian (prob. Chomutov), ca. 1440–50. Wood, leather, gesso, silver foil, polychromy, 42½ × 20½ in. (107.9 × 52 cm). The Metropolitan Museum of Art, New York, Bashford Dean Memorial Collection, Funds from various donors, 1929 (29.158.595)

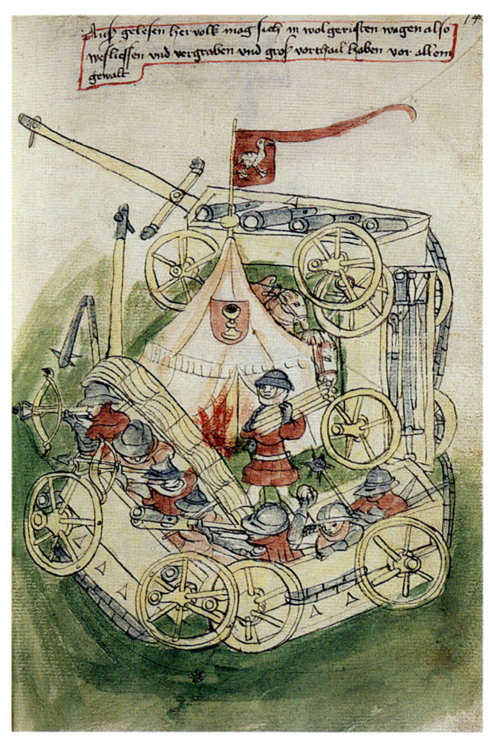

Figure 6 Attributed to Johannes Hartlieb (Austrian, ca. 1410–1468). A Hussite wagon fort. Illuminated page from a treatise on the art of warfare, ca. 1440. Watercolor on paper, ca. 12¹⁄₃₂ × 8³⁄₁₆ in. (30.5 × 20.7 cm). Österreichische Nationalbibliothek, Vienna (Cod. 3062, fol. 148r)

Figure 7 Chess figure of a bishop, accompanied by a bodyguard of crossbowmen. Southern German, ca. 1350–1450. Ivory, H. 3¾ in. (9.3 cm). The British Museum, London (1857,0804.34)

and aimed in a spanned position for prolonged periods of time.[2] The rate of discharge was not as critical in hunting as it was in war—although the ability to shoot quickly certainly was. To minimize this disadvantage, aristocratic hunting parties sometimes included servants who spanned one weapon while another weapon was being shot.

Although crossbows appear to have been used as hunting weapons during the late Roman period—an observation based only on the two reliefs from France cited above—continuous documentation for them is not available until about the tenth or eleventh century, when they were evidently used for stalking game. In most parts of Europe, the hunting of large prey such as bear, deer, and wild boar, as well as certain birds, was a privilege of the nobility, referred to in German and Spanish as the "high hunt." Numerous smaller animals and most birds, on the other hand, were regarded as lesser prey, and in many regions of Europe could also be hunted by members of the humbler classes, who no doubt supplemented their diet with fowl and small game whenever the possibility presented itself.

For the nobility, hunting provided an important occasion for self-representation, including the demonstration of physical ability. Requiring an expenditure of money, time, and effort, it was an entertainment befitting the social status of the ruling elite, while providing opportunities for forging (political) friendships and conducting informal diplomacy. As one of the foremost hunting weapons, crossbows were prized possessions, symbols of high rank, and, as such, exchanged as personal presents and diplomatic gifts. During the Renaissance, when conspicuous consumption and display were quasi-virtues, their costly embellishment often reflected their owners' prestige (cats. 3, 4, 11, 27, 31).

The ruling classes usually hunted large game on horseback and on foot, assisted by groups that included beaters and packs of dogs. Manuscript illuminations from the famous *Livre de la chasse*, written between 1387 and 1389 by Gaston III (1331–1391), comte de Foix, known as Phoebus, illustrate how self-bows and crossbows were used for stalking prey (figs. 8, 9). These techniques included artificial hedges and nets for laying traps and ambushes; even decoys and hunting carts are depicted (fig. 9).

By the sixteenth century, beaters were increasingly driving swift prey such as deer toward nets, or fences, or into bodies of water so that hunters could shoot them more easily (fig. 10). Not only did this method allow royalty and the high nobility to stage large-scale hunts as prestigious pastimes, but, because of the reduced risks, almost the entire court could participate, including women, children, and guests (fig. 11).

During the medieval period small animals were hunted with crossbows that were either correspondingly smaller than those normally used for war or hunting or else shot blunt stunning bolts, in order not to damage a valuable pelt or destroy the animal completely. Since at least the fourteenth century, self-bows discharging stones or pellets from a pouch fitted to a double bowstring were used for this purpose, and pellet-shooting crossbows probably appeared about the same time, although neither documents, visual evidence, nor extant examples appear to survive from before the sixteenth century (cats. 19–24).

After 1600, firearms became the preferred hunting weapon of the nobility. The invention of the flintlock mechanism in France at that time quickly led to the development of lighter and more elegant weapons, which were especially suited to shooting birds in flight, or "on the wing." However, large game such as deer and wild boar was still hunted with crossbows in England, Spain, and certain German-speaking regions. Hunters also continued to shoot small mammals, such as rabbits and squirrels, and birds, especially waterfowl, with either blunt stunning bolts or pellets, and pellet crossbows of various types retained their

Figures 8, 9 Wild boar hunt and deer hunt with a camouflaged cart. Illuminations from Gaston III Phoebus, comte de Foix (1331–1391), *Livre de la Chasse*. French, ca. 1406–7. Mixed media on vellum, 15 × 11⁷⁄₁₆ in. (38.1 × 29 cm). The Morgan Library and Museum, New York (M.1044, fols. 105r. 103r). Bequest of Clara S. Peck, 1983

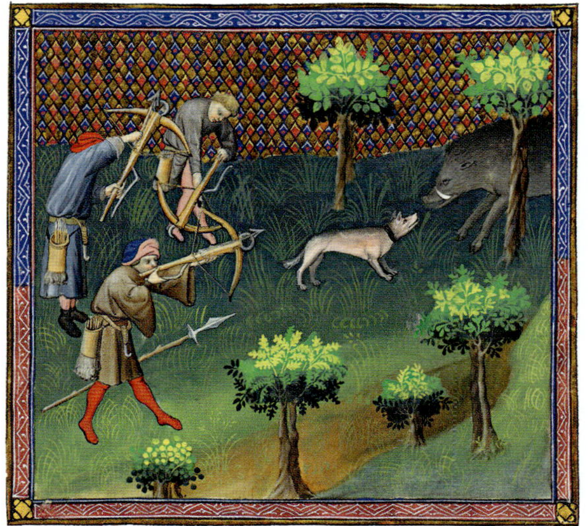

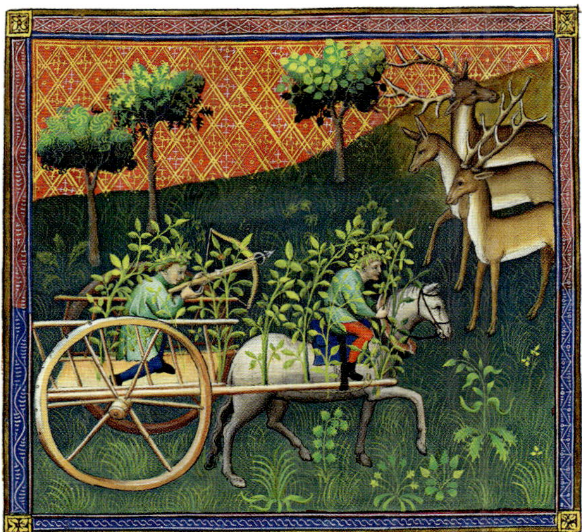

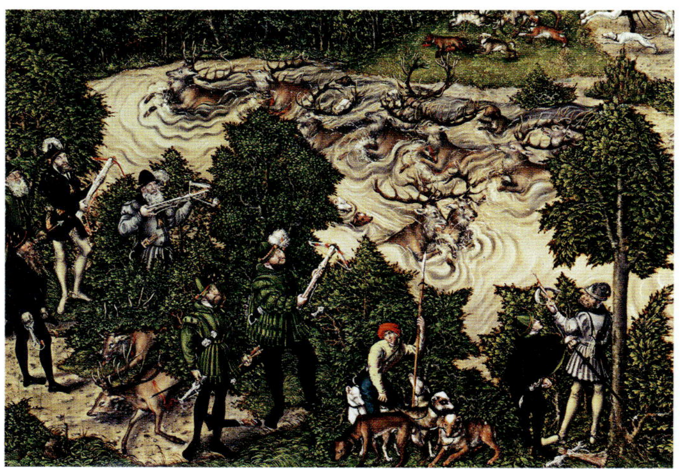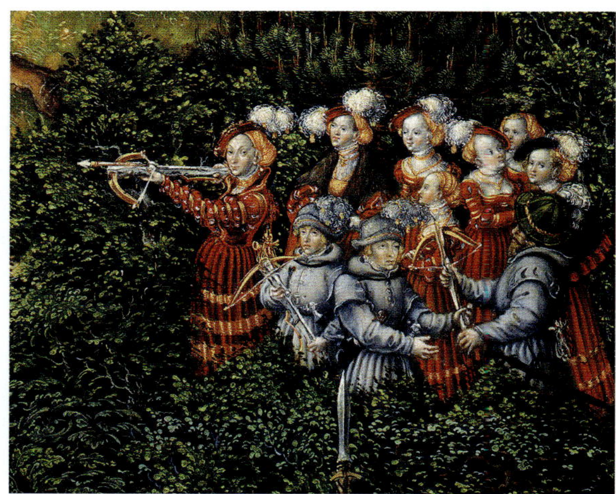

popularity in some regions—England, for example—until well into the first half of the nineteenth century.

Civilian Life and Competitions

The history of the European crossbow is closely connected with the rise of medieval and early modern cities, from the twelfth through the fifteenth century, an age during which conflicts ranged from frequent large-scale warfare to incessant local feuds. In order to defend not only their physical existence but also their political interests and growing mercantile wealth against other cities and the nobility, many urban communities throughout Europe obliged their inhabitants to purchase and maintain arms and armor. To ensure that an adequate number of functioning weapons would be available at all times, additional crossbows were stored in urban arsenals and maintained by crossbow makers paid by the city. Legal provisions regulating the possession and use of crossbows, as well as their frequent occurrence in inventories and wills, indicate the weapon's wide dissemination.

The crossbow was well suited to a civilian population, as it required little training, compared with the self-bow or sword, for example. Nevertheless, city councils often officially supported regular practice, mostly through financial aid and legal provisions, and in many cases even mandated it. It is probably from such gatherings that local and regional shooting competitions developed, and that the men who regularly came together began to form societies of crossbowmen, as did archers, and later, handgunners. The earliest associations of crossbowmen may have originated during the twelfth century, although substantial documentary evidence, such as charters, lists of members, and commissioned artworks, survives only from the fourteenth century on, in particular for France and the Netherlands. By that time, many of the larger towns or cities in continental Europe were home to at least one of these societies.

The establishment of such an association required approval by the city council, the ruling noble family, or, in some cases, both. These local authorities thereby gained a well-trained urban militia, capable of serving on the battlefield, and that, in peacetime, could be called upon to perform police and guard duties. At the same time, the new bodies could be controlled, with the number of members often restricted so that they did not become too powerful. For its part, the association was endowed with social status, and frequently also received financial and material support, as well as privileges for its individual members, including clothing, alcoholic beverages for any gatherings, or tax exemptions. Their role as military forces and urban police, their wealthy and influential members, and, last but not least, the political patronage and sporting enthusiasm of the nobility—who occasionally joined the societies and frequently participated in regional shooting competitions—ensured that crossbow associations rose to social and political prominence, especially in France, the Low Countries, and the German-speaking regions.

Most crossbow societies organized annual competitions to determine the best marksman among them. The winner was declared "king" for a year; became the head, or captain, of the society; and had to organize the following year's competition. The "king" might also enjoy privileges such as additional tax exemptions.

A society's annual event, like the large regional crossbow competitions, was an important occasion for social gatherings and public entertainments, not infrequently on a very lavish scale. These hugely popular contests were a matter of civic pride, sometimes associated with diplomatic efforts, and city councils often contributed to the costs of hosting the more important events, or they might pay the travel expenses of local members, allowing them to compete in other cities. By the fifteenth century, crossbow associations were influential social bodies; the membership and patronage of the high nobility brought exclusivity and guaranteed political protection against the influence of rival societies, for example. The presence of noble members also made the societies attractive to their peers and to wealthy patricians, endowing even members belonging to the urban bourgeoisie with an elite status. All members were entitled to wear the society's prestigious badge (figs. 12, 13) and held privileged positions in civic and religious festivals. For example, at the Procession of the Relic of the Holy Blood in Bruges—one of the largest festivals of its kind in the Low Countries—members of the local Crossbow Society of Saint George walked on either side of the relic to protect it. Commissions by individual members, or the entire society, ranged from paintings and goldsmith works by local artists to shooting ranges and prestigious buildings. By the seventeenth and eighteenth centuries members of several French crossbow societies even referred to themselves as *chevaliers d'arbalète*, or "knights of the crossbow" (fig. 14).

The shooting ranges of these urban crossbow societies were usually outside the city, but close to it, for example, in the moat by the city walls. By the sixteenth century, a shooting ground might comprise a primary range, adjacent to the society's building, and a number of practice ranges, as well as one or more associated buildings nearby that could be used for indoor shooting, festivities, and storage.

During the fifteenth century, the nobility also began to frequent archery and crossbow shooting ranges, or had them built for their exclusive use. By the sixteenth century, some of the wealthiest princes of the Holy Roman Empire, such as the dukes of Württemberg and those of Saxony, so enjoyed crossbow shooting as a pastime that they built prestigious "shooting houses" near their main residences.

Shooting competitions with crossbows can be divided into two kinds. The first type, target shooting, was popular throughout Europe: participants shot horizontally at a target set up at a certain distance (fig. 15). The requirements varied in the number of bolts to be shot, the distance to the target, and whether contestants were to be standing or seated.

Informal gatherings had taken place since the early Middle Ages but were rarely recorded; beginning in the 1300s, however, local, regional, and interregional shooting competitions became frequent, ranging from smaller events to large festivities that lasted days or even weeks. Since the latter especially attracted great numbers of participants and spectators, some of them visitors from outside the town, they required almost the same kind of organization as chivalric tournaments or large fairs. Handwritten or printed invitations were sent out to

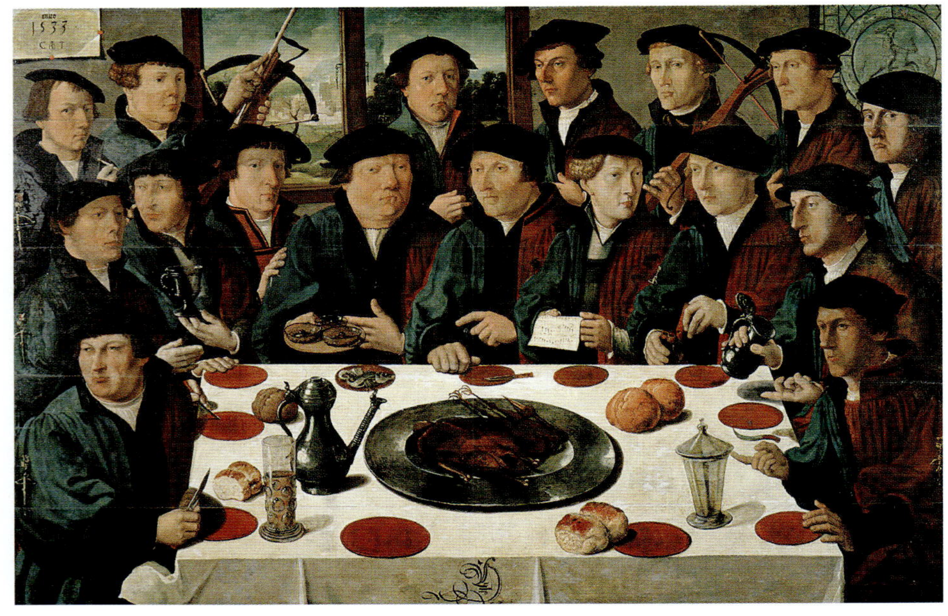

Figure 12 Cornelis Anthonisz. (Netherlandish, ca. 1505–1553). *Banquet of Members of Amsterdam's Saint Joris Civic Guard of Crossbowmen*, dated 1533. Oil on panel, 51³⁄₁₆ × 81¹¹⁄₃₂ in. (130 × 206.5 cm). Amsterdam Museum (SA 7279)

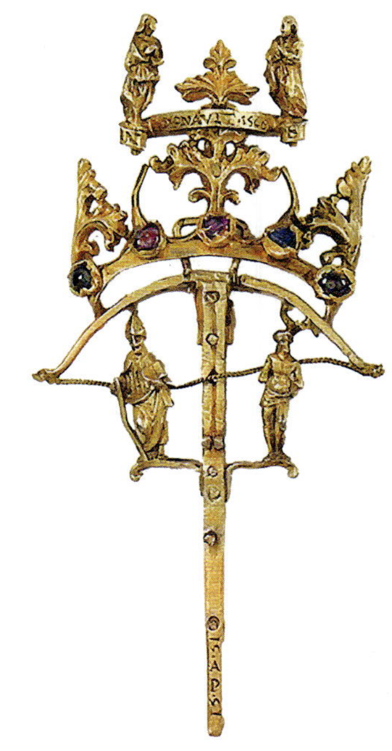

Figure 13 Badge of an unidentified society of crossbowmen. Probably Netherlandish, ca. 1525–75 (with later alterations). Gilded silver with stones in gold settings, H. 3¾ in. (9.5 cm). The Victoria and Albert Museum, London (2276-1855)

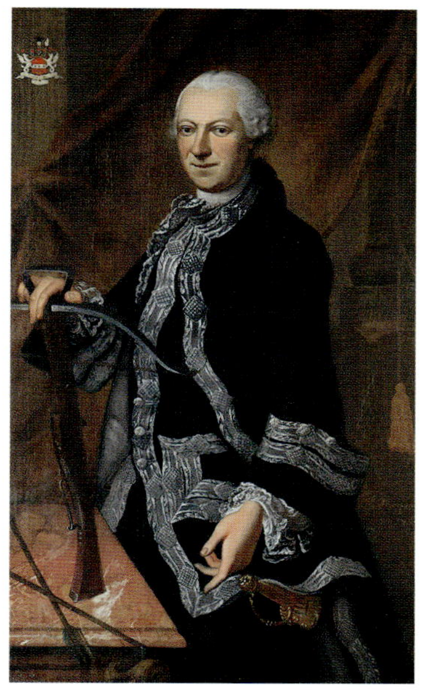

cities, their crossbow societies, and the nobility, sometimes as much as a year in advance. Surviving examples show the detailed information they contained: the weapons to be employed—self-bows, crossbows, firearms, or any combination of these—the size of the target, the distance to it, the number of shots allowed per contestant, and the permissible diameter of each bolt (fig. 16). These announcements almost invariably identify the prizes, which might be items of clothing, silver- and goldsmith works, substantial sums of money—even a live bull.

The second type of competition is known by descriptive terms such as "shooting at the bird" or "shooting at the popinjay"; the latter English word is probably a corruption of the Anglo-Norman, French, or Germanic word *papegei* (parrot), which exists in numerous spellings.[3] The practice of shooting at a bird (initially a live animal, later replaced by a target in the form of a bird) was already known in antiquity and either survived to or was revived in the Middle Ages. There are few specific documentary references before the sixteenth century, and the sport appears to have been more popular north of the Alps, from Scotland and the Low Countries in the north, to Switzerland in the south, France in the west, and Saxony and Bohemia in the east. Shooting almost vertically at the figure of a bird—most often of wood, but sometimes of leather or clay—that had been mounted atop a high pole, the contestants attempted to shoot off parts of the bird, for each of which they would be rewarded with a prize (fig. 17).

Historical accounts of these events, as well as the invitations mentioned above, provide details confirming the accuracy and efficiency of medieval and early modern crossbows. The pole supporting the popinjay varied in height from about 49 feet (15 m) to about 137 feet (42 m), while the dimension of the target ranged from lifesize to a bird that could be several feet tall on the highest poles; the largest popinjays measured 13 feet (4 m) in height and were used in nineteenth-century Dresden, where

Figure 14 A. Marquardt (Netherlandish, act. 1761–84). *Portrait of Pieter van Leyden*, dated 1765. Oil on canvas, 52⅜ × 33¹⁄₁₆ in. (133 × 84 cm). Gorcums Museum, Gorinchem (4971)

Figure 15 Matthias Gerung (German, ca. 1500–ca. 1568). Target shooting with crossbows, bows, and firearms (among other pastimes), detail of *Melancholy in the Garden of Life*, dated 1558. Mixed media on panel (limewood), 34²¹⁄₃₂ × 26¹³⁄₁₆ in. (88 × 68 cm). Kunsthalle, Karlsruhe (2619)

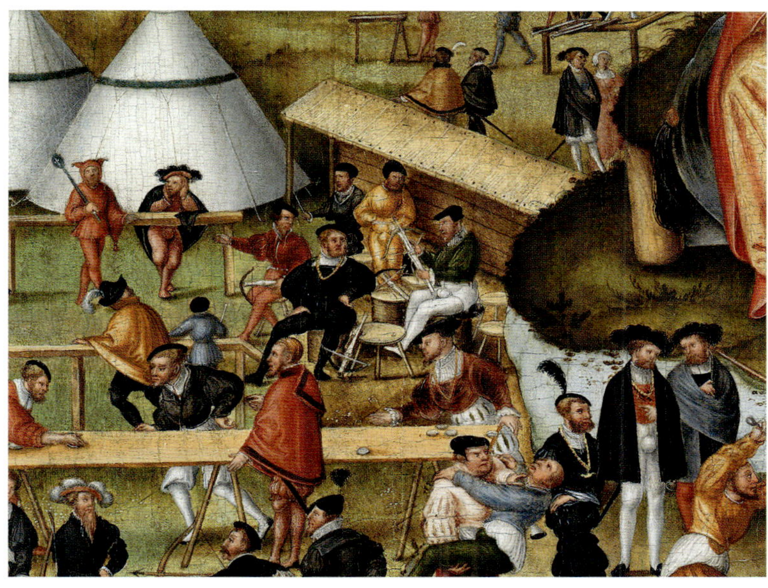

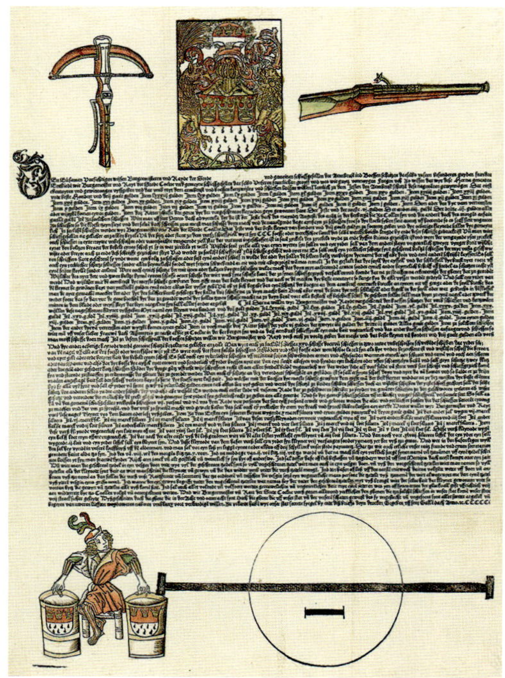

Figure 16 Broadside: An invitation to a target-shooting contest with crossbows and firearms. German, dated 1501. Hand-colored woodcut. National Gallery of Art, Washington, D.C. (Rosenwald Collection, 1951.16.4)

Figure 17 *Shooting Ground for the Annual* Vogelschießen *in Dresden.* German, ca. 1830. Pencil and gouache on paper, 7⁵/₁₆ × 10¹⁵/₁₆ in. (18.6 × 27.7 cm), private collection. Note the three targets mounted at different heights.

contestants stood some 98 feet (30 m) from the pole and thus shot diagonally upward at the bird from 169 feet (52 m) away.[4] For target shooting, the distance could be almost twice that, and the targets were much smaller: at a target-shooting contest in Nuremberg in the summer of 1458, participants had fifty shots each to hit a mark nearly 300 feet (91 m) away; the target measured less than 6 inches (15 cm) in diameter. The winner of the competition—out of 321 contestants—managed to hit the mark eleven times.[5]

By the early seventeenth century, crossbows had been all but replaced by firearms as weapons of war. Hunters, too, were exchanging large, heavy crossbows for lighter firearms with modern ignition systems; only light crossbows continued to play a small role in hunting. From the fifteenth century on, firearms had also become steadily more important for both leisurely and competitive target shooting, often appearing alongside crossbows in the same event, and by the nineteenth century they had largely replaced the latter as

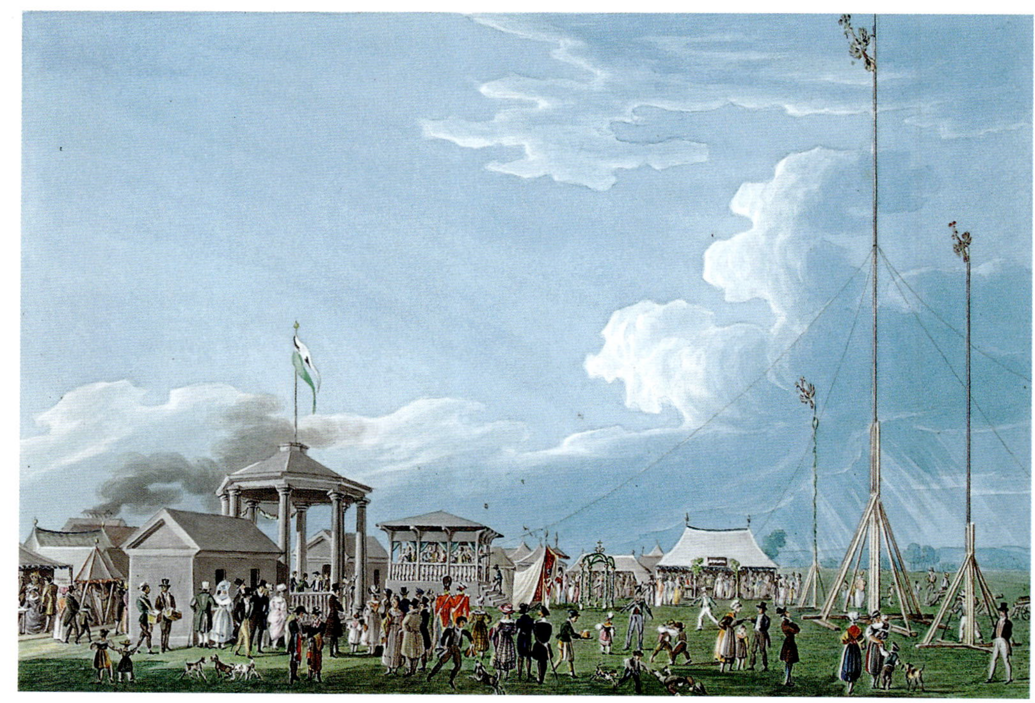

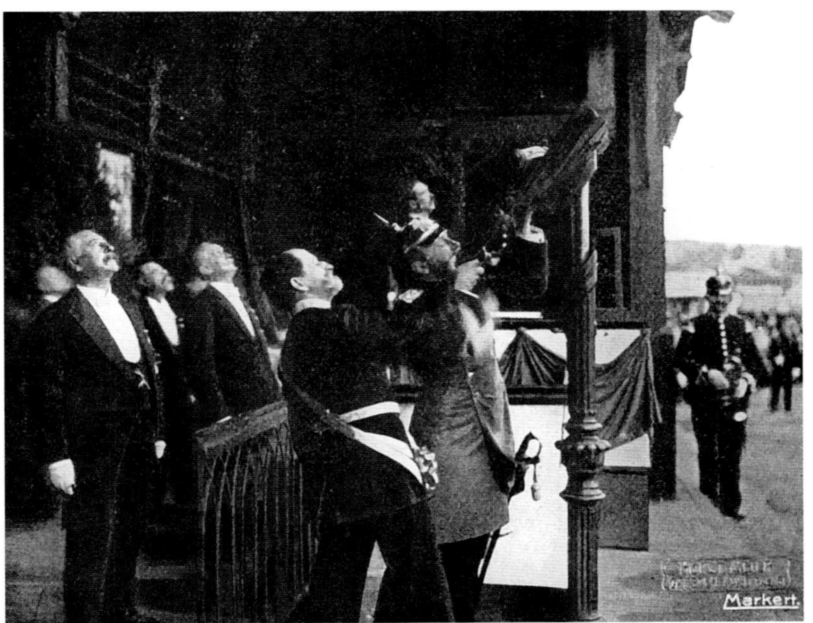

Figure 18 King Friedrich Augustus III of Saxony shooting a crossbow during the annual *Vogelschießen* in Dresden. German, ca. 1905. The king is assisted by Friedrich Julius Theodor Hänisch (1845–1928), Royal Master of Arms (*Königlicher Schützenmeister*), the last of his line and a direct descendant of Johann Gottfried Hänisch the Elder, who made catalogues 14, 15, and 16 and to whom catalogues 12 and 13 are attributed.

target weapons. In several parts of Europe, political events such as the Thirty Years War (1618–48), the French Revolution and the Napoleonic Wars (1789–1815), and the national democratic upheavals in France and Germany during the mid-nineteenth century accelerated the gradual decline of many crossbow societies, usually owing to government restrictions and general loss of membership. Nevertheless, crossbow competitions survived in some areas, retaining their importance as social events, for example in Saxony, and in certain Dutch, Belgian, and Italian cities.

Beginning in the late nineteenth century, the crossbow has made occasional appearances once more in the areas in which it once reigned supreme. During World War I, crossbows and crossbow-like devices were used by French and German troops in trench warfare for hurling hand grenades, and since World War II crossbows have been employed by snipers and other special forces. When the possession of firearms was widely banned in Germany following World War II, hunters and forest rangers used crossbows instead, and they have since also reemerged as alternative hunting weapons in other parts of the world, including Russia and both South and North America.

The crossbow's popularity as a target weapon may, at times, have dimmed, but as a sport or pastime target-shooting has never vanished entirely. In addition to Italy, the Low Countries, and the German-speaking regions (fig. 18), crossbows have, during the twentieth century, also appeared in contests in the United States.

1 | Early Crossbows

The study of early crossbows is difficult, since no complete examples survive from before the mid-fourteenth century.[1] Research on medieval examples must therefore rely largely on the scant archaeological evidence (cat. 1), and on documentary and pictorial sources such as inventories and book illuminations (fig. 1.1). These suggest that crossbows of this period were fitted with wooden bows and triggers made of wood. Some of these early weapons had very simple release mechanisms, consisting of a transverse groove in the top of the tiller to retain the bowstring; the shot was released when the trigger pushed a peg upward through a hole in the groove. From about the thirteenth century onward, wooden bows were gradually replaced by stronger, composite examples. These consisted of strips of horn, mostly ibex and goat (cow horn is not well suited for this purpose, as it is generally too short), which were glued together lengthwise to form a strong core; layers of frayed animal tendons were glued to the outer side to provide additional elasticity. The horn core's ability to be compressed, together with the stretchability of the outer layer of tendons, allowed for considerable energy to be stored and released, but since this laminate was held together by animal glue it was susceptible to moisture. In order to protect this construction against the elements, therefore, it was wrapped in one or two layers of birch bark (fig. 1.2). The emergence of weapons with composite bows in Europe was probably the result of intensified contact with the Near East during the Crusades. Owing to their main component, period documents and modern authors alike often refer to them as "horn bows." They were secured to the front of the tiller in the same way as their earlier counterparts—by means of a hemp-cord binding that was threaded through a transverse hole in the tiller and then tightly wrapped around the bow at either side of the fore-end, and finally waxed to increase durability and water resistance.

Tillers were invariably made of wood and remained characteristically slim until the late fifteenth century.

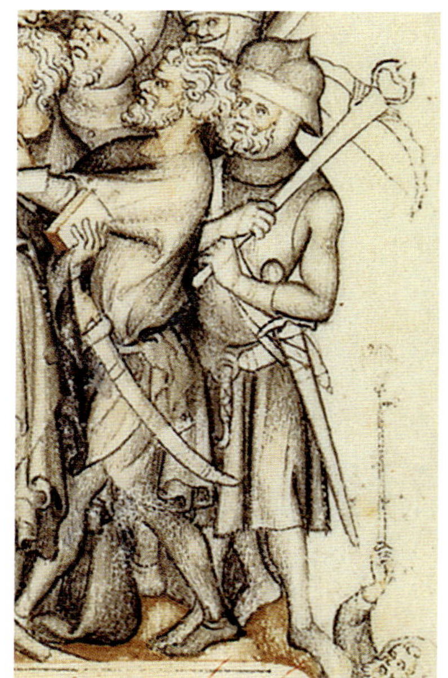

The most common type of release mechanism was a simple lock that may date as far back as the late Roman period, that is, the fourth or fifth century A.D. (fig. 2.6). The lock consisted of a rotating cylinder, the nut, which held and released the bowstring, and a lever trigger that pivoted around a single axis. Set into a cavity—the nut well—in the top of the tiller, the nut had a transverse central hole through which a string binding was threaded, forming a flexible axis that allowed the nut to rotate; the binding continued through holes on either side of the tiller and around the underside, thus preventing the nut from falling out accidentally. The nut had a transverse groove for the bowstring, while a small notch on the opposite side engaged the forward end of the lever trigger. A second notch, set at a right angle to the bowstring groove, permitted the rear of the bolt to touch the string directly. Composite bows were much more powerful than wooden ones, having draw weights of several hundred pounds, the force of which, when spanned, rested on the nut and the end of the trigger that engaged it. Accordingly, weapons with horn bows required stronger triggers, which were made of steel, and of greater length, in order to provide enough leverage for a smooth release. As early as the mid-thirteenth century, increasingly powerful bows also resulted in the appearance of two other technical features: reinforced nuts and stirrups. Made from staghorn, nuts were susceptible to wear and tear, and even to breakage; crossbow makers sought to alleviate this problem with iron-alloy insets that reinforced especially the notch for the trigger (cat. 1). Stirrups were attached to the front of the weapons, usually by interlaced leather straps, in order to facilitate the spanning of powerful bows and to prevent the bow or its binding from being damaged through repeated contact with the ground during the spanning process. Beginning in the late fifteenth century, the nut and trigger were sometimes separated by an internal iron-alloy tumbler to reduce the trigger pull. This tumbler had to be set before each shot, by pulling a string issuing from the right side of the tiller; because the tumbler pivoted around an additional axis, this variation is known as a two-axis lock (cats. 4, 5). Since the reduced trigger pull facilitated the release but could also lead to accidental discharges, it is during this period that the first safety mechanisms appear: a small foldable peg in the underside of the tiller, which, when extended downward, prevented the lever trigger from being pushed or pulled upward.[2]

Medieval inventories, wills, and correspondence occasionally mention the specific region in which a crossbow was made, but since particular features are not described, and contemporary depictions suggest a relatively uniform appearance across Europe during that period, the different types and characteristics remain largely unknown. By the late fifteenth century, however, general stylistic differences had developed between crossbows used in central

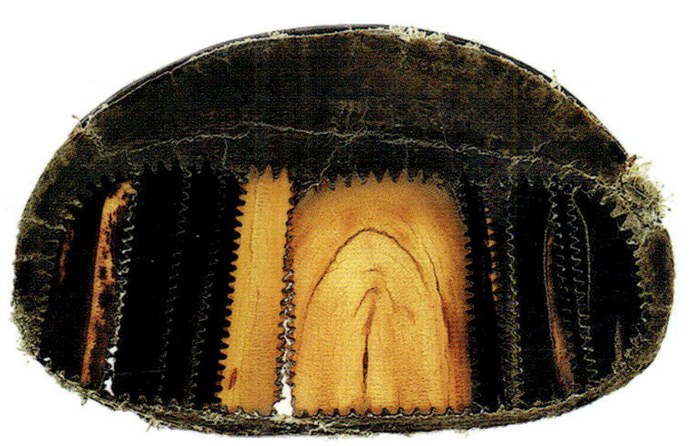

Figure 1.2 Cross section of a composite bow, possibly South German or Swiss, ca. 1450–1500. Horn, animal sinew, birch bark, 1 7/16 × 1 29/32 in. (3.7 × 5.9 cm). The Metropolitan Museum of Art, New York, Museum Accession (X.800)

Europe and a type that had emerged on the Iberian Peninsula and became popular in other parts of western Europe.[3]

Most central European crossbows were fitted with composite bows, which by the late fifteenth century were usually thick, stout, and extremely powerful, with the result that tillers were made slightly sturdier, especially around the center, which was weaker because it accommodated the internal lock mechanism. The lock and binding areas were usually reinforced with panels of horn or staghorn inlay. Initially, the rear of the tiller had been symmetrical, but during the second half of the fifteenth century a slight cheek appeared, almost invariably on the left, allowing a more comfortable fit against the archer's own cheek and thus a better aim. Depending on the spanning device used to operate a given weapon, its tiller was usually fitted with some kind of a support: the most common was either a small steel hook at the back, usually on top—for a rope-and-pulley system or for a cranequin fitted with an anchoring plate—or else a transverse metal lug, one end of which protruded from either side of the tiller at some distance behind the lock, for a cranequin with a cord loop. (See Section 5, "Spanning Devices" and cats. 2–4.)

Western European crossbows, today sometimes referred to as of the "Spanish" type, differed from the central European weapons in both appearance and construction (cat. 6). At first they seem to have been fitted with wooden and composite bows similar to those of their central European counterparts, but soon after the mid-fifteenth century steel bows became prevalent—apparently somewhat earlier than elsewhere. (See Section 2, "Crossbows with Steel Bows.") Until about 1500, most bows of the Spanish type were still bound to the tiller, but this technique was largely replaced by a pair of metal brackets before the turn of the century. Unlike in central Europe, the tiller stayed very slender and rectangular in section throughout; it did not swell at the lock because this area was usually reinforced with copper- or iron-alloy side plates. Spanish-type crossbows also retained simple nut-and-lever-trigger locks. The nut was not held in the cavity by a binding; it thus rotated freely and could be removed when necessary by moving it into a position in which its diameter was smaller because of the bowstring groove. Western European crossbows were spanned with either a particular type of cranequin or a pull lever—both required the tiller to be fitted with a transverse lug at the rear, but at different distances: lugs for levers are always integrated into the reinforces of the nut well, while those for cranequins are set farther back (cats. 30, 31, 40–43).

Although the development may well be older, it was also during the fifteenth century that differences in the sizes of handheld crossbows apparently emerged throughout Europe (fig. 1.3). Larger examples lent themselves to siege warfare, while smaller ones were better suited to the open battlefield or scouting on horseback; likewise, hunters stalked large

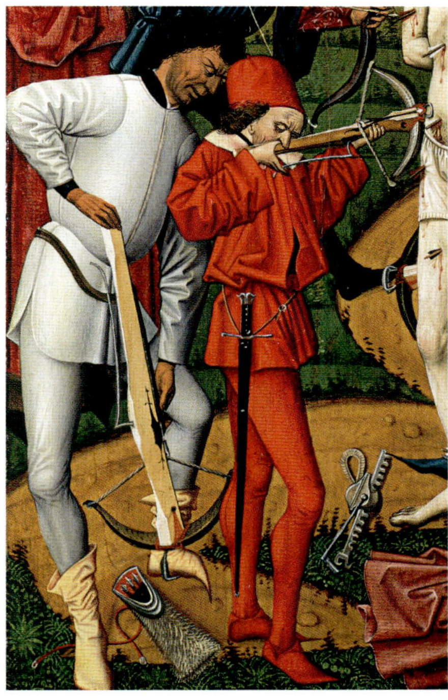 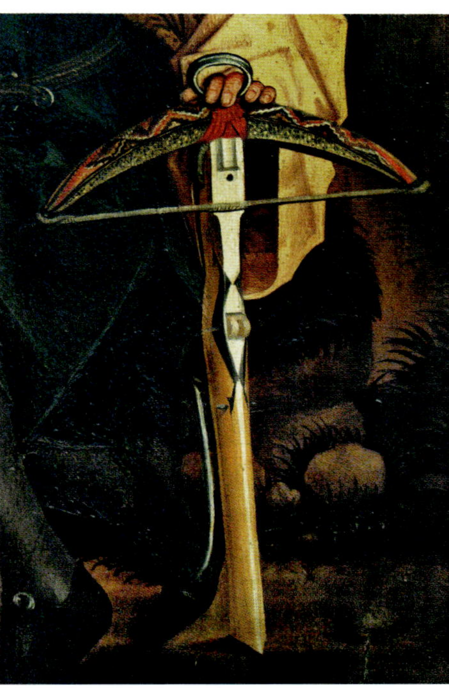

prey with heavier weapons, and small game with lighter pieces (compare, for example, the dimensions of cat. 2 with those of cats. 3 and 4). Another innovation, probably of earlier Near Eastern origin but not introduced into Europe until the late fifteenth century, was the bolt clip.[4] This was a small arched strip, usually made of horn, that was secured to the upper side of the tiller just behind the nut. The bolt clip reached over the nut, applying enough pressure to the rear of the bolt to prevent it from falling off.

In general, the decoration of early crossbows seems to have been comparatively modest, particularly in western Europe.[5] On central European weapons, it usually consisted of a dotted pattern, stenciled or printed on the bow's birch-bark covering, while panels of polished stag-horn and horn inlaid flush on the tiller not only reinforced certain areas but also enriched its overall appearance. Sometimes, the embellishment was more exuberant, including elaborately painted bows (fig. 1.4) and more extensive inlays, which might be decoratively shaped (cat. 2) or, in rare cases, even ornately carved (cats. 3, 4).

1. Archaeological Finds from Montfort Castle/Starkenberg Castle

Western Europe or Near East, before 1272
Parts of release mechanisms (nuts): staghorn, iron alloy
a. W. ¾ in. (1.9 cm); Diam. 1⅛ in. (2.9 cm); Wt. .28 oz.
(8 g) (.28)
b. W. ⅝ in. (1.3 cm); Diam. 1⅛ in. (2.9 cm); Wt. .24 oz.
(7 g) (.29)

Projectile shafts: wood, polychromy
c. L. 10¼ in. (25.9 cm); Diam. ¹³⁄₃₂ in. (1 cm) (.38a)
d. L. 6⅜ in. (16.2 cm); Diam. ⁷⁄₁₆ in. (1.1 cm) (.38b)
e. L. 5¼ in. (13.1 cm); Diam. ⅜ in. (.9 cm) (.38c)
f. L. 4½ in. (11.2 cm); Diam. ⅜ in. (.8 cm) (.38d)
g. L. 2⅝ in. (6.6 cm); Diam. ⅜ in. (.8 cm) (.38e)

Bolt heads: iron
h. L. 3¹⁄₁₆ in. (7.8 cm); W. 1 in. (2.6 cm); Wt. 1.5 oz. (42 g) (.30)
i. L. 2⁵⁄₁₆ in. (5.9 cm); W. ¹³⁄₃₂ in. (1 cm); Wt. .5 oz. (13 g) (.31)
j. L. 2 in. (5.1 cm); W. ½ in. (1.3 cm); Wt. .5 oz. (16 g) (.32)
Gift of Clarence H. Mackay, Archer M. Huntington,
Stephen H. P. Pell, and Bashford Dean, 1928 (28.99.28–.29,
28.99.38a–e, 28.99.30–.32)

Ex coll.: Armory of the Teutonic Knights at Montfort
Castle/Starkenberg Castle, Palestine, and/or arsenal of the
besieging Mamluk army under Sultan Baybars I (also at
Montfort Castle/Starkenberg Castle)

References: Dean 1927, p. 38; Nickel 1989, pp. 35–36;
Boas 1999, p. 178; Breiding forthcoming

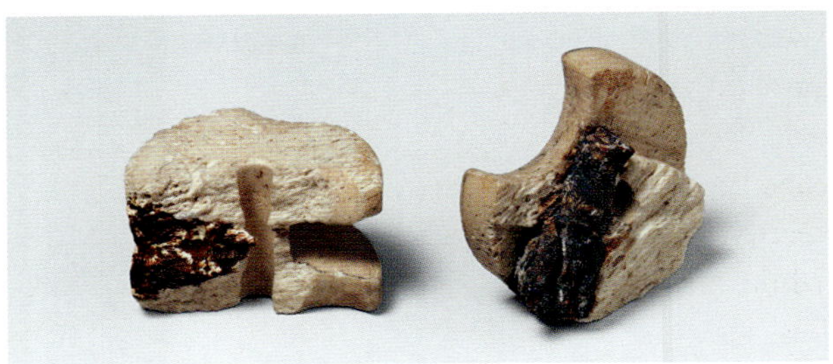

Catalogue 1a Fragments of release mechanisms (a, b)

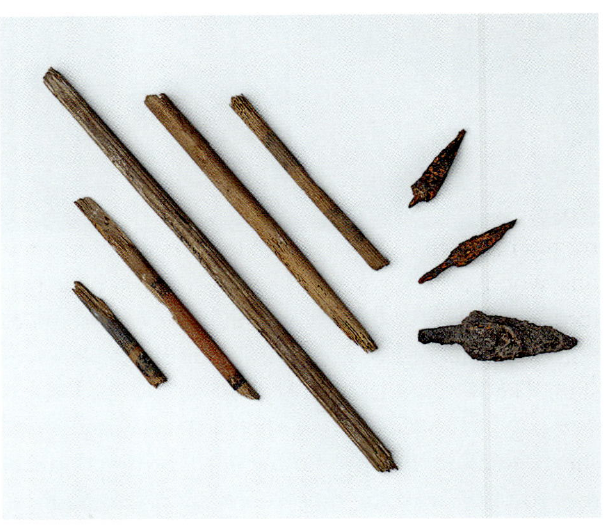

Catalogue 1b Projectile shafts and bolt heads (c–j)

Excavated in 1926 at Montfort Castle in Palestine,[1] these fragments include parts of crossbow release mechanisms (nuts), projectile heads, and what appear to be shafts. Despite their poor condition, the present objects are important for the study of early crossbows, since they date from before the castle's destruction in 1271/72, and are thus the earliest crossbow remains of European type in the Metropolitan Museum's collection.

The nuts of staghorn are noteworthy for two reasons. First, they are among the earliest recorded examples to be fitted with an iron-alloy reinforce, and, second, they are decorated, however simply, with incised lines that encircle each cylinder. The projectile heads, all made from iron alloy and pyramidal in shape, would originally have been secured to their shafts by their tangs. The Metropolitan Museum holds five accessioned examples and about twenty unaccessioned specimens (their advanced state of corrosion makes it difficult to clearly identify some of them as projectile heads or to establish their former dimensions). About half of these heads are relatively small and sharply pointed (cats. 1i, 1j), while the other examples are noticeably larger and heavier (cat. 1h); among the latter, about half a dozen heads appear to be of a medium size and weight and may constitute a third group. It is difficult to distinguish clearly between certain types of arrow and bolt heads that have become separated from their shafts;[2] in this case, however, it seems likely that the smallest heads were for arrows, the medium-size heads were intended for crossbow bolts, and the large, heavy examples came from great-crossbow or springald bolts (cat. 44d). The five shaft fragments in the Museum's collection are of coniferous wood and hardwood, respectively; almost perfectly circular in section and with surfaces worked to a smooth finish, they demonstrate superior workmanship. The thicker ones with plain surfaces were presumably crossbow bolts, while the more slender ones showing painted decoration most likely belonged to arrows.

Montfort Castle was originally built by French Crusaders, who, in 1220, sold it to the Order of the Knights of the Hospital of Saint Mary of the Germans in Jerusalem, known as the Order of the Teutonic Knights. As the Knights' largest and most important stronghold, it became the Order's official seat in 1229, and its French name, meaning strong mountain, was translated into German: Starkenberg. In 1271, the castle was besieged by Mamluks under Sultan Baybars I (r. 1260–77), taken, and destroyed. One slightly larger nut, more shaft fragments, and numerous projectile heads from the same site are today in Jerusalem.[3] While the shafts and projectile heads were probably made locally—perhaps at Montfort Castle itself—it is at present impossible to say whether the nuts were produced in the Near East or brought to the castle from Europe.

2. Crossbow

Central Europe (possibly Austria), ca. 1425–75
Wood (European hornbeam), horn, animal sinew, animal glue, birch bark, staghorn, iron alloy, hemp, leather
L. 37⅝ in. (95.6 cm); W. 29¾ in. (75.5 cm); Wt. 8 lb. 12 oz. (3,989 g)
Bashford Dean Memorial Collection, Funds from various donors, 1929 (29.158.647)

EX COLL.: Bashford Dean, Riverdale, N.Y.

REFERENCE: Paterson 1990, p. 72, fig. 13 (and possibly p. 41)

Large crossbows were widely used throughout fifteenth-century Europe for both war and the hunt. This example has a powerful composite bow, whose present forward curve is due to later deformation. Originally, the bow's birch-bark covering was decorated with a simple pattern of light dots on a dark ground; it was painted black at a later date. The long, slender tiller is decorated with inlaid panels of polished staghorn. This inlay is noteworthy for its meandering, or flame-shaped, extensions; the unusual length of the reinforce at either side of the seat of the nut; and the bolt guide carved from a piece of the inlay (fig. 1.5). The single-axis release mechanism includes an extremely long steel trigger that changes in section from diamond shape to circular. Laced to the front of the bow by means of interwoven leather bands is a well-made steel stirrup with a prominent medial ridge and edges decorated with incised roping. A small iron-alloy hook on the tiller's upper side served as the anchoring point for a

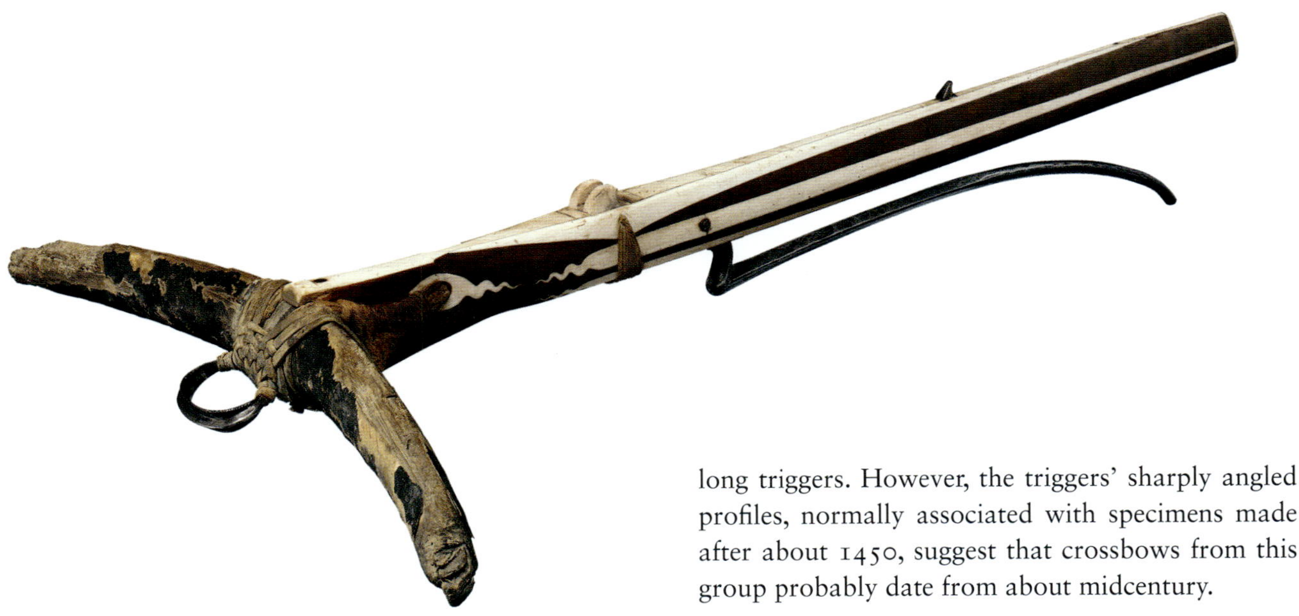

spanning device, either a rope-and-pulley system (cat. 29) or a cranequin fitted with a hinged and pierced anchoring plate instead of a hemp loop.

Few surviving crossbows date from before the mid-fifteenth century, and, among these, examples showing near-identical decoration are rare. The Metropolitan Museum's weapon belongs to a group so similar in size, construction, and decoration that it is likely they were made in the same workshop. The group includes two crossbows in Scena[1] and one at Spiš Castle in northern Slovakia.[2] Another example, less well preserved and partly composite, but with a tiller from the same workshop, is in Vienna.[3] Related to this group—probably from the same region and made about the same time—is a crossbow in Kremsmünster.[4] It is similar in size and appearance, showing a comparable arrangement of elongated staghorn panels, though the latter do not end in flame-shaped extensions but taper to straight points.

The slender outlines of these powerful weapons, especially the tillers' high fore-ends and elongated rear portions, are characteristic of early fifteenth-century crossbows, as are the carved bolt guides and

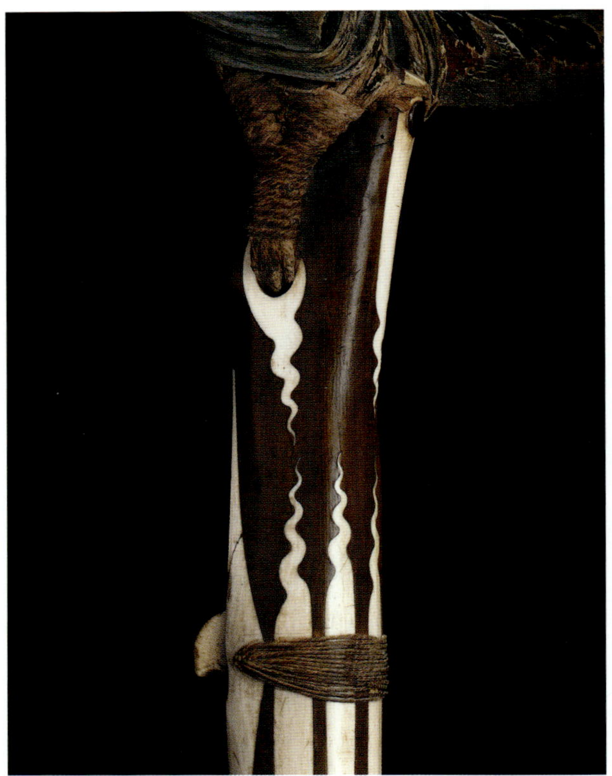

Figure 1.5

3. Crossbow of Ulrich V, Count of Württemberg

Germany (probably Stuttgart), dated 1460
Wood (European hornbeam), horn, animal sinew, staghorn, birch bark, iron alloy, copper alloy, pigment
L. 28 1/16 in. (71.2 cm); W. 25 5/8 in. (65 cm); Wt. 6 lb. 9 oz. (2,972 g)
Rogers Fund, 1904 (04.3.36)

Ex coll.: Count Ulrich V of Württemberg, Stuttgart; Count James-Alexandre de Pourtalès-Gorgier, Neuchâtel and Paris; anonymous collection, Paris; Charles Alexander, baron de Cosson, London; Maurice de Talleyrand-Périgord, duc de Dino, Paris

References: de Cosson 1893; de Cosson 1901; Dean 1905, p. 123; Laking 1922, vol. 3, pp. 135–36; Dean 1925, pp. 154–57; Metropolitan Museum of Art 1975, p. 222, no. 236; *Metropolitan Museum of Art Guide* 1983, p. 65; Nickel 1991, p. 40; Paterson 1990, p. 68; Frakes 2004, pp. 68–69; Richter 2006, pp. 42–43; Breiding 2007, pp. 104–5; Breiding 2009; Dahlström 2011, p. 78; Pyhrr 2012a, pp. 202–3, fig. 43; Pyhrr 2012b, pp. 7–8

This crossbow is remarkable for the extensive decoration of its hornbeam tiller, which identifies the original owner and the year of manufacture, 1460. The plain composite bow, which retains only traces of a birch-bark covering decorated with a simple dot pattern, is from the fifteenth or early sixteenth century but it is probably not original to this weapon; a stirrup is missing.[1] The single-axis lock mechanism comprises a string-rotating nut of staghorn with several iron-alloy reinforces (the nut is a later replacement), and a sharply angled iron-alloy lever trigger partially sheathed with copper alloy.

Even among the lavishly decorated crossbows of the fifteenth century, this example is noteworthy

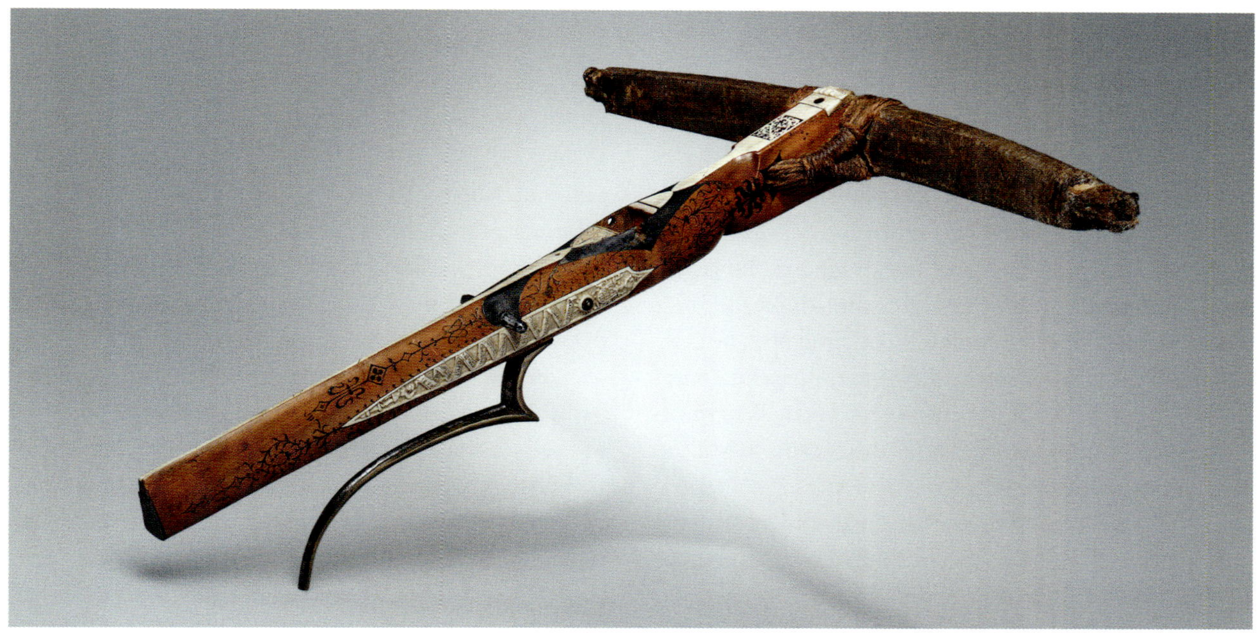

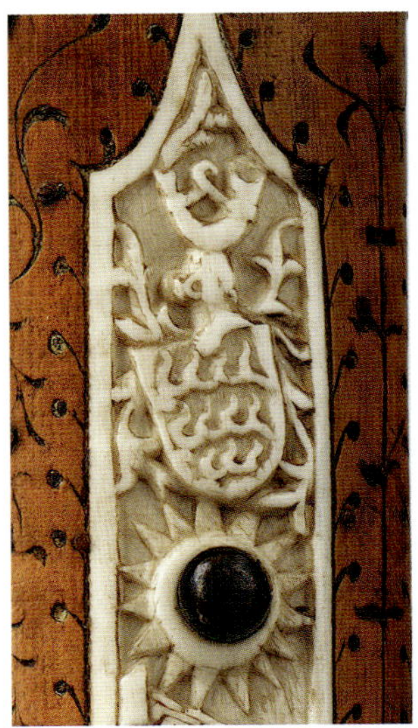

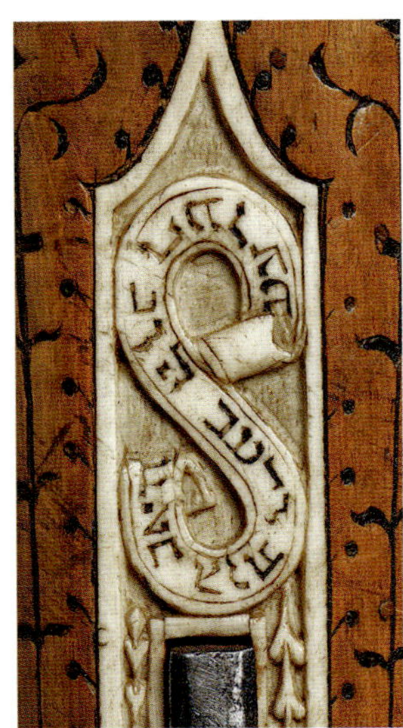

Figure 1.6

Figure 1.7

for the presence of carved staghorn and the extent to which the embellishment is individualized, with intricately carved figural decoration, heraldry (fig. 1.6), and inscriptions (fig. 1.7). In addition to the inlay, almost the entire surface of the tiller is covered with a floral pattern, engraved and filled with a mastic-like substance, that includes stylized fleurs-de-lis, pomegranates, knots, and quatrefoils, as well as small leaves reminiscent of the crockets of Gothic tracery.

Except for a small panel with scrollwork in low relief on the chase and the monogram of Jesus, IHS, just behind the nut, the upper side of the tiller is plain so as not to distract the user's eye. On either side, the elongated lancet-shape panels are carved with a coat of arms at the top, followed by a sun-like frame for the trigger axis, and below that—issuing from above a small human figure—a scroll bearing a Latin religious inscription in Gothic minuscules and the year of manufacture.

On the right panel, beneath the arms of Württemberg (in gold, three black stags' antlers [fig. 1.6]), the inscription reads: GLORIA . / IN EXCELSIS / DEO . ET . / IN . TERRA . / PAX . HO / MINIBUS / BONE VO / LUNTATIS / . LAUDA / M⁹ . TE . / BENE / DICTIM⁹ / . TE / 1460 (Glory be to God in the highest, and on earth peace to men who enjoy His good will. We praise thee. We bless thee. 1460). Except for the addition of the year, this inscription is a quotation from the beginning of one of the most famous hymns in Christendom, also known as the Greater Doxology, which is based on Luke 2:14, the angels' announcement of the birth of Christ to the shepherds.[2]

On the left panel, beneath the arms of Savoy (in red, a silver cross), the inscription reads: O / MA / RIA . GRA / CIO / SA . D / EI . MR . GE / NE / ROSA . / DIGA . // LAUDE / . GLORIOSA . / SIS . / PRO . / NOBIS . SP / ECIO / SA . / AD [?] M . CCCC / . LX . (O gracious Mary, generous mother of God. Worthy of glorious praise. Be beautiful [to behold] for us. [In the year/In the year of the Lord] MCCCCLX). The words form four lines of a rhyming verse from a prayer or hymn to the Virgin Mary.

The two panels on the tiller's underside show Saint Michael as Weigher of Souls on the fore-end as well as the most remarkable decorative motif of this crossbow, an S-shaped scroll bearing an inscription in Hebrew letters: האב ג[?]ו[?]ת ליעב ה[?]ו[?]כ הער[?]ע[?] (fig. 1.7). When read phonetically from right to left, they reveal a German phrase: *hab gut lieb hoch herze.*

The lavish use of staghorn, the inscriptions, and its specific iconography distinguish this weapon as an extraordinary commission. The heraldry identifies the original owner as Ulrich V, count of Württemberg (1413–1480; figs. 1.6, 1.8). Known as "the Much-Beloved," Count Ulrich was one of the most powerful nobles in southern Germany, a generous patron

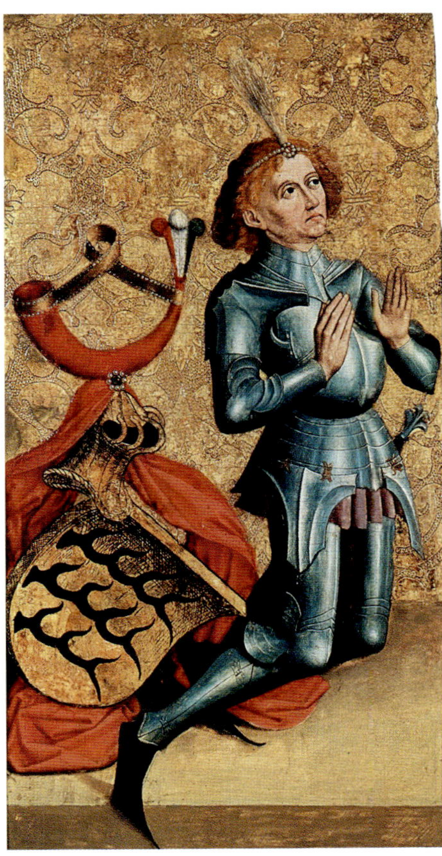

Figure 1.8 Ludwig Fries (Master of the Sterzing Altar) (German, rec. 1460–84). Ulrich V "the Much-Beloved," count of Württemberg. Left panel from a votive altar, ca. 1470. Tempera on panel, 31¼ × 18¾ in. (79.5 × 47.5 cm). Landesmuseum Württemberg, Stuttgart (WLM 13721)

of the arts, and an avid huntsman. In 1453, he married his third wife, Margaret of Savoy (1420–1479), who patronized several renowned manuscript workshops, at least one of which was presumably located near the principal Württemberg residence in Stuttgart.

The meaning of this inscription—probably intended as a cryptogram—is likely to have been intentionally ambiguous and has long evaded interpretation. Its first three words, *hab gut lieb*, were based in part on a popular fifteenth-century religious saying and are found, albeit followed by different, often individualized texts, in a number of German manuscripts, several of which are attributable to Margaret of Savoy's patronage. The entire inscription was perhaps intended as a personal motto, "Hold God dear and be high-hearted!" or "Hold God dear, high-hearted one!"[3] The connection between the countess' manuscript commissions and the inscriptions on this crossbow suggests the possibility that it may have been a present, possibly for Christmas, from Countess Margaret to her husband.[4]

Documentary evidence—in particular letters of appointment and lists of court artists—from the Württemberg court also suggests a name for the maker of this weapon. From 1454 to 1460 a certain Heinrich Heid von Winterthur is recorded in Stuttgart as Count Ulrich's crossbow maker and "master of works"; the latter title may imply that he made and maintained not only the count's crossbows, but also other weapons and siege engines, as well as perhaps overseeing these functions when carried out by others.[5] Given the coincidence of dates and the absence of other crossbow makers recorded in Stuttgart during that time, Heid is the most likely candidate. The fact that he lived near other court artists may explain where this crossbow maker could have received help with the design and execution of the weapon's lavish embellishment.

The few highly decorated crossbows that have survived from the fifteenth century include one made for Matthias Corvinus in the Metropolitan Museum's collection (cat. 4) and an example in London with a painted steel bow from the last quarter of the century, its tiller bearing the arms of the Tyrolean Colonna-Vels family.[6] Also worth noting are three examples with somewhat similar decoration, in Leeds, New York, and Toronto;[7] a heavily damaged tiller in Grandson, near Yverdon-les-Bains,[8] whose now-missing inlay was once shaped and arranged in a way similar to that found on all these weapons; and, finally, for its sumptuously painted bow, the large crossbow with an undecorated tiller of Baron Andreas Baumkircher, dating from about 1460–70, in Vienna.[9] Among these, Count Ulrich's weapon is the earliest known dated crossbow and the only example from the fifteenth century to which a maker can be attributed with reasonable certainty.

4. Crossbow of Matthias Corvinus, King of Hungary

Central or eastern Europe (possibly Vienna), dated 1489
Wood,[1] horn, animal sinew, staghorn, birch bark, iron alloy
L. 29 in. (73.7 cm); W. 24 in. (60.9 cm); Wt. 5 lb. ½ oz. (2,284 g)
Rogers Fund, 1925 (25.42)

Ex coll.: Matthias Corvinus, king of Hungary, Vienna (and/or possibly his son, János Corvinus); [Julius Böhler, Lucerne]

References: Dean 1925; Grancsay 1935, pl. 15; Blair 1962, fig. 240; Kalmár 1971, pp. 141–42, fig. 15; Zolnay 1971, pp. 49–52; Richter 2006, pp. 60–62; Breiding 2009, p. 62; Radway 2009, p. 27; Dahlström 2011, pp. 80–81.

Like catalogue 3, this crossbow is remarkable for the extensive decoration identifying it as belonging to an illustrious owner who undoubtedly used it for hunting or ceremonial purposes rather than warfare. The weapon comprises the remains of a composite bow and a richly embellished wooden tiller with a two-axis lock.[2] Small areas of the bow's birch-bark covering indicate that it was once adorned with a simple geometric pattern, while both nocks were originally painted black. Inlaid panels of polished staghorn set closely around the tiller's center are carved in shallow relief, mostly on a hatched ground. Motifs include a stylized floral vine, possibly a strawberry plant; grotesque dragon heads; Saint George and the dragon; heads of Wild Men; and two depictions of Adam and Eve. Toward the front of the tiller, an intricate Gothic arch contains a scroll inscribed with the year 1489 above a crowned helmet with a large coat of arms below; the latter is flanked by a smaller shield on either side. An interesting detail of the decoration is the treatment of the panel borders, also toward the front, which are carved in the shape of quivers. The sides of the fore-end and rear of the tiller, finally, are embellished with a lightly incised floral pattern that extends from the front and rear points of the side panels and that has been filled with a dark mastic-like substance.

Although ambitious and wide-ranging in iconography, the crossbow's decoration lacks sophistication and a coherent overall design. Elements on the same panels face in different directions, and the execution of the carving is of rather modest quality. Nonetheless, the weapon belongs to a small number of highly decorated fifteenth-century crossbows whose motifs include heraldry identifying the original owner, and it is one of only two known dated examples from that period (cat. 3).

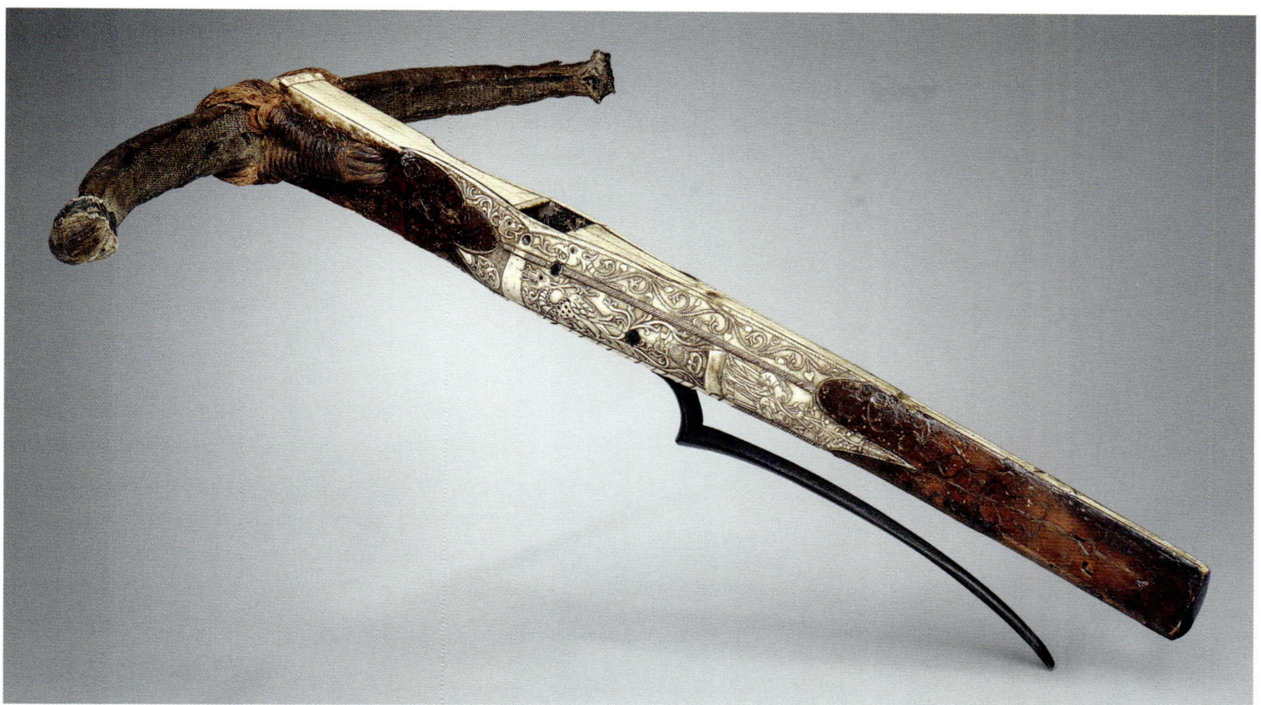

The heraldry—placed so as to be read when the weapon is either held or hanging upright—identifies its former owner as a member of the noble Hunyadi family of Hungary. The large central shield bears a version of the arms of the kings of Hungary (fig. 1.9): divided horizontally; the upper field is further divided vertically; in the first upper field the old arms of Hungary (eight alternating bands of red and silver); in the second upper field the new arms of Hungary (in red, a silver patriarchal cross); and in the lower field the arms of the Hunyadi family (in blue, a silver raven on a silver branch with a golden ring in its beak); the crest, on a barred helmet, consists of a golden crown; the mantling is red and silver.[3]

The arms placed in the heraldically more important position to the right (dexter) of those of the king of Hungary are the arms of Dalmatia (in blue, three frontal golden leopard heads with red tongues).[4] The arms to the left (sinister) of the royal arms are presumably those of Bohemia (in red, a rearing silver lion with two crossed tails [the crossing of the tails is not shown here], and with golden claws, tongue, and crown).[5] In 1489, the royal arms of Hungary, as composed on this weapon, could only have referred to the then king of Hungary, Matthias Hunyadi (r. 1458–90), called by the Latin epithet "Corvinus" (of the raven) (fig. 1.10).[6]

The remaining decoration does not relate specifically to the king or the Hunyadi family. The repeated depiction of dragons may allude generally to the Order of the Dragon, of which Matthias was a grand master.[7] However, none of the dragons shows any of the characteristics of devices associated with the order.[8] The figure of Saint George appears frequently

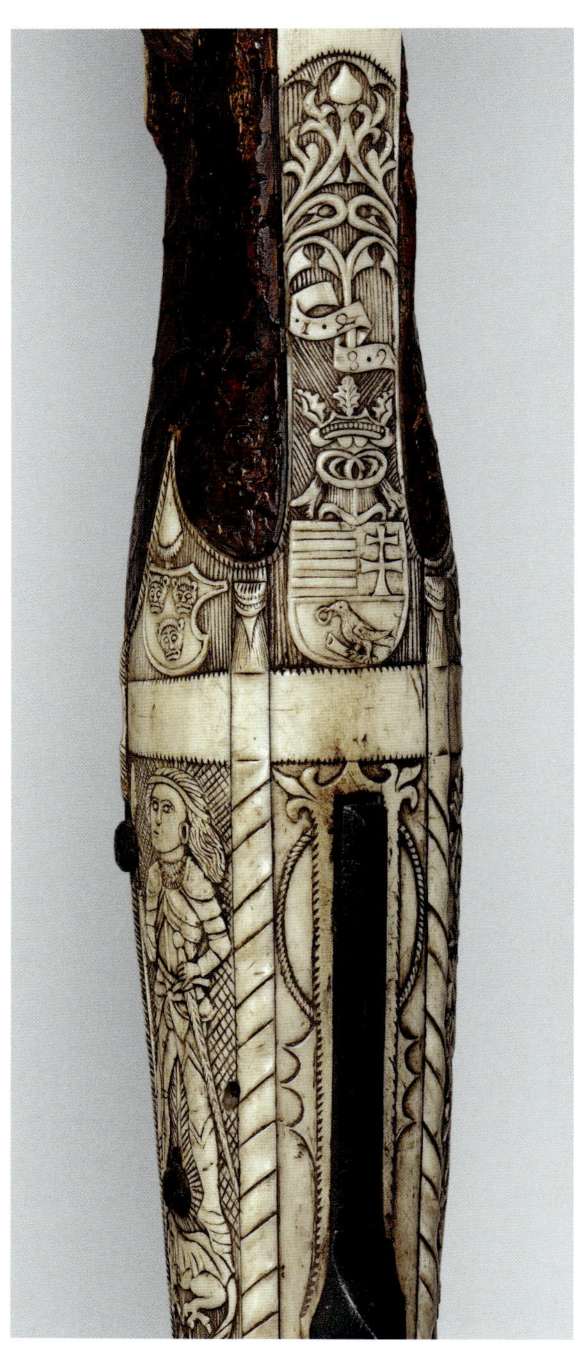

Figure 1.9

in fifteenth-century iconography, and, as the chivalric patron saint par excellence, he is found especially in the decoration of weapons. The depictions of Adam and Eve before (naked) and after (clothed) the Fall are doubtless intended as a reminder of original sin and, by extension, as a memento mori.

Closest in comparison to the Metropolitan's weapon is a late fifteenth-century crossbow in London.[9] It is fitted with a painted steel bow and has a tiller entirely clad in panels of polished staghorn carved in shallow relief. Of superior craftsmanship and composition, its iconography includes Saints George and Sebastian, as well as several religious

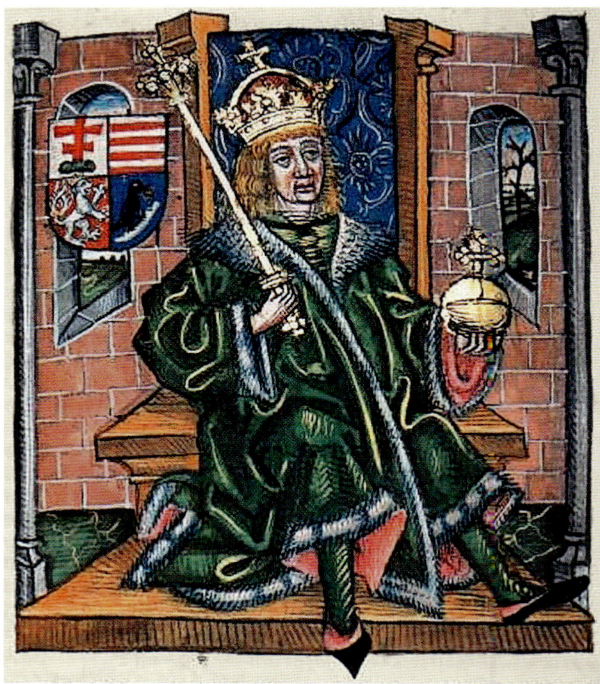

Figure 1.10 Matthias "Corvinus" Hunyadi, king of Hungary. Hand-colored woodcut from Johannes de Thurocz (Hungarian, ca. 1435–1488/89), *Chronica Hungarorum*, dated 1488. Ink, mixed media, and gold on parchment. National Széchényi Library, Budapest (Inc. 1143)

and secular moralizing scenes, a stag hunt, dragons, and an extensive display of heraldry. One coat of arms, prominently painted onto the chase, identifies the weapon's original owner as a member of the Colonna-Vels family from southern Tyrol, while another eight carved and painted shields, placed around the tiller in an arrangement similar to that on the Corvinus example, display the family's far-reaching connections. There are two other known crossbows from the same period, with similarly elaborate decoration incorporating the heraldry of their original owners: one with an unidentified coat of arms in Leeds,[10] and another with the arms of the Fuger, or Fügen, family from Schwaz in Tyrol (western Austria), today in a private collection in New York.[11] A third crossbow, with similarly extensive decoration but lacking any heraldry, is in Toronto.[12]

The practice of applying carved and painted panels of staghorn was not confined to crossbows: similar decoration also embellished objects such as the small boxes often given as lovers' tokens.[13] Most prominently, however, this kind of decoration is found on a group of more than twenty saddles dating probably from about 1425 to about 1475, three of which are in the Metropolitan's collections (fig. 1.11). Certain iconographic details suggest that these saddles were manufactured either in Bohemia or possibly in Hungary or northern Italy,[14] although it cannot be excluded that the method of decoration was practiced over a wide geographical area.

Matthias Corvinus resided in Vienna for most of 1489, suggesting that this crossbow was perhaps made there, either by local craftsmen or by a Hungarian crossbow maker in the king's employ. As well as by its rich embellishment, the quality and sophistication of this weapon are demonstrated by

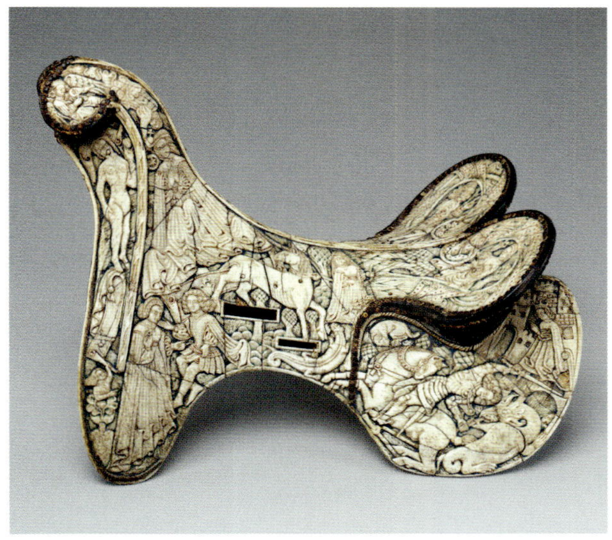

Figure 1.11 Parade saddle. German or Tyrolean, ca. 1440–50. Wood, staghorn, iron alloy, leather, and polychromy, L. 22 in. (54.8 cm); H. 16½ in. (41.9 cm); W. 17 in. (43.2 cm). The Metropolitan Museum of Art, New York, Rogers Fund, 1904 (04.3.250). Note the carved and polychrome decoration.

the two-axis lock—one of the earliest recorded instances of this type—and the fact that the trigger is offset slightly to the right, to make it more easily accessible to the user's right hand. Another unusual technical characteristic of the Metropolitan's crossbow is the system for supporting a spanning device, either a rope-and-pulley system or a cranequin: instead of a transverse lug, this tiller is fitted with a pair of wedge-like protrusions carved from the same material as the staghorn panels into which they have been set and decorated to match. Since they are an extremely rare feature, these protrusions may be characteristic of crossbows made in eastern Austria or Hungary.[15]

2 | CROSSBOWS WITH STEEL BOWS

Figure 2.1 Jörg Kölderer (Austrian, act. by 1497–d. 1540). Crossbows with steel bows and horn bows. Page from an illuminated inventory of the arsenals of Maximilian I. Austrian, bet. 1504 and 1508. Yale Center for British Art, New Haven, Paul Mellon Collection (Folio A 2011 36). Note the central European weapons with composite bows, held by a hemp binding, and the slender, more western-European-looking examples with steel bows, held by iron-alloy bow irons and "unsecured" nuts.

Soon after 1300 the first crossbows with steel bows appear in documentary sources[1]—one of the earliest mentions a weapon with a bow "of steel, gilded" among the (stolen) possessions of Mathilda of Brabant (1268–1329), countess of Artois, in 1316.[2] However, they remained rare until the fifteenth century: no early examples are known to have survived, and few are mentioned in written sources. Composite bows, being relatively light and very effective, though difficult and time-consuming to produce, continued to be used through the early sixteenth century, but in the decades about 1500 steel bows rapidly became prevalent throughout most of Europe (fig. 2.1).

The successful manufacture of steel bows became possible with the production of high-quality steel, comparatively rich in carbon and as free from inclusions as possible.[3] The material had to store large amounts of energy, while maintaining enough strength and elasticity to not break under the strain. Perfected through generations of trial and error, the manufacturing process resulted in bows of astonishing sophistication; for example, modern research has shown that the tapered arms are essential to achieving an even distribution of strain throughout the bow during the spanning process.

Steel bows had several advantages over composite examples: they were less susceptible to the elements, in particular, moisture, and, because they needed less maintenance, they did not have to be replaced as frequently as horn bows. Moreover, advances in technology made possible the production of more steel bows of increasingly better quality at faster rates and more affordable prices. The steel bow's main disadvantage was its greater weight, and—probably in rare circumstances only—the fact that, when the material or workmanship was of poor quality, it could break, with potentially disastrous consequences. Central European bows were therefore often fitted with a braided safety cord.

After about 1500, the general types of crossbows that had developed in western and central Europe during the previous century changed little in terms of overall appearance. The most noticeable innovations occurred in the areas of technology and decoration, in particular the release mechanisms of central European crossbows and the embellishment of their tillers.

The western European, or "Spanish," features that had taken shape over the course of the fifteenth century came together as a distinct type (fig. 2.2). In comparison to those on central European crossbows, most western European

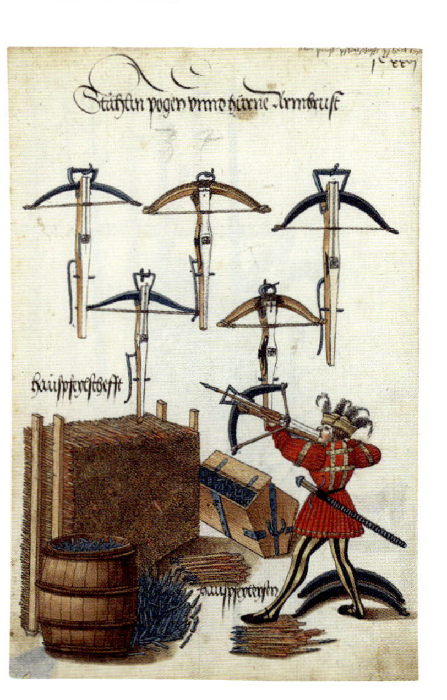

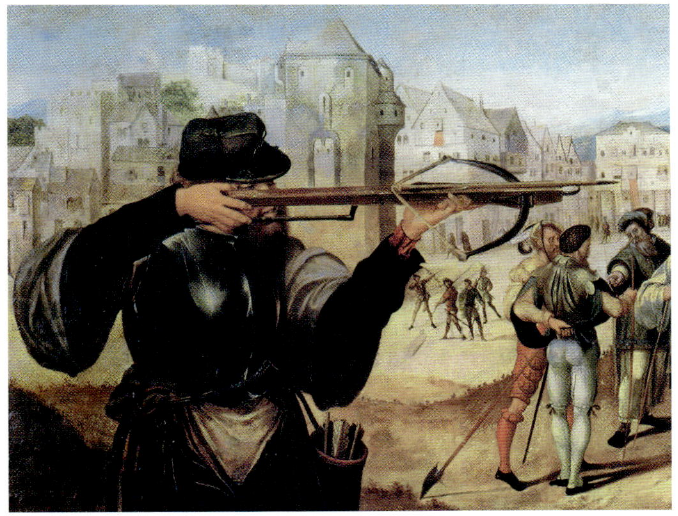

Figure 2.2 Gregório Lopes (Portuguese, ca. 1490–1550). Man-at-arms using a crossbow of western European type, detail of *The Martyrdom of Saint Sebastian*, ca. 1536–39. Oil on panel, 46⅞ × 96⅛ in. (119 × 244 cm). Museo de Arte Antigua, Lisbon (80 Pint)

gle-axis lock (cat. 6). Weapons of different sizes were employed throughout the Iberian Peninsula, both in warfare and for hunting, and the type strongly influenced the appearance of crossbows in Italy, France, the Netherlands (fig. 2.3), and England (cat. 9).

In the sixteenth century a variation of the western European type emerged, probably in Belgium, that was based on a larger version originally used in war and spanned with a windlass. Characterized by a massive steel bow and a heavy wooden tiller, often with a more or less developed protrusion on its underside, it became a weapon used exclusively for target shooting and served as a model for such weapons throughout the Low Countries (fig. 2.4). Because of their sparse and generic decoration, examples of the type rarely offer information about the time and place of their manufacture, so that they are still sometimes erroneously identified as fifteenth-century crossbows for war.[4]

In central Europe, most crossbows maintained the same overall characteristics for centuries, that is, a steel bow that tends to be heavier than its western or southern European counterpart, is always secured by the traditional hemp binding, and has a bowstring with knotted ends. The tiller, somewhat stockier than its "Gothic" predecessor, has a fore-end of rectangular section, is fitted with a nut lock, around which the tiller swells noticeably in thickness, and exhibits a slightly shorter, tapering rear part that changes in section to form a cheek. Beginning in the late sixteenth century, German-language inventories and other period documents sometimes refer to this type of bolt-shooting crossbow as a *Rüstung*, which came in "full," "half," and "quarter" sizes (*ganze Rüstung*, *halbe Rüstung*, and *Viertelrüstung*)—a classification that originally corresponded to the distances at target-shooting competitions (fig. 2.5).[5] Also during the sixteenth century a lighter version of the weapon appeared, which shot either bolts or pellets: the *Schnepper* (probably an onomatopoeic term akin to the English "snapper"). As

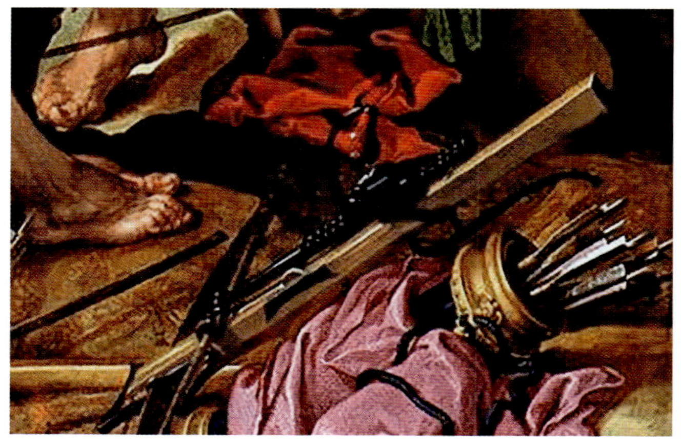

Figure 2.3 Joachim Anthonisz Wtewael (Netherlandish, 1566–1638). Crossbow and cric of western European type, detail of *The Martyrdom of Saint Sebastian*, dated 1600. Oil on canvas, 66⅝ × 49¼ in. (169.3 × 125.1 cm). The Nelson-Atkins Museum of Art, Kansas City, Missouri. Purchase: Nelson Gallery Foundation (F84-71)

Figure 2.4 Jan Josef Horemans the Elder (Flemish, 1682–1759). Crossbow practice, detail of *Figures at Rest by a Classical Building*, dated 1750. Oil on canvas, 23 × 19¼ in. (58.5 × 48.9 cm). Private collection

with the *Rüstung*, variations of the *Schnepper* were sometimes categorized by the projectiles they shot and by their intended use, such as the *Wandschnepper* and *Vogelschnepper*, for shooting at a wall-mounted target (*Wand* = wall) and at the popinjay (*Vogel* = bird), respectively (cats. 13–15).[6]

When a crossbow is in a spanned position, the bow's draw weight rests on the lock holding back the bowstring (see Section 5, "Spanning Devices"). In order to release a shot, a certain resistance has to be overcome to disengage the trigger or the part of the release mechanism that holds the bowstring. The "trigger pull" describes the force necessary to overcome this resistance—to "pull" the trigger (in fact, a trigger should be squeezed, not pulled). The more strength required to squeeze the trigger, the greater the risk of shaking or jerking the weapon. The introduction of one or more levers between the trigger and the part that releases the bowstring allowed the strength of the bow to be distributed along several axes restraining the internal levers, resulting in a noticeably reduced trigger pull. This development, begun in the decades before 1500, produced the two-axis lock (cats. 4, 5) and, in the second half of the sixteenth century, culminated in internal-release mechanisms ultimately involving four axes. Readying a crossbow with a four-axis lock and set trigger was a complicated process involving a number of time-consuming steps and an additional instrument, the pricker, or cocking pin (cat. 39 and figs. 2.6–2.8). Even in the hands of an expert, the entire sequence could take several minutes. This period also witnessed the introduction of a variety of sight systems. Traditionally, the crossbowman covered the target with the tip of the bolt, positioning his cheek against the rear of the tiller and the thumb of the hand holding it (fig. 2.2). Weapons from the late fifteenth century on show one or more notches for the thumb; this system remained in use throughout the period under discussion. Beginning in the sixteenth century, the bolt clip was sometimes notched to act as a rear sight. Probably before 1600, but cetainly during the seventeenth century, the foldable rear sight emerged.[7]

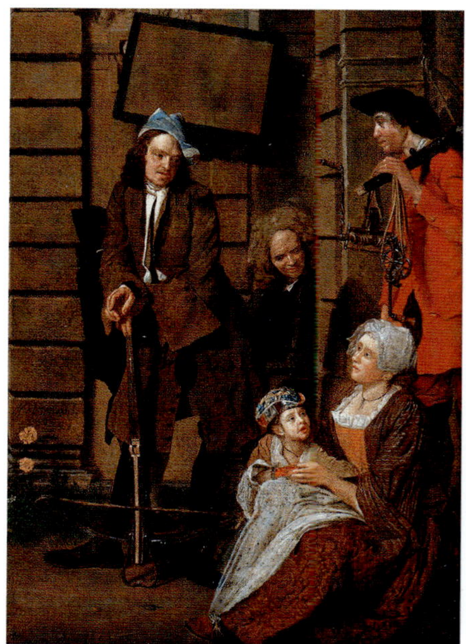

While the reduction of the trigger pull and the resulting increased sensitivity of the release mechanism dispensed with the need for long lever triggers, they also made accidental discharges more likely. The former lever trigger, or a metal fixture of the same shape, was now secured to the tiller in a fixed position to form a trigger guard. At the same time, the earliest form of safety catch—a short, foldable peg that prevented the lever trigger from being pressed up against the tiller—disappeared, except in areas where single-axis release mechanisms remained in use, as in England, for example (cat. 9). On central European examples the foldable peg was replaced by a small swiveling plate that could be turned to engage the underside of the tumbler, thus arresting it and the nut.

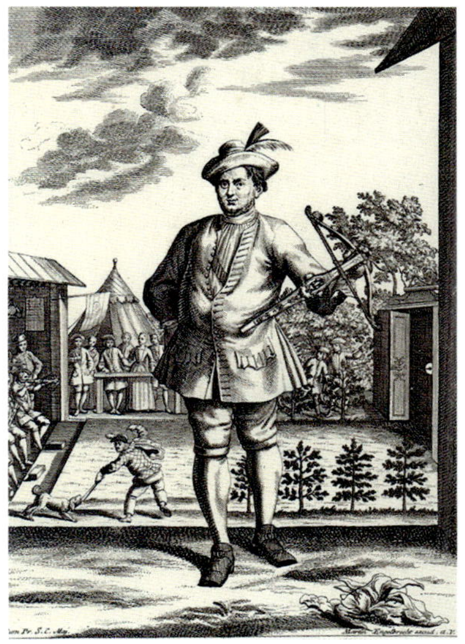

Figure 2.5 Martin Engelbrecht (German, 1684–1756). Man holding a crossbow, detail of a print entitled *Die zur Ergötzung dienliche Armbrust* (The Regaling Crossbow), 1720. Etching, sheet 14½ × 8¹³⁄₁₆ in. (36.9 × 22.4 cm). The Metropolitan Museum of Art, New York, The Elisha Whittelsey Fund, 1957 (57.559.23)

Another, simpler form of catch, the snap lock, first appeared during the early sixteenth century but only became widespread during the seventeenth century. It is usually found on smaller weapons with lighter bows, like the *Schnepper*, which, instead of a nut, have a transverse groove across the tiller for the bowstring; this was held in position by an open, claw-like trap, which was connected in turn to a set trigger by a single internal lever (fig. 2.8).

The decoration of crossbows made for the hunt and competitions reached its pinnacle during the sixteenth and seventeenth centuries, but the ornament was mostly concentrated in the tiller. The majority of steel bows—unlike their predecessors of composite construction—were left plain, their surfaces either polished bright or darkened (blued or browned) as a simple rust-prevention measure. Initially, the decoration of the few steel bows that were embellished mimicked that of earlier horn bows: the steel bows were either wrapped in parchment and then painted, or the paint was applied directly onto the steel surface. During the first half of the sixteenth century these practices were mostly replaced by etching (cats. 24, 27) or, occasionally, engraving. In rare cases this decoration, which might consist of simple ornament, inscriptions, or more elaborate figurative scenes, was partially or entirely gilded. However, etching and engraving carried the risk of weakening the steel surface to such an extent that the bow might become liable to breaking, but whether bow makers recognized this danger, and thus employed this decorative medium only infrequently, is not known. In any case, with few exceptions, the adornment of bows all but ceased after the seventeenth century.[8]

However, the tillers of steel crossbows, like those of their predecessors, were embellished with the same variety of techniques, frequently in combination and sometimes lavishly. The most common forms of decoration—flush inlays or veneers, usually of polished staghorn—became increasingly elaborate and extensive, at times covering the entire surface of the tiller. Roughly before 1500, the inlay consisted of panels, while thereafter it was often applied in an intricately carved intarsia technique of varying extent. Analogously with other works of art, such as furniture and firearms, as the engraved inlay on tillers came to cover more of the surface, the decoration was not infrequently inspired by or copied from contemporary prints (cats. 12, 16, 26). On a few early sixteenth-century examples, the staghorn veneer was left in its natural, rugged state around the lock area, a trend that was taken up again in Germany during the 1650s for gunstocks and firearm-related accessories; when the practice was revived in Saxony during the first half of the eighteenth century, it was perhaps done as a deliberate harking back to earlier decorating practices (cat. 16). Precious, often exotic materials, such as imported woods, ivory, and mother-of-pearl, subtly enhanced the overall visual effect (cats. 9–11). The embellishment of tillers also varied by region, with western European crossbows displaying greater restraint than the more densely ornamented examples of the north-western areas. Although metal surfaces such as the visible parts of the lock might be chiseled or engraved and subsequently gilded, it is extremely rare to find decoratively forged and chiseled trigger guards or the use of gilded copper-alloy appliqués (cat. 18 and fig. 2.30). A constant decorative element from the sixteenth century, at least on central European crossbows, are pom-poms of dyed wool, usually green or featuring the heraldic colors of their owner, and still found on early twentieth-century weapons.

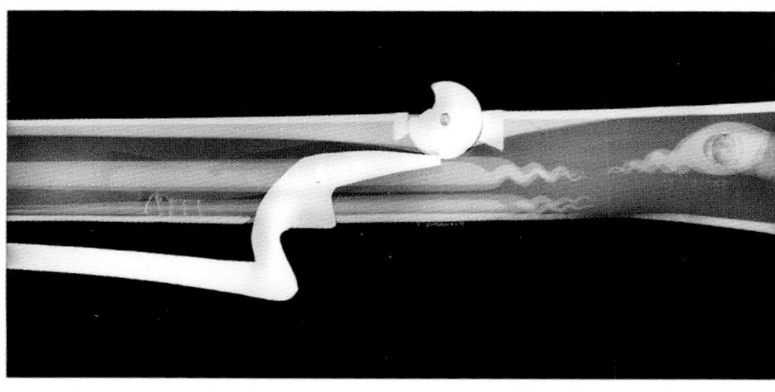

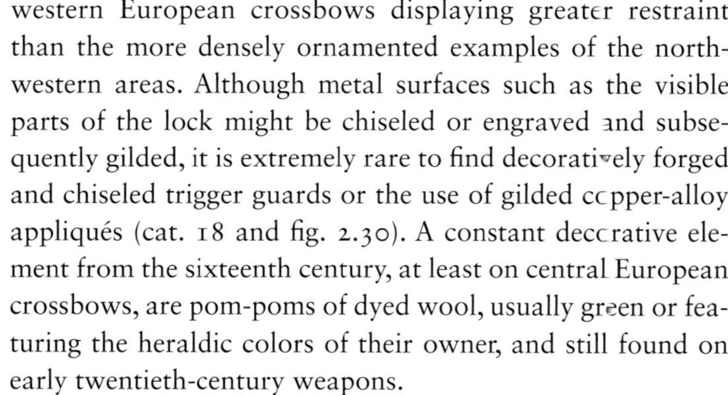

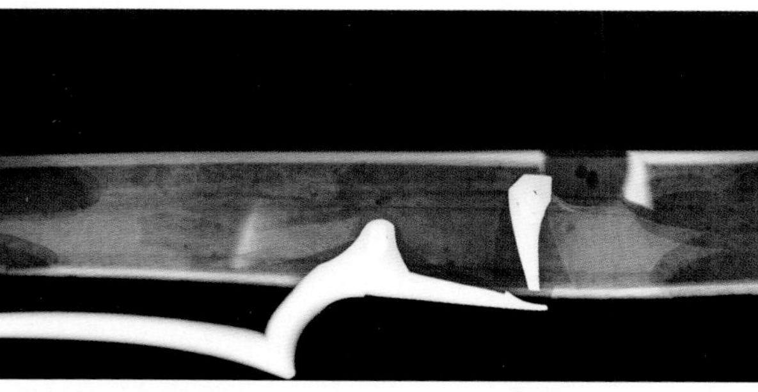

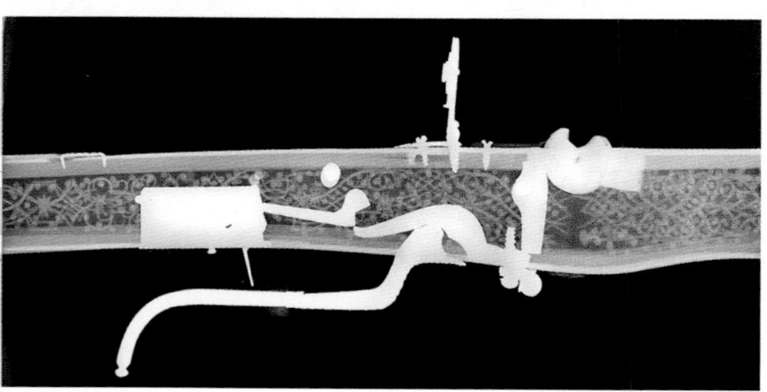

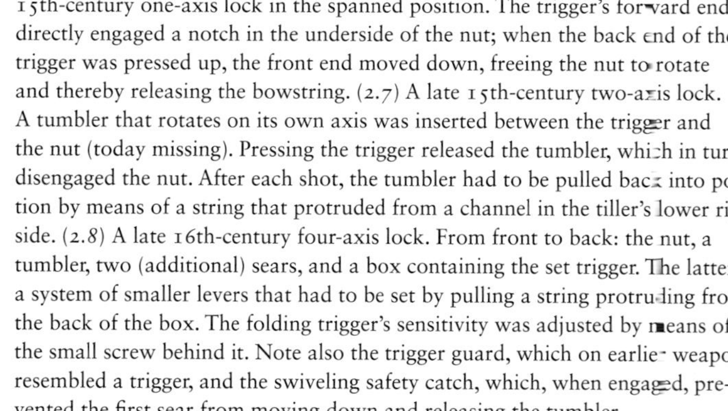

Figure 2.6–2.8 X-rays of catalogues 2, 4, and 8, all from the right. (2.6) A 15th-century one-axis lock in the spanned position. The trigger's forward end directly engaged a notch in the underside of the nut; when the back end of the trigger was pressed up, the front end moved down, freeing the nut to rotate and thereby releasing the bowstring. (2.7) A late 15th-century two-axis lock. A tumbler that rotates on its own axis was inserted between the trigger and the nut (today missing). Pressing the trigger released the tumbler, which in turn disengaged the nut. After each shot, the tumbler had to be pulled back into position by means of a string that protruded from a channel in the tiller's lower right side. (2.8) A late 16th-century four-axis lock. From front to back: the nut, a tumbler, two (additional) sears, and a box containing the set trigger. The latter is a system of smaller levers that had to be set by pulling a string protruding from the back of the box. The folding trigger's sensitivity was adjusted by means of the small screw behind it. Note also the trigger guard, which on earlier weapons resembled a trigger, and the swiveling safety catch, which, when engaged, prevented the first sear from moving down and releasing the tumbler.

5. Crossbow

Central Europe (possibly southern Germany), late 15th or early 16th century, and later
Date 1584 engraved probably during the 19th century
Steel, wood,[1] staghorn, hemp
L. 29 in. (73.7 cm); W. 24⁹⁄₁₆ in. (62.4 cm); Wt. 6 lb. 10 oz. (3 kg)
Gift of William H. Riggs, 1913 (14.25.1572a)

Ex coll.: William H. Riggs, Paris

References: Stone 1934 (1961 ed.), p. 12; Grancsay 1964, p. 35, no. 44; Nickel 1974, p. 228; Stevens 1978, p. 9

At first glance a typical sixteenth-century crossbow, this example comprises a plain, unmarked steel bow, a wooden tiller veneered overall with polished and extensively engraved staghorn, and a snap lock with a folding trigger. Yet, closer examination reveals several unusual features. The weapon was originally fitted with a different release mechanism, a two-axis lock made up of a nut, an internal tumbler, and a long lever trigger. The tumbler was set by pulling a short string that issued from a small hole on the lower right side, and the lock was released with the lever trigger. At some point, probably in the late sixteenth or seventeenth century, the nut was removed, a transverse groove for the bowstring was cut through the nut seat, and a small folding trigger was installed just behind the opening for the lever trigger, thereby creating a snap lock. What was probably the original lever trigger, now secured in place, became a trigger guard. Repairs to the fore-end suggest that the steel bow, too, is not original, though they probably represent working-lifetime alterations and the

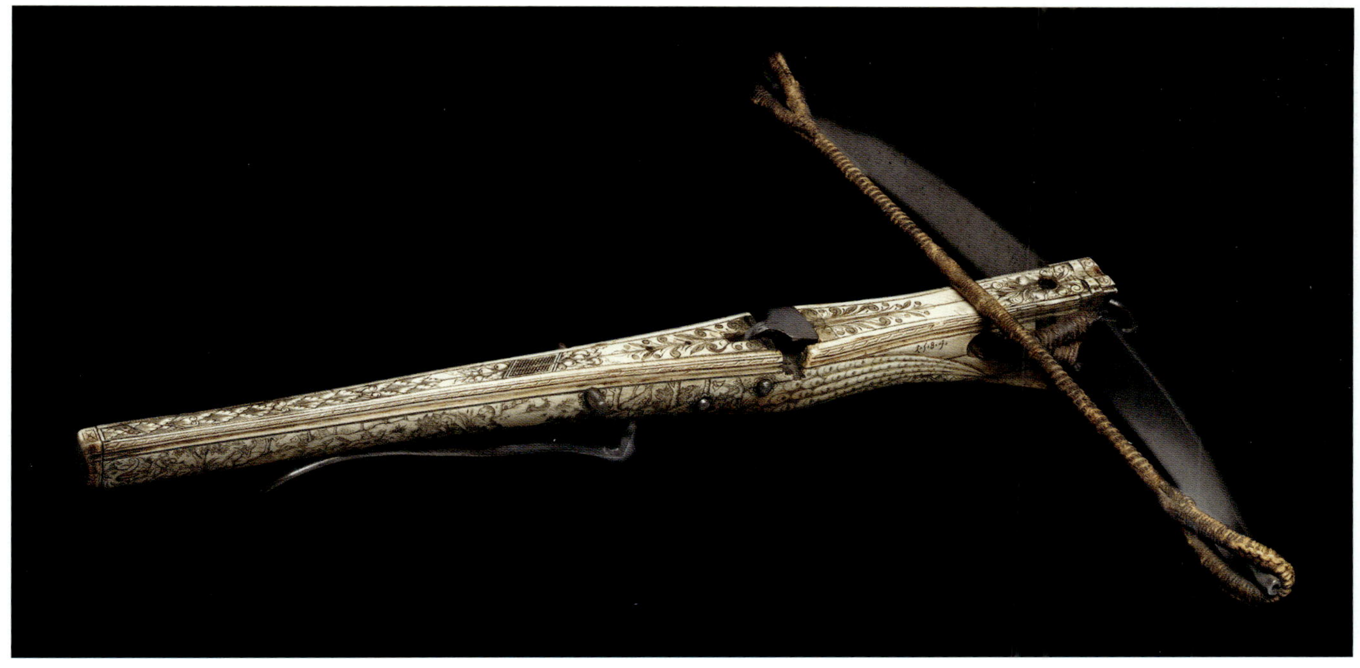

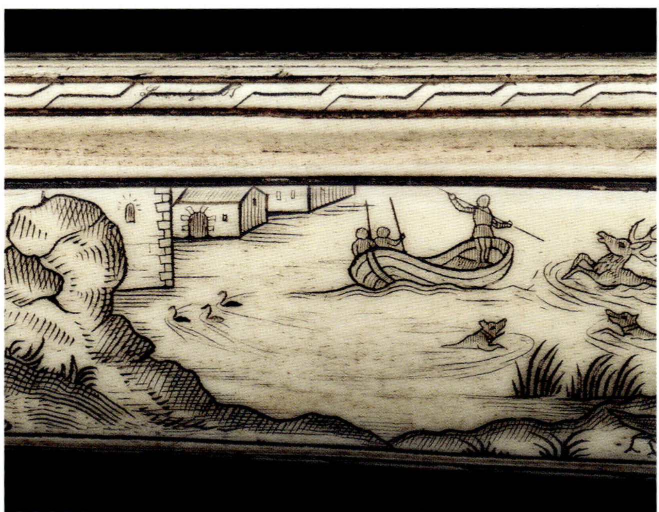

Figure 2.9

At least the hunting scenes must be later than the late fifteenth- or early sixteenth-century tiller and its bone veneer, since the costume depicted is of a style not found before about 1550. Moreover, the ornament clearly accommodates all the openings for the axes of the new lock mechanism, including the folding trigger, and some of the foliage on the top surface of the tiller was probably also engraved at the time the lock was converted.

Yet, there are reasons to doubt the ostensible date of the decoration. The engraving is very crisp, and its black color unfaded, the figures are rather awkward and stiff in their execution, and the mix of styles for the initials is highly anachronistic.[4] Most significant is the recent discovery of an inscription in what appears to be a modern hand, that is, from some time after 1800, located on the rear upper right edge of the tiller. It is minute, some $\frac{1}{32}$ in. (9 mm) in length, and was rendered largely illegible by the guilloche pattern that was engraved over it. The word or words appear to begin with a cursive L.[5]

The Museum's crossbow thus underwent several alterations: as a late fifteenth- or early sixteenth-century weapon it was originally fitted with a two-axis nut lock and presumably had a bow of composite construction; at first, the horn bow was replaced with the present one, perhaps as early as the beginning of the sixteenth century, then, at some point during that or the following century, the release mechanism was converted from a nut lock to a snap lock. Thus, both changes most likely happened during the weapon's working lifetime and attest to a long period of use, as is evident on many crossbows. The majority of the engraved decoration, however, was added during the nineteenth century, perhaps in an attempt to make this crossbow more attractive for sale.[6]

replacement of an earlier, possibly composite bow. The binding and suspension ring presumably date from the same time as these repairs.

The two-axis lock evidently was short-lived, since depictions are found only from the late fifteenth and very early sixteenth centuries, and surviving examples are quite rare (cat. 4).[2] And, indeed, the tiller of this elegant weapon shows all the main characteristics of a crossbow from this period: the elongated, slender shape, a rather high fore-end, and the overall veneer of polished staghorn.[3]

The tiller's extensive embellishment includes sprays of peacock feathers carved in shallow relief, as well as engraved ornament, including a zoomorphic grotesque face; hunting scenes with deer (fig. 2.9), wild boar, bears, a fox, a wolf, and quail; and stylized floral and geometrical patterns. At the fore-end, the tiller is engraved, on the left with the letters F.G.E., and on the right with the year, 1584.

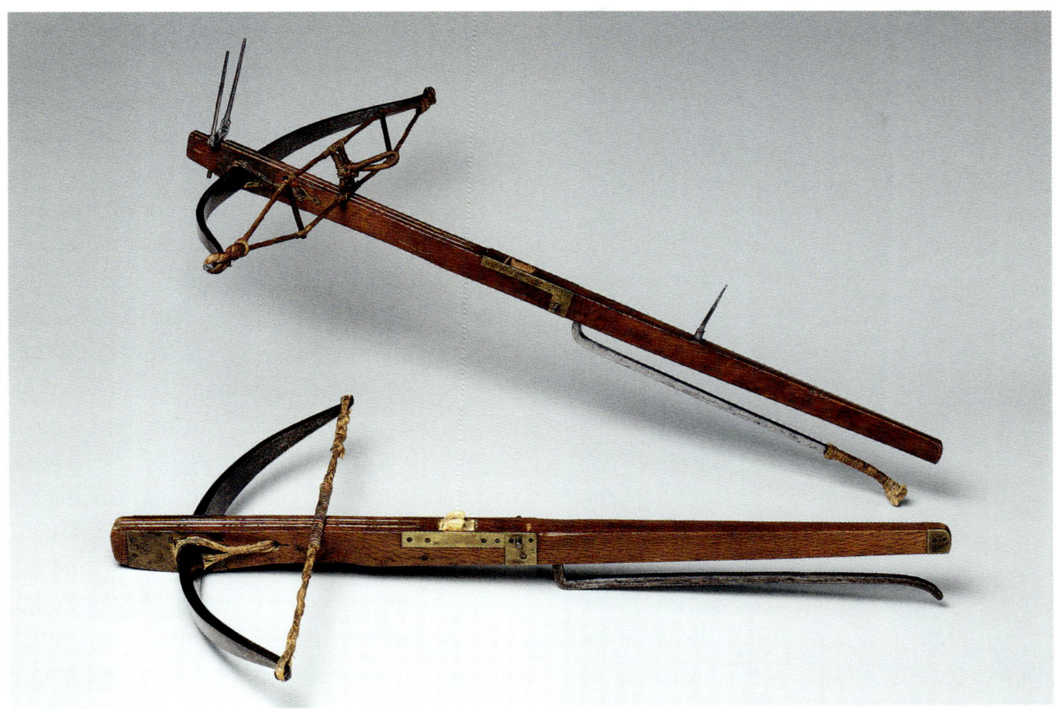

Catalogues 6a (foreground) and *6b*

6. Two Crossbows of Western European Type

a. Spain (possibly Valencia or Toledo), ca. 1540–60
Steel, wood (holly oak), staghorn, copper alloy, hemp, leather
L. 32⅝ in. (82.9 cm); W. 21½ in. (54.6 cm); Wt. 6 lb. (2,726 g)
Gift of Archer M. Huntington, 1927 (27.160.19a)
b. Spain (possibly Madrid), ca. 1540–60 and later
Steel, wood (fruitwood, probably pear), staghorn, copper alloy, hemp
L. 36¼ in. (92.1 cm); W. 25⁷⁄₁₆ in. (64.4 cm); Wt. 4 lb. 13 oz. (2,183 g)
Gift of Archer M. Huntington, 1927 (27.160.18a)

Ex coll.: Guillermo Casanova, marqués de Dos Aguas, Valencia

References: (6a) unpublished; (6b) Stevens 1978, p. 11

Mark:

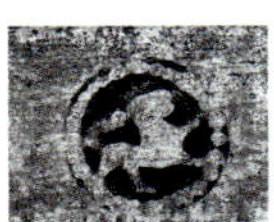

These two crossbows belong to a type that developed in western Europe and is usually referred to as "Spanish" but that was disseminated throughout the western Mediterranean and eventually also to Africa and the colonies in America. The type is characterized by powerful steel bows more curved than central European examples, and by slim wooden tillers that remain rectangular in section for their entire length. The reinforces are often made of metal rather

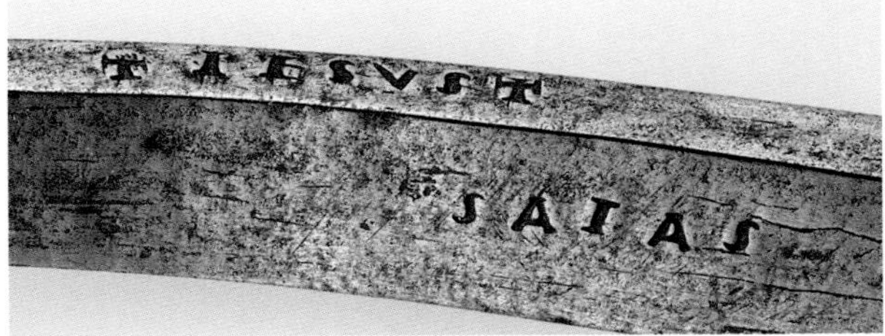

Figure 2.10

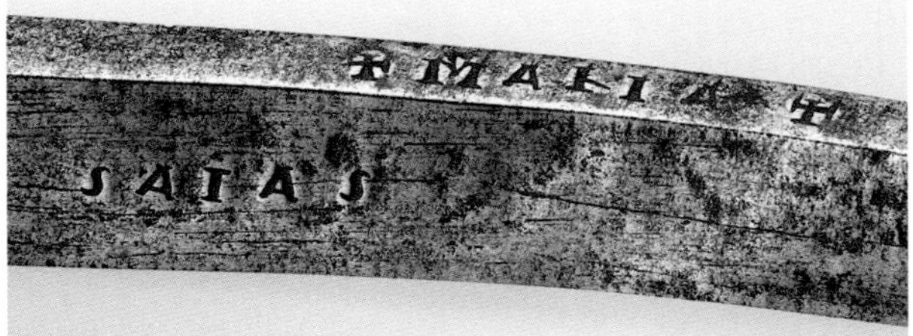

Figure 2.11

than of organic materials, and the release mechanism is usually a simple one-axis lock consisting of an unsecured nut. Both the present examples are plain and utilitarian except for a few strips of sparsely decorated staghorn inlay along the chase. The two weapons here differ in several ways: catalogue 6a is somewhat smaller but noticeably heavier than catalogue 6b, their bows bear different marks and inscriptions, and their tillers are made of different woods; catalogue 6b, finally, was at some point converted into a pellet crossbow (see Section 3, "Pellet Crossbows").

The bow of catalogue 6a was struck four times with the same slightly defaced mark: a crowned lion or leopard passant guardant (or possibly rampant) within a circle of dots. Catalogue 6b displays four short inscriptions: on the bow's upper edge, †IESUS† (left; fig. 2.10) and †MARIA† (right; fig. 2.11), and, on the corresponding inner face, SAIAS, likely a reference to Zayas, a village near Soria in Old Castile.[1]

Both crossbows are nearly identical to two others, in Chicago, one of which is also a converted pellet crossbow.[2] All four weapons originally came from the collection of Guillermo Casanova, marqués de Dos Aguas, Valencia.[3] Similar examples survive in collections in Madrid,[4] Valletta,[5] Turin,[6] Sluderno,[7] and Albuquerque.[8] Distinguishing features of this group include a bow secured by a hemp binding, not metal brackets; L-shaped reinforces of the lock area; and a comparatively long lever trigger that extends almost to the rear end of the tiller. Documentary and archaeological evidence indicates that these crossbows are Spanish and date from about the mid-sixteenth century. This is confirmed by one of the surviving crossbows in Madrid, whose trigger bears the signature of the Valencia crossbow maker Juan Guillén, while the bow—by a different artisan—is dated 1557.[9] Lion marks like the one on catalogue 6a are found on the bows of four crossbows and a pull lever in Madrid, all of which are also probably the work of mid-sixteenth-century Spanish crossbow makers.[10] Some or all of these marks might refer to the kingdom of León.

The present appearance of the two pellet crossbows, finally, is unconvincing, most likely the result of a later, poorly executed conversion. Apart from the fact that the angles of both bows do not allow for the use of a double bowstring, no attempt was made to convert the nut seats or release mechanisms to a system appropriate for pellet crossbows. Since both weapons are now nonfunctional the modifications they underwent were most likely done for appearance only, perhaps in the late nineteenth century.[11] No other extant pellet crossbows of western European type are recorded, although surviving examples of pull levers with only a single claw and their contemporary documentation prove that they must have existed (cat. 38).

7. Crossbow (*Halbe Rüstung*)

Probably Germany (perhaps Bavaria), ca. 1560–80
Steel, wood (core: probably fruitwood, possibly pear; repair
at cheek includes walnut), staghorn, copper alloy, hemp,
leather, polychromy
L. 27¾ in. (70.5 cm); W. 24 in. (60.9 cm); Wt. 8 lb. 14 oz. (4,016 g)
Bequest of George D. Pratt, 1935 (48.149.36a)

Ex coll.: Richard Zschille, Grossenhain, Saxony; Henry
G. Keasbey, Eastbourne, East Sussex; George D. Pratt,
Glen Cove, Long Island, N.Y.

References: Forrer [1894], vol. 1, p. 27, no. 1019, vol. 2,
pl. xxiii; Imperial Institute 1896, p. 70, no. 262; Zschille
sale 1897, p. 62, lot 350; Zschille sale 1900, p. 18, lot 139;
Helbing sale 1902, p. 53, lot 832; Keasbey sale 1924,
lot 277; Grancsay 1931, p. 106; Grancsay 1933b, p. 42,
cat. no. 284; Priest 1940, p. 238; Grancsay 1953, p. 29,
cat. no. 116

Mark:

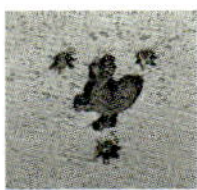

During the sixteenth century, decorated crossbows
became more widespread, no longer an exclusive
privilege of the high nobility. The plain steel bow on
this example is probably a later replacement, as it is
mounted—incorrectly—upside down; the binding
and bowstring are modern. The wooden tiller is
veneered nearly overall with polished and carved
staghorn and includes a four-axis nut lock with a set
trigger. At the back, the butt and cheek have been
repaired; the lock plate around the trigger and the
safety catch are missing.

Except for the chase, almost the entire surface of
the tiller is carved in shallow relief, its ornament
standing proud against a sunken background stained
a dark green. Scenes from the Old Testament along

the sides are oriented so as to be read when the
weapon is held upright (fig. 2.12). They include, front
to back, on the left: God creating the world, the creation of Adam, God instructing Adam, and the
creation of Eve; at least one more scene is missing.
On the right are: the Fall, Adam ashamed of his
nakedness, the Expulsion, Adam and Eve laboring,
Cain and Abel sacrificing, and Cain slaying Abel.
In addition to a variety of stylized floral patterns,
the underside displays two female figures: a naked
woman stabbing herself and a woman in early
sixteenth-century dress, holding an archaic sword, a
falchion, and the severed head of a bearded man.
The former undoubtedly refers to Lucretia, the
ancient Roman matron who, raped by an enemy of
Rome and believing herself to be thereby dishon-
ored, took her own life; the latter is most likely the
biblical heroine Judith, who decapitated Israel's
Assyrian enemy Holofernes. Both are commonplace

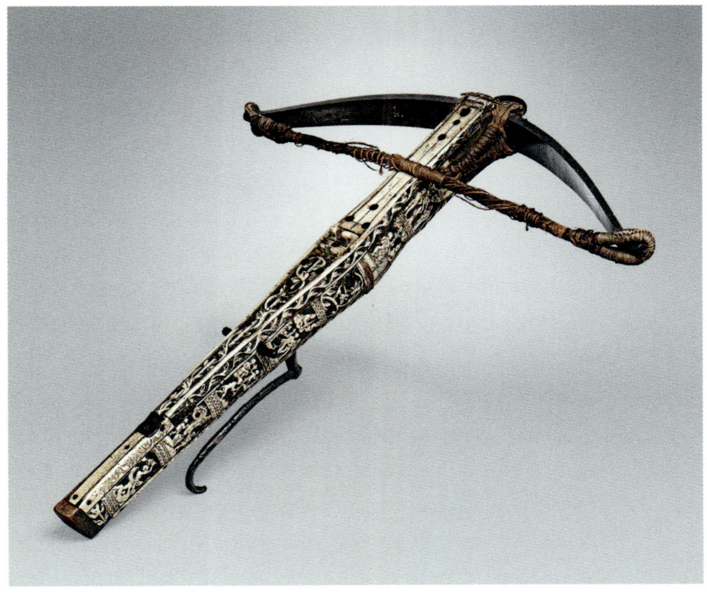

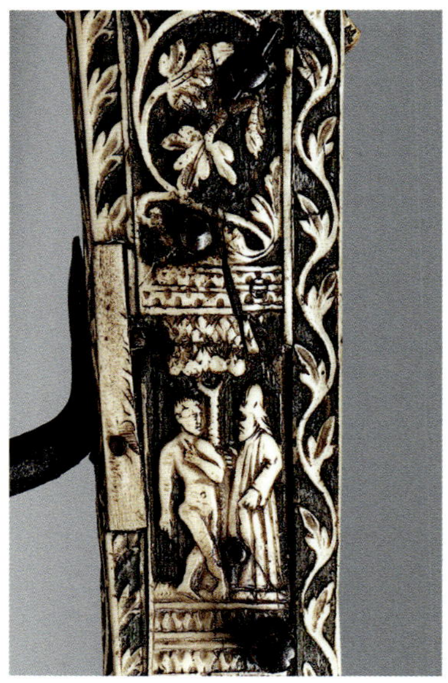

Figure 2.12

examples of womanly virtue and self-sacrifice. Some of the metal furniture—the trigger guard, cranequin lugs, and one side of the tumbler axis—has been decorated with sparse chiseling. The bow is struck on the belly side of the left arm with an upside-down mark: a rooster surrounded by three six-pointed stars.

Decorative relief carving, found on crossbow tillers from as early as the mid-fifteenth century (cats. 3, 4), continued through the sixteenth century, and the present crossbow may be compared to a small number of similarily embellished weapons. The religious scenes found on an example in Paris closely resemble those on the Museum's crossbow.[1] Another, in Berlin, dated 1567, differs somewhat in the overall composition of the tiller's decoration, which features both hunting and biblical scenes polychromed and oriented to be read with the weapon in a horizontal position.[2]

The highest quality of this type of shallow relief work among surviving examples is displayed on two crossbows in Leeds and Prague.[3] Instead of figural scenes, the motifs consist mainly of stylized floral and candelabra patterns inhabited by animal grotesques and a few human figures; the two crossbows, probably of mid-sixteenth-century date, bear the arms of the dukes of Bavaria but do not form a pair. Finally, a crossbow in Basel, dated 1565 on the tiller, shows the carved staghorn only on its underside, but the arrangement of two allegorical females front and back recalls the composition on the underside of the Metropolitan Museum's crossbow.[4] The dated examples in Basel and Berlin further support the suggestion that most weapons belonging to this group were made in the second half of the sixteenth century. The year 1627, accompanied by an unidentified coat of arms containing a bird, engraved on the butt plate of the Paris crossbow was probably added by a subsequent owner, while a second date, 1656, on the weapon in Berlin probably refers to a working-lifetime refurbishment.[5] Finally, it is noteworthy that the bows on some of the weapons in this group are extensively decorated: those in Paris and Berlin are painted with floral ornament, and the one in Leeds is etched overall with floral vines and strapwork cartouches containing trophies.

The mark on the bow of the Museum's weapon has been recorded, for example, on two target crossbows in Delft, which are believed to be Belgian and to date from the seventeenth or eighteenth century.[6] This has led to the suggestion that bows struck with this mark may have been made in Belgium.[7] However, the emblem, or charge, of a rooster surrounded by three stars can be found in heraldry as far ranging as that of Silesia/Poland, Hungary, Switzerland, and France, so that any attribution must remain tentative.[8] Nonetheless, the assessment that bows struck with this mark date to the seventeenth or eighteenth century, if correct, would confirm that the bow mounted on the Museum's crossbow is a later replacement.

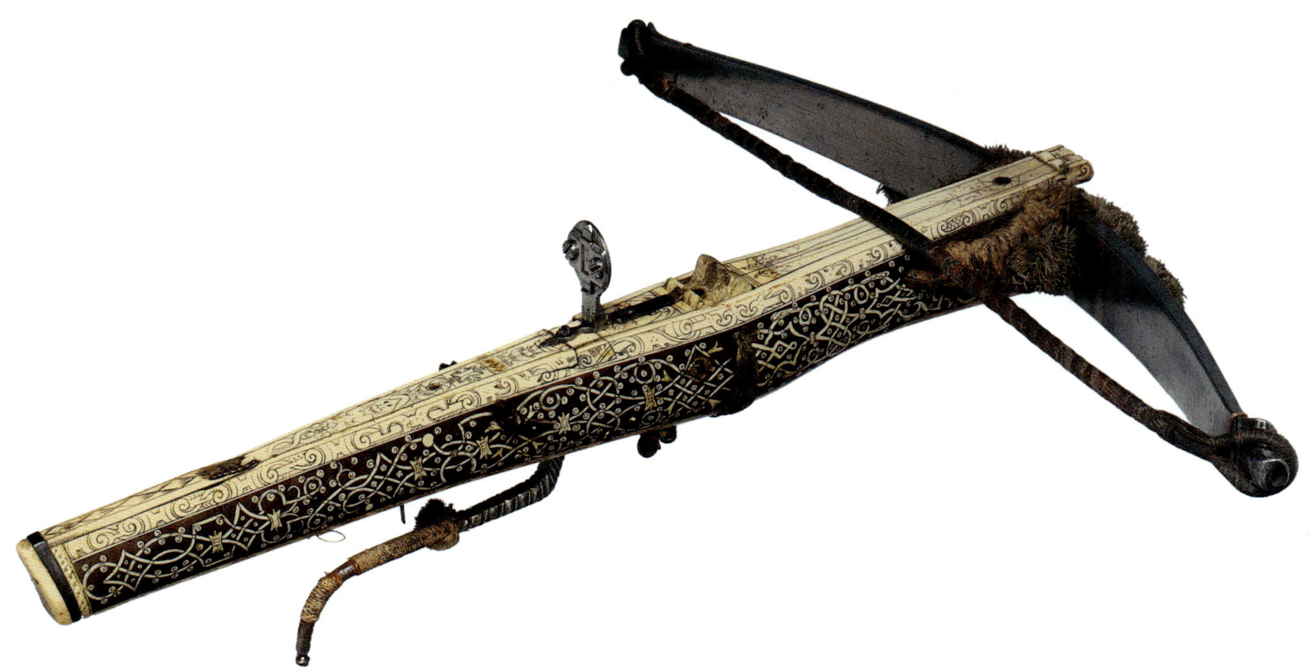

8. Crossbow (*Halbe Rüstung*)

Central Europe, probably Germany (possibly Saxony),
ca. 1575–1650
Steel, wood (fruitwood veneer, probably cherry), staghorn,
copper alloy, hemp, wool
L. 24 13/16 in. (63 cm); W. 23 7/16 in. (59.5 cm); Wt. 8 lb. 7 oz.
(3,775 g)
Gift of William H. Riggs, 1913 (14.25.1574a)

Ex coll.: Prince Peter Soltykoff, Paris; William H. Riggs,
Paris

References: Stone 1934 (1961 ed.), p. 12; Grancsay 1955,
p. 23, no. 85; Nickel 1974, p. 229; Nickel, Pyhrr, and
Tarassuk 1982, pp. 129–30, no. 87

Mark:

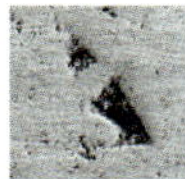

This crossbow is characteristic of a type that was
popular throughout central Europe from the mid-
sixteenth until at least the late seventeenth century.

Fitted with powerful steel bows, these weapons were
used for both hunting large game and shooting
competitions. This particular example is noteworthy
for its decoration, which, although comparatively
simple and not of the highest quality, covers almost
the entire surface of the tiller.

The bow is plain but very well made, as indicated
by the chamfered edges; it is struck on the belly side
of the right arm with a mark, now much worn and

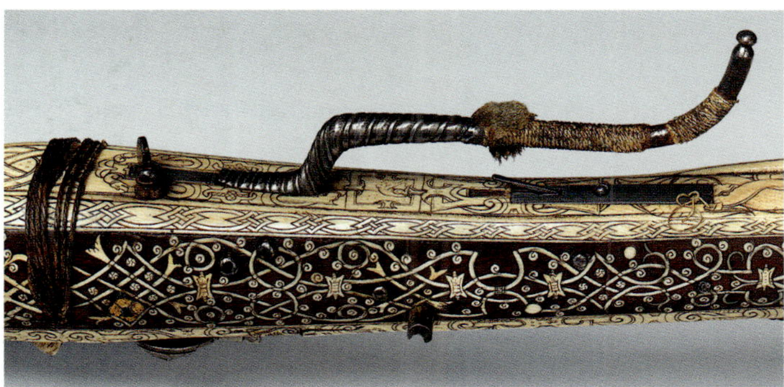

Figure 2.13

illegible. The bowstring is a modern replacement. Made with flanged upper and lower edges and a distinctly concave cheek, the tiller's core is made of an unidentified wood, probably veneered with cherry, and fitted with a four-axis lock with a set trigger and a rear sight.

The panels of polished staghorn covering the top and underside of the tiller are engraved with cartouches, architectural elements, and grotesque faces on top, while the underside features braided bands, strapwork, and a curling, elephantine sea monster. The sides are inlaid with polished and engraved staghorn forming dense strapwork interlace, from which issue sparse floral extensions and scrollwork. Apart from the curling sea monster, there is little figural ornament: a pair of small strapwork extensions in the shape of dogs' heads, in front of the trigger, and a depiction within a cartouche of a simian creature, apparently holding its nose, near the set trigger. Sculptural embellishment includes the trigger guard, decoratively chiseled with a spiraling double-band motif (fig. 2.13), and the head rivet and the right side of the main tumbler axis, which are shaped like four-petaled flowers. All of these retain traces of gilding, as do the axes of the lock mechanism, the safety catch, and the cranequin lugs.

There are no other recorded examples closely comparable to the Museum's crossbow. The overall shape, release mechanism, and general style of decoration suggest that this weapon was made in the later decades of the sixteenth century, possibly in the Saxon region of Germany. Whether the monkey motif—despite its unobtrusive location—was intended to have any particular meaning is impossible to determine. Its presence may have had a moralizing significance or may allude to a coat of arms or a name;[1] on the other hand, it might simply be an artistic whim, reflecting the general popularity of monkeys in early modern iconography.

9. Crossbow

Probably England (possibly London), ca. 1600–1625
Steel, wood (Indian rosewood), staghorn, mother-of-pearl
L. 27¾ in. (70.5 cm); W. 18⅜ in. (46.6 cm); Wt. 8 lb. 9 oz. (3,890 g)
Bashford Dean Memorial Collection, Funds from various donors, 1929 (29.158.649)

Ex coll.: Seymour Lucas, R. A., Blythburgh, Suffolk; his estate sale, Sotheby, Wilkinson & Hodge, London, Dec. 5 and 7, 1923, lot 195; [Fenton and Sons, London]; Bashford Dean, Riverdale, N.Y.

Reference: Sotheby's sale 1923, p. 27, lot 195

Crossbows had been employed in the British Isles long before the Norman Conquest. And despite an English predisposition toward longbows, and repeated attempts at regulating the possession and use of crossbows, the latter remained a favorite hunting weapon well into the Victorian age.[1]

This example's plain, unmarked steel bow is heavy and powerful for its size. The slender tiller of Indian rosewood is fitted with a single-axis release mechanism and a steel belt clip. An unusual detail of the lock mechanism is the fact that the axis for the lever trigger protrudes far enough on either side to serve as lugs for the spanning device, a pull lever. The weapon is missing its bowstring, nut, and a bolt clip, as well as the small foldaway safety catch that was formerly mounted to the underside of the tiller; the coat of dark paint on all metal

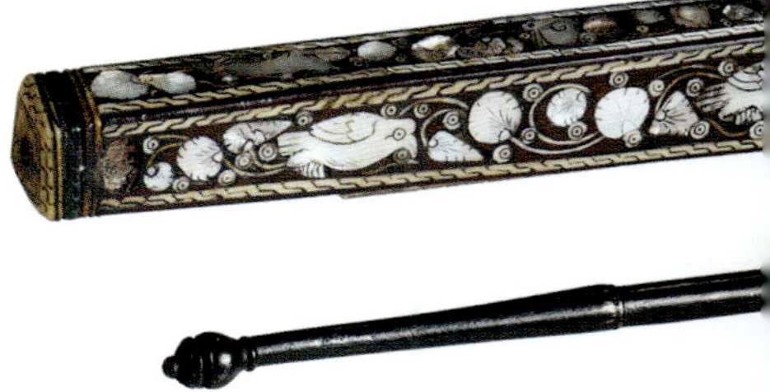

surfaces is modern. All four sides of the tiller are profusely inlaid with strips and small plaques of polished staghorn and mother-of pearl, most of which
are engraved with floral vines, petals, blossoms, and
guilloche patterns. On the sides, the inlay features
several birds—perhaps ravens[2]—and there are three
hounds and three snails on the top of the tiller. The
groove of the chase is inlaid in staghorn engraved
with a bold guilloche pattern and green-stained central dots; just behind the nut seat is a large mother-
of-pearl plaque in the shape of a plain, angular shield
(fig. 2.14). Most of the metal parts are plain, except
for the simple loops of the suspension ring, the decoratively shaped lever trigger, and the small perforated
and chiseled finial of the belt clip (fig. 2.15).

The Museum's crossbow belongs to a small
group of similar weapons that are likely to be of
English manufacture. The characteristics that some
scholars have described as "English"
include the combination of a straight
tiller with a slight medial ridge and a
belt clip on the underside of the fore-
end, a chase protruding forward beyond
the fore-end, the specific type of decoration,
an elongated oval (in the present case) or round
suspension ring to protect the extension of the chase,

and a long lever trigger. The fact that the general
appearance of these crossbows is almost identical to
examples made in France and the Netherlands can
be explained by the strong presence of French-
Burgundian and Flemish artisans and craftsmen—
crossbow makers, gun makers, stock carvers, and
joiners—who worked in London during the sixteenth and seventeenth centuries.

The most distinguished of the group are several
crossbows of royal provenance. Three of these, some
with matching levers and gold- or silver-embroidered
covers, were included in two gifts of weapons, horses,
hounds, and other luxurious goods sent by James I
of England to Philip III of Spain in 1604 and 1614
respectively. The two examples from the first gift
and one from the 1614 shipment, which originally
included six crossbows, still survive in Madrid.[3]
While these presentation weapons feature much
more sumptuous decoration—including etched and
gilded decoration on the bows, bow brackets, and
trigger levers—plainer examples, similar in appearance to the Museum's weapon, are in Leeds
and other public and private collections in Great Britain. Among

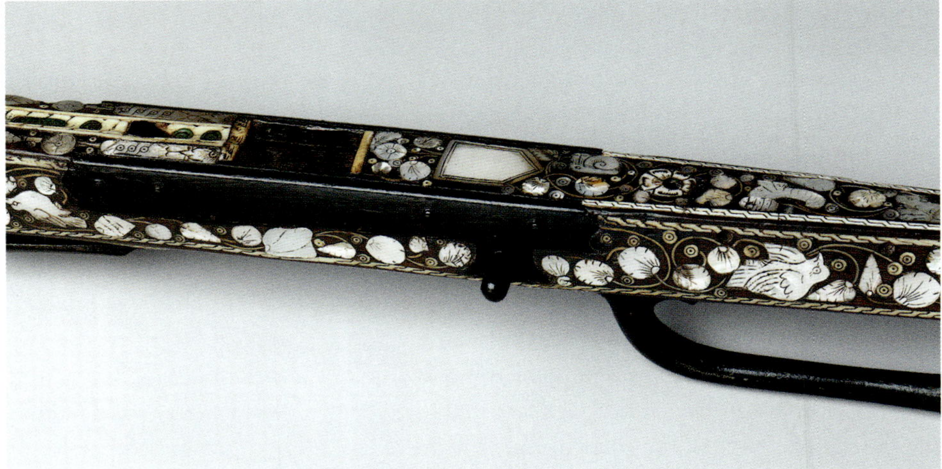

Figure 2.14

these a crossbow dated to about 1600, now in Leeds, most closely resembles the Museum's example.[4] As indicated by a painting at Lamport Hall in Northamptonshire, crossbows of this type remained in use at least until the mid-seventeenth century.[5]

The characteristic form of the staghorn and mother-of-pearl inlay also embellishes contemporary

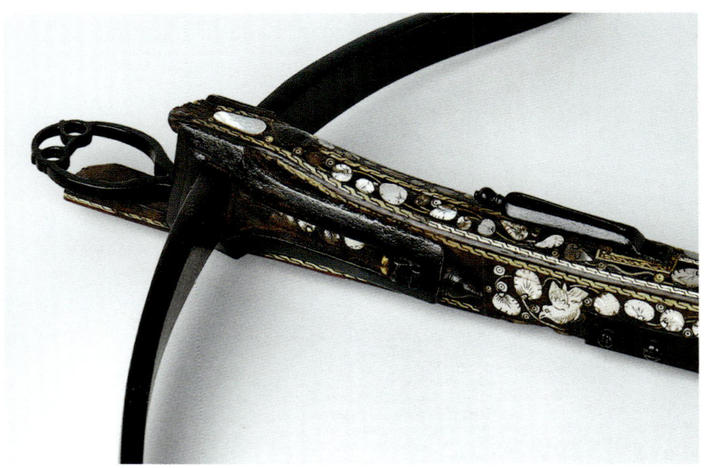

Figure 2.15

English and Continental firearms and furniture.[6] Among such firearms is a group of ceremonial muskets, apparently made for members of trade guilds, or Worshipful Companies, of the City of London at different times during the first half of the seventeenth century.[7] Several of these feature the shield-shaped mother-of-pearl plaques, some of which are left plain, while others bear the owner's initials, the Company's coat of arms, or both. Some or all of these muskets would have been made, or at least decorated, in London. If this assumption is correct, the resemblance of their escutcheon-like shields to those found on some of the English crossbows would indicate that the same London craftsmen—some certainly of Continental origin—were responsible for the work on both types of weapons. The similarity in shape between the belt clip and lever trigger on the Museum's crossbow and that of their counterparts on weapons from the English shipments to Spain also supports the likelihood that the Museum's crossbow was made in London during the first quarter of the seventeenth century.[8]

10. Crossbow (*Halbe Rüstung*)

Central Europe (southern Germany or perhaps Tyrol),
ca. 1600–1650
Steel, wood (probably cherry), ivory (probably elephant), horn,
mother-of-pearl, iron alloy
L. 26⅞ in. (68.3 cm); W. 24⁹⁄₁₆ in. (62.4 cm); Wt. 9 lb. 6 oz.
(4,258 g)
Gift of Mrs. Ridgely Hunt in memory of William Cruger Pell,
1907 (07.24.48a)

Ex coll.: William Cruger Pell, New York

References: Dean 1907; Heath 1972, p. 304

Mark:

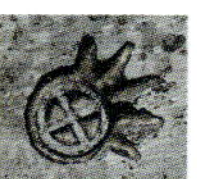

The distinguishing features of this weapon are a
four-axis release mechanism that includes a particular type of set trigger and a metal nut, the decoration
of dense inlay executed in ivory and mother-of-pearl,
and several indications that this crossbow remained
in use for a long time.

The plain steel bow, although not very large, is
stout and strong, and—for its size—has relatively
large nocks. Since the binding is modern, and the
saddle block too small, the bow is probably a later
replacement; the bowstring appears to be old. On
the belly side the bow's right arm is struck with a
mark: a quartered circle crowned by five rays.[1]

The sturdy tiller, probably made of cherry, has a
strong fore-end that is almost square in section and
a small left cheek. Of four-axis type, the release
mechanism comprises a set trigger, a nut, a trigger
guard in the shape of a lever trigger, and a safety
catch, all of iron alloy. Remarkable are particulars of
the nut, the axis for the tumbler, and the set trigger.
The nut is fitted across the groove for the bowstring
with a flat rectangular iron plate held in place by
two screws. The tumbler axis protrudes slightly on
either side, and it is retained in the tiller by a pin
passing through a small hole on the left. The user
would have been able to disassemble the front of the
release mechanism quickly by removing the pin and
axis. Instead of a set trigger operated by a short

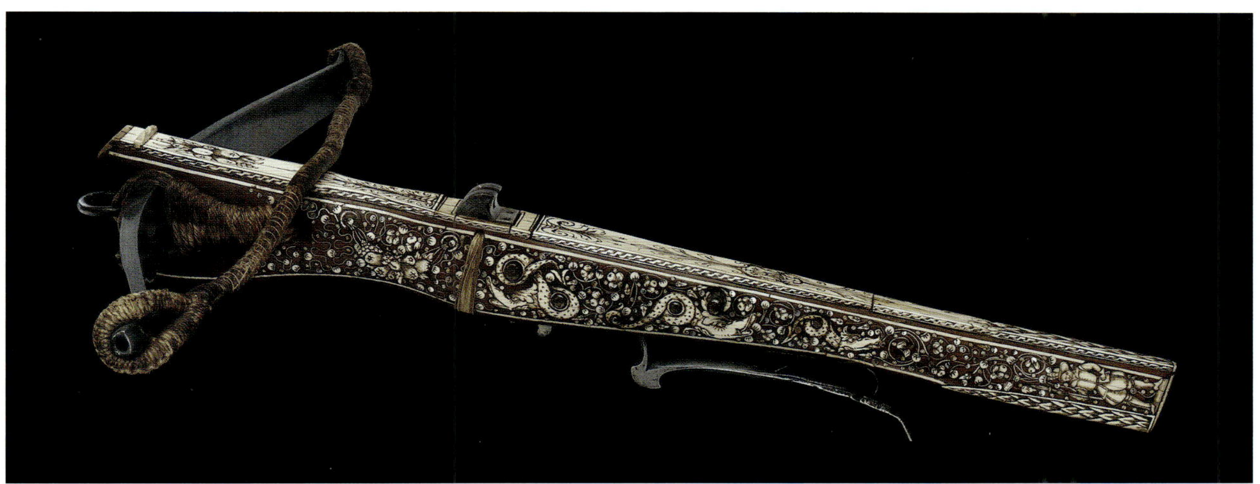

string (cats. 8, 11, 12, 16), the one on this weapon is set, or prepared, by a second trigger, like those more commonly found on late seventeenth- and eighteenth-century firearms and snap-lock crossbows (cats. 13–15). Since neither the trigger proper nor its setting mechanism can be folded flat against the stock, the weapon could not be spanned by means of a cranequin with a conventional hemp loop. In light of these observations it is likely that this set trigger is a late seventeenth- or eighteenth-century addition, and that the weapon was then spanned with a modified cranequin whose loop had been replaced by a pair of hooked claws.

The top of the tiller is entirely faced with polished ivory engraved with stylized floral ornament, a grotesque face, and a bunch of fruit and foliage, which on either side is bordered by narrow bands engraved with a guilloche pattern. The sides and underside are inlaid with engraved ivory and mother-of-pearl. On the sides, curling floral vines with leaves and flower buds are inhabited by large dragon-like creatures with fish tails, three on the left and four on the right, their tails curling around the cranequin lugs and the axes of the release mechanism. In addition, festoons of fruit and vegetables hang from two rings at the front just behind the bridle hole. Larger ivory panels, probably

of later date, were added by cutting into the inlay on the underside at the front, the rear, and around the openings for the set trigger, trigger guard, and tumbler. These panels, too, are engraved, with variations of the same stylized floral pattern found on the top of the tiller. A butt plate, also of polished ivory, caps the end of the tiller, and the upper flange of the fore-end is faced with a horn plaque.

The Museum's crossbow belongs to a common central European type that was used throughout the late sixteenth and seventeenth centuries; the weapon was probably made in the later years of that range. The features associated with a date of manufacture after about 1570 are the tiller's markedly stout silhouette, a short fore-end of almost square section, and the ease with which the tumbler axis may be removed. The mark on the bow of the Museum's weapon is one of the most widely found stamps on central European crossbows. Most of the recorded examples are nearly identical to this one, while others show variations in size or the number of rays, or they do not show a quartering.[2] Just as noteworthy as the number of surviving examples is their wide temporal, as well as geographical, distribution: they are struck into bows mounted on weapons dating from the sixteenth to the eighteenth century. Yet

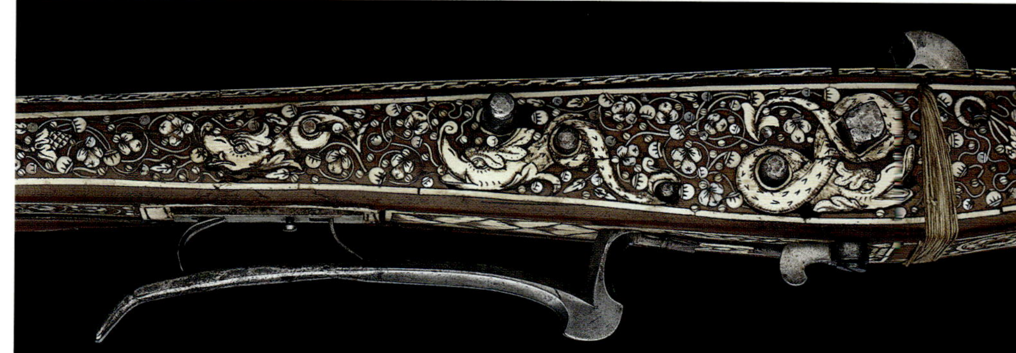

Figure 2.16

despite the mark's frequent occurrence, it has so far been impossible to identify even the geographical origin of bows struck with it, nor is it clear whether it represents a single maker or a workshop, or even an official proof or city stamp.

The difficulty of dating this weapon is further complicated by the fact that several alterations and repairs suggest that the Museum's crossbow remained in use for a considerable time, notably the replaced bow, the addition of an iron-alloy nut and the particular set trigger, and several changes to the decoration. Most of the upper facing is a replacement, as are the two larger panels at the front and rear of the underside and the inlay framing the set trigger opening. All of the later inlay was inserted into the original ornament.

An unusual feature of the inlay, apart from the costliness of the materials, is the presence of festoons on either side of the fore-end (fig. 2.16), which might help to date this weapon.[3] A very similar treatment of this motif—especially the suspension of the garlands from three tendrils—appears on the stock of a wheel-lock arquebus in Saint-Étienne, the barrel of which is signed ADAM SCHUG, and dated 1645.[4] Although nothing more is known about the gun maker, this arquebus provides at least an approximate date for crossbows adorned with similar ornaments.

Crossbows generally similar to the Museum's example in silhouette and type of decoration are today in Buenos Aires,[5] Bad Wildungen,[6] Geneva,[7] and Dresden.[8] Among these, one of the weapons in Buenos Aires bears a significantly close resemblance to the Museum's example: the tiller displays the same stout silhouette, bands of guilloche along the edges, and curly-tailed dragons on the sides. The fact that the Buenos Aires crossbow has a snap lock further supports the assessment that these weapons are probably of seventeenth-century date.

11. Large Crossbow (*Ganze Rüstung*) of Johann Georg, Baron von Rechenberg

German (probably Dresden), dated 1663
Steel, wood,[1] wood veneer (snakewood), ivory (elephant), staghorn, horn, copper alloy, gold, wool, leather
L. 32¾ in. (83.2 cm); W. 32⅞ in. (83.5 cm); Wt. 25 lb. 11 oz. (11,656 g)
Gift of William H. Riggs, 1913 (14.25.1576a)

EX COLL.: The armory of Johann Georg, baron von Rechenberg, Dresden; von Löwen, Dresden; William H. Riggs, Paris

REFERENCE: Sensfelder 2012, pp. 42–43, figs. 9, 10

MARKS:

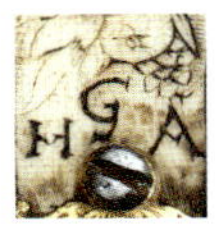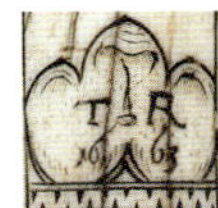

Large and exceptionally heavy crossbows like the present example are known in German as *ganze Rüstungen* (full-size equipment). They developed from the oversize weapons employed in war and for hunting large game, but after the late sixteenth century their use appears to have been restricted to the German-speaking areas, where they served exclusively in competitions. A crossbow this large, even with modest decoration, would have been so expensive that only a few could afford it; this may explain the rarity of examples of this type.

The Museum's weapon consists of a plain, unmarked steel bow that is extremely thick and heavy, and a well-proportioned wooden tiller with a four-axis release mechanism that includes an ivory nut, a set trigger, and a heavy trigger guard. The decoration consists of an exotic snakewood veneer and panels of polished and engraved staghorn, as

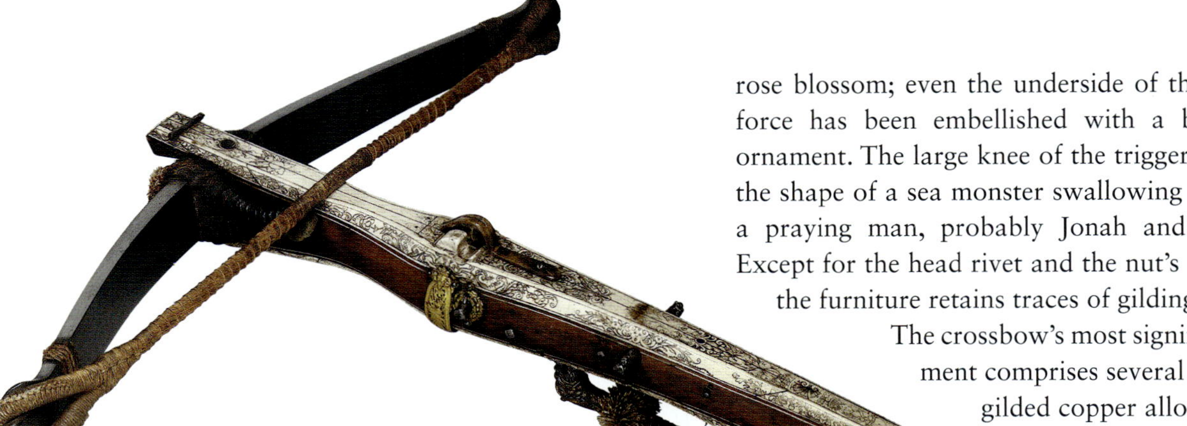

well as chiseled steel furniture and gilded copper-alloy appliqués.

The engraved ornament includes grotesque figures among splays of fruit, festoons, and floral vines terminating in animal heads and interspersed with mascarons and occasional birds; various monsters and other creatures appear on the butt: a fish-tailed griffin at the top left, a bird extending from the floral vine at the top right, a similar extension in the shape of a dragon at the lower right, and two addorsed sea horses at the lower left edge. Also visible on the underside are two sets of initials, probably those of the crossbow maker and the artist responsible for the tiller's decoration. At the fore-end, just below a cluster of fruit, can be found the letters HGA, while at the butt a separate field below an owl on a broken tree trunk contains the initials TR above what appears to be the weapon's year of manufacture, 1663.

The ornament extends to almost all the tiller's steel furniture: the suspension ring is chiseled with two bust-length human figures placed head to head and the ends of the cranequin lug resemble lions' heads. The safety catch is decoratively pierced, and the upper end of the head rivet displays an etched rose blossom; even the underside of the nut's reinforce has been embellished with a brace-shaped ornament. The large knee of the trigger guard takes the shape of a sea monster swallowing the figure of a praying man, probably Jonah and the Whale. Except for the head rivet and the nut's reinforce, all the furniture retains traces of gilding.

The crossbow's most significant adornment comprises several appliqués of gilded copper alloy, in particular a panel set flush into the center of the staghorn butt plate. The panel is pierced and engraved with a coat of arms below an *Adelskrone*, that is, the crown of the untitled lower nobility, accompanied by a series of letters. The arms on the butt plate of the present example are those of the Rechenberg family: quartered, in 1 and 4 on a golden ground a halved double-headed black eagle with red talons and tongue; in 2 and 3 on a red ground a crowned black ram's head with golden horns and a red tongue, with three ostrich feathers issuing from the crown, alternately red, black, and silver (figs. 2.17, 2.18).[2] Together with the letters I.G.F.V.R.C.S.O.H.M.W.G.R.V.O.C., they identify the crossbow's original owner and a list of the most important offices he held: Iohann Georg Freiherr Von Rechenberg Churfürstlich Sächsischer Ober Hof Marschall Wirklicher Geheimer Rat Vnd Ober Cämmerer (Johann Georg, baron von Rechenberg, Electoral Saxon Lord Steward, True Privy Councilor, and Lord Chamberlain). Further pierced and engraved appliqués, on the covers of the lower end of the head rivet and the binding of the nut, depict trophies of classical and later arms, all of which—including those on the butt plate—are backed by thin sheets of gilded copper-alloy foil.

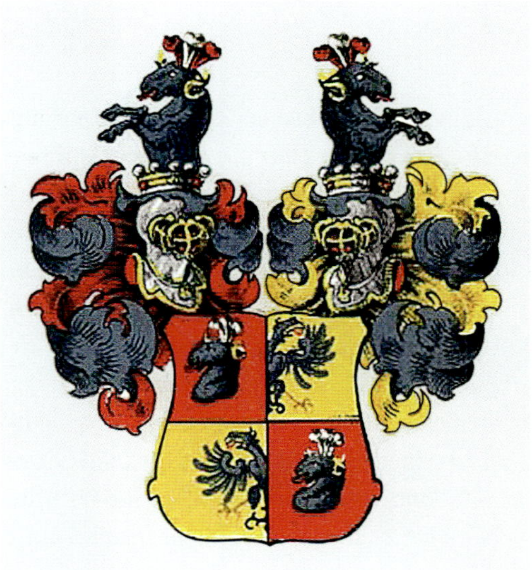

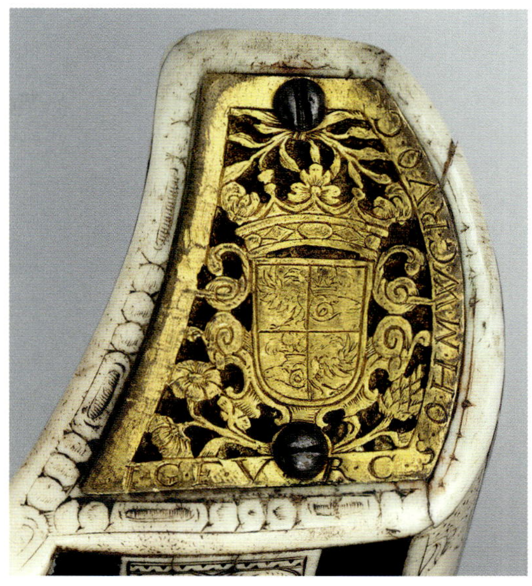

Figure 2.17 Arms of the barons (*Freiherren*) von Rehenberg.

Figure 2.18

Other appliqués are embossed. Two are shaped like rose blossoms and overlay the ends of the tumbler axis, and pairs of holes flanking each axis of the lock mechanism show that they were all formerly capped by similar appliqués, now lost. Another two, placed atop either side of the protective band on the nut binding, are embossed in the shape of a crowned ram's head, another allusion to the Rechenberg baronial arms.

Finally, a number of woolen pom-poms are attached to the security cord, binding, and trigger guard. The three (of originally at least four) that adorn the security cord, together with a single pom-pom attached to the trigger, are faded but appear to have once been green or yellow green, the chief color of the Saxon family coat of arms. Interestingly, the two pom-poms on either side of the fore-end, like traces of others formerly fitted near the binding hole, are red and yellow, referring to the main colors in the Rechenberg baronial arms.

Although examples survive in several public and private collections, crossbows of this size and weight were not common, and they have received little scholarly attention. Noteworthy among known examples are three *ganze Rüstungen*, one in Dresden and two at Skokloster Castle, dated 1582, 1592, and 1593, respectively;[3] another late sixteenth-century example in Philadelphia;[4] and large crossbows of the seventeenth, eighteenth, and nineteenth centuries in Grandson, Coburg, Heidelberg, Poznan, and Dresden.[5] Their dimensions and the extent of their decoration vary, the latter ranging from relatively sparse to an exuberant use of engraving on more or less extensive staghorn inlay, but the Metropolitan's crossbow is exceptional in the quality and variety of its embellishment. Gilded appliqués are occasionally found on other crossbows, but they are usually confined to a protective band over the nut binding (cats. 12, 16), while figuratively shaped and chiseled trigger guards are even scarcer: only three other instances are recorded to date, and those are on crossbows of ordinary size.[6]

Equally unusual for a *ganze Rüstung* is the fact that the decoration includes not only the heraldry of its original owner and the year in which it was made but also the initials of at least two of the artisans involved in its manufacture. The first set of initials,

HGA, may refer to the crossbow maker, that is, the person who made tillers and fitted them with locks and with steel bows bought from a bow maker. The second set of initials, TR, is likely to be those of an artisan working for the Saxon court, either a stock maker or else an artist specialized in the decoration of gun stocks and tillers: a number of seventeenth-century pistol and gun stocks in Dresden bear polished staghorn or horn panels engraved with the same initials.[7] Although it has not yet been possible to identify either one of these artists, the crossbow was most likely made and decorated in Saxony, possibly in Dresden.

The original owner of the Museum's crossbow, Johann Georg von Rechenberg (1610–1664), was a Saxon nobleman who rose to power and fame at the Dresden court, became a close confidant of both Duke Johann Georg I and his son, Duke Johann Georg II, and was described as one of the court's most illustrious cavaliers (fig. 2.19).[8] In 1656, the same year in which he was created a baron,[9] Rechenberg was appointed to his most important position, *Oberhofmarschall*, probably in recognition of more than twenty years in ducal service as chamberlain and personal attendant, making him the highest official at the Dresden court, responsible for the material needs of the court and charged with oversight of all aspects of ceremonies and festivities. In light of his important position at the Dresden court, it is possible that the *Oberhofmarschall* commissioned this crossbow because he participated in shooting competitions, or he could have received it as a gift from Duke Johann Georg II in recognition of almost three decades of loyal service.

Rechenberg's will makes no mention of arms or armor, and it has so far been impossible to trace the history of the Museum's crossbow after his death. William Riggs reported acquiring the crossbow in the 1860s from a "Director von Löwen in Dresden," a person and provenance as yet unconfirmed.[10]

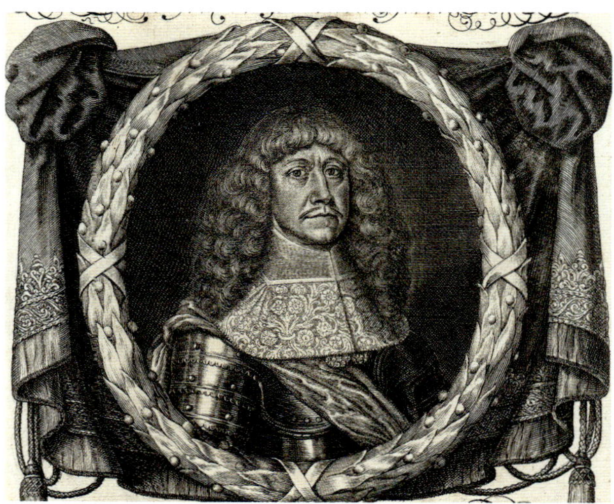

Figure 2.19 Johann Caspar Höckner (German, 1629–ca. 1670/71). Johann Georg von Rechenberg, detail of the title page of his eulogy, 1664. Engraving. Staatliche Kunstsammlungen Dresden/ Kupferstichkabinett

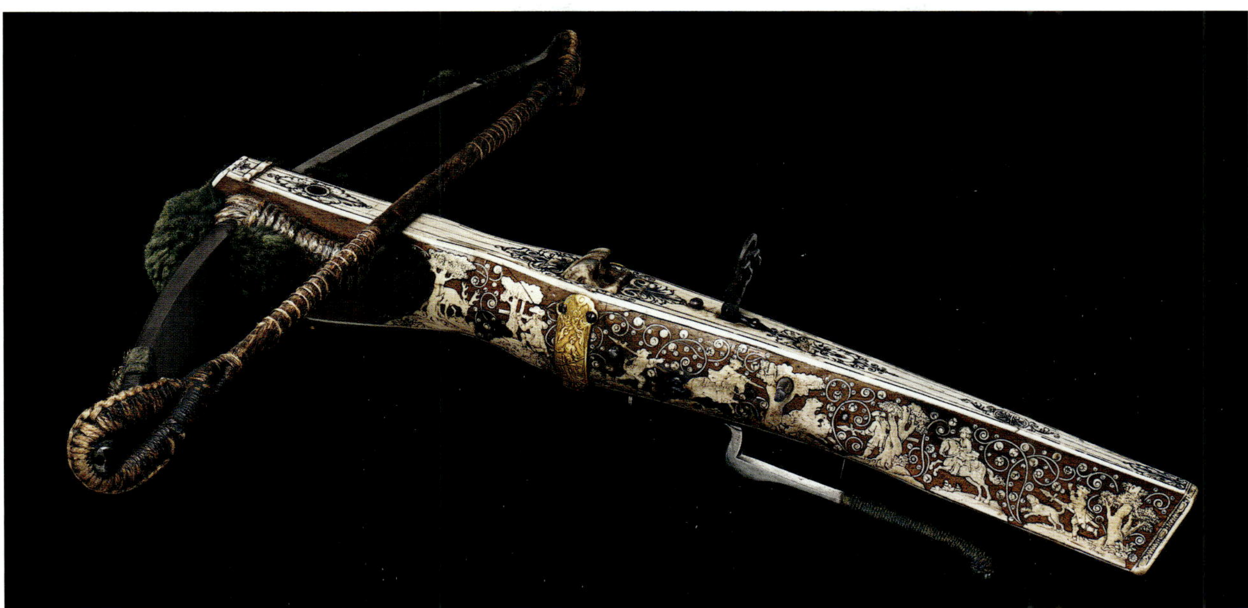

Attributed to Johann Gottfried Hänisch the Elder
German (Dresden), 1696–1778

12. Crossbow (*Halbe Rüstung*)

German (probably Dresden), ca. 1720–30
Steel, wood (walnut), staghorn, copper alloy, hemp, leather,
silk, gold, iron alloy, wool
L. 26 15/16 in. (68.4 cm); W. 29 7/8 in. (75.8 cm); Wt. 13 lb. 15 oz.
(6,329 g)
Bashford Dean Memorial Collection, Funds from various
donors, 1929 (29.158.650a)

Ex coll.: Anonymous collection, South Germany; Bashford
Dean, Riverdale, New York

References: Helbing sale 1919, lot 153; Grancsay 1933a,
pp. 241–45, no. 197

Although the lighter and more elegant *Schnepper*
became increasingly popular throughout central
Europe after the mid-seventeenth century, the heavier
Rüstungen remained in use and continued to be produced, especially for the shooting competitions held
regularly in Saxony. This early eighteenth-century
example of a *halbe Rüstung* is noteworthy not only
for its extensive decoration, which indicates that it
was made by one of the Saxon court crossbow makers, but also for its remarkable state of preservation.

The plain, heavy steel bow is of superior quality
but unmarked. It preserves its braided security cord
of green silk, now faded, and what is presumably the
original bowstring, and it is secured to the tiller by a
hemp binding, which includes a wooden saddle block,
a leather wrapping at the center to prevent the bow
from slipping, and an iron-alloy suspension ring.

The walnut tiller is stout and of typical mid-
sixteenth- to seventeenth-century shape, with a slight
downward curve at the rear. Its furniture is all of iron
alloy, including the four-axis release mechanism with a
set trigger, the trigger guard and safety catch, and the
foldable sight. The nut is made of staghorn, its binding
protected by a copper-alloy band. A screw behind
the nut seat indicates that the tiller was formerly fitted with a bolt clip, now missing. A thick butt plate

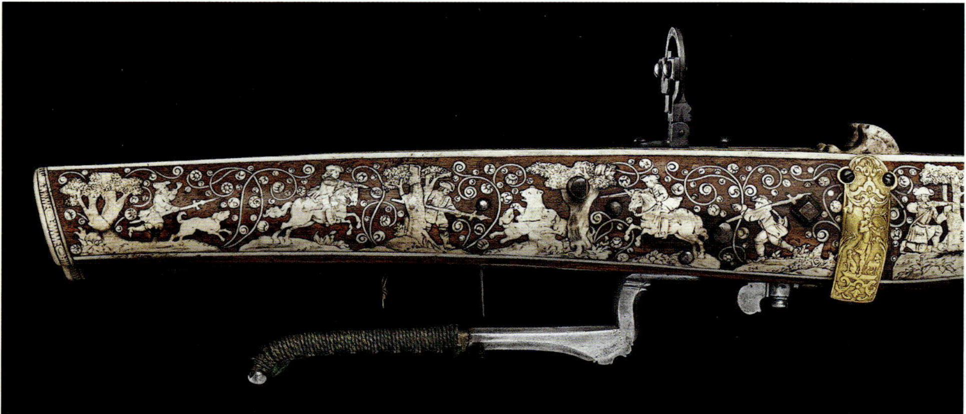

Figure 2.20

of staghorn is engraved with the letters No., but the inscription is not followed by any numeral.

The top of the tiller is entirely faced with polished staghorn, the relatively modest engraving of which displays floral scrollwork, a grotesque mask, and the shell-shaped thumbrest. Further engraved staghorn inlay on the remaining three sides is more ambitious: on either side (mirroring each other), a bear hunt amid a wooded landscape and generic floral vines extends from the rear to just below the nut, including two men on horseback and several footmen and hounds (fig. 2.20), while in front of the nut seat a kneeling hunter rests his gun in the fork of a tree, taking aim at a grazing stag. On the underside, among a few string-like vines, several larger panels of inlay are engraved with Baroque architectural ornament and another grotesque mask; two individual figures, at the shoulder and butt, respectively, represent huntsmen in tricorne and knee-length hunting frock. But while the first holds a boar spear and is accompanied by a hunting dog, the second is armed with a short hunting sword and—ironically—carries a light crossbow, a *Schnepper*, and a blunt hunting bolt (fig. 2.21).

Noteworthy amid the additional embellishment are the gilded copper-alloy band covering the nut binding and a similar ornamental appliqué on the underside of the fore-end. The band is embossed and chased with a boar hunt flanked on either side by a single figure and a pair of hounds (fig. 2.22): a man blowing a large hunting horn on the right and a woman holding a spear (Diana?) on the left; the appliqué is shaped as a stylized festoon drapery and human mask. The remaining decorative elements include a running wild boar engraved on the lock plate of the set trigger; a small grotesque face chiseled into the forward end of the tumbler's underside; traces of gilding on the binding, saddle block, leather wrapping, and suspension ring; and the green pom-poms on the security cord. A pair of similar pom-poms were probably once attached to the wrapped rear part of the trigger guard.

This crossbow is well preserved and shows no signs of alterations or repair, except perhaps for the engraved lock plate of the set trigger. Its decoration, in particular the style of engraving and the use of gilded copper-alloy appliqués, suggests that it was made in Dresden, and although the

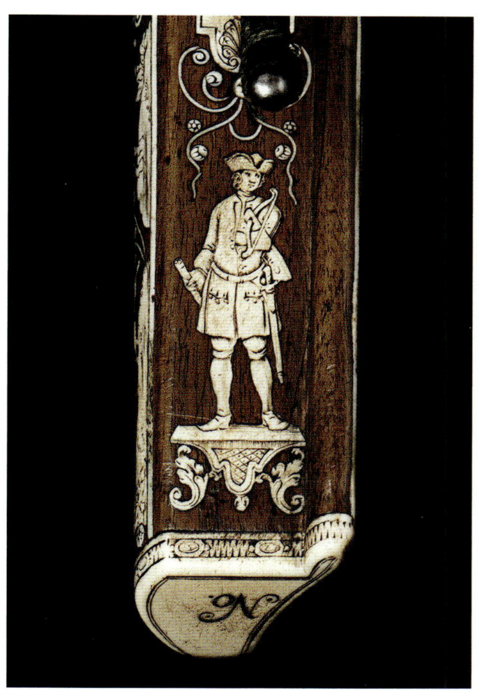

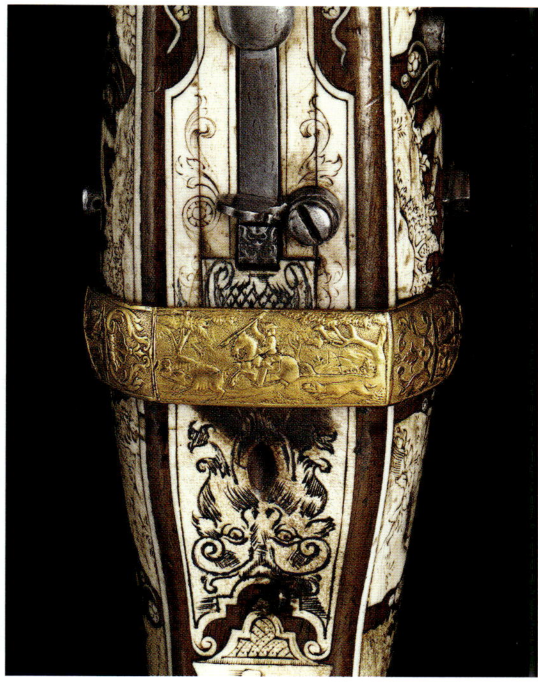

Museum's weapon is unsigned, it can be attributed to Johann Gottfried Hänisch the Elder (1696–1778), court crossbow maker to the electors of Saxony (cats. 13–16). For more than three hundred years, members of the Hänisch family were employed by the Saxon court and other clients. Johann Gottfried, the most prolific member of this remarkably successful dynasty, appears to have been active from at least 1718 until about 1770.[1]

A *halbe Rüstung* in Dresden similar to the Metropolitan's but even more lavishly embellished with a painted bow, ornamental inlay and engraving, gilded and blued furniture and appliqués, and red pom-poms, is signed IGH (Iohann Gottfried Hänish) on the underside and dated 1718 at the fore-end.[2] The Dresden example is mentioned in a 1733 inventory as a target crossbow that "His Royal Majesty," that is, Frederick Augustus I "the Strong," duke of Saxony (1670–1733), and, as August II, king of Poland (r. 1697–1704; 1709–33), "once bought from the master of arms Hänischen [*sic*]," who at that time can only have been Johann Gottfried Hänisch the Elder.[3] On another, similar crossbow, also signed IGH and today in Cracow, the inlay on the sides represents a mixture of the figural scenes on the Museum's weapon and the strapwork found on the Dresden example.[4] Further support for the attribution of the Museum's crossbow to the court crossbow maker is provided by its inlay; a similar huntsman and hound as on the fore-end of this weapon, differing only in that the figure is blowing a horn instead of holding a spear, are found on a push lever in Dresden associated with a *Schnepper* also signed IGH and dated 1730.[5]

Attributed to Johann Gottfried Hänisch the Elder
German (Dresden), 1696–1778

13. Light Crossbow (*Schnepper*) and Lever from the Armory of Moritzburg Castle

Germany (Dresden), 1728
a. Crossbow
Steel, wood (walnut), staghorn, horn, wool, silk
L. 27¹⁵⁄₁₆ in. (70.9 cm); W. 26¾ in. (67.9 cm); Wt. 4 lb. 6 oz. (1,975 g)
b. Push lever
Wood (possibly hornbeam), steel
L. 24⅜ in. (61.9 cm); W. 2⁷⁄₁₆ in. (6.2 cm); Wt. 1 lb. 1 oz. (480 g)
Purchase, Bashford Dean Gift, 1970 (1970.102.1a, b)

Ex coll.: Armory of both Frederick Augustus I "the Strong," duke of Saxony, and, as August II, king of Poland, and his son Frederick Augustus II (1696–1763; r. 1734–63), who succeeded to both titles, at Moritzburg Castle; Royal Gun Cabinet, Dresden; Historisches Museum, Dresden

References: Sotheby's sale 1970, p. 8, lot 2; Nickel 1970, p. 66; Nickel 1974, p. 229

Mark:

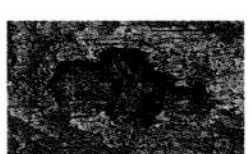

This crossbow and catalogues 14 and 15 belong to a type known in German as a *Schnepper*, indicating a lighter crossbow than those of the *Rüstung* type (see, for example, cats. 12, 16). This variety of *Schnepper* is distinguished by a slender steel bow that passes through a transverse opening in the front of the tiller, to which it is secured by a traditional hemp binding; an elegant wooden tiller with an angular butt similar in shape to those found on the heavier German hunting guns beginning in the seventeenth century; and a simple snap lock with a set trigger. A few examples show extensive decoration on the tiller and bow, but a relatively modest embellishment on the tiller only is more common. As on the present example, the ornament usually consists of polished staghorn inlay engraved with floral and figural motifs and some carving; the butt plates are either of horn or polished staghorn. A light crossbow of this type was invariably spanned with a simple wooden lever fitted with a steel hook at the front that engaged the suspension or spanning ring at the crossbow's fore-end; pulling the lever arm toward the user caused the wooden fork to push the bowstring back toward the lock.

The Museum's weapon retains an old horn bolt clip, an adjustable steel rear sight, and its hemp bowstring, as well as the original silk security cord and pom-poms of green and white wool. In addition to the typical engraving of stylized leaves on the chase and more engraved staghorn inlay on the sides and at the rear of the tiller, a panel behind the sight displays a minute architectural representation, while another, on the underside, is inscribed MORITZBURG (fig. 2.23). On the butt plate of dark horn the inscription No 8 is engraved and filled with white pigment; this is presumably the original inventory number.[1] The bow is struck on the right inner side with an unidentified maker's mark: an acorn. The lever is inscribed in dark ink with what is presumably its original inventory number, No: 17, indicating that the lever did not originally belong to this crossbow.[2]

Moritzburg Castle had been the favorite hunting residence of the dukes of Saxony, prince-electors of the Holy Roman Empire, since the sixteenth century. Together with Pillnitz Castle and the Baroque palace at Sedlitz, it was one of several ducal residences located in the vicinity of Dresden. In 1720, Duke Frederick Augustus I "the Strong" (1670–1733)—who also reigned as king of Poland as August II (r. 1697–1704; 1709–33)—undertook an extensive building program that envisaged Pillnitz as the Saxon court's residence for general diversion, while, beginning in 1723, Moritzburg was enlarged so that it could continue to serve as the court's foremost hunting palace (fig. 2.24). By the early eighteenth century, firearms had replaced crossbows as the hunting weapons of choice throughout most of Europe, but crossbows remained popular, especially for target shooting, and at many of the Saxon palaces competitions with crossbows and guns were held regularly for the amusement of the court.

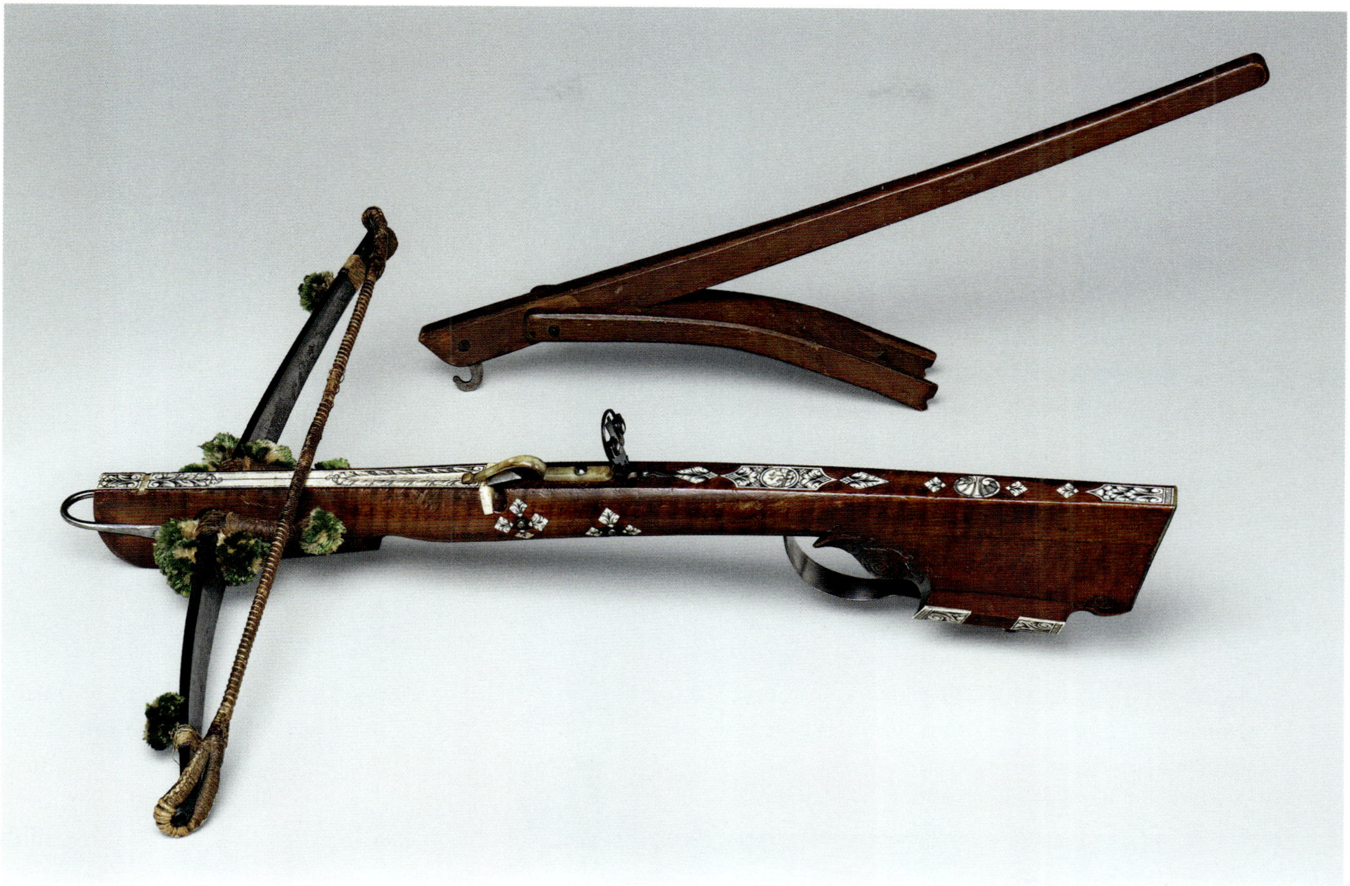

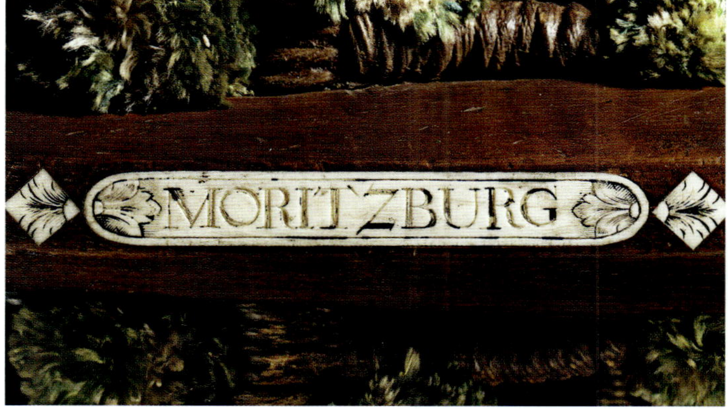

Figure 2.23

An inventory of the armory at Moritzburg Castle, drawn up in 1733, lists twenty-four "*Schnepper* and accessories made and hereto delivered in 1728," most likely by Johann Gottfried Hänisch the Elder, court crossbow maker to the dukes of Saxony in Dresden.[3] The delivery consisted of two sets of twelve weapons, linen crossbow covers, metal canisters for bolts, spare bowstrings, tools, and two types of projectiles: blunt bolts (*Cron-Bolzen*) and pointed ones (*Spiz-Bolzen*). This distinction between bolt types indicates that the Moritzburg crossbows were intended both for shooting at the popinjay and for target shooting (cat. 46). More than twenty weapons from the Moritzburg sets survive, eighteen of which are today in Dresden.[4] Several examples are dated 1728, and the bows of at least three are struck with the same acorn mark as the one found on the Museum's *Schnepper*.[5] For a wooden bolt box from Moritzburg Castle, see catalogue 50.

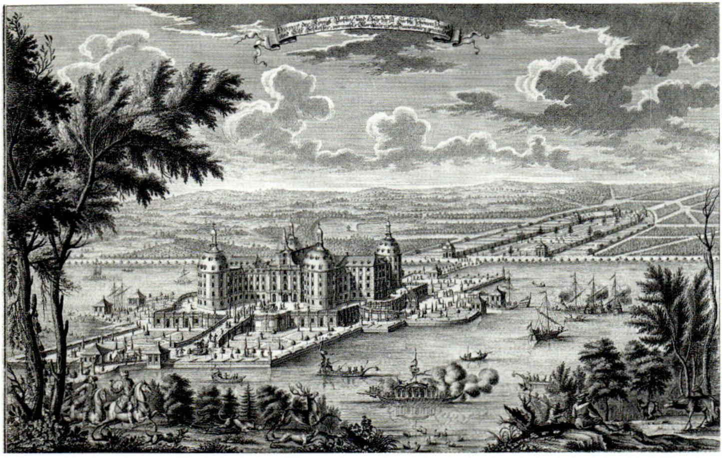

Figure 2.24 Johann August Corvinus (German, 1683–1738). *Moritzburg Castle*, dated 1733. Engraving, 20¹¹⁄₁₆ × 33¼ in. (52.5 × 84.5 cm). Staatliche Kunstsammlungen Dresden/Kupferstichkabinett, Dresden (Sax. top. I-VIII.3)

Johann Gottfried Hänisch the Elder
German (Dresden), 1696–1778

14. Light Crossbow (*Schnepper*) from the Armory of Sedlitz Palace

Germany (Dresden), dated 1733
Steel, wood (walnut), staghorn, hemp, wool, gold
L. 27¹¹⁄₁₆ in. (70.3 cm); W. 22½ in. (57.1 cm); Wt. 4 lb. 5 oz. (1,949 g)
Purchase, Arthur Ochs Sulzberger Gift, 2010 (2010.315)

Ex coll.: Armory of Frederick Augustus II, duke of Saxony, and, as August III, king of Poland, at Sedlitz Palace; Royal Gun Cabinet, Dresden; Historisches Museum, Dresden; [Anton Hofstätter, Vienna]

References: Lepke sale 1920, lot 1739 (possibly this crossbow); Sensfelder 2007, p. 199; Richter 2008a, p. 84; Richter 2008b, p. 57

Mark:

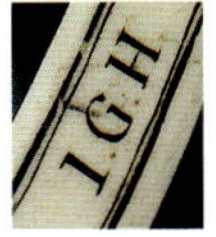

Like catalogue 13, this *Schnepper* belonged to a set of light crossbows and accessories kept in the armories of one of the Saxon ducal residences near Dresden, where it was used for the leisure amusement of target shooting. This weapon came from Sedlitz Palace. Of the same construction and nearly the same dimensions and weight, it, too, exhibits a slender steel bow (albeit unmarked), wooden tiller, and snap lock with a set trigger.

The present weapon differs significantly from the Moritzburg example, however, in the extent and quality of its decoration, notably the panels of polished and engraved staghorn inlay. The latter displays, on the cheek, a stag in a wooded landscape; on the lower edge of the cheek, a minute landscape with

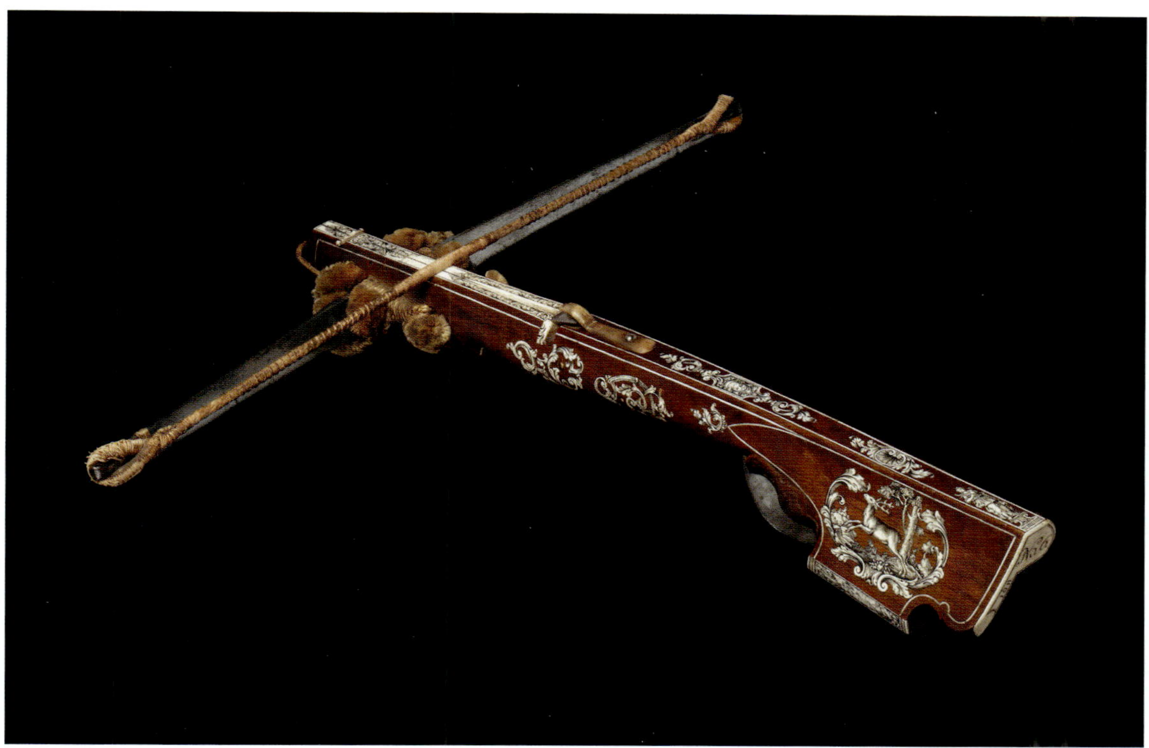

a castle and town; and, on top, floral scrolls on the chase, a female head, a shell-shaped thumbrest, and a figure of Diana, the goddess of hunting, with a dog. In addition to a thin band of staghorn inlay that borders the main outlines of the tiller, the sides feature

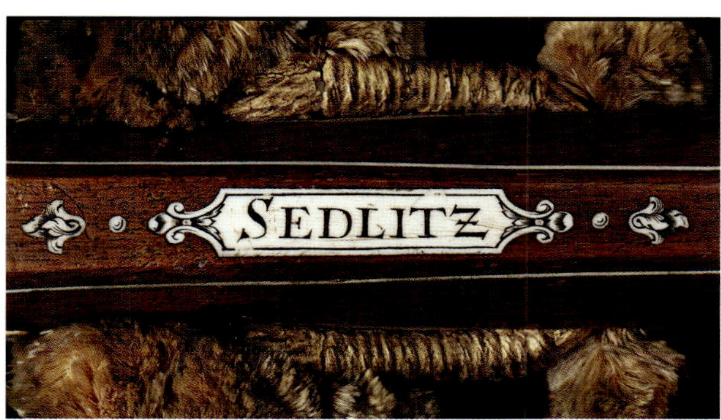

Figure 2.25

cut and pierced floral scrollwork, while the inscription SEDLITZ is engraved on a staghorn panel on the underside of the tiller's fore-end (fig. 2.25). Finally, the binding of the bow, the spanning loop, and the ends of the axes have been gilded, and both the bow's binding and its security cord are fitted with decorative pom-poms of green wool. On the butt plate, the crossbow is signed I.G.H., for "Iohann Gottfried Hänisch," and inscribed NO. 6., while the front reinforce of the bowstring groove bears the year 1733.[1] Except for these markings, the embellishment is iconographically nearly identical on all known crossbows from the set.

The palace and Baroque gardens of Sedlitz (today Gross-Sedlitz) were originally commissioned in 1719 by Count August Christoph von Wackerbarth. In 1723, Frederick Augustus I "the Strong," duke of

Saxony (1670–1733)—and, as August II, king of Poland (r. 1697–1704; 1709–33)—purchased the property and continued the building work. It subsequently became one of several ducal residences in the vicinity of Dresden, but while others, such as the castles at Moritzburg and Pillnitz, had long been hunting and leisure residences, Sedlitz Palace was conceived by Augustus the Strong as a site for festivities associated with the Polish chivalric Order of the White Eagle. The order had been founded by Duke Augustus in 1705 as an honor for those members of the nobility who had supported him as king of Poland, in the face of a threat of forced deposition by King Charles XII of Sweden.[2] Celebrations surrounding meetings of the order included shooting competitions with guns and crossbows in the Lower Orangery, one of Sedlitz's famous gardens.

While the armories at Moritzburg and Pillnitz held sets of twenty-four crossbows with accessories, the palace armory at Sedlitz appears to have contained a set of only twelve *Schnepper* with their related equipment. The engraved initials and year on several examples show that these weapons were made in 1733 by Johann Gottfried Hänisch the Elder, court crossbow maker to the dukes of Saxony in Dresden.[3]

Nine of the Sedlitz crossbows survive in Dresden.[4] It is possible that the set was originally commissioned by Frederick Augustus I, but given that the duke lost interest in his Saxon palaces toward the end of his life—construction at Sedlitz ceased in 1732—and that he died in early February 1733, it is more likely that the commission came from his son. Frederick Augustus II (r. 1733–63) would host the order's festivities at Sedlitz twelve more times, until 1756, when the palace and gardens were occupied by Prussian troops for the duration of the Seven Years War (1756–63).

Johann Gottfried Hänisch the Elder
German (Dresden), 1696–1778

15. Small Crossbow (*Schnepper*), Probably for a Woman or Child

Germany (Dresden), dated 1738
Steel, wood (fruitwood, probably plum or cherry), staghorn, hemp, wool, gold, horn
L. 22 7/32 in. (56.4 cm); W. 16 15/16 in. (43 cm); Wt. 1 lb. 14½ oz. (866 g)
Purchase, Arthur Ochs Sulzberger Gift, 2010 (2011.429)

Ex coll.: Presumably Royal Gun Cabinet, Dresden, and subsequently Historisches Museum, Dresden; Clay P. Bedford, Paradise Valley, Ariz.; [Eric Vaule, Bridgewater, Conn.]

Reference: Christie's sale 1977, p. 31, lot 151, pl. 19

Mark:

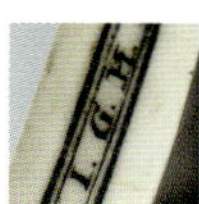

This *Schnepper*, like catalogues 14 and 16, was made by Johann Gottfried Hänisch, court crossbow maker to the dukes of Saxony at Dresden. Noticeably smaller and lighter than the previous examples, the weapon consists of a slender, unmarked steel bow, with its original bowstring and security cord. The delicate wooden tiller is fitted with a spanning loop at the front, a snap lock and set trigger, a trigger guard, and an adjustable rear sight, all of steel. The bolt clip of dark horn is a replacement, either working-lifetime or modern. The tiller shows extensive decoration recalling that found on catalogue 14.

Plain on the underside, the tiller is decorated with a carved floral scroll on the cheek and flush inlaid panels of polished and engraved staghorn. The panels display figural scenes, such as a stag attacked by two hounds amid a wooded landscape, a minute

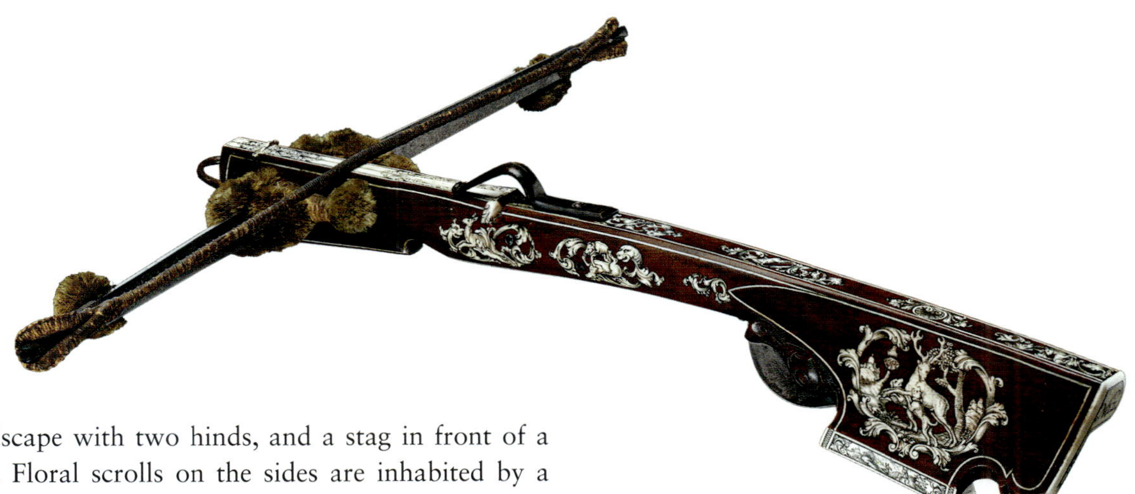

landscape with two hinds, and a stag in front of a tree. Floral scrolls on the sides are inhabited by a hind and a dog, and a single thin band follows the lines of the tiller. Finally, the front and rear finials of the trigger guard are decoratively cut and chiseled, and the binding of the bow, the spanning loop, and the ends of the axes retain traces of gilding; both the bow's binding and its security cord are fitted with decorative green wool pom-poms.

The *Schnepper* is engraved with Hänisch's initials, I.G.H., and NO. 2 on the butt plate, and with the year 1738 on top of the reinforce of the bowstring groove (fig. 2.26). Whether the numeral 2 indicates that this example was originally one of a pair or that it belonged to a set is at present impossible to say. If the crossbow was once owned privately, it was probably accompanied by a similarly decorated push lever;

if it belonged to an armory, a plain, utilitarian lever would have been provided from storage.

Comparatively small crossbows such as this one are rare, especially those with ornate embellishment. They are commonly thought to have been made for women or children (fig. 2.27), and were presumably used in informal competitions and other pastimes, some of which were held indoors. The elegant and finely engraved inlay and the court crossbow maker's initials and date distinguish this *Schnepper* as a weapon of high quality intended for use at the Saxon court in Dresden or at one of the court's satellite residences, such as Moritzburg, Sedlitz, Pillnitz, or Königsberg.

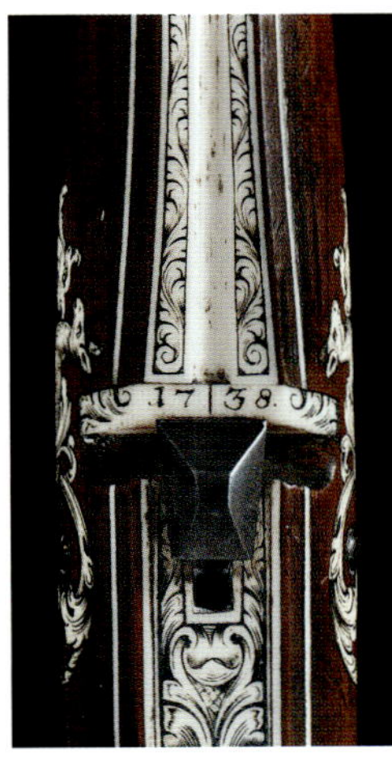

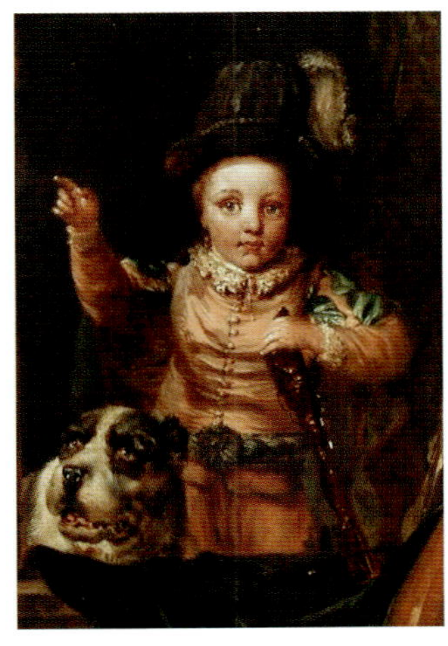

Figure 2.26

Figure 2.27 Johann Eleazar Zeissig, called Schenau (German, 1737–1806). *Dietrich von Miltitz, Age 4, with a Small Crossbow*, ca. 1773. Oil on panel, ca. 13¼ × 9³⁄₁₆ in. (33.7 × 23.3 cm). Private collection

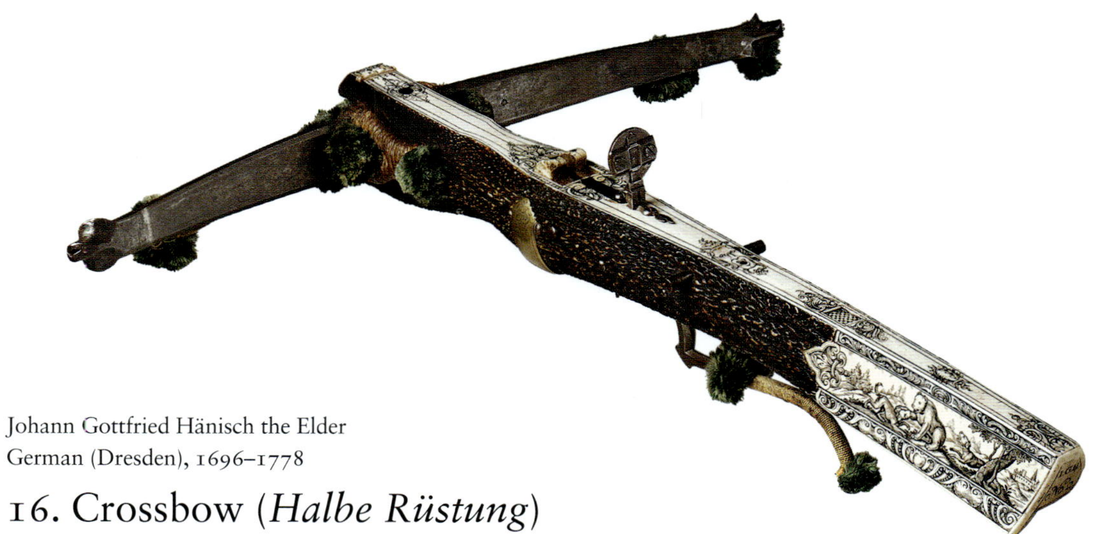

Johann Gottfried Hänisch the Elder
German (Dresden), 1696–1778

16. Crossbow (*Halbe Rüstung*)

Germany (Dresden), dated 1742
Steel, wood,[1] staghorn, copper alloy, hemp, wool, gold,
iron alloy
L. 28 13/16 in. (73.2 cm); W. 24 15/16 in. (63.3 cm);
Wt. 10 lb. 7 oz. (4,817 g)
Purchase, Louis V. Bell Fund and Bequest of
Stephen V. Grancsay, by exchange, 1985 (1985.248a)

Ex coll.: The armory of Frederick Augustus II, duke of
Saxony, and, as Augustus III, king of Poland, Dresden;
Royal Gun Cabinet, Dresden; Historisches Museum, Dres-
den; Earlshall Castle, Leuchars, Fife (part of a collection
formed in modern times, probably by R. W. R. Mackenzie);
[Peter Finer, Ilmington, Warwickshire]

References: Nickel 1986; Finer 2005, no. 32; Richter 2008a,
pp. 32, 34

Mark:

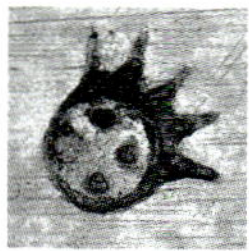

In Saxony, especially at the court in Dresden, crossbow shooting enjoyed an unparalleled popularity
until the early twentieth century. By the eighteenth
century, the lighter *Schnepper* had become the favorite weapon, but variations of the traditional, heavier
Rüstung type remained in use and continued to be
made by local artisans. The present example is
noteworthy for its powerful bow and an overall
rugged appearance combined with sparse but elegant
decoration. Its plain, massive steel bow displays superior workmanship, for example in the flanged edges;
the wooden saddle block, steel suspension ring, and
substantial remnants of the braided security cord are
original. The wooden tiller is almost entirely veneered
with panels of natural, or "rough," staghorn and fitted
with a steel bolt clip (damaged) and an adjustable steel
rear sight.[2] The four-axis lock consists of a reinforced
nut made from staghorn, and a set trigger, safety catch,
and trigger guard, all of iron alloy; the nut's string binding is protected by a copper-alloy band. A rare feature—or perhaps a later alteration—is an elongated
spring-loaded push button of iron alloy set firmly
into the channel in front of the trigger guard into
which a cocking pin would normally have been
inserted in order to set the tumbler (fig. 2.28).[3]

The bow is struck on the belly side of its right
arm with a mark that is frequently encountered: a
quartered circle crowned by five rays.[4] At the front
of the chase, just behind the bolt rest, the engraving
includes the year, 1742, and on the butt plate the
maker's initials, I.G.H. (Iohann Gottfried Hänisch),
together with a No. 2 (fig. 2.29).

Apart from the natural staghorn veneer, this crossbow's decoration is relatively restrained and consists mainly of engraving. On the cheek, framed by ornamental friezes, is a scene of a bear in a wooded landscape under attack front and rear by two hounds (fig. 2.29). The top of the tiller bears stylized floral and shell motifs, rocaille ornament, the gaping mouth of a grotesque face, and a laurel and a palm branch bound in a wreath. Further embellishment includes shell motifs and a mascaron engraved on the copper-alloy band protecting the nut binding (fig. 2.28); traces of gilding on the bow binding, saddle block, and suspension ring; and several green wool pom-poms.

The Museum's crossbow belongs to what is probably a group of about a dozen similar weapons, several of which are signed by Johann Gottfried Hänisch the Elder and bear dates between 1736 and 1742. The group's characteristic feature is a cheek of polished staghorn inlay, engraved with animal-combat scenes, but individual examples differ in a number of details other than the varied iconography of their cheeks, for example, the presence or absence of engraved staghorn panels opposite the cheek and the placement of the year and Hänisch's initials. Some examples are fitted with steel sights, while on others the bolt clip is notched on top for that purpose, and the majority of the wooden tillers are not sheathed in natural staghorn veneer.[5] In fact, only four crossbows compare closely to the Museum's weapon, in that their tillers are veneered with natural staghorn: two in Dresden,[6] one in Vitoria-Gasteiz,[7] and another that came onto the art market in recent years.[8]

The purposes of these weapons apparently varied in the eighteenth and nineteenth centuries. A Dresden inventory of 1765 mentions four "small birding crossbows for fight hunting" ("*kleine Vogel-Rüstungen zum Kampf-Jagen*"), comprising one pair with "yellow-stained" tillers and one pair veneered with staghorn, numbered "No. 100 through No. 103." The term *Vogel-Rüstung* (birding crossbow) seems to imply that these weapons were intended for shooting at the popinjay.[9] And, indeed, the weapons' powerful bows would have been necessary to drive a bolt

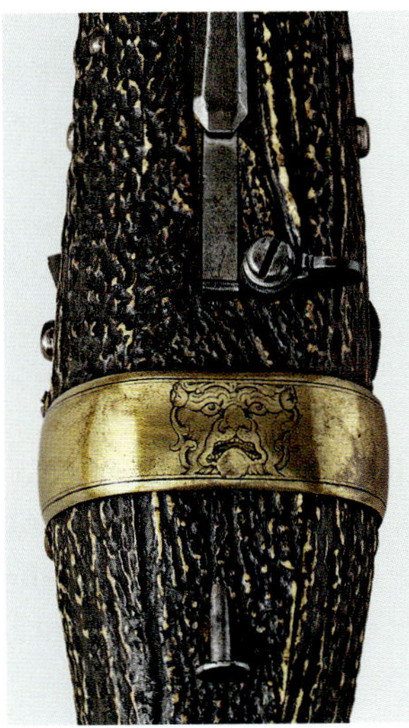

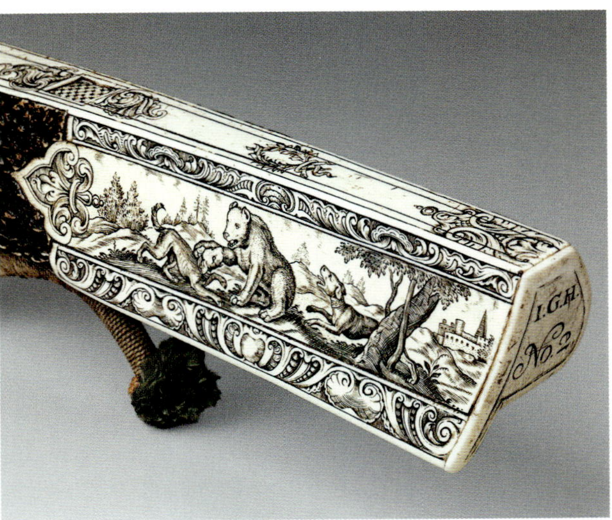

Figure 2.28

Figure 2.29

upward with enough force to strike off parts from the target. However, the same inventory specifies that these crossbows and other weapons like it were also employed for a particularly cruel courtly entertainment, the *Kampfjagen* (fight hunting). This involved large wild animals such as bovine bulls, bears, lions, and boar, which were pitted against each other in an enclosed arena, while spectators shot at them to further provoke the fighting. Whatever their purpose, since natural staghorn veneer is a decorative feature more commonly found on mid-seventeenth-century objects, the four recorded crossbows with such veneer, made almost a century later, must have looked old-fashioned, presenting a noticeable contrast to the more modern style of the *Schnepper*.

17. Target Crossbow with Windlass

Probably Belgium or Holland
a. Crossbow, probably mid-18th century
Steel, wood (possibly padauk), copper alloy, staghorn, horn, mother-of-pearl
L. 44½ in. (113 cm); W. 31¾ in. (80.7 cm); Wt. 19 lb. 3 oz. (8,712 g)
b. Windlass, dated 1741
Steel, copper alloy, hemp, wood (boxwood, pearwood)
L. upper part only, overall 22¹⁄₁₆ in. (56 cm); W. 16⅝ in. (42.2 cm); Wt. 9 lb. 12 oz. (4,430 g)
Gift of William H. Riggs, 1913 (14.25.1579a, b)

Ex coll.: William H. Riggs, Paris

Reference: Mayer 1935, p. 70, no. 72

Marks:

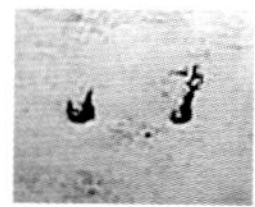 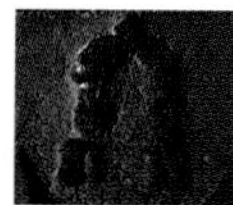

Powerful windlass crossbows had been employed in war since at least the late fourteenth century, but owing to size and weight their use was mainly restricted to siege warfare. After becoming obsolete as military weapons during the sixteenth century, windlass crossbows continued to be used for target shooting, especially in western Europe. They developed into weapons such as the present example and catalogue 18, whose distant bellicose ancestry is still echoed by their size, the overall utilitarian form and simple lock, and the somewhat cumbersome spanning method. A characteristic feature of these late successors is the prominent stand, or rest, on the underside of the tiller. Intended solely for competitive and ceremonial use, these weapons are known as target crossbows.

Catalogue 17 consists of a large steel bow that passes through an opening in the front of the tiller, to which it is secured with a pair of bow irons. The tiller, made of what is possibly padauk, a rather expensive wood imported from Africa or Asia, features a large flat rest with a contemporary extension at the bottom, and an elongated rear section encased in copper alloy and capped with a butt plate of horn; the tiller is fitted with a three-part steel stirrup, a small rear sight of polished staghorn, and a single-axis release mechanism consisting of a nut made of staghorn and a spring-loaded steel lever trigger. Apart from the ornamental shape and sporadic chiseling of some of the steel and copper-alloy furniture, the tiller is comparatively plain. Its decoration consists of a few thin, parallel bands, inlaid in a light-colored wood, and five plain pieces of mother-of-pearl—two shield-shaped, the remaining three diamond-shaped—laid flush into the top of the rear section. The bow's right arm, on the belly side, shows traces of a mark, struck twice: a bull's head.[1]

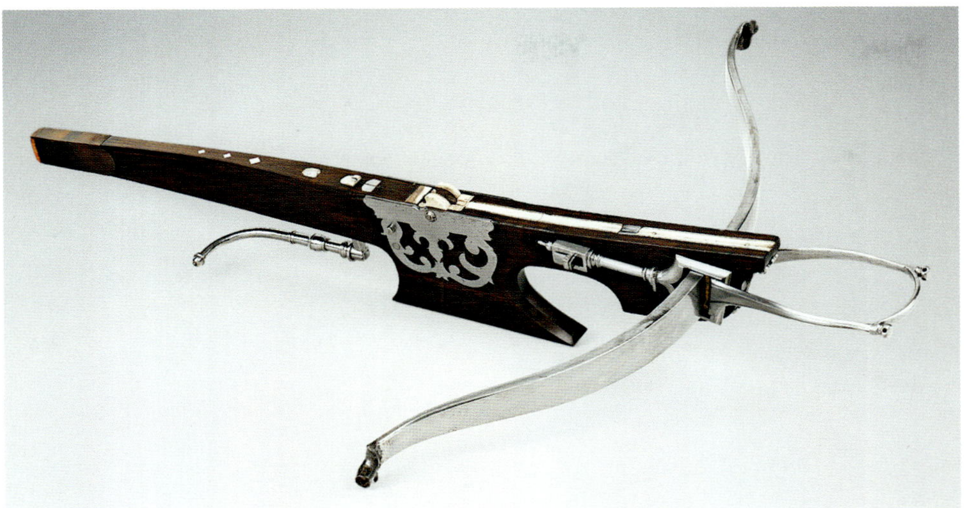

Catalogue 17a

The windlass consists of an upper part, which includes a square socket that fits over the rear end of the tiller, and the lower part, or pulley. The former is flanked by a pair of copper-alloy wheels on either side and contains the rope spindle, or axis, which is turned by two steel crank arms with wooden handles; the right one, of boxwood, is original, the left, of pearwood, is a later replacement. Connected to the upper part by two strands of modern hemp rope, the pulley comprises a grapple and a strong frame, the two arms of which contain a pair of copper-alloy wheels each. In addition to the turned wooden grips and the color contrast between the iron and the copper alloy, the decoration of the windlass consists of scattered chiseling overall and, on the upper part, cut-and-pierced ornament, which includes the year, 1741. The spindle frame is struck with an unidentified mark: a domed tower.[2]

In general, this crossbow is similar to a group of weapons that appeared in northwestern Europe during the seventeenth century and are generally thought to be Belgian or Dutch. Details such as the downward curve of the rear of the tiller and the shape of the lever trigger indicate a later date of manufacture,

probably the mid-eighteenth century. The bows of a number of target weapons are struck with the same bull's-head mark, including another example in the Museum's collection.[3] Among these, two examples—one in Delft and one in Bern—are dated on their tillers 1756 and 1766, respectively.[4] The windlass associated with the target crossbow in Delft is stamped with a clover-leaf mark, but, generally, marks on windlasses are rare; the one on the Museum's windlass is unrecorded.

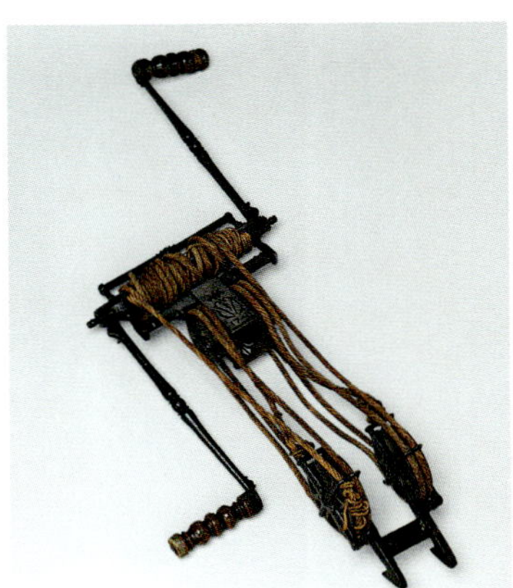

Catalogue 17b

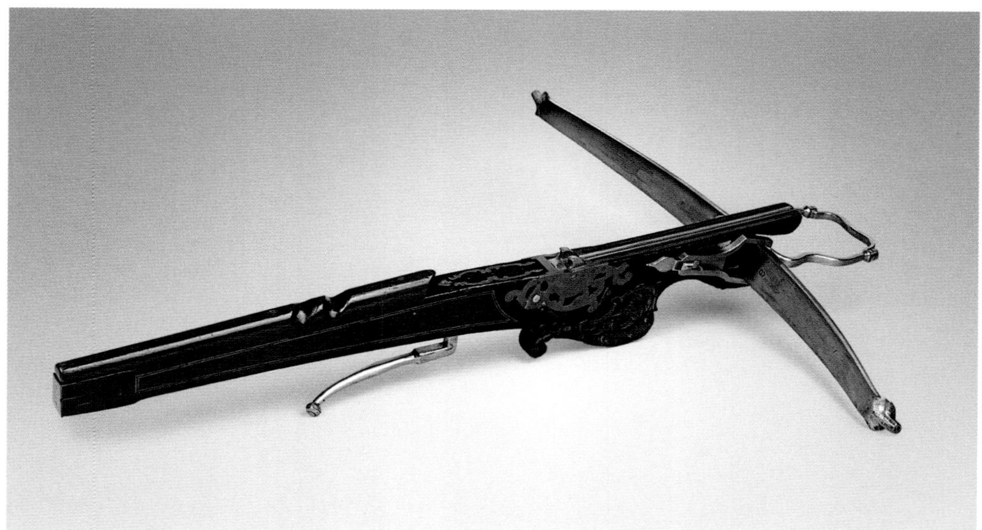

Catalogue 18a

18. Target Crossbow with Windlass

Probably Belgium or Holland
a. Crossbow: tiller: mid-18th century; bow: probably 19th century
Steel, wood (possibly mahogany), copper alloy
L. 42⁷⁄₁₆ in. (107.8 cm); W. 31⁹⁄₁₆ in. (81.2 cm); Wt. 17 lb. 7 oz. (7,912 g)
b. Windlass, ca. 1600–1750
Steel, staghorn, hemp
L. upper part only, overall 20³⁄₈ in. (51.7 cm); W. 16 in. (40.6 cm); Wt. 6 lb. 1 oz. (2,744 g)
Gift of William H. Riggs, 1913 (14.25.1578a, b)

Ex coll.: William H. Riggs, Paris

References: Unpublished

Mark:

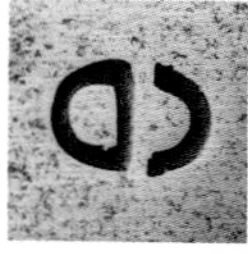

The majority of western European target crossbows were not elaborately decorated. This example is typical, with its plain but powerful steel bow, long wooden tiller with steel furniture, single-axis lock, rounded rest on its underside (with old repairs), and thumbrest at the top rear. However, it is also unusual for the extensive carved ornament on its tiller. Moreover, the weapon appears to have been so treasured by its former owner(s) that it remained in use for a considerable time, was repaired during its long working life, and was at some point fitted with a replacement bow, probably during the nineteenth century. On the belly of its left arm, the bow is struck twice with the same unidentified mark: probably the capital letters CD in reverse.

The two-axis release mechanism comprises a copper-alloy nut, two internal sears, and a lever trigger.

The crossbow's main decoration consists of carved rococo ornament on the bottom and sides of the rest, and openwork copper-alloy side plates (fig. 2.30). The latter complement other elements of the same metal, such as the nut, the chase, and, in front of the thumbrest, a spade-shaped inlay framing a hole of as-yet-undetermined function. The rear of the tiller is further decorated with two thin bands of light-colored wood inlay.

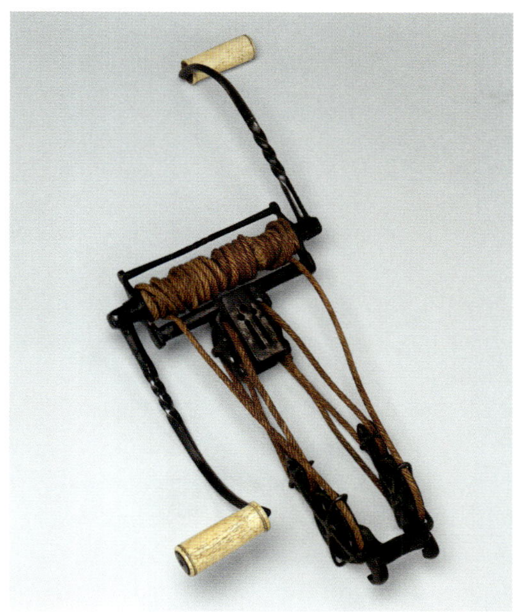

Catalogue 18b

Except for the staghorn grips and hemp rope, all the parts of the accompanying windlass are made of steel; the surfaces have been browned as a simple prevention against rust. The upper part comprises the axis frame with its two curved cranks and a socket fitted with a three-armed guard on either side, each containing a wheel with six spokes. The pulley's arms are in the shape of elongated five-barred guards, each containing two six-spoked wheels and fitted with frontal claws. In addition to the polished staghorn on the handles, the decoration on the windlass includes twisted motifs on the cranks and upper bar of the axis frame, sparse chiseling and flanged edges overall, and the cut-and-pierced Gothic-style ornament on the front and rear sides of the tiller box.

Only a few target crossbows with closely comparable decoration have been recorded to date.[1] The style of ornament and the apparent age of the wood suggest that the tiller dates from the middle or second half of the eighteenth century. The bow, on the other hand, is probably of more recent manufacture and thus a replacement. This assumption is supported not only by the modern appearance of the mark, but also by the existence of another bow by the same maker, or at least from the same source. This second bow is struck once with the same CD (?) mark, mounted on what is believed to be a nineteenth- or twentieth-century Belgian target crossbow in Delft.[2] The style of the bow irons and especially their wedges also resemble those of the Museum's weapon.

The date of the windlass is more difficult to establish. It may have been made as early as the beginning of the seventeenth century, since very similar examples are depicted in the art of that period.[3] On the other hand, windlasses of this type and decoration were apparently still in use—and probably continued to be made in this fashion—well into the eighteenth and perhaps even into the nineteenth century. Among surviving windlasses, there is a comparable example associated with a crossbow, also in Delft; the windlass's upper part is almost identical, except for the handles, while the pulley differs slightly in construction.[4]

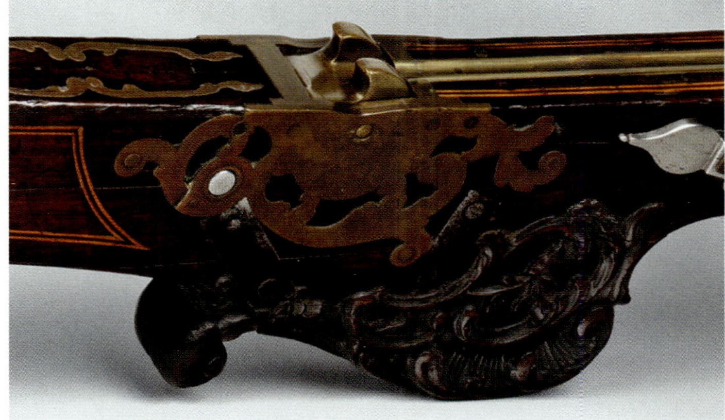

Figure 2.30

3 | Pellet Crossbows

Some crossbows, instead of shooting bolts, discharged small stones, balls, bullets, or other pellets made from clay, marble, or metals like lead and iron alloy (see Section 6, "Projectiles and Their Storage"). Accordingly, the weapons are referred to as "pellet" or "bullet" crossbows, and—somewhat misleadingly—as "stone" bows. The term "prodd" is also frequently used by modern writers, but since its origin is an eighteenth-century misreading and misinterpretation of an earlier text it should not be mistaken for a period term or a modern technical expression (in this publication, only the terms "pellet" and "stone" crossbow are used).[1] Probably introduced into Europe from the Near East, self-bows discharging small round projectiles are mentioned in European documents as early as the fourteenth century, and pellet crossbows may have appeared about the same time. Yet, to date no pictorial evidence or examples of such crossbows dating from before the sixteenth century have come to light.[2]

Beginning in the sixteenth century, pellet crossbows became increasingly popular but were used exclusively for hunting rather than in war or competitions. During the first half of that century, a distinctive type of pellet crossbow developed in Italy. Its characteristic features are the delicate overall silhouette and comparatively light weight, a noticeably curved front half of the wooden tiller, and a light, slender steel bow that can be spanned by hand (fig. 3.1). The bow is usually secured to the tiller by a pair of vertical steel brackets and fitted with a double bowstring. The release mechanism is a variation of

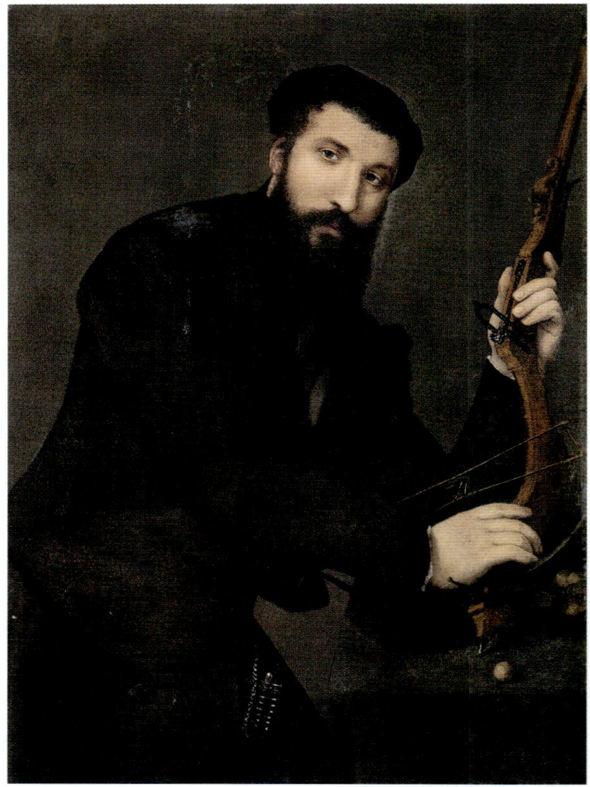

Figure 3.1 Lorenzo Lotto (Italian, ca. 1480–1556). *Portrait of a Crossbow Maker (Master Battista di Rocca Contrada)*, ca. 1551. Oil on panel, ca. 37 × 28⅜ in. (94 × 72 cm). Pinacoteca Capitolina, Rome (PC 40)

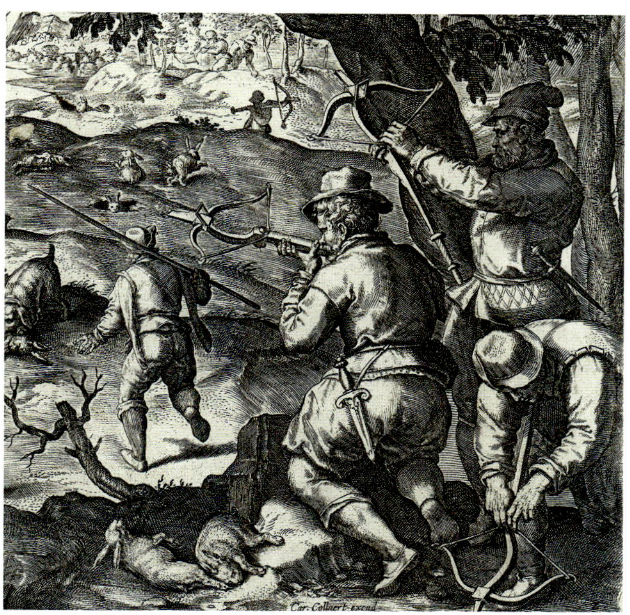

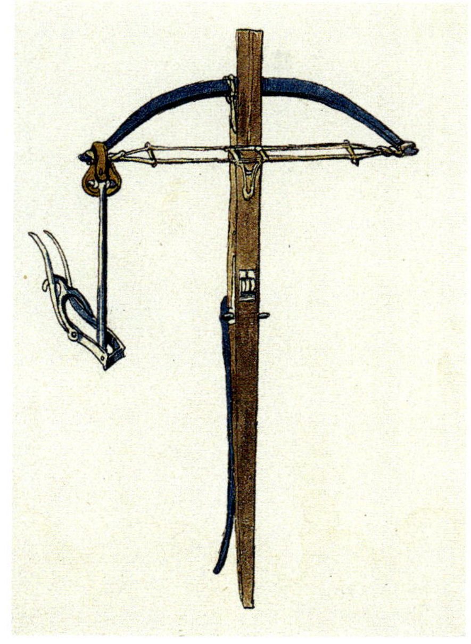

the two-axis lock: instead of a nut, the upper side of the tiller contains a small pivoting arm with a single hook at the front for the bowstring, while the back of the arm is flattened and pierced with a rectangular hole; this hole engages a hook at the end of the vertical extension at the front of the lever trigger. Such pellet crossbows, of various sizes, remained a favorite hunting weapon, especially throughout southern Europe, but also in France and southern parts of Germany, well into the seventeenth century (fig. 3.2). Their decoration is often sparse, consisting only of carved ornament on the back of the tiller—sometimes complemented by additional carving at the front—as well as some chiseling, chasing, etching, and/or gilding of the steel furniture, that is, the bow brackets, release arm and trigger, and front and rear sights (cats. 21, 22, 24, 27).

During the same period, another variation of the pellet crossbow developed on the Iberian Peninsula, although to date only one artistic representation has come to light (fig. 3.3), and extant examples are extremely rare (and in some cases dubious; see cat. 25). The type is very similar in appearance to other crossbows from western Europe, with a straight, narrow tiller and a stronger steel bow, which, although fitted with a double bowstring, also required spanning with a pull lever. The latter, however, had a single central hook instead of a double claw, or grapple (cats. 6b, 43).

Perhaps influenced by these western European examples, a somewhat heavier and distinctly different variety of pellet crossbow appeared in central Europe sometime about 1600. Characteristic of this "German" type are a relatively strong steel bow and a thin, almost skeletal tiller of steel that is fitted at the rear with a wooden butt, usually shaped not unlike the cheeks of contemporary gunstocks. Since the stronger bow does not allow for spanning

Figure 3.2 After Jan van der Straet, called Stradanus (Netherlandish, 1523–1605). Rabbit hunting with pellet crossbows, detail of pl. 2 of a set of six hunting scenes published by Carel Collaert in Antwerp, ca. 1574–76. Engraving, 8½ × 11¾ in. (21.5 × 29.8 cm). The British Museum, London (1948,0410.4.221)

Figure 3.3 Pellet crossbow and spanning lever, detail of a page from the *Inventario Iluminado*, an illustrated inventory of the armory of the Holy Roman Emperor Charles V (including objects formerly belonging to his father, Philip I of Castile, and to his grandfather and predecessor, Maximilian I). German, ca. 1544–58. Watercolor on paper. Patrimonio Nacional/Real Armería, Madrid (N.18.B, fol. 85v)

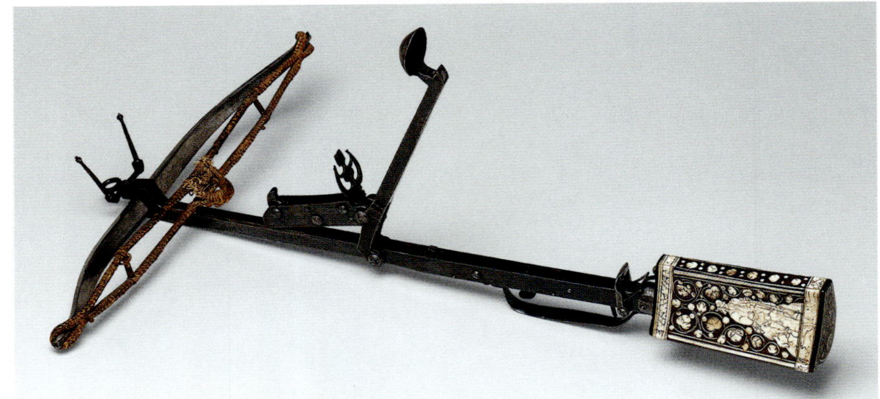

Figure 3.4
Catalogue 23,
with raised lever

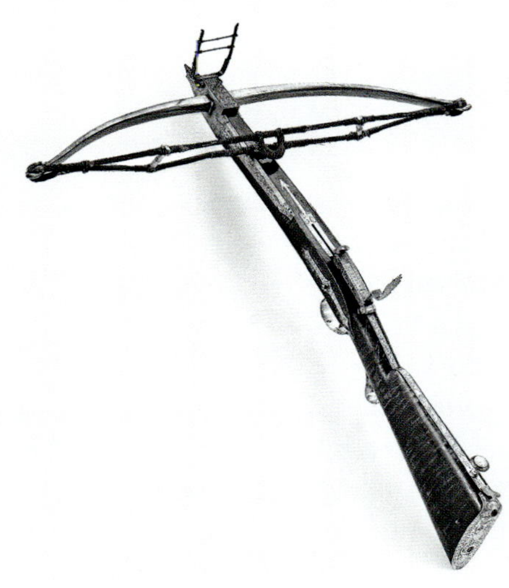

Figure 3.5 Joseph Egg
(English, born in France,
1775–1837). Pellet
crossbow, probably made
1818–19 for Sir Astley
Paston Cooper, 1st baronet
Cooper of Gadebridge,
surgeon to King George IV,
King William IV, and
Queen Victoria. Royal
Armouries Museum, Leeds
(XI.97)

by hand, a combination of lever spanner and release mechanism is permanently secured to the top of the tiller by means of a pivot (fig. 3.4). When the lever arm is raised, a small box containing part of the release mechanism is pushed forward until the hook engages the bowstring; pushing the lever down again brings the string and box back until the latter lines up with the rear part of the release mechanism within the tiller proper. The hook also serves as the bowstring release: the weapon is shot by pulling the trigger after the rear mechanism has been set by means of a push button on the tiller's underside. Like pellet crossbows of the "Italian" type, their northern counterparts come in varying sizes (cats. 23, 24).

The decoration of pellet crossbows is usually quite modest. Most weapons of the Italian type are rather plain, rarely showing any embellishment other than a simple rear tiller ornament and sparse chiseling, chasing, or etching of their metal furniture. In a very few instances, the dorsal figure is of extraordinary quality, the carved ornament extends to other parts of the tiller, and the metal parts are gilded; decorated bows are the exception (cats. 24, 27). The same is true for pellet crossbows of the German type: their bows and iron-alloy tillers are generally unadorned, with only their wooden butts occasionally showing forms of inlay similar to that found on contemporary gunstocks and the tillers of the heavier central European crossbows. Examples with etched ornament, gilding, or both on their bows and tillers, or with butts that feature inlay other than of polished staghorn are very uncommon (cat. 24).

By the eighteenth century, the popularity of pellet crossbows appears to have all but vanished throughout continental Europe. Only in England, where a particular type emerged that married the typically slim wooden tiller of western European weapons with the built-in spanning mechanism of their counterparts of the German type, would pellet crossbows remain in use as hunting weapons until well into the nineteenth century (fig. 3.5).

19. Pellet Crossbow

Probably Italy or France, ca. 1550–1600
Steel, wood (walnut), staghorn, hemp
L. 40³⁄₁₆ in. (102.1 cm); W. 25⁹⁄₁₆ in. (64.9 cm); Wt. 7 lb. 8 oz.
(3,388 g)
Gift of William H. Riggs, 1913 (14.25.1581)

Ex coll.: Count James-Alexandre de Pourtalès-Gorgier,
Neuchâtel and Paris; William H. Riggs, Paris

References: Stone 1934 (1961 ed.), p. 13; Nickel, Pyhrr, and
Tarassuk 1982, pp. 131–32, no. 90

An elegant version of the pellet crossbow developed
in Italy in the first half of the sixteenth century. It
came in various sizes and remained a favorite weapon
for hunting birds and other small game, especially
in southern Europe, but also in France, the Low
Countries, and parts of southern Germany, well into
the seventeenth century.

This example is fitted with a steel bow, the center
section of which is shaped like an angular arch. This
shape is probably intended to lower the bow's center
section below and out of the way of the projectile's
trajectory, a feature that is highly unusual and to
date remains the only recorded example of its kind;
the double bowstring is likely a later replacement.
The walnut tiller is fitted with fore-end reinforces,
lock plates, a single-axis lock, and front and rear
sights, all of steel.

A grotesque animal head at the front of the fore-
end and a finely carved basilisk at the rear (fig. 3.6)
are the tiller's main decoration. Except for the fore-
end reinforces, all the parts of the steel furniture—
lock plates, front and rear sights, and the trigger—
show modest chiseling, and the front finial is shaped
like an acorn.

Pellet crossbows, in particular those of Italian
type, have not received much scholarly attention,
and the dating and geographical attribution of individual examples remain difficult.[1] Most are quite
plain, rarely showing any embellishment other than
a simple rear tiller ornament and sparse chiseling,

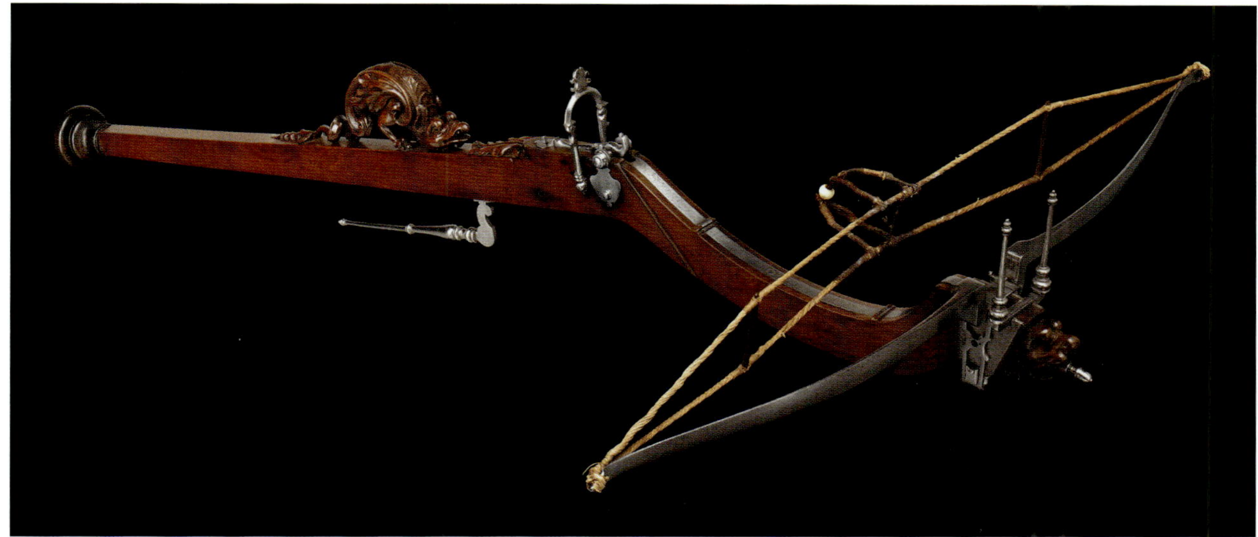

chasing, etching, and/or gilding of their metal parts. However, some of these weapons are distinguished by an extraordinary quality and diversity of the sculptural decoration on the tiller's top rear, ranging from simple bosses and raised scrolls to animals and monsters, or groups of different creatures. On a few examples, large areas of the tiller's surface display inlay, usually of staghorn, or shallow relief carving.

A particular characteristic of the sculptural tiller ornament of these weapons is their variety: near-identical or even similar figures are scarce. A weapon in Vienna features, among other comparable elements, a basilisk-like creature (accompanied by a small frog in front) that is quite close to the one on the present crossbow, but the Vienna example differs in a few details, such as the frontal spike issuing from a blossom instead of an animal head; the shape of the trigger; and the decoration of the forward and rear sights.[2] Another weapon with a similar basilisk on top of its tiller is depicted in a portrait by Lorenzo Lotto of an Italian crossbow maker (fig. 3.1). Its presence in the portrait demonstrates that this type of crossbow must have already been fully developed by the mid-sixteenth century, since Lotto died in 1556.

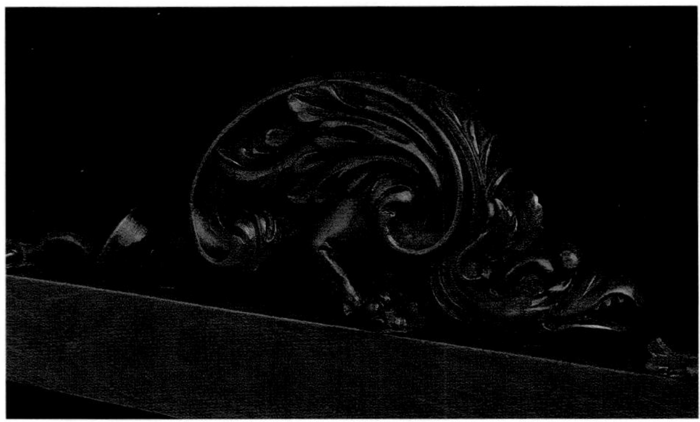

Figure 3.6

20. Pellet Crossbow

Italy (or possibly southern Germany), probably 1550–1600
Steel, wood (rosewood), iron alloy, copper alloy
L. overall 32⅞ in. (83.5 cm); W. 21⅛ in. (53.5 cm); Wt. 3 lb. 4 oz. (1,476 g)
Bashford Dean Memorial Collection, Funds from various donors, 1929 (29.158.651)

Ex coll.: Bashford Dean, Riverdale, N.Y.

References: Grancsay 1955, pp. 24–25, no. 90; Flint Institute 1967, no. 55

According to the scarce pictorial evidence available from the sixteenth and seventeenth centuries, most pellet crossbows were utilitarian and comparatively plain. This example is unusual in several respects: not only is the tiller made of rosewood, an exotic and therefore rare and expensive material, but most of its surfaces are decorated with subtle relief ornament, and the tiller can be taken apart (fig. 3.7).

The steel bow is fitted with an old double bow-string, and its slightly curved arms show traces of having been blued or blackened. The bow irons and the wedge (or wedges) or screw that originally secured the bow to the fore-end are missing; a modern wedge made of wood is currently holding the bow in place. The tiller is reinforced with iron-alloy plates at the front, contains the conventional single-axis lock, and is fitted with front and rear sights—only the base of the forward sight remains. Just behind the middle, the tiller has a joint that can be unscrewed so that the rear part can be taken off; three thin sheets of modern copper alloy ensure a tight fit. An old split in the wood at the lock area has been repaired with an iron-alloy collar, in all likelihood during the weapon's working life.

The decoration of the tiller consists mainly of leaves and floral scrolls, grotesque masks, and

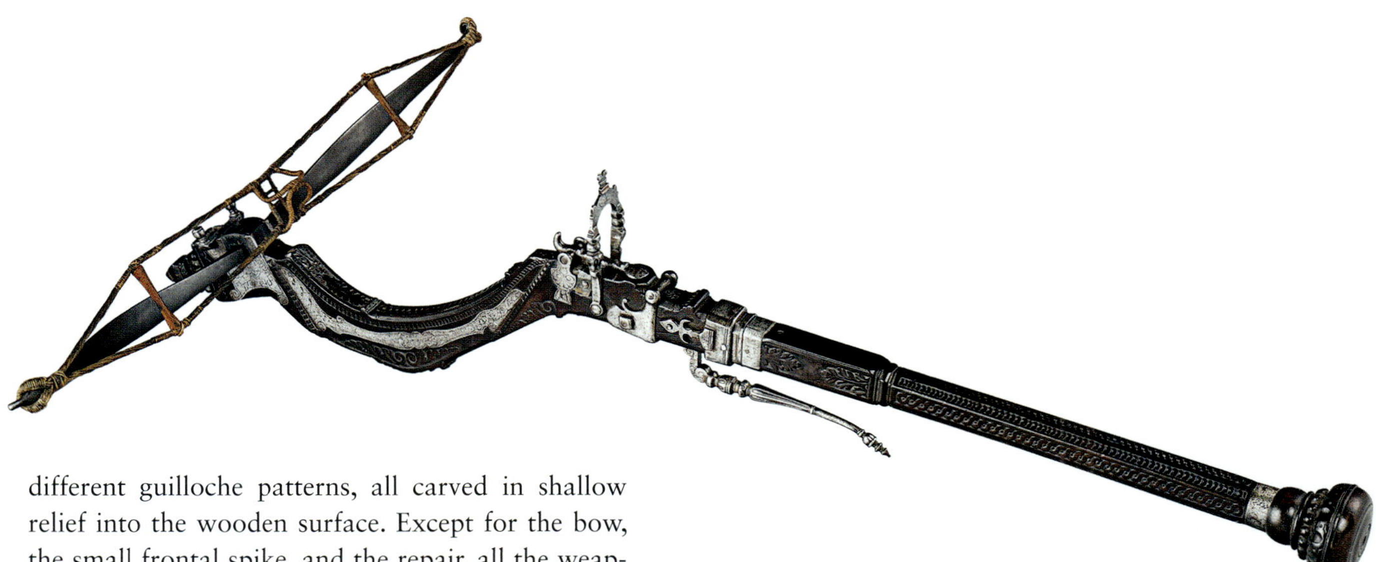

different guilloche patterns, all carved in shallow relief into the wooden surface. Except for the bow, the small frontal spike, and the repair, all the weapon's metal parts are decorated with various degrees of engraving, in the form of floral, strapwork, and further guilloche patterns, occasionally accompanied by ornamental chiseling.[1]

This crossbow's capability to be taken apart, together with the relatively extensive but subtle decoration, is a most unusual combination. In fact, to date only two other pellet crossbows that can be dismounted have been recorded. The first, in Vienna, is of the Italian type, dating from about 1600–1625, and its tiller is decorated only with a plain dorsal scroll.[2]

The tiller cannot be disassembled, but its rear part can be folded: it is made in three sections, which are joined by two lockable hinges; a small key unlocks these hinges, allowing the rear of the tiller to be collapsed (fig. 3.8). The other recorded example is a pellet crossbow of English type, probably dating from the seventeenth century, in Oxford.[3] Its straight wooden tiller shows a steel-capped joint like the one on the Museum's example, but located in front of the lock. However, the joint on the Oxford weapon is of

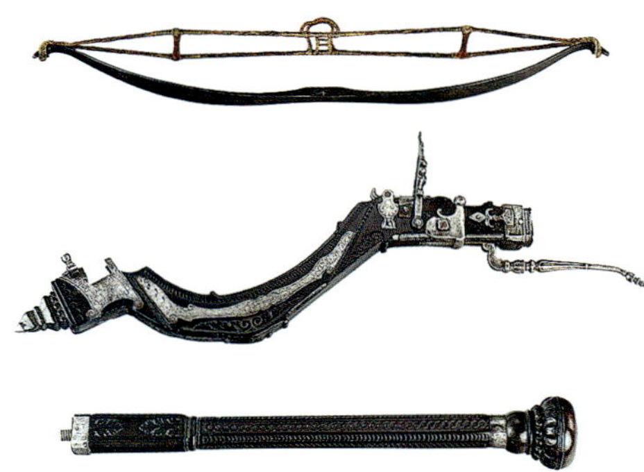

Figure 3.7 Catalogue 20, disassembled

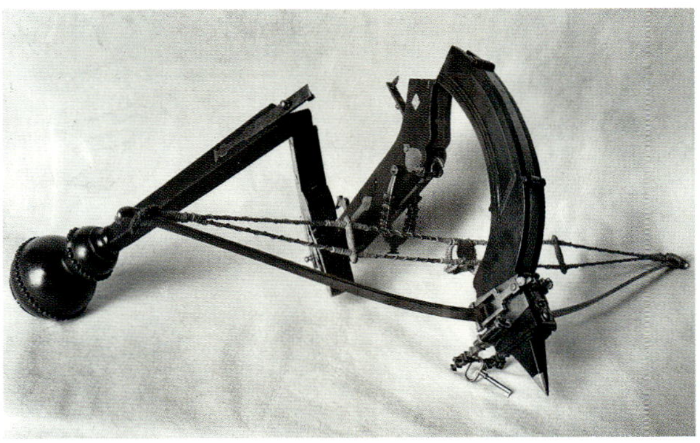

Figure 3.8 Pellet crossbow with foldable tiller. Probably Italian, ca. 1600. Kunsthistorisches Museum/Hofjagd- und Rüstkammer, Vienna (D 212)

a more permanent kind: it is secured by a strip of metal on the underside, held in place by two screws; disassembly of this weapon therefore required a tool and somewhat more time.[4]

In theory, the purpose of taking apart or collapsing a tiller would undoubtedly have been to facilitate storage and transport. Yet given the dearth of recorded examples, the quality of workmanship on the Vienna crossbow, and the use of rosewood for the Metropolitan Museum's tiller, it is more probable that these weapons, although usable, were made for their novelty appeal and as collectors' objects rather than practical considerations. The Vienna example in particular appears to have been part of the Habsburg art collections (*Kunstkammer*), where it would have been admired for its technical sophistication and its maker's ingenuity.

As for the Metropolitan Museum's example, it is at present impossible to establish whether the tiller was made to be taken apart, or whether the feature is a later modification, perhaps executed when the damage at the lock area was repaired. In the latter case, the tiller may originally have had a dorsal ornament that was lost in the alteration; the remaining decoration, in particular the foliage and scrollwork motifs, suggests a date of manufacture sometime in the later part of the sixteenth century.

21. Small Pellet Crossbow, Probably for a Woman or Child

Probably Italy, ca. 1575–1650
Steel, wood (probably walnut and ebony), gold
L. 29 1/16 in. (73.8 cm); W. 18 3/8 in. (46.6 cm); Wt. 5 lb. 1 oz. (2,304 g)
Gift of William H. Riggs, 1913 (14.25.1586)

Ex coll.: [H. Baum, Paris]; William H. Riggs, Paris

Reference: Grancsay 1933b, p. 42, no. 287

Some weapons made for women, and especially those for children, are often smaller and lighter than arms made for men. It is reasonable to assume that comparatively robust, plain ones were given to children, while elaborately decorated examples—such as the present crossbow—are more likely to have belonged to women. Exceptions are, of course, to be expected, especially in the extent and quality of the decoration on weapons made for the children of the high nobility.

This pellet crossbow comprises a delicate steel bow with unusual spatula-shaped nocks and a wooden tiller fitted with a reinforced fore-end, a rear pommel of ebony, the conventional single-axis lock, and front and rear sights. The tiller's main decoration consists of a finely carved lion's head with an open mouth at the front of the fore-end and a dorsal ornament in the shape of a dolphin-like sea monster; the latter has a curled, scaly body with a second face on its back, and it is accompanied by a small lizard or salamander in front. Except for the bow, all the metal parts and furniture are embellished, including the forward sight, which is shaped and engraved as a pair of dolphin-like sea monsters; the pierced and etched floral scrolls terminating in animal heads that form the lock plates; and the chiseled decoration of the trigger and rear sight (fig. 3.9). The gilding on the

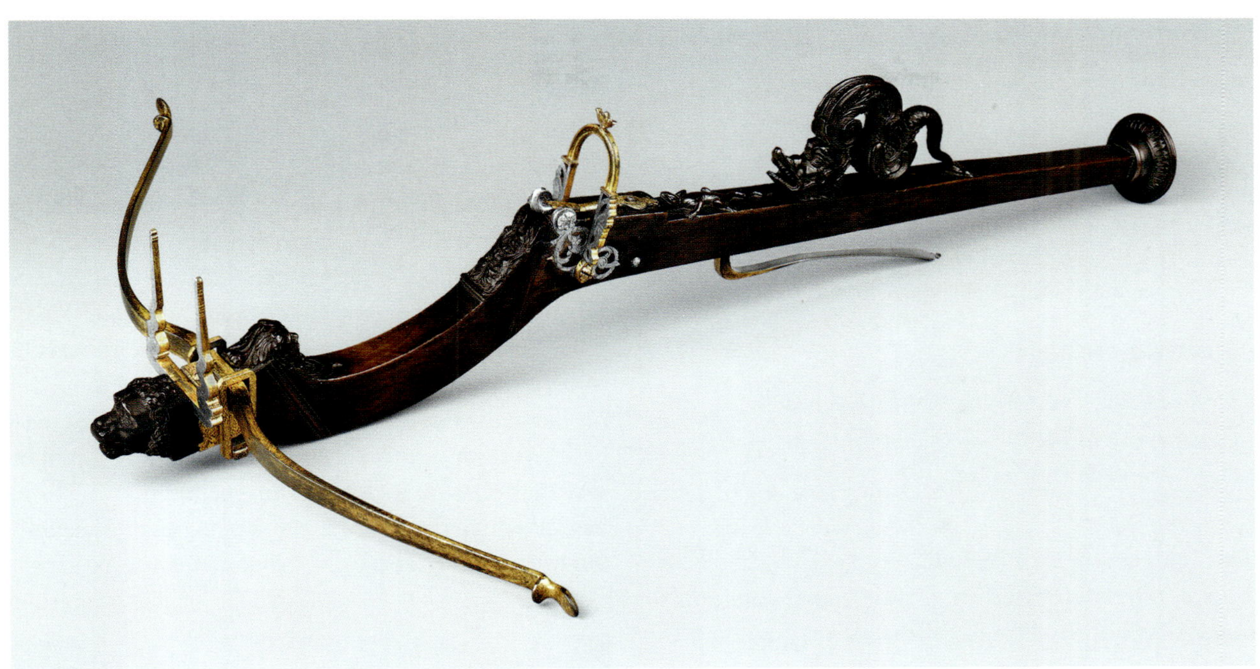

bow, fore-end reinforces, bow irons, and release hook—all of which are also clumsily etched, or re-etched—is most likely modern.

Sea monsters were a popular theme in the decorative arts of the Renaissance and Early Modern periods, and they are often found among the engraved inlay and sculptural embellishment of crossbow tillers and firearm stocks.[1] In addition to the present example and a nineteenth-century copy in the Metropolitan's collection (cat. 27), the weapons displaying these beasts include a small one in London,[2] as well as two in Paris: an example with an otherwise only sparsely decorated tiller and the exceedingly ornate pellet crossbow thought to have belonged to Catherine de Médicis.[3]

The pellet crossbow of Italian type, with a dorsal sculpture on the tiller, was fully developed by the mid-sixteenth century (cat. 19), but it remained in use for a considerable period. The delicate lock plates of the Museum's example are reminiscent of those found on Italian firearms from the middle of the seventeenth century, and suggest that the present weapon probably also dates from that period.

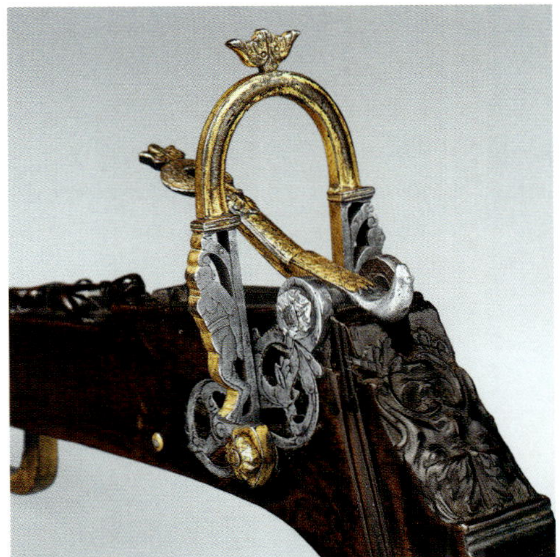

Figure 3.9

22. Pellet Crossbow

Probably France, late 16th or early 17th century
Steel, wood (fruitwood, probably cherry), ivory, mother-of-pearl, gold, hemp, iron alloy
L. 36³⁄₁₆ in. (92 cm); W. 22¾ in. (57.7 cm); Wt. 3 lb. 3 oz. (1,432 g)
Gift of William H. Riggs, 1913 (14.25.1584)

Ex coll.: Joseph Fau, Paris; William H. Riggs, Paris

References: Fau sale 1884, p. 55, lot 194; Stone 1934 (1961 ed.), p. 13; Nickel 1974, p. 230

This is an example of an Italian-type pellet crossbow with a tiller decorated in a style more commonly found north of the Alps (see also cat. 27). Showing an unusual recurve, the plain, unmarked steel bow is mounted onto the tiller by a pair of oblong bow irons, which are secured by a pair of spacers and a wedge, all made of iron alloy; these pass through a transverse opening in the fore-end, rather than being wedged against the underside. The hemp bowstring shows signs of age and is missing its two spacer pegs; the present pegs are modern.

The fruitwood tiller has a forward half of vertical-rectangular section with a comparatively flat curve. The forward curve features decorative carving, and the underside is fitted with a small transverse stag-horn stand or rest. At present, the fore-end has no frontal spike, no plates strengthening the mounting

area of the bow, and no forward sight. The absence of reinforcing plates appears to be original, but some kind of finial in front and the foreward sight were probably lost due to damage and subsequent repairs to the fore-end; the latter include the bolt guide, a plaque on the fore-end's underside, and the small finial button, all made of staghorn, and all appearing to be replacements. The unusual bow, accordingly, is probably also not original to this crossbow but may be a working-life replacement. The tiller's straight rear half has a lock area of rectangular section, behind which the tiller becomes octagonal in section. On top, the tiller displays a prominently carved scroll,

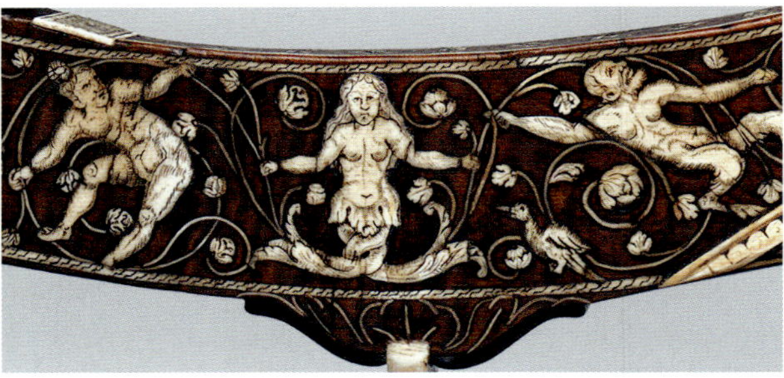

Figure 3.10

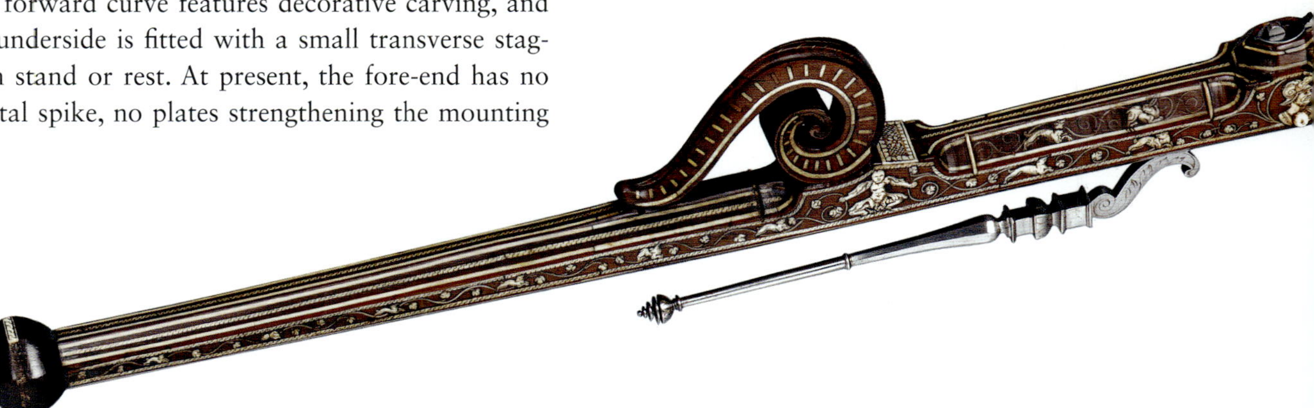

and it terminates at the rear in a multifaceted pommel with a small, inset butt plate of mother-of-pearl. The single-axis lock, made entirely of iron alloy, comprises a release hook, a lock plate on either side, and a lever trigger with a particularly blunt angle; the lever axis is made of staghorn. A pivoting, arch-shaped rear sight, also of iron alloy, is fitted to the tiller just behind the lock plates.

All the parts of the release mechanism are decoratively shaped and chiseled, and the trigger also displays some modest etched ornament exhibiting traces of gilding; only the bow and its fittings are unadorned. In addition to the molding and the carved ornament, the tiller is inlaid flush with bands and panels of polished and engraved staghorn; some of these are missing and some have been replaced. The bands vary in width; the thinner ones are either plain or show a guilloche pattern, while the few wider ones feature a scalloped motif. The panels display grotesques and mythical figures, heads of warriors wearing helmets *all'antica*, nudes (fig. 3.10), dogs giving chase, and—on either side of the fore-end—a courtier dressed in late sixteenth-century French fashion. The figure on the left is partially restored and its engraving probably refreshed, that is, recut; the head of the figure on the right is a replacement. These costumed figures allow for a relatively precise dating of this weapon—to the late sixteenth century—and indicate that the weapon was likely made in France.

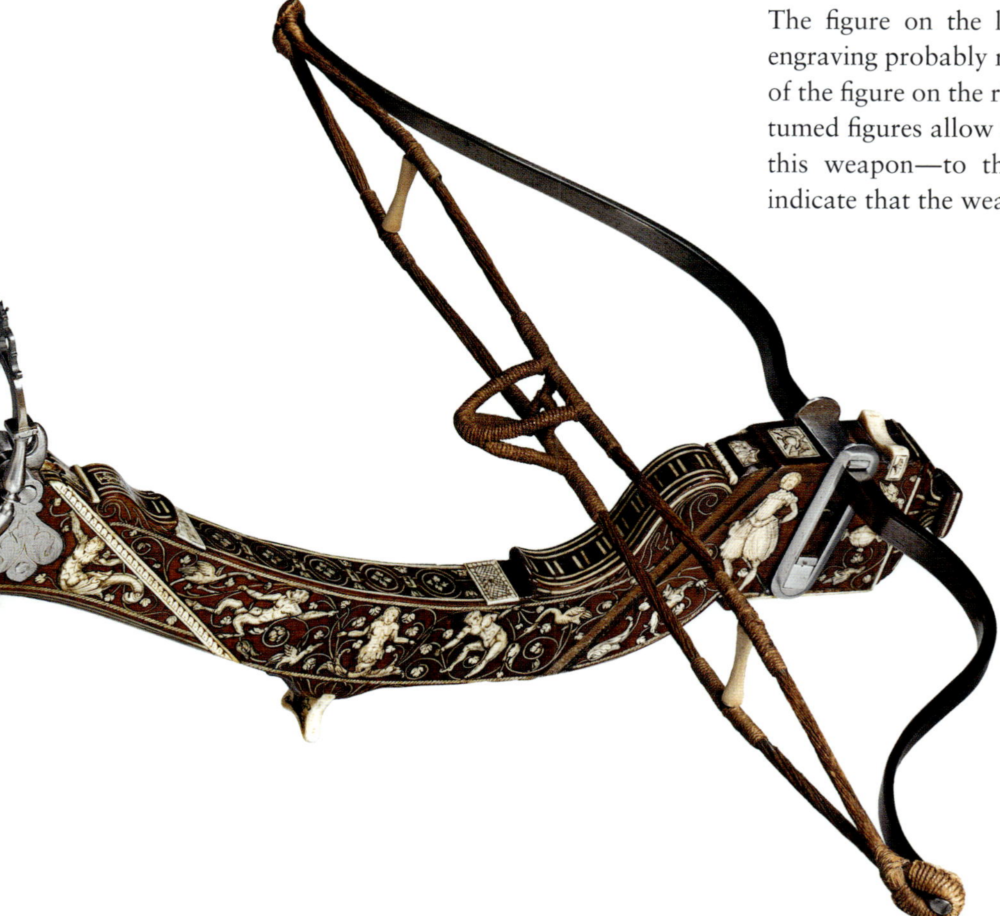

23. Pellet Crossbow

Central Europe (Germany), ca. 1600–1650
Steel, wood,[1] staghorn, hemp, leather
L. 26⅞ in. (68.2 cm); W. 17⅜ in. (44.1 cm); Wt. 5 lb. 1 oz.
(2,302 g)
Gift of William H. Riggs, 1913 (14.25.1587)

Ex coll.: William H. Riggs, Paris

References: Grancsay 1933b, p. 42; Stone 1934 (1961 ed.), p. 13

Mark:

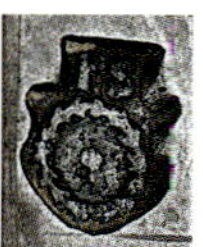

Unlike the pellet crossbows of "Italian" type (cats. 19–22), which have wooden tillers and light steel bows that could be spanned by hand, a heavier and distinctly different variety emerged in central Europe about 1600. Characteristic of the "German" type, or *Kugelschnepper* (pellet snapper), are a stronger steel bow and a thin, almost skeletal steel tiller fitted at the rear with a wooden butt resembling the cheeks of contemporary gunstocks. Since the stronger bow did not allow for spanning by hand, a

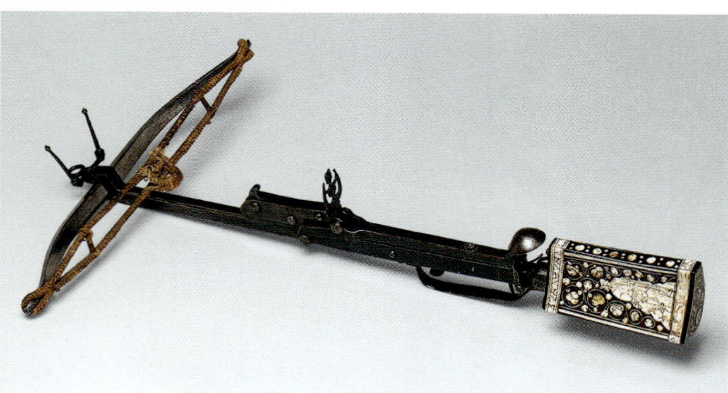

combination lever spanner and release mechanism was permanently secured to the top of the tiller by means of a pivot. Raising the lever arm resulted in the pushing forward of a short box containing part of the release mechanism until the hook in front could engage the bowstring; when the user pushed the lever down again, it brought the string and box back until the latter lined up with the rear part of the release mechanism within the tiller proper. The hook also served as the bowstring release: the user shot the weapon by pulling the trigger after setting the rear mechanism by means of a push button on the tiller's underside. Like pellet crossbows of Italian type, their northern counterparts came in varying sizes.

This rather plain example is made up of a strong steel bow of square rectangular section with a double bowstring of hemp (damaged); a steel tiller, fitted with an integrated spanning and release mechanism; and a wooden butt covered front and rear with a horn plate. Any accidental release was prevented by the spring-loaded safety catch just in front of the butt and the trigger guard; the present guard and the screw-headed axes are later replacements. The upper surface of the lever is struck once with a maker's mark: the letters PS above a wreath of leaves.[2]

The decoration includes traces of bluing on the bow and on all parts of the otherwise plain tiller, and the rear sight is pierced and engraved with the figure of a double-tailed mermaid; a series of small circles is engraved on the spring of the release hook. The polished and engraved staghorn inlay of the butt displays floral vines and blossoms containing, on the cheek, a large figure of a hunter with his dog and a wheel-lock gun, and, on the opposite side, a grotesque face above a sea monster, as well as bands of guilloche and scenes of dogs chasing hares; the last band has been partially replaced.

More than half a dozen *Kugelschnepper* bearing the same mark are recorded, including examples in London,[3] Stockholm,[4] Nuremberg,[5] Frankfurt,[6] Darmstadt,[7] Prague,[8] Cracow,[9] and Paris.[10] Another was formerly in Eisenach.[11] Except for the Cracow and Paris examples (which display extensive decoration on their respective tillers and wooden butts), the majority of weapons from this group have plain tillers and spanning mechanisms, while their butts show decoration of varying accomplishment, but which—in every case—appears to be unique. Despite the fact that only a small number of late sixteenth- and early seventeenth-century German crossbow makers with these initials are recorded in contemporary documents—for example, Peter Senger/Peter Schneider (rec. 1594), who worked for Landgrave Moritz of Hessen[12]—it has so far been impossible to identify the maker of these pellet crossbows.

24. Pellet Crossbow

Central Europe (Germany), ca. 1600–1650
Steel, wood (probably maple), gold, iron alloy
L. 28⅝ in. (72.6 cm); W. 17⅝ in. (44.7 cm); Wt. 6 lb. 8 oz. (2,944 g)
Gift of William H. Riggs, 1913 (14.25.1588)

Ex coll.: William H. Riggs, Paris

References: Grancsay 1933b, p. 42, no. 285; Grancsay 1955, p. 24, no. 89; Grancsay 1964, p. 35, no. 45

Marks:

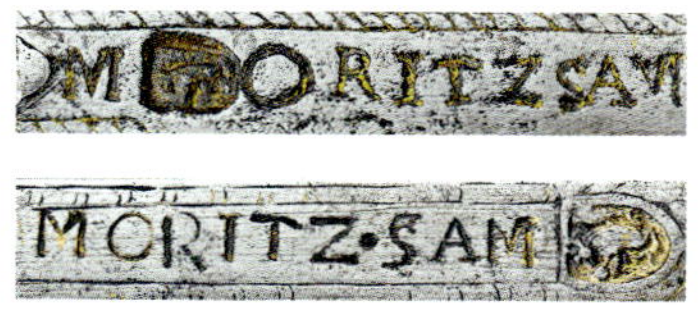

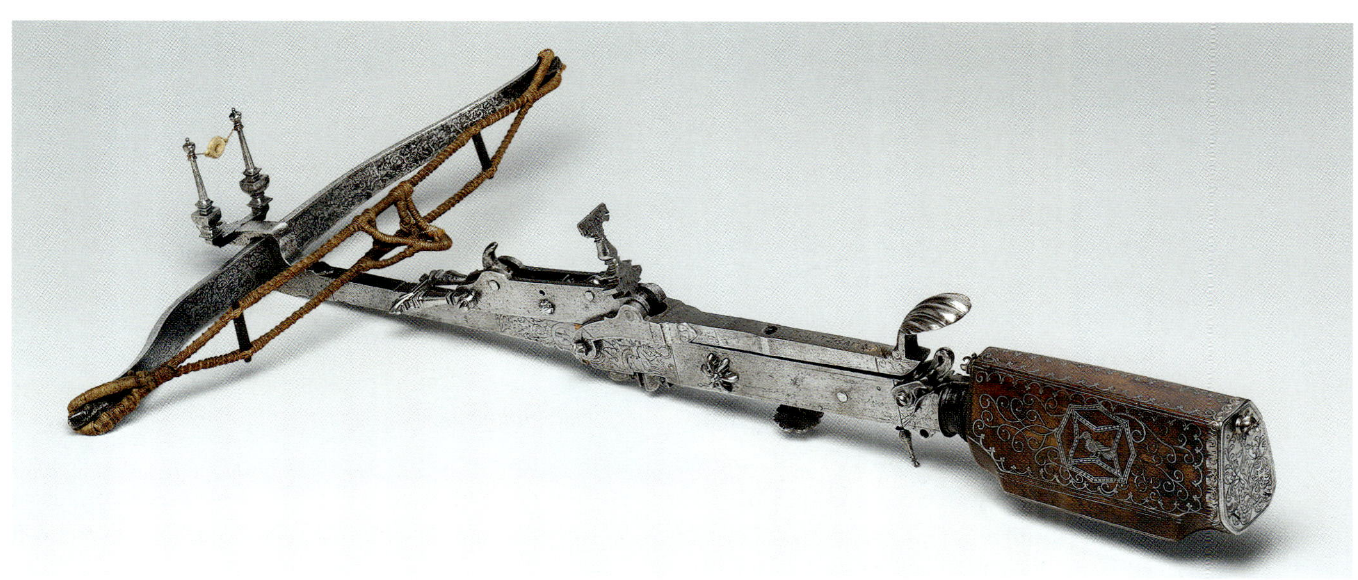

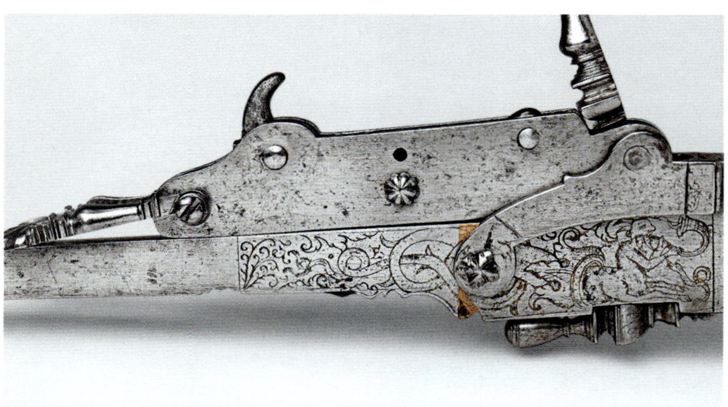

Like catalogue 23, this pellet crossbow is of the "German" type (*Kugelschnepper*) but slightly larger and heavier and more extensively decorated. It is constructed in the usual manner, with a strong steel bow and its double bowstring; a steel tiller with an integrated span-and-release mechanism; and a butt, probably of maple and at least in part veneered, with an iron-alloy butt plate. The butt appears to be a working-lifetime replacement; at the time of writing, the safety catch for the lever arm was not working, and the trigger guard was missing. The lever arm and tiller proper are each struck once with the same maker's mark: within a shield a seated squirrel, holding a nut[?]; each mark is accompanied by the deeply engraved inscription MORITZ SAM, showing traces of gilding in both cases.[1]

All four sides of the bow are etched, displaying scenes of deer-, bear-, and hare-hunting amid floral vines. In addition to the shell shape of the lever handle, the heart shape of the suspension ring, the setting button, and the spiral heel knob, several parts of the tiller and lever bear chiseled ornament and delicately engraved grotesque figures, birds, and foliage, all of which show traces of gilding (fig. 3.11). The decoration of the wooden butt consists of what seems to be maple veneer, flush iron-alloy wire inlay

in the shape of a central cartouche containing a bird, and bands of stylized fleurs-de-lis bordering the principal edges; the butt plate is engraved with foliage.

This pellet crossbow belongs to a small group of weapons of similar quality, all bearing the same squirrel mark and inscription, MORITZ SAM, including examples in Leeds,[2] Paris,[3] and Guernsey,[4] and another, formerly in the collection of the dukes of Brunswick.[5] The last two are almost identical in decoration and also bear the squirrel mark, but on both weapons the inscription MORITZ SAM is engraved not on the tiller, but on panels of polished staghorn inlay on the top of the butt. A number of pellet bows are struck on the lever arm, tiller, or both with a similar mark—a squirrel flanked by the initials MS—but lack the accompanying inscription.[6] Finally, several weapons of the same type are struck with the squirrel mark only.[7]

The initials MS in the marks found on weapons from the second group correspond to the first letters of the inscription MORITZ SAM, indicating that pellet crossbows from the first and second groups are, in all probability, by the same maker, or from the same (family) workshop. Whether examples from the third group are remains to be identified, as do the exact geographical origin of these weapons and their maker.[8]

25. Small Pellet Crossbow

Probably France (possibly Paris), ca. 1850–90 in
16th-century style
Steel, copper alloy, gold
L. 25⅞ in. (65.7 cm); W. 16⁹⁄₁₆ in. (42 cm); Wt. 2 lb. 1 oz. (925 g)
Rogers Fund, 1955 (55.185.5)

Ex coll.: Frédéric Spitzer, Paris; Collection of William
Randolph Hearst/The Hearst Corporation, New York

References: Spitzer 1890–93, vol. 6 (1892), pl. XLIII,
no. 294; Spitzer sale 1895, p. 32, no. 294

Although this weapon would seem to be an Italian
pellet crossbow of the sixteenth century (cat. 19),
there are several indications that it is a nineteenth-
century copy or fake. The clues include a tiller of cast
metal rather than wood, the unusual shape of the
arms of the bow, the prominent release hook, and,
last but not least, the somewhat stiff and awkward
execution of the decoration.

This crossbow was once owned by Frédéric Spitzer
(1815–1890), a celebrated Paris art dealer and collector (cat. 49), and notorious purveyor of elaborate
fakes in medieval and Renaissance style. Doubts
about the weapon's authenticity, perhaps even certain
knowledge of its modern manufacture, may already
be inferred from the way in which the weapon was
published in the nineteenth-century catalogues of the
Spitzer collection and its subsequent dispersal after
the collector's death. In the first publication (1892), it
is the only crossbow among seven for which no
approximate date is offered, while the sale catalogue
(1895) explicitly refers to it as "*Style Renaissance*" (in
the style of the Renaissance). However, any reserva-
tions (or certainty) must have been either forgotten or
ignored during the course of the first half of the twentieth century, for when the Metropolitan Museum
purchased this pellet crossbow from the Hearst
Corporation in 1955, it was believed to be genuine.

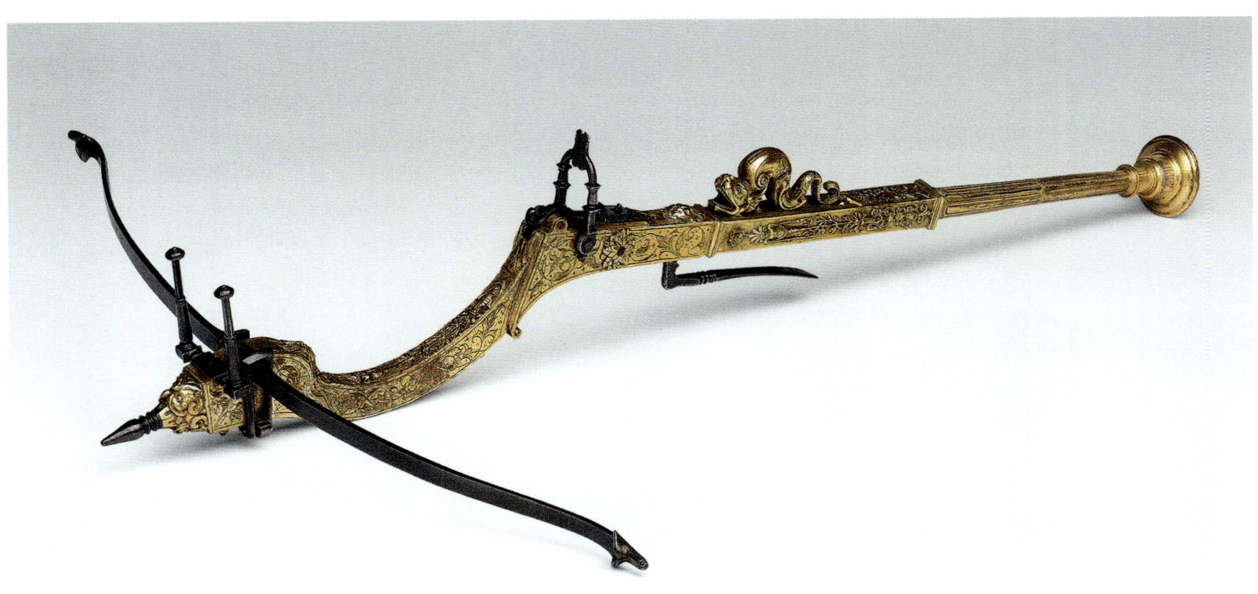

4 | SPECIAL TYPES OF CROSSBOWS

A few crossbows differ in construction and function from the ordinary forms of bolt- and pellet-shooting weapons to such an extent as to constitute special types. The Metropolitan Museum possesses three extraordinary European examples.[1] The practice of combining crossbows with other weapons has a long tradition, although both documentary references and surviving objects are extremely rare: only a dozen extant examples are recorded to date.[2] As early as the late twelfth century a spear-mounted crossbow was depicted in an Islamic treatise on weapons and tactics written for Salah al-Din (Saladin, r. 1169–93).[3] In Europe, the marriage of a crossbow and a firearm was probably first undertaken in Italy during the late fifteenth or early sixteenth century. Three crossbows in Venice, originally from the armory of the Doge's Palace, appear to be the earliest of these hybrids, which were made with steel tillers and incorporated some of the first recorded wheel-lock mechanisms.[4] Within a decade or two, that is, during the first half of the sixteenth century, the technology spread to the German-speaking regions north of the Alps, and the very few survivors, as well as occasional documentary references, indicate that they continued to be made in both regions through the sixteenth and into the seventeenth century.[5]

The plain Venetian weapons were likely intended for utilitarian use, presumably by a bodyguard, as was the even rarer—possibly unique—combination of a crossbow and a hunting sword, probably of German construction, today in Rome.[6] Most of the other known combination crossbows, however, show an exceptional degree of embellishment. Among the finest is one made for Archduke Ferdinand I of Austria (later Holy Roman Emperor, r. 1558–64; fig. 4.1); its painted and etched decoration features the owner's name and heraldry, the latter dating the weapon to between 1521 and 1526.[7] Another imperial member of the Habsburg family, Ferdinand's predecessor, Charles V (r. 1519–58), apparently also owned an ornate combination crossbow, today in Churburg.[8] Admired as conversation pieces for their technological ingenuity, rather than intended for actual use, these singular weapons were probably made exclusively for noble patrons and hence decorated to reflect their owners' status.

A most unusual crossbow in the Metropolitan's collection could shoot pellets as well as bolts, has a large lever trigger built into its profusely decorated tiller, and is combined with a self-spanning wheel-lock pistol (cat. 26). A weapon in Vienna is so similar in construction and decoration that there can be little doubt that both originally came from the same workshop and may have once formed a pair. Indeed, taken in conjunction with the examples in

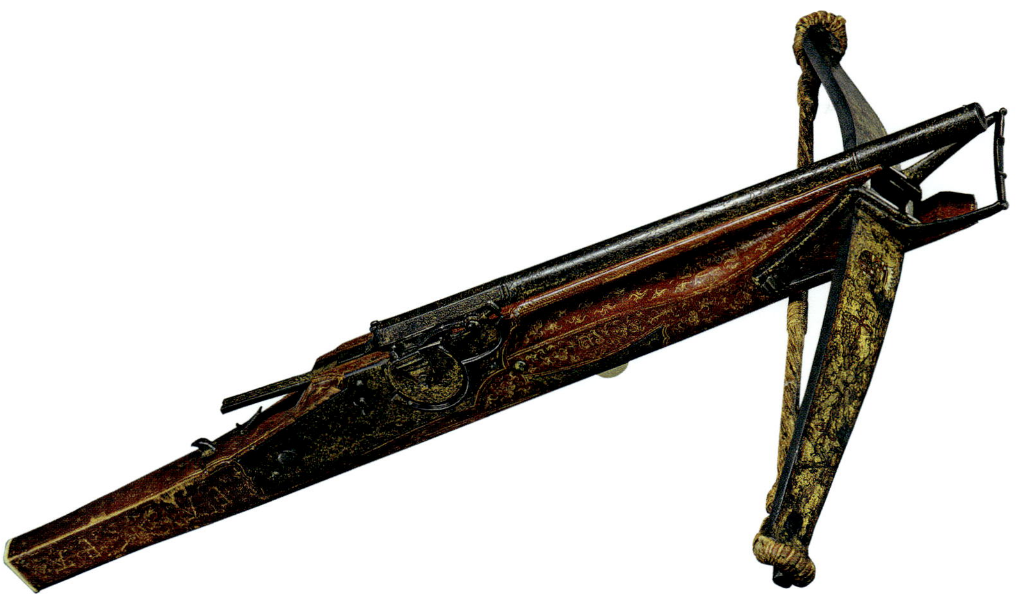

Munich and Churburg, the circumstantial evidence provided by the Metropolitan's combination crossbow and its mate in Vienna suggests that both may once have also belonged to
members of the imperial Habsburg family.

Another form of combination crossbow is exemplified by a small group of weapons that
can be adapted to shoot either pellets or bolts. This special type has been mentioned in passing by a few scholars, but so far only pellet crossbows of central European, or "German,"
type have been identified as displaying this feature, the removable support for a bolt—a "bolt
bridge" or "quarrel rest."[9] However, pellet crossbows of "Italian" type were occasionally also
fitted with a bolt bridge, and Italy may in fact be the origin of this feature.

A crossbow in the Metropolitan Museum's collection, whose tiller is of the Italian shape but
whose inlaid decoration suggests that it was made in the region of eastern France or southern
Germany, has a curved fore-end that is pierced centrally by a vertical hole and further cavities
at the front and rear (cat. 27). An explanation for the function of these enigmatic features
was provided by a very similar crossbow formerly in the collection of Frédéric Spitzer, Paris,
and today in a different private collection (fig. 4.2):[10] the hole and cavities accommodated a
long central screw and two short prongs that secured a wooden support across the weapon's
curved fore-end, allowing it to also shoot bolts instead of the (usual) pellets. Together with

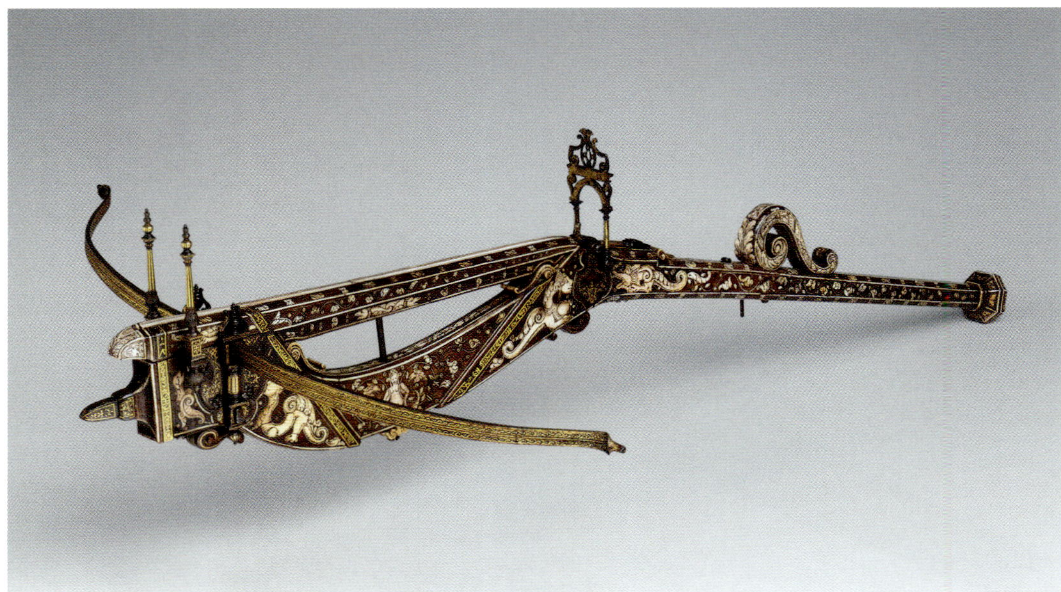

one other, the two crossbows remain the only recorded examples of this type to date, and so far no documentary reference or representation in art has come to light.

Very small crossbows constitute another special type, an individual example of which is known by the Italian term *balestrino* (little crossbow) or by the modern epithet "assassin's crossbow" (fig. 4.3).[11] Documentary evidence points to a probable origin in Italy, in at least the early fifteenth century, although no examples appear to survive from before 1500. In general, *balestrini* were smaller than the crossbows intended for use by women or children (cats. 15, 21) but larger than miniature weapons; they usually had an all-metal tiller and some form of internal spanning mechanism. Easily concealable and, like all crossbows, nearly silent, these small but effective weapons presented a potential danger clearly recognized in surviving sixteenth- and seventeenth-century documents: some of their bows could have a draw weight of more than three hundred pounds (136 kg). As a result, a number of Italian laws banned their possession on pain of such draconian penalties as several years' galley service.[12]

A seventeenth-century account gives some indication of the power and accuracy of these weapons and suggests that, on one occasion at least, a *balestrino* had been exported to a European colony. In his memoirs, published posthumously in 1690, the French nobleman Guichard Déageant (1574–1642) related the account of a visitor to the French court who had observed, in one of the Spanish colonies, "a young Indian boy with a steel crossbow so small it fitted inside his pouch, and with which he shot so accurately that he never failed to hit from twenty or twenty-five paces a disk the size of a *denier* [a coin], with a sharp arrow that penetrated with great force and well forward into [a] plank. . . ."[13]

Since the dating of individual *balestrini* remains difficult, and documentary references are scarce, it is still not clear how long these weapons remained in use. Many surviving examples are plain and unmarked, and the difficult task of their dating and geographical attribution must therefore rely largely on stylistic comparisons. Despite the lack of any continuous evidence, however, it is reasonably certain that the *balestrino* was the direct ancestor of the pistol crossbows of the eighteenth and nineteenth centuries.

Finally, mention ought to be made of several other examples, which may form their own special types, but which cannot be examined in detail here. These include the plain, sturdy crossbow trap, which was mounted outdoors in a stationary position and rigged with bait and a trip wire, and the famous Chinese repeating crossbow, which appears to date back about two thousand years, and of which nineteenth-century examples survive in several collections.[14] In addition, there are crossbows made as engineering marvels that could be folded or taken apart; the Metropolitan has one in its collection (cat. 20), but since it is not clear whether its special feature is original or a later, working-life modification, this weapon is discussed in Section 3, "Pellet Crossbows." Similarly intriguing are enigmatic references in period documents, such as the crossbow "without a nut that shoots two bolts," in a 1316 inventory of objects stolen from Mathilda of Brabant (1268–1329), countess of Artois (see the introduction to Section 2), and the "slurbows" in a 1599 inventory of the armories in the Tower of London; especially the latter are probably military weapons fitted with barrels for the discharging of incendiary projectiles.[15] All these special types await further detailed scholarly attention.

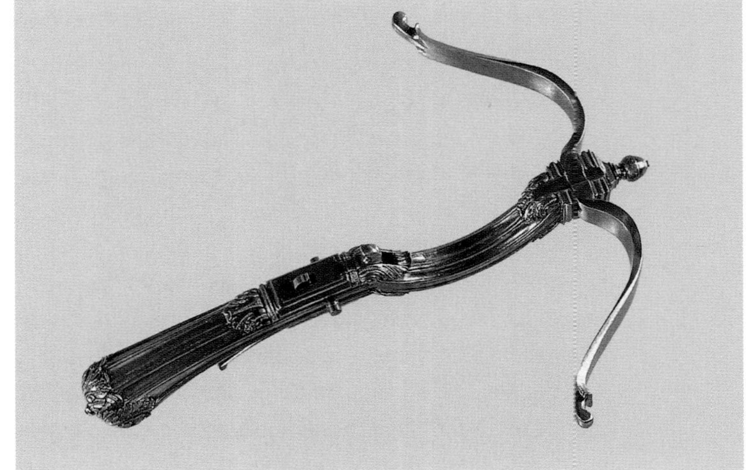

Figure 4.3 Small crossbow (*balestrino*). Italian or French, probably 17th century. Musée le Secq des Tournelles, Rouen (LS-1414)

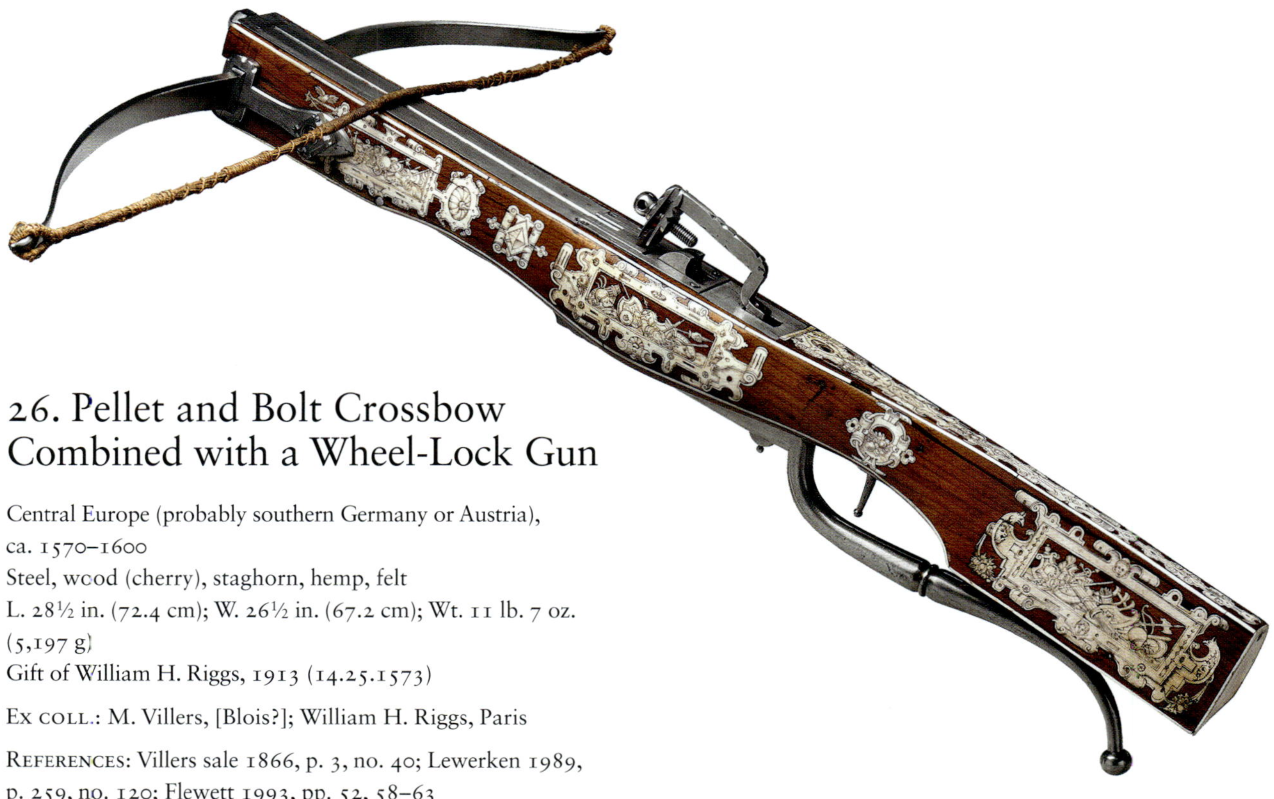

26. Pellet and Bolt Crossbow Combined with a Wheel-Lock Gun

Central Europe (probably southern Germany or Austria),
ca. 1570–1600
Steel, wood (cherry), staghorn, hemp, felt
L. 28½ in. (72.4 cm); W. 26½ in. (67.2 cm); Wt. 11 lb. 7 oz.
(5,197 g)
Gift of William H. Riggs, 1913 (14.25.1573)

Ex coll.: M. Villers, [Blois?]; William H. Riggs, Paris

References: Villers sale 1866, p. 3, no. 40; Lewerken 1989,
p. 259, no. 120; Flewett 1993, pp. 52, 58–63

The combination of a crossbow and a firearm into a single weapon was probably first undertaken in Italy during the late fifteenth or early sixteenth century. Such weapons soon spread to the German-speaking regions north of the Alps, where they continued to be made well into the seventeenth century. However, the small number of surviving examples and the scarce documentary evidence suggest that this type of combination weapon was rare.

This example consists of a slender, unmarked steel bow and a large, hollow tiller, made of cherrywood and lined with green felt, which contains an extraordinary combination of crossbow spanning-and-release mechanism, gun barrel, and self-spanning wheel lock, all of steel. The bow, bow irons and screw, and possibly the cock, that is, the hammer, of the wheel lock are later replacements, as is probably also the felt lining.

Inside the tiller, the main body of the spanning-and-release mechanism is a block of triangular section freely suspended within the fore-end. Grooved with a shallow depression down the middle, the flat upper surface serves as the crossbow's chase; two small holes at the front mark the position of a missing bolt guide. Embedded within the underside of the block is a smooth-bore barrel of pistol length, the muzzle of which can be closed with the hexagonal domed screw cap, and the central wheel-lock mechanism. The entire block is connected at the back to a large Z-shaped lever system, which in turn is attached with pins to the front and rear of the tiller. When lowered, the lever moves the block forward until the nut catches the bowstring; when the lever is raised, the block retreats into the tiller, and the crossbow is spanned. Only the heavy spanning lever is fitted with a safety catch.

The lock comprises the combined wheel lock and crossbow release and is covered by an H-shaped upper lock plate. Within the forward cutout is the opening for the pan and the internal wheel of the first mechanism, which are concealed beneath a sliding pan-cover; the wheel is spanned by pulling the cock back. The nut is situated between the wheel and the cock. When both mechanisms are spanned, pulling the trigger discharges the crossbow then fires the gun.

Except for modest chiseling on the bow irons, wheel-lock cock, lever, and trigger, and the addorsed baluster shape of the lower lever arm, the steel components of this weapon are plain. All four sides of the tiller, on the other hand, are richly embellished with flush inlay of polished and engraved staghorn. On either side are three rectangular scrollwork cartouches, each containing a different trophy of arms (fig. 4.5); the top rear of the tiller shows a continuous strap-work panel adorned with festoons and a caryatid-like upper torso of a nude female. Simpler cartouches and small individual festoons alternating with grotesque mascarons decorate the tiller's underside.

The Museum's weapon is one of only two recorded crossbow-and-wheel-lock combinations fitted with this extraordinary internal spanning-and-release mechanism. The other, from the collection of Archduke Ferdinand II of Tyrol (1529–1595) at Ambras Castle near Innsbruck and now in Vienna (fig. 4.6), matches the Museum's example so closely in construction and appearance that there can be little doubt that both came from the same work-shop.[1] The two weapons vary slightly in their bows, the way in which these are mounted, and a small detail in the operation of the lever construction— all owing to later modifications on the Museum's example—and slightly in the shape of their cheeks and the iconography of their respective inlays.

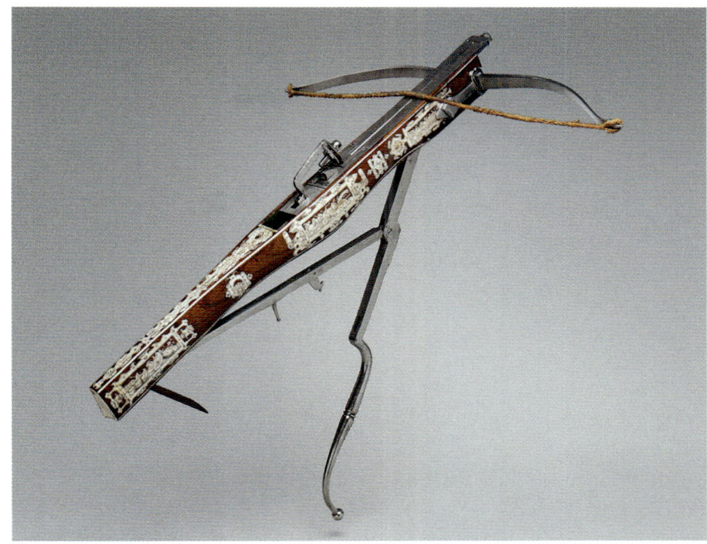

Figure 4.4 Catalogue 26, with lever raised

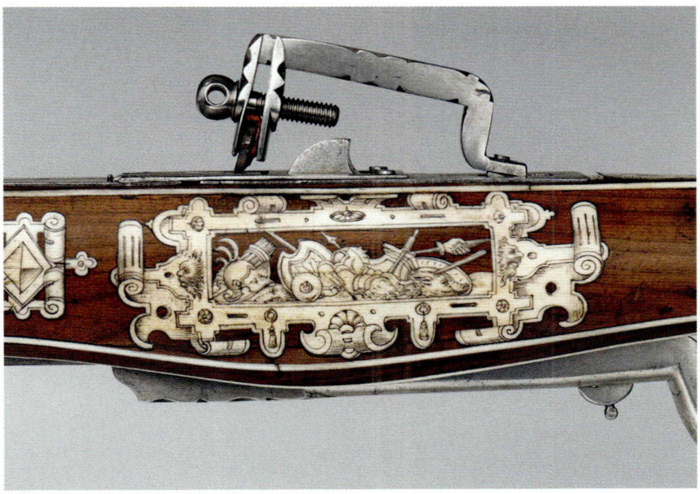

Figure 4.5 Detail of catalogue 26, with inlaid trophy of arms

The strong steel bow of the Vienna crossbow is struck four times with an unidentified mark (the Gothic letter M within a circle; fig. 4.7) and mounted to the tiller by a hemp binding; the general appearance of the bow, especially the near-square section, and its marks suggest that it was probably made by

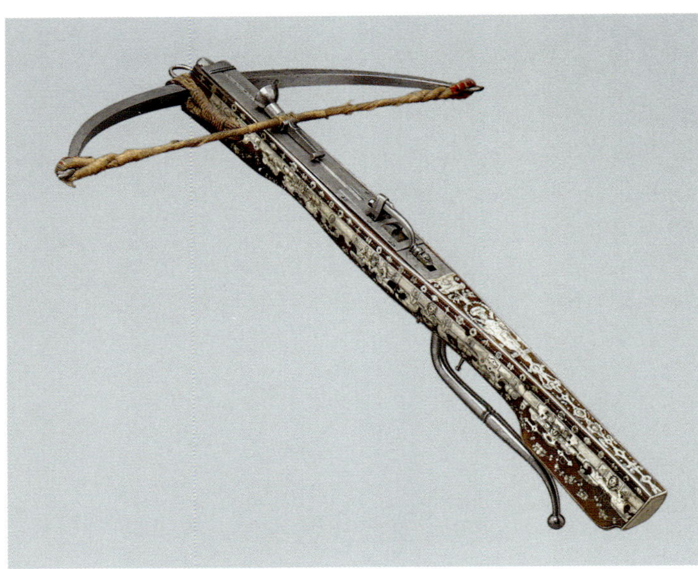

Figure 4.6 Pellet crossbow combined with a wheel-lock pistol, probably Austrian, ca. 1570–1600. Steel, cherrywood, staghorn, hemp. Kunsthistorisches Museum/ Hofjagd- und Rüstkammer, Vienna (D 200)

Figure 4.7

a Spanish bow maker.[2] A single bowstring, also of hemp, is fitted in the middle with an iron pellet cup; the latter has an extension at the rear terminating in a handle-like crossbar that fits into the groove of the nut. The Vienna bow appears to be original, and it may be assumed that a similar one was once mounted onto the Museum's tiller, probably also secured by a binding. The pellet cup, which is detachable, confirms that both weapons could shoot pellets as well as bolts.

The decoration on the Vienna tiller consists mainly of continuous architectural bands, rather than cartouches, along the sides; these are adorned with scrollwork, mascarons, and small nude figures, while

the band on top displaying the caryatid is more delicate than on the Museum's example. Nonetheless, the artistic medium and execution appear to be by the same hand on both tillers.

The scrollwork cartouches and trophies of arms on the sides of the Museum's crossbow are closely influenced by a series of designs by Jacob Floris the Elder (1524–1581), titled *Veelderhande cierlijcke Compartementen . . .* (Manifold delicate cartouches . . .) and engraved in Antwerp by Herman Müller in 1564 (fig. 4.8).[3] While the model for the caryatid-like figure on the tiller's upper side has not been identified, the one on the tiller in Vienna is clearly copied from one of the figures included in a collection of caryatids designed by Hans Vredeman de Vries (1527–1606 [?]) and published in 1565, also in Antwerp.[4]

Generally similar inlay, ranging from modestly executed individual motifs to accomplished cartouches accompanied by figures and elaborate ornament, is also found on a number of late sixteenth-century southern German firearms.[5] These comparisons—together with the terminus post quem provided by the Antwerp designs and the fact that self-spanning wheel locks are rare before about 1570—allow a dating of both combination weapons to the last decades of the sixteenth century.

However, since only the Vienna bow is marked, and neither crossbow bears any other signatures, inscriptions, or coats of arms, it has so far not been possible to establish their maker or workshop. Equally elusive is the identity of their original owner or owners, though one may assume that such extraordinary weapons must have been made for persons of considerable social status. Notwithstanding their ingenious construction and the high quality of the decoration, the weapons are rather heavy, and the spanning process is not only cumbersome but—as is evident on the Museum's example—causes considerable strain on the parts of the tiller to which the mechanism is attached. Since other crossbow-and-firearm combinations are lighter and could certainly be used, the present weapons were probably meant to be conversation pieces, perhaps for a *Kunstkammer* or as impressive gifts. In this light, it is tempting to speculate that a Spanish bow, mounted in central European fashion to a tiller of southern German or Austrian manufacture, coupled with the Ambras provenance of the Vienna example (as well as those in Munich and Churburg Castle; see the introduction to this section), points to a connection with the Habsburg court.

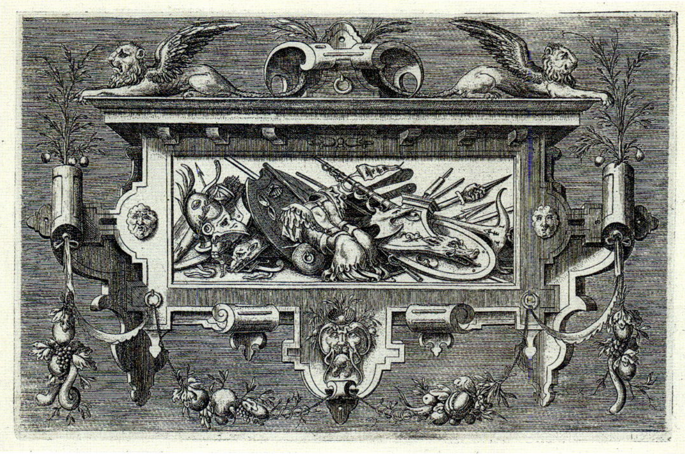

Figure 4.8 After Jacob Floris the Elder (Flemish, 1524–1581). Ornamental print from *Veelderhande cierlijcke Compartementen* . . . (Manifold delicate cartouches . . .), a pattern book for painters, goldsmiths, and sculptors, engraved by Herman Müller, published by Hans Liefrinck. Flemish, dated 1564. Engraving, ca. 11 × 7⅞ in. (28 × 20 cm). The Metropolitan Museum of Art, New York, The Elisha Whittelsey Collection, The Elisha Whittelsey Fund, 1948 (48.13.4 [41])

27. Pellet and Bolt Crossbow

Northern Italy or France (probably Savoy), dated 1573
Steel, wood (cherrywood), staghorn, ivory (probably elephant)
L. 37¾ in. (95.9 cm); W. 25⁵⁄₁₆ in. (64.3 cm); Wt. 4 lb. 6 oz. (1,977 g)
Gift of William H. Riggs, 1913 (14.25.1583)

Ex coll.: M. E. Vaïsse, Marseilles; William H. Riggs, Paris

Reference: Vaïsse sale 1885, p. 9, lot 73

It is extremely unusual to find the dates of manufacture and features identifying the original owner on Italian pellet crossbows. This example not only bears both a date and a coat of arms, but it is further distinguished by having once been able to shoot both pellets and bolts, and by its elaborate decoration. Accordingly, despite significant restorations, it is an important example for the study of this particular type of weapon.

The Museum's crossbow consists of a slightly curved steel bow and a cherrywood tiller with a reinforced fore-end and a long rear part terminating in an onion-shaped, faceted pommel; the part behind the scroll, including the pommel, is a later repair made from mahogany. The weapon is fitted with front and rear sights and with a release mechanism that has been converted from the conventional single-axis, lever-trigger release system. The latter is composed of a modified release hook, lock plates on the sides and underside, an internal lever, a trigger proper, and a trigger guard. Three holes pierce the curved fore-end vertically, one at the center, one toward the front, and one in front of the release. This unusual feature once allowed this weapon to be fitted with a bridge-shaped addition (now missing) for shooting bolts rather than pellets.

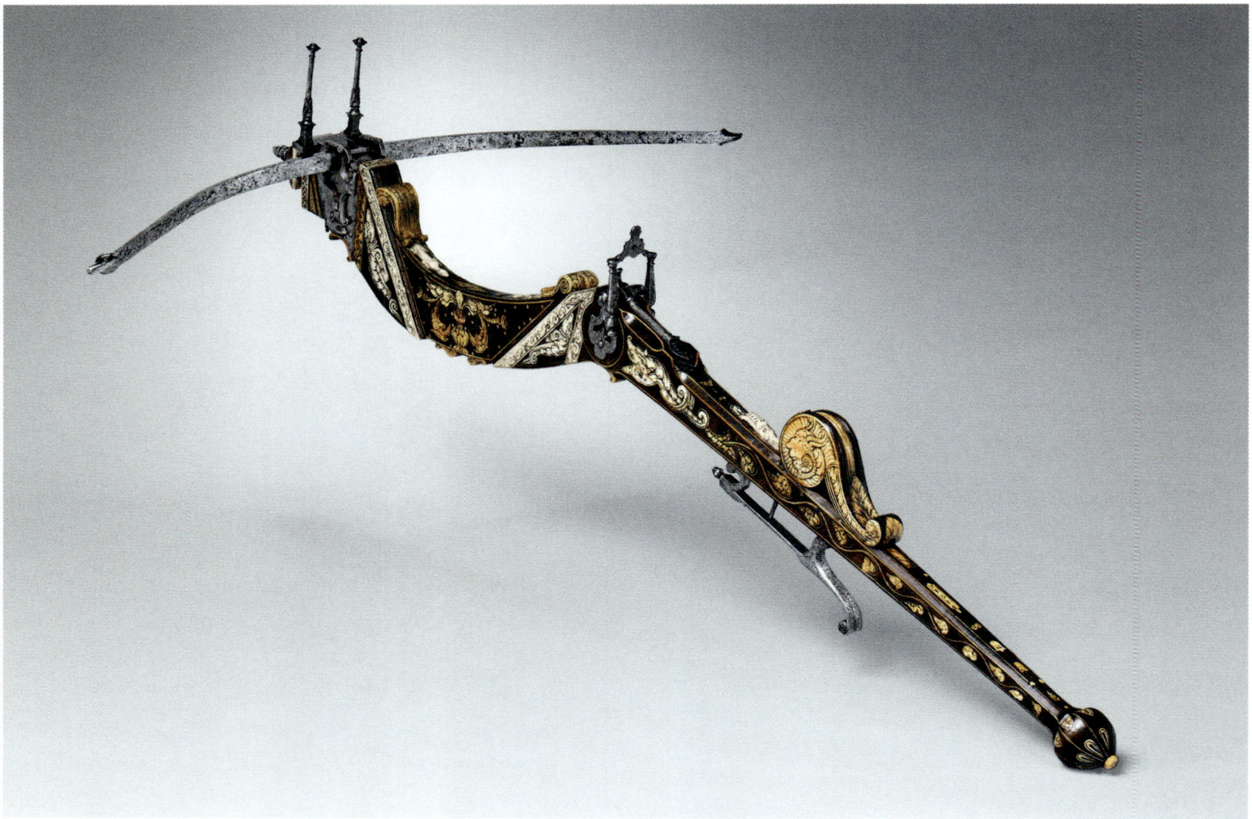

Every part of this crossbow is embellished. Near the middle, the bow is etched on all four sides with guilloches and stylized leaves, while the front finial, foreward sight, bow irons, release hook, and trigger guard are either sculpted or chiseled and engraved. The side plates of the lock are decoratively pierced and engraved, and the lower lock plate shows the same etched guilloche pattern as on the upper and lower sides of the bow. In addition to the carved molding and a scroll on top, the tiller is adorned by a flush inlay of polished and engraved staghorn, mainly bands of floral scrollwork and guilloche patterns, as well as individual panels cut and engraved in the shape of sea monsters and foliage. A few bands and panels are later restorations, some of

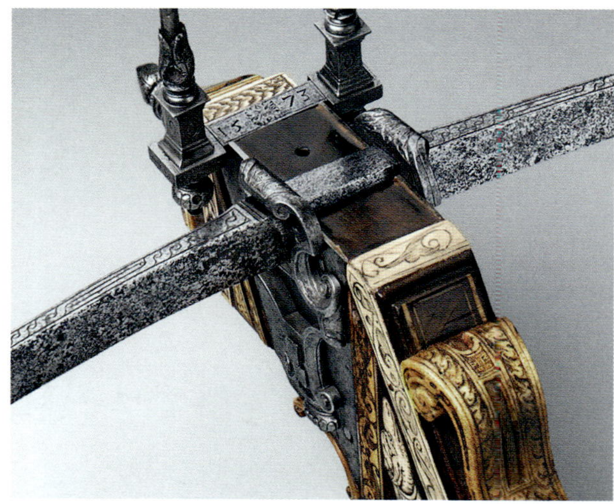

Figure 4.9 Detail of catalogue 27. Note date and decoration of bow

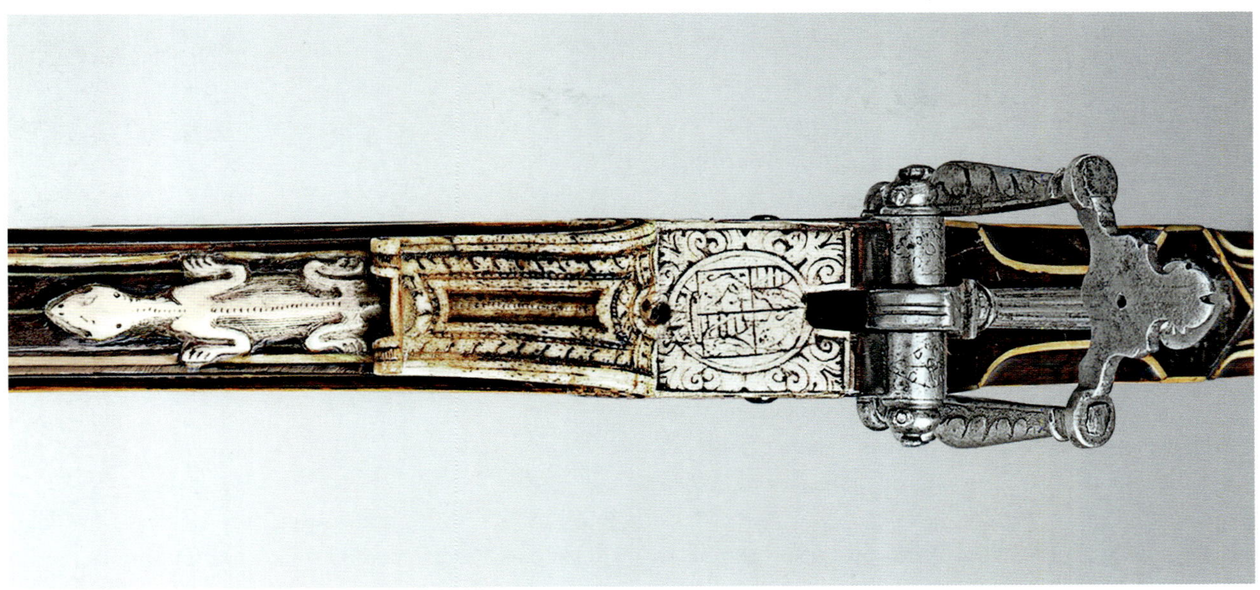

Figure 4.10 Detail of catalogue 27 showing coat of arms

which—like the salamander-like creature in front of the scroll—are made of ivory.

The flat base of the foreward sight is engraved with the year 1573 (fig. 4.9), and a square plaque of polished staghorn just in front of the release hook shows a crudely engraved coat of arms beneath a crown—identifiable as a version of the arms used by some members of the house of Savoy (fig. 4.10).[1]

The Museum's weapon is particularly noteworthy, as it belongs to a type not previously recorded, and of which fewer than a handful of surviving examples can now be identified.[2] These pellet crossbows could be adapted to shoot bolts by the addition of a piece that would bridge the gap of the curve between the release hook and the fore-end. This piece, for which the term "bolt bridge" is here suggested, was secured by a central screw and two prongs; the screw passed through a vertical hole in the curve of the tiller, while the prongs at the front

and rear fitted into corresponding holes to add further stability. Until pictorial evidence for this type is available, it will remain uncertain whether the bowstring would have had to be changed from a double to a single string for the conversion to work.

If the crude arms and the rather crisply engraved date of 1573 can be trusted—and in light of the crown above the escutcheon—the Museum's weapon probably belonged to a member of the ducal family of Savoy, perhaps Duke Emmanuel Philibert (1528–1580) or his cousin Jacques of Savoy, duke of Nemours (1531–1585).[3] Whether the modifications to the lock mechanism and the repair to the rear end of the tiller were working-life repairs, indicating that the weapon remained in use for a considerable time, or a later restoration is at present difficult to ascertain.

A pellet crossbow very similar to the Museum's weapon in general appearance, dimensions, and decoration, and retaining what appears to be its original bolt bridge, was formerly in the Frédéric Spitzer collection and is now in another private collection in the United States (fig. 4.2).[4] Its tiller (which also shows some repairs), including the bolt bridge, is also of cherrywood and inlaid with polished and engraved staghorn, as well as with small bands of iron alloy that have been blued and damascened with gold; it is signed PONT DE VOILLE (Pont-de-Veyle, in today's Rhône-Alpes region of France) on the underside of the release arm, struck with an indistinct mark on the bow, and dated 1579 at the front of the bolt bridge.

The style of inlaid decoration on both weapons is more often found on crossbow tillers and gunstocks made and decorated north of the Alps. It is probable, therefore, that these convertible crossbows were made somewhere in the Savoyard regions of northern Italy or southeastern France; in fact, they may be a type particular to that region, since so few have been recorded to date.

28. Small Crossbow (*Balestrino*)

Probably Italy, probably 17th or 18th century, with later modifications
Steel
L. 11½ in. (28.6 cm); W. 8⅝ in. (21.8 cm); Wt. 1 lb. 8 oz. (692 g)
Bequest of Alan Rutherfurd Stuyvesant, 1954 (54.46.4a)

EX COLL.: Rutherfurd Stuyvesant, Allamuchy, N.J.; Alan Rutherfurd Stuyvesant, Allamuchy, N.J.

REFERENCES: Unpublished

Crossbows this small were not always intended merely as models or demonstration examples. Some bows have a draw weight of more than two hundred pounds (91 kg), and tests with modern replicas suggest that they may have had capabilities comparable to those of their full-size cousins, in relative terms. Easily concealable, the near-silent weapons presented a danger clearly recognized in the few surviving sixteenth- and seventeenth-century references to crossbows of this type. The same realization has led some modern writers to classify these weapons as "assassin's crossbows."[1] However, the only recorded period reference that may be regarded as a technical term is *balestrino* (little crossbow; plural: *balestrini*), which can be found in Italian inventories and other documents beginning in the early fifteenth century.[2]

The Museum's *balestrino* has a plain, unmarked steel bow, terminating in hooked nocks, that is secured to the tiller by a central screw; the bowstring is missing. The short tiller, also made entirely of steel, is fitted with a tube shaped like a short gun barrel that acts as a bolt guide; the tiller's hollow interior contains a trigger and spanning-screw combination. Turning the rear screw counterclockwise moves the lock forward until it reaches an upward curve on the bottom that pushes the lowered hook up, allowing it to engage the

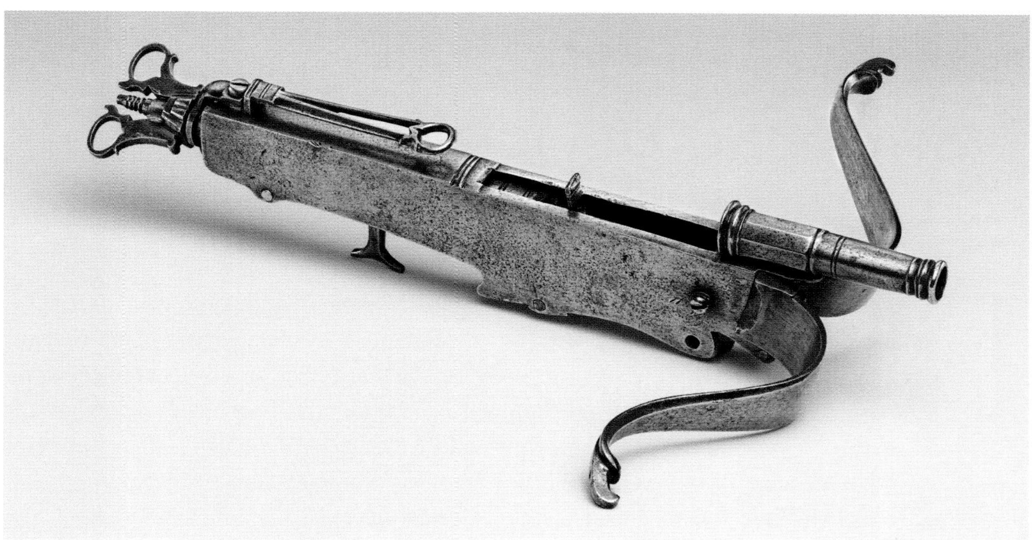

bowstring. Pulling the trigger down while turning the screw clockwise draws the entire release mechanism and bowstring back; the weapon can then be shot by pressing the trigger up. At the top rear, the crossbow is fitted with a forward-pointing belt hook. Overall, the weapon is relatively plain, but the subtle embellishment includes a few engraved lines, the moldings and faceting on the breech of the bolt guide, the fishtail shape of the trigger, and the ornamentally cut-and-pierced wings of the spanning screw and belt hook.

Surviving *balestrini* are relatively scarce; only about two dozen extant examples have been recorded to date, several of which may be reproductions, however.[3] It is perhaps significant that a number of the weapons believed to be genuine are in Italian collections, in Florence,[4] Turin,[5] Venice,[6] and Naples.[7]

The general appearance and spanning mechanism of the Museum's *balestrino* are similar to a number of examples that have been described and classified as types B, C, and D in a typology proposed by W. E. Flewett.[8] The present weapon, however, shows some details rarely found on any other recorded *balestrino*. The barrel-like bolt guide, for example, has only a distant equivalent in the small "roofs" of half-tube shape on several other weapons, all classified by Flewett as Type C. And while almost all recorded *balestrini* have an internal spanning mechanism and a belt hook, the shape of the trigger and the mounting of the belt hook on the top of the tiller are also scarcely found elsewhere.

What appear to be the closest comparisons to the Museum's crossbow are two *balestrini* (Flewett Type D), one in Florence and the other in a private collection in Great Britain.[9] Particularly similar are the profiles of the tillers, which are vaguely reminiscent of those of large target crossbows (cat. 25), and the method of securing the bow to the tiller by means of a hinged plate and screw.

The tiller's shape and the internal spanning mechanism suggest a tentative date of manufacture for the three weapons during the seventeenth or early eighteenth century. However, in light of their rarity and scarce documentation it must be emphasized that the dating of *balestrini*, and with it the differentiation of genuine examples from later reproductions, or fakes, remains difficult.

5 | Spanning Devices

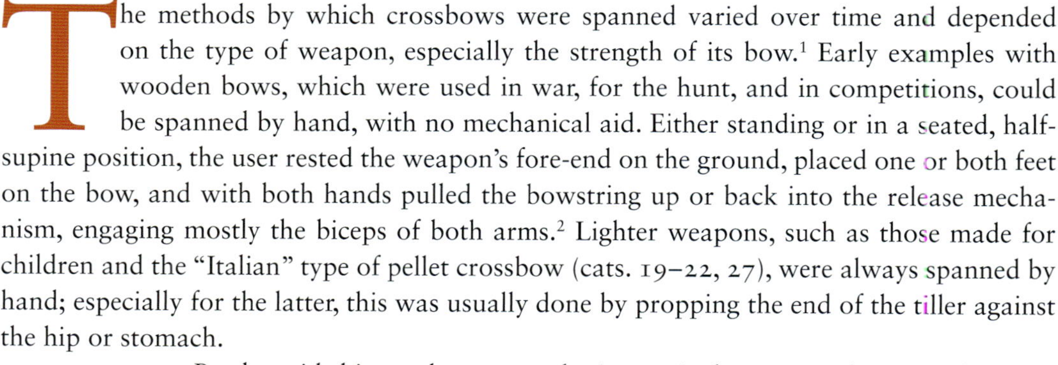

The methods by which crossbows were spanned varied over time and depended on the type of weapon, especially the strength of its bow.[1] Early examples with wooden bows, which were used in war, for the hunt, and in competitions, could be spanned by hand, with no mechanical aid. Either standing or in a seated, half-supine position, the user rested the weapon's fore-end on the ground, placed one or both feet on the bow, and with both hands pulled the bowstring up or back into the release mechanism, engaging mostly the biceps of both arms.[2] Lighter weapons, such as those made for children and the "Italian" type of pellet crossbow (cats. 19–22, 27), were always spanned by hand; especially for the latter, this was usually done by propping the end of the tiller against the hip or stomach.

By the mid-thirteenth century, the increasingly stronger bows made either of wood or of composite construction required modifications to the spanning process—the stirrup and belt hook—that appear to have been introduced from the East. The stirrup, mounted to the front of the tiller, not only protected the bow and fore-end from damage by lifting them off the ground but it helped to stabilize the weapon and the archer's foot more securely on the ground. The belt hook was most often made of steel; at first a single hook and later also a two-fingered claw, it was attached to a sturdy belt worn around the hips (fig. 1.1). The crossbowman set his weapon firmly on the ground, put a foot in the stirrup, bent his knees, and, leaning over, grabbed the bowstring with his belt hook. When he straightened up again, he was utilizing the combined strength of his thigh and lower-back muscles to pull up the bowstring, using one or both hands to guide the belt hook and provide additional power. Alternatively, several depictions show that experienced archers sometimes reversed the process: standing up straight and holding the weapon in front of the body, the crossbowman placed the belt hook over the bowstring; lifting one foot and inserting it into the stirrup, he spanned the bow by pushing it down with the strength of the thigh alone.

Because they were easy to use, belt hooks remained popular well into the fifteenth century, despite the introduction of more powerful spanning devices. During the late fourteenth and fifteenth centuries the drawing power of the belt hook was increased by combining it with a pulley system operating with ropes

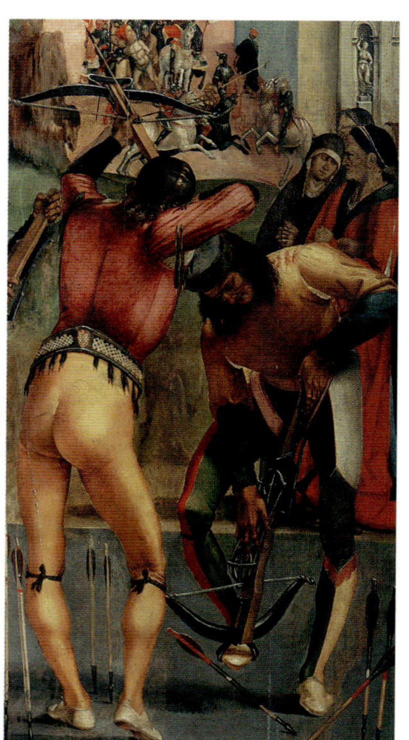

Figure 5.1 Luca Signorelli (Italian, act. by 1470– d. 1523). Crossbowman using a rope-and-pulley spanner, detail of *The Martyrdom of Saint Sebastian*, 1498. Oil on panel, 113⅜ × 68⅞ in. (288 × 175 cm). Pinacoteca Comunale, Città di Castello

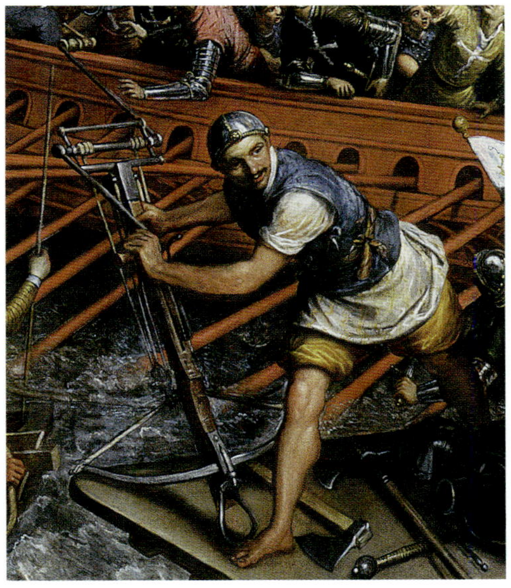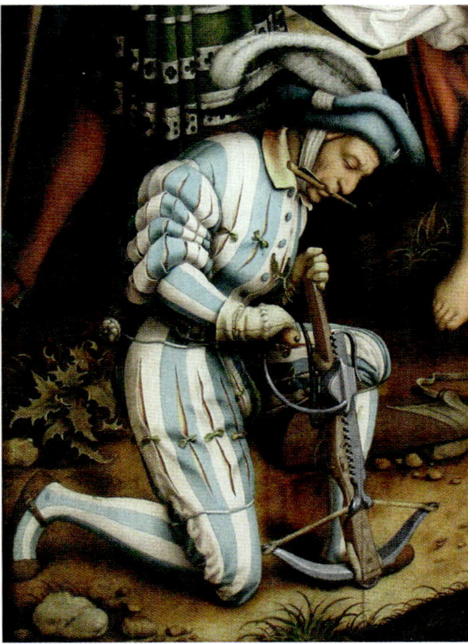

Figure 5.2 Jacopo Tintoretto (Jacopo Robusti) (Italian, 1519–1594). Crossbowman using a windlass, detail of *The Capture of Constantinople in 1204*, ca. 1580. Oil on canvas. Great Council Hall, Palazzo Ducale, Venice

Figure 5.3 Hans Holbein the Elder (German, ca. 1465–1524). Crossbowman using a cric, detail of *The Martyrdom of Saint Sebastian*, ca. 1516. Oil on panel (limewood), 60¼ × 42⅛ in. (153 × 107 cm). Alte Pinakothek, Munich (5352)

or a leather strap (fig. 5.1). An Islamic source states that the belt-and-pulley system could be adapted for spanning crossbows on horseback,[3] and frequent European depictions of mounted crossbowmen during the period indicate that the simple belt-hook-and-stirrup method was probably also employed in these circumstances. Decorated devices appear to be extremely rare, although later examples occasionally display modest chiseling (cat. 29).

The increased presence of crossbows on the battlefield and the appearance of, first, the stronger composite bows and then the steel bows, about the late thirteenth or early fourteenth century, resulted in more complex and powerful spanning devices. Large stationary crossbows spanned with a winch, introduced in all likelihood from the East, had been adopted throughout Europe by the thirteenth century. It was probably the combination of a winch with a belt hook or a rope-and-pulley system sometime in the fourteenth century that led to the development of the windlass for the spanning of handheld crossbows (fig. 5.2). The winch contained a socket that—with the ropes unwound—fitted over the rear of the tiller; the claws of the lower pulley were placed over the bowstring, and the weapon was spanned by turning the two handles with both hands, thus winding up the ropes. Slow and cumbersome to use, windlasses were ill suited to situations where speed was essential, such as the open battlefield and the hunt. They were mainly employed in siege warfare and, after crossbows were no longer used in war, windlasses were used only for spanning target weapons, especially in northwestern Europe (cats. 17, 18). Any embellishment of windlasses is usually modest. Occasionally, the upper part displays openwork designs, and the handle arms can be decoratively twisted or sparsely chiseled, while the grips are made of either turned and carved wood or more elegant materials such as polished staghorn.

Figure 5.4 Lucas Cranach the Elder (German, 1472–1553). Spanning a crossbow on horseback using a cric, detail of *Stag Hunt*, 1506. Woodcut, sheet 13 15/16 × 19⅞ in. (35.4 × 50.5 cm). The Metropolitan Museum of Art, New York, Rogers Fund, 1922 (22.67.45)

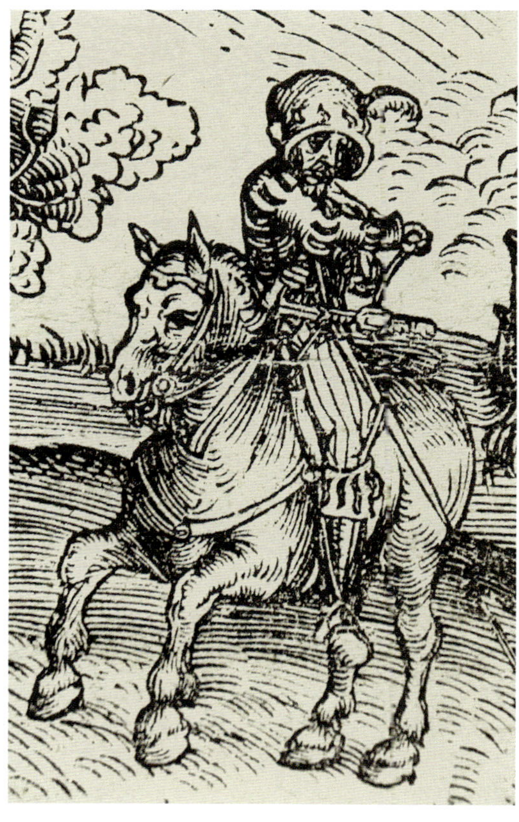

The other mechanical spanning device invented during the late fourteenth or early fifteenth century was the winder, also known as a "rack," "cranequin," or "cric." Operating on the rack-and-pinion principle, a cranequin consists of a steel bar, or rack, and a wheel case, or gearbox. The rack has a grapple of two claws at the front and teeth cut into one side; the wheel case contains a cogwheel operated by a handle arm and grip and on the underside it is usually fitted with a loop (fig. 5.3). When the handle arm was turned in one direction, the rack extended forward, the loop of the cranequin was slipped over the rear of the tiller until it came to rest against a transverse lug, and the grapple engaged the bowstring. When the handle arm was turned in the opposite direction, the rack retreated, drawing the bowstring back until it could be brought to rest in the groove of the nut.

Crossbow winders can be divided into two types. Western European examples, or "Spanish," cranequins, are comparatively light and distinguished by a slender rack with teeth on the top, a vertically mounted wheel case, and a steel loop on the underside (cat. 30); they were predominantly used throughout the fifteenth and sixteenth centuries on the Iberian Peninsula and areas under Spanish influence, for example, the Netherlands. Most of the surviving winders are of the "central European" type, which remained popular, especially in the German-speaking regions, until the early twentieth century. Of a somewhat heavier build, they are characterized by a rack with teeth cut into the side, usually on the user's right; a horizontally mounted wheel case; and a loop of braided hemp cord. Cranequins were robust, relatively easy to service, and often interchangeable; due to their compact size they could also be used on horseback (fig. 5.4). Like the embellishment of crossbows, the decoration of cranequins varied widely according to period taste and regional preferences. The grapple on some examples was decoratively forged, while the other steel surfaces could be etched, chiseled, or engraved; adorned with openwork; or—less frequently—inlaid with (engraved) copper alloy; silvered or gilded; or blued. Frequently, a combination of ornamental techniques can be found, and, occasionally, the decoration extends to the grip, loop, and belt hook (cats. 31, 34, 35, 38). Since individual winders often saw use for long periods of time, many examples show evidence of repairs, modifications, or later embellishment.

Sometime during the fourteenth century, another simple but powerful spanning device was developed: the lever, or gaffle (cats. 40–43). It consists of a lever arm with a handle and an anchoring fork with a pivoting grapple; allegedly because when it is extended its profile resembles the hind leg of the eponymous animal, this type is today often referred to as a "goat's-foot" lever. The arm and fork are usually joined by a hinge, which permitted the lever to be collapsed and suspended from the belt by a hook when not in use. To span a crossbow the grapple was placed over the bowstring, with the lever arm pointing toward the bow and the arms of the fork pointing back; the arms, placed on either side of the tiller, engaged and rested against a transverse lug in the tiller similar to that required for a cranequin but closer to the lock. When the archer pulled the lever arm back, the fork arms slid down, pressing against the transverse lug extensions and thus providing the leverage that pulled the grapple and bowstring back and into the lock's release. Because of the spanning motion, this device is also called a "pull" lever.

A variation that seems to have been popular in Italy was fitted with a slightly curved T bar at the end of the lever arm, which allowed it to be rested on the thigh or against the hip. The crossbowman could then use both hands to push the weapon down, thus spanning the crossbow (fig. 5.5). In order to accommodate the different bow strengths, pull levers came in a normal and a large size, the latter apparently intended to be used predominantly with the large hunting crossbow of "Spanish" type. Rare among pull levers are those fitted with a single hook, rather than a grapple, which were evidently used for spanning pellet crossbows (cat. 43). About 1600 yet another variety of lever appeared, displaying a long lever arm with a hook in front and a hinged fork arm, which was simply notched at the bottom, rather than fitted with a pivoting grapple. With the hook of the lever arm secured to the front of the crossbow—usually by being anchored in the suspension or spanning ring—and the notched bottom of the fork arm against the bowstring, the lever arm was pulled back, and the fork arm pushed the string back toward the lock. Some of these "push" levers were made almost entirely of wood (cat. 13b), while later examples were also made of steel.

Quick and easy to use, pull levers were employed both in war and for the hunt until at least the late seventeenth century, especially on the Iberian Peninsula. They were also used in Italy, the Netherlands, England, and Scandinavia, and colonial expansion introduced them to West Africa, the Americas, and possibly the east coast of India. Push levers, on the other hand, were used from the seventeenth century on. Together with several further variations that emerged during the eighteenth and nineteenth centuries, they were especially popular for target crossbows in the Netherlands, Germany, and Italy, where they remain in use today. Most levers were utilitarian and therefore not extensively decorated; some examples for use

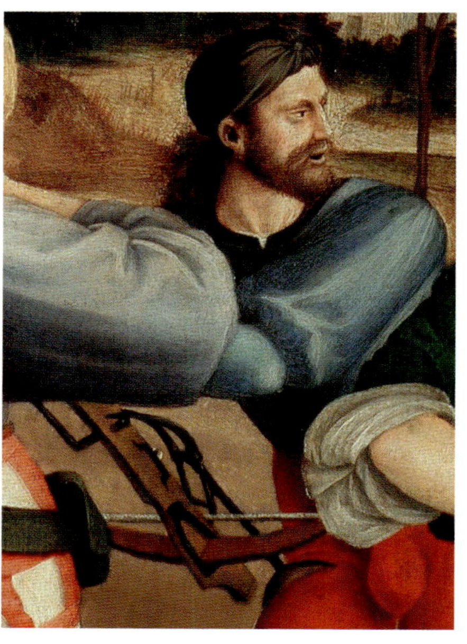

in hunting and with target crossbows, however, show varying degrees of chiseled ornament, gilding, bluing, and even damascening, when made of steel (cats. 40, 42); when made of wood, a few feature the same inlay as on the crossbows they accompanied.

Since at least the late fourteenth century, spanning mechanisms were also built into or permanently attached to individual crossbows.[4] One of the earliest versions was an internal screw mechanism operated by an external wheel at the rear of the tiller, a feature perhaps inspired by large siege weapons. The capability of this mechanism was relatively limited, however, and it survived beyond the fifteenth century only on very small weapons such as the *balestrino* (cat. 28). The most common variety emerged during the sixteenth century, when levers combined with release mechanisms were attached to the upper side of tillers. Although these are found mainly on central European pellet crossbows (cats. 23, 24), they also spread to western Europe, where they are occasionally found on target crossbows, but remained especially popular on English bullet crossbows until the mid-nineteenth century (fig. 3.5).

29. Anchor Plate from a Rope-and-Pulley System

Europe (possibly England), ca. 1475–1525
Steel, copper alloy
L. 7 in. (17.7 cm); W. 3 in. (7.7 cm); Wt. 8 oz. (224 g)
Gift of William H. Riggs, 1913 (14.25.1611)

Ex coll.: William H. Riggs, Paris

References: Unpublished

This anchor plate is all that remains of a rope-and-pulley device that combined an easy-to-use spanning hook with the additional drawing power of a pulley system. Originally, the device would have also included two ropes, a corresponding pulley with a grapple of one or two claws to hold the bowstring, a belt attachment, and the belt itself—all missing. The Museum's example is made from a single steel plate with an anchoring extension, or tongue, by which it was attached to a hook on the back of a tiller (cat. 2), and a forked base with short arms, each securing a deeply grooved copper-alloy wheel, or runner, with four spokes. Five openings in the anchor plate's extension made this device adaptable to both crossbows of varying sizes and the height of individual users. Its superior quality is indicated by the protective hoops and extensions for the runners, as well as by the overall decoration on the front; the rear is flat and plain. The decorative chiseling is reminiscent of Gothic tracery, and the sculptural ornament at the base of the fork is similar to that found on the grapples of fifteenth-century cranequins.

Surviving examples of rope-and-pulley systems are rare. Only two complete systems are recorded, both of which comprise a leather belt, a rope of twisted leather, and a two-runner pulley and are probably of much later date, probably sixteenth to

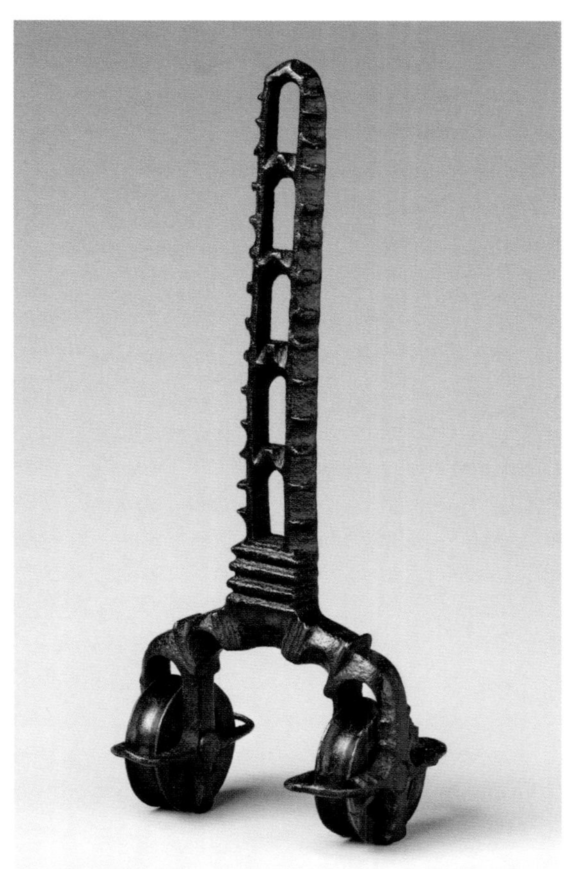

eighteenth century. One is in Stockholm,[1] the other in Helsinki.[2] Individual components, usually archaeological finds, survive in a number of collections, particularly in Scandinavia; most of these are two-runner grapple pulleys, though without a context it is nearly impossible to determine whether these pulleys once belonged to a windlass or to a rope-and-pulley system.[3] Less common are single-runner claw or anchor pulleys.[4] According to its former owner William H. Riggs, the Museum's anchor pulley is English, of fifteenth-century date, having been dredged from the Port of Bordeaux.[5]

30. Cranequin

Western Europe (probably Spain), 16th century
Steel, wood (possibly pear)
L. 16³¹⁄₃₂ in. (43.1 cm); W. 2⁹⁄₃₂ in. (5.8 cm); W. 3 lb. 10 oz.
(1,638 g)
Gift of William H. Riggs, 1913 (14.25.1575b)

Ex coll.: William H. Riggs, Paris

References: Gay 1887, vol. 1, p. 488; Stone 1934 (1961 ed.),
p. 12; Peterson 1962, p. 24; Nickel 1974, p. 230; Stevens
1978, p. 9

Cranequins like this one were common in western
Europe, especially in Spain, Portugal, and the Netherlands. Among their identifying characteristics are a
slender steel rack with a long neck at the front and
teeth cut into the top of the main part, as well as a
vertically mounted steel wheel case fitted with a belt
hook and a steel loop by which the winder can be
mounted over the rear of a tiller. Plain and unmarked,
the Museum's example has a rack with a neck that is
hexagonal in section, and a small drop-shaped wheel
case; a rear stop plate for the rack is missing, and
the handle arm and wooden grip are probably old,
possibly working-lifetime replacements.

This type of cranequin likely appeared during the
early fifteenth century and remained in use at least
until about 1600; the few known depictions date
mostly from after 1540. About a dozen extant examples are recorded, among them, three winders that
probably came from the personal armory of Emperor
Maximilian I: one in the Metropolitan Museum's
collection (cat. 31), another in Vienna,[1] and a third
in Madrid.[2] Plain cranequins of this type reside, for
example, in Vézac,[3] Vitoria-Gasteiz,[4] and Manchester
in the United Kingdom.[5]

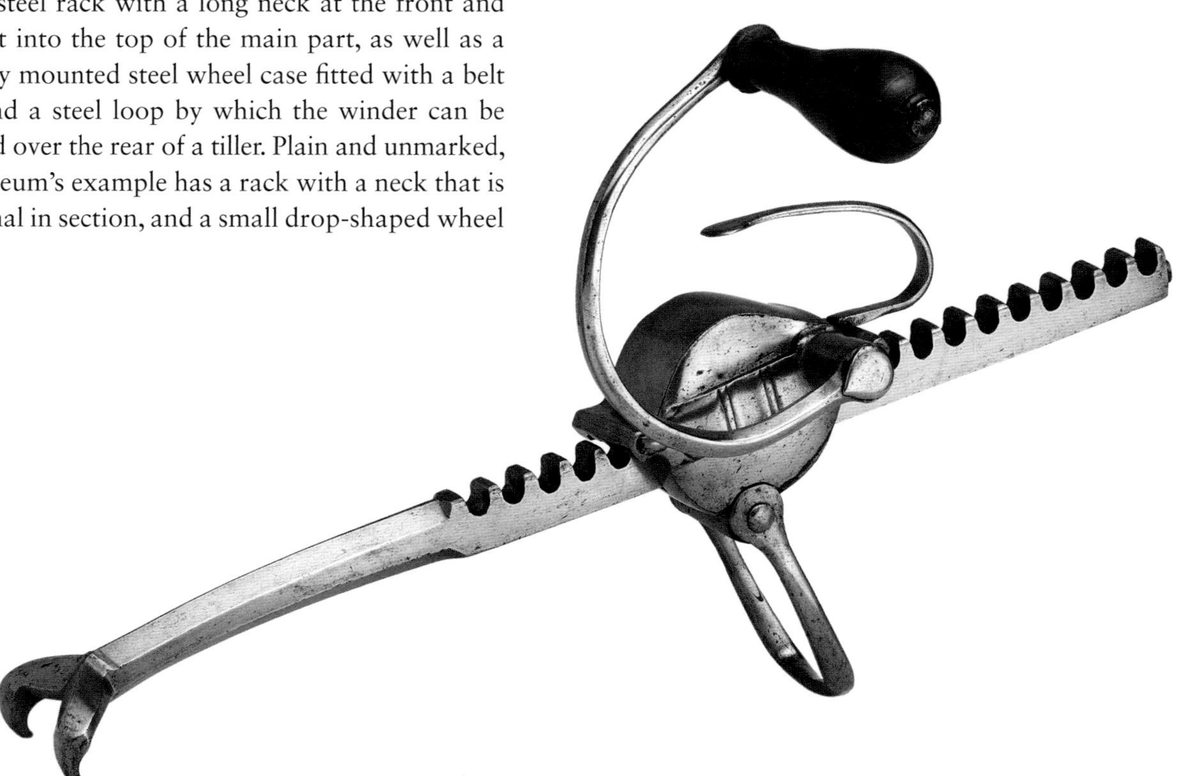

31. Cranequin from the Armory of Emperor Maximilian I

Western or central Europe (the Netherlands or Austria),
ca. 1505–19
Steel, wood (fruitwood, possibly pear), copper alloy
L. 14⅞ in. (37.7 cm); W. 6⁵⁄₁₆ in. (16 cm); Wt. 3 lb. 3 oz.
(1,435 g)
Purchase, Arthur Ochs Sulzberger Gift, 2012 (2012.4)

Ex coll.: Armory of Maximilian I (archduke of Austria,
king of Germany from 1486, Holy Roman Emperor
from 1508); private collection (anonymous), Germany (?)
or Austria (?); [Galerie Fischer Auktionen, Lucerne];
Collection of Hans von Schulthess-Rechberg, Zurich;
von Schulthess family, by descent; [Andrew Lumley]

References: Grafenegg sale 1934, p. 20, lot 165; Thomas
and Gamber 1976, p. 207

Mark:

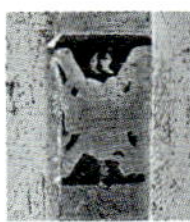

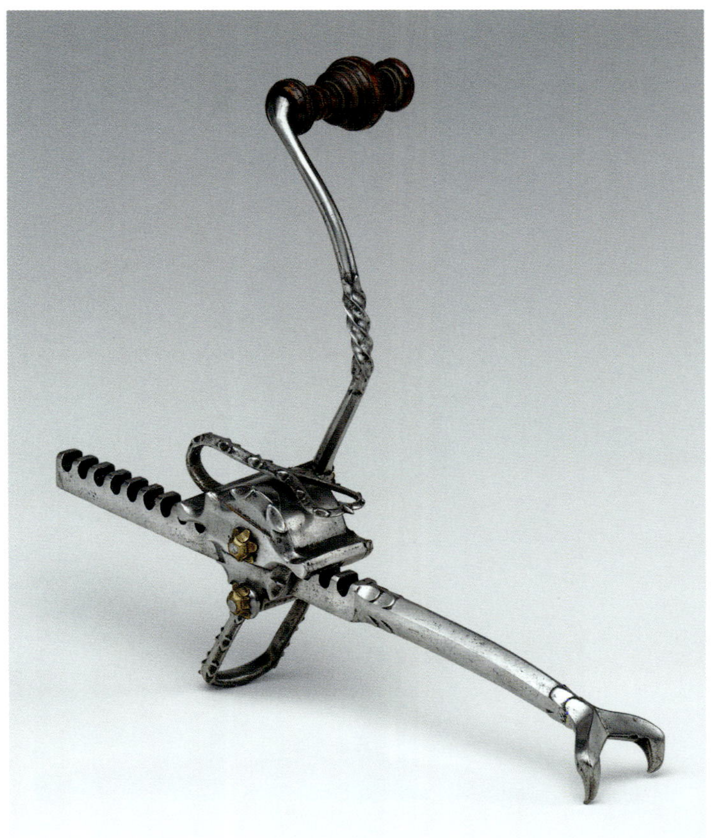

Like catalogue 30, this is a cranequin of western
European type, consisting of a characteristically long-
necked steel rack and a small, vertically mounted
steel wheel case with a loop, belt hook, and curved
handle arm.[1] For its type, however, this winder displays an unusal extent of decoration.

In addition to the twisted handle arm and the
decoratively turned fruitwood grip, the rack, wheel
case, loop, and belt hook are chiseled in a style generally reminiscent of Gothic architectural ornament.
Moreover, the lower part of the belt hook is split and
shaped like an inverted heart, while a number of
flower-shaped copper-alloy washers add color to
the overall embellishment. The neck of the rack is
struck with a mark, a fire steel over a Saint Andrew's
cross, with sparks above and below.

The Saint Andrew's cross and fire steel are charges,
or emblems, from mid-fifteenth-century Burgundian
heraldry, which Maximilian of Habsburg (fig. 5.6),
the future Holy Roman Emperor (r. 1493/1508–19),
adopted in 1477, after his marriage that year to
Mary, duchess of Burgundy (r. 1477–82), daughter
and heiress of Charles "the Bold," duke of Burgundy
(r. 1465–77). It has therefore been suggested that
this mark may be an imperial ownership or inventory mark.[2] On the other hand, it is more likely to be

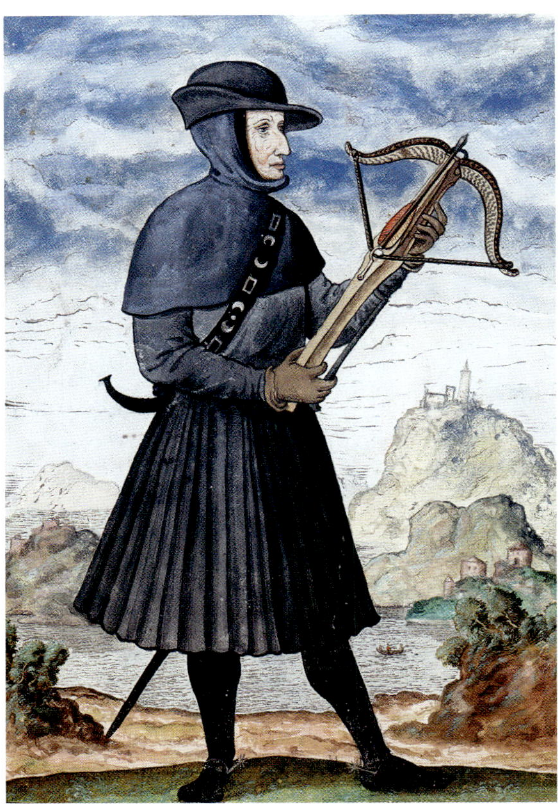

Figure 5.6 Emperor Maximilian I, detail of a page from the illuminated manuscript *Ehrenspiegel des Hauses Österreich* (Mirror of Honor of the House of Austria). German, 1555. Bayerische Staatsbibliothek, Munich (Cgm 896, fol. 338r)

be found in the *Inventario Iluminado*, an illustrated inventory of the armory of Maximilian's grandson and successor, Emperor Charles V, that was compiled between about 1544 and 1558.[5]

The Museum's cranequin is the most extensively decorated of the three, the only one bearing any chiseled ornament. In the context of Habsburg ownership it is worth noting that the Vienna winder seems to be one of a group of three originally supplied and used with three crossbows of western European type made for Emperor Maximilian I sometime between 1508 and his death in 1519, and still extant in Vienna. It has been suggested that the Metropolitan Museum's winder may also have belonged to this group, and recent measurements have shown that it would indeed fit these weapons.[6] Maximilian is known to have taken an interest in Netherlandish crossbow making, and he employed at least one Burgundian crossbow maker in Austria, a certain Balthasar Grot (d. 1520), who worked as "court bowyer" in Innsbruck.

Regardless of whether the mark indicates ownership or the artisan responsible for the winder's production, its iconography, combined with the Habsburg provenance for two of the three extant examples, leaves little doubt that the present cranequin was made for the Habsburg emperor by one of his court artists. Pictorial evidence indicates that noble hunters and their guests were accompanied by servants who spanned the crossbows for their respective lord or lady. However, Maximilian was a most avid hunter who is recorded as enjoying stalking prey on his own, accompanied only by a local hunter. Given the extent of the decoration on the Museum's piece, which is unique among winders of this type, it is quite conceivable that this particular cranequin was used—at least on occasion—by the emperor himself.

a maker's mark, since it is on the neck of the rack, where other cranequins of this type sometimes also bear similar stamps. In fact, this mark has so far been recorded only on winders—not on crossbows or any other weapons—and only two other cranequins struck with this mark are known, one in Vienna,[3] the other in Madrid.[4] All three examples share similar flower-shaped copper-alloy washers and near-identical handles; a depiction of such a winder can

32. Cranequin

Central Europe (probably southern Germany), first half of
the 16th century
Steel, copper alloy, wood, hemp, pigment
L. 14⅛ in. (35.9 cm); W. 3½ in. (8.8 cm); Wt. 5 lb. 3 oz. (2,343 g)
Bequest of George D. Pratt, 1935 (48.149.36b)

Ex coll.: Richard Zschille, Grossenhain, Saxony; Henry
G. Keaseby, Eastbourne, East Sussex; George D. Pratt,
Glen Cove, Long Island, N.Y.

References: Forrer [1894], p. 27, no. 1028, pl. 206; Imperial Institute 1896, p. 70. no. 262; Zschille sale 1897, p. 62,
no. 350; Zschille sale 1900, p. 18, no. 139; Helbing sale 1902,
no. 828; Keasbey sale 1924, no. 277, pl. XXIX; Grancsay
1933b, p. 42, no. 284; Grancsay 1953, p. 29, cat. no. 116

Mark:

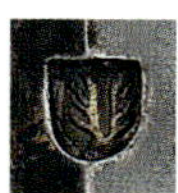

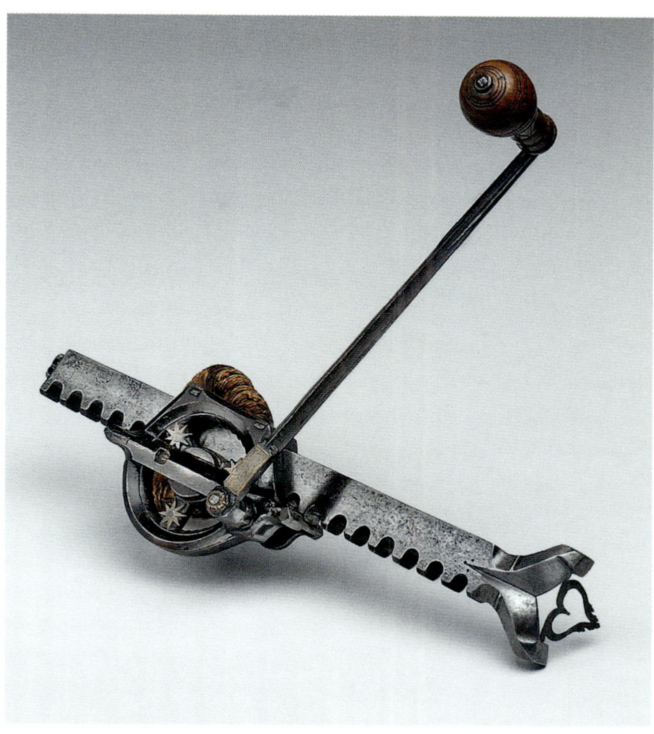

Crossbow winders like this one were predominantly
used in central Europe; since they are especially common in the German-speaking regions, they are sometimes
referred to as of "German" type. Their characteristic
features are a sturdy steel rack with teeth, usually cut
into the right side; a belt hook fitted at the rear,
which also stopped the wheel case from coming off
the rack; and a horizontally mounted steel wheel
case, usually circular, semicircular, or semihexagonal, fitted with a hemp loop by which the winder was
mounted over the rear of the tiller.

Noteworthy on this example is the open wheel
case (covered in later paint), revealing the internal
cogwheel, its axis, and the spindle of the handle arm,
as well as the modest decoration consisting mainly
of copper-alloy applications (fig. 5.7). These include
an eight-pointed star on each of the cogwheel's three
spokes, a flower-shaped washer above the base of
the handle, and a flat panel at the base of the handle
arm, which shows faint traces of an engraved figure;
the barely discernible face, halo, tree, and naked

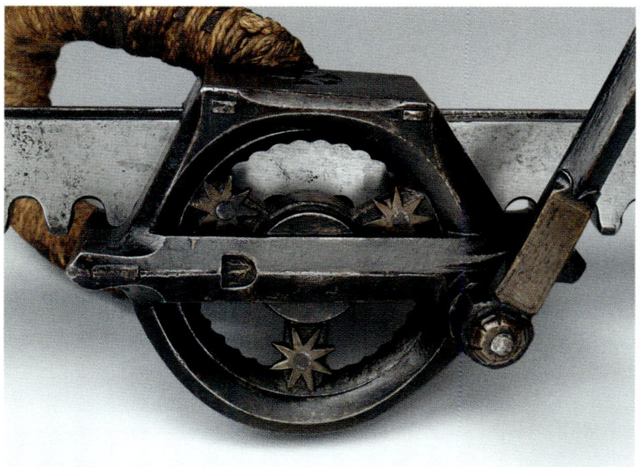

Figure 5.7

legs indicate that the subject was probably Saint Sebastian. The center of the wheel-case reinforce bears a deeply sunken mark, inlaid in copper alloy: a pair of stag's antlers. What are probably the initials of a former owner, the letters PM, are roughly engraved upside down on the wooden grip. The mark's placement on the central reinforce, the straight handle arm decorated with wolf's-teeth molding, and decorative applications of copper alloy indicate that this wheel case is of early sixteenth-century date. The wooden grip and hemp loop are probably old, possibly working-lifetime replacements; the belt hook is missing.

A cranequin from the same maker or workshop is in Bern; it has a near-identical wheel case, and the rack is struck with the same mark.[1] One of its inlaid copper-alloy panels shows traces of what is likely the year of its manufacture: [15]32. A related example in Turin is similar in general construction and decoration—the open wheel case, wheel spokes decorated with a star, and wolf's-teeth molding on the handle arm—but it bears a different mark, a crowned star.[2] Probably as a result of efforts to make them lighter and easier to clean and repair, some cranequins show an extreme version of the open construction: a winder in Darmstadt has a wheel case consisting only of a lower base, a lower wall, and an upper central reinforce to guide and contain the cogwheel, which is otherwise completely exposed.[3] The Darmstadt winder's principal decoration consists of an eight-pointed star on the spokes and reinforce and flush copper-alloy panels engraved with figures in early to mid-sixteenth-century costume. Another cranequin, in Liège, with a similarly exposed cogwheel but decorated with extensive etching, demonstrates that the Darmstadt winder is not unique.[4] In addition to practical considerations, this fashion also attests to the period's fascination with technology and its manifold applications.

33. Cranequin

Central Europe (probably Germany or Switzerland), dated 1556
Steel, wood (possibly service tree), copper alloy, hemp
L. 14⅝ in. (37 cm); W. 3⁹⁄₁₆ in. (9 cm); Wt. 5 lb. 1 oz. (2,297 g)
Gift of Mrs. Ridgely Hunt, in memory of William Cruger Pell, 1907 (07.24.48b)

Ex coll.: William Cruger Pell, New York

References: Dean 1907; Heath 1972, p. 304 (ill.)

Mark:

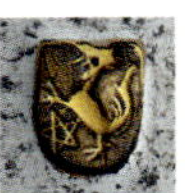

This cranequin is typical of the winders used most commonly in central Europe. It comprises a rack and a horizontally mounted wheel case, both of steel. The rack has a slightly elongated grapple and is fitted with a belt hook at the rear, while the wheel case is semihexagonal and semicircular, stepped on the right side, and fitted with an S-shaped handle arm;

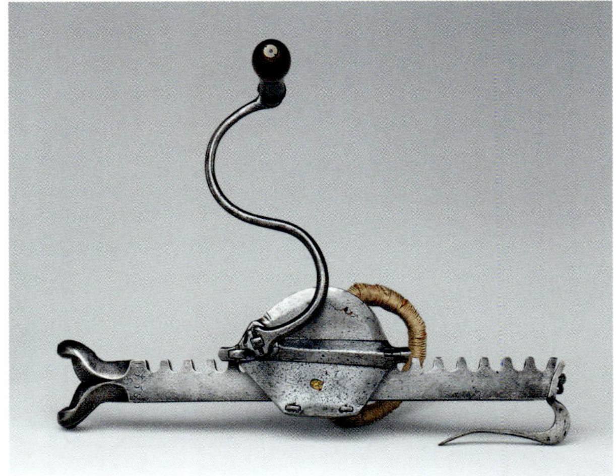

the handle arm and wooden grip are later replacements, the thin hemp loop is modern.

Otherwise entirely undecorated, the winder is engraved on the rack with the year 1556, and the top face of the wheel case bears a deeply struck maker's mark, inlaid in copper alloy: a rampant rooster with a pentagram under the raised leg.[1]

More than a dozen cranequins with this mark survive, struck either on the rack or on the wheel case.[2] What appears to be the earliest example,[3] an undecorated winder with the year 1531 on the rack, is today in Heidelberg.[4] Other examples in European collections display years from each consecutive decade, with the latest recorded winder, in Berlin, engraved with the year 1584.[5]

This long span between the earliest and latest recorded examples is remarkable. Although such a conclusion appears unlikely, it may be proof of the successful career of a single extraordinary cranequin maker, extending over five decades. It is more plausible, however, that the mark continued to be used by a relative, apprentice, or colleague of the original maker, or that it was copied by a competitor. Indeed, on earlier examples the mark is usually found on top of the wheel case, whereas the cranequins dating from 1545 or later bear the mark on the rack; the Museum's example and one formerly in the Visser collection—both with marks on the wheel case and the date 1556 on the rack—are the only known exceptions.[6] Most winders with this mark are undecorated, except for four examples, in Saint Petersburg, London, Rothenburg, and Bern.[7]

The mark has been assigned to a Zurich cranequin maker,[8] but its origin has also been attributed tentatively to Henneberg (*Henne* [hen] + *Berg* [mountain]), the name of a noble southern Thuringian family, their castle, an adjacent town, and the surrounding county.[9] No documentary evidence was offered in either case, however, and given the absence of other information, such as a maker's initials, both attributions remain speculative.

34. Cranequin

Probably Germany, dated 1562
Steel, wood (fruitwood, probably plum), staghorn, copper alloy, hemp
L. 13¾ in. (34.8 cm); W. 4⅛ in. (10.4 cm); Wt. 5 lb. 11 oz. (2,567 g)
Gift of William H. Riggs, 1913 (14.25.1574b)

Ex coll.: Prince Peter Soltykoff, Paris; William H. Riggs, Paris

References: Stone 1934 (1961 ed.), p. 12; Grancsay 1955, p. 23, cat. no. 85; Nickel, Pyhrr, and Tarassuk 1982, pp. 129–31, cat. no. 88

Mark:

This cranequin is composed of a rack, a stepped semicircular and semihexagonal wheel case, and a slender curved handle. Made with nineteen teeth on the right, the rack has a deep channel on the left, a frontal grapple fitted with holes for a missing indicator, and a small, bilobed extension at the rear, now damaged, for a missing belt hook. The wheel case is of the open type, with a detachable lid that consists only of an outer rim and a central reinforce, thus revealing the top surface of the cogwheel inside. The underside of the cogwheel is covered by a semicircular lower lid, while a thin side strip encloses the cogwheel and handle-spindle axes, respectively. The

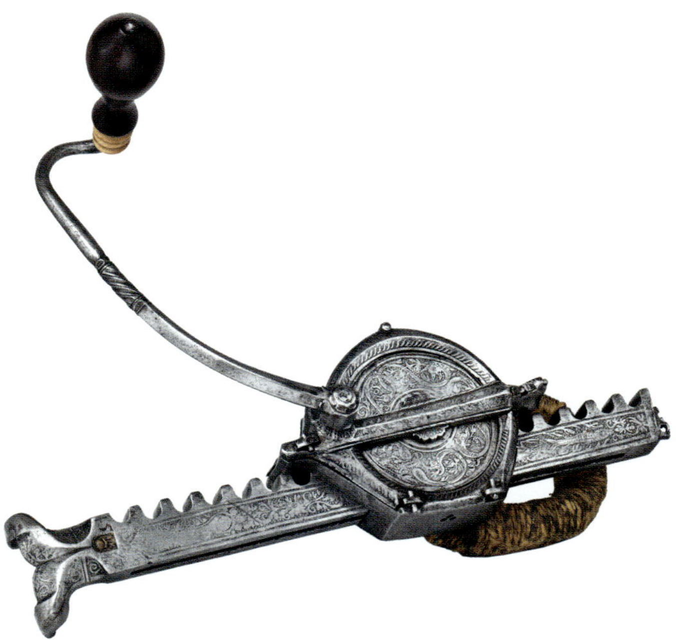

two covers may be removed by detaching three small screws. The turning handle has a hexagonal base and an arm that is slightly arced and of lozenge section before curving in almost a right angle and changing to a round section toward the grip. The slight curve may represent an adjustment, perhaps by a former owner, or by later damage. The turned fruitwood grip, possibly of plum, is fitted with a collar of polished staghorn, and seems to be old. The cord loop of natural hemp is probably also original.

Just above its grapple, the rack is dated 1562 and struck with a maker's mark, inlaid in copper alloy: the initials IK above a purse.[1]

In addition to the elegantly shaped grapple, twisted midsection of the handle, and cut-and-pierced ornament on the left side of the wheel case, this winder is noteworthy for the extent of its etched decoration. Rendered with a blackened and mostly dotted background, the embellishment covers the lid, the visible upper surface of the cogwheel, and both removable parts of the right side of the wheel case, as well as the grapple and top of the rack; small

traces indicate that the base and upper flanges of the handle arm were also once etched. The ornament includes guilloche bands and stylized plants on the lid; vines terminating in bird-like animal heads on the cogwheel (fig. 5.8); three birds, including an owl, on the lower lid; and further stylized plants, a crawfish or lobster, and a fish on the rack.

It is difficult to attribute the Museum's winder to a specific maker or even to a place of production, since its type, shape, and decoration are characteristic of the mid-sixteenth century, and so far the IK mark has not been documented elsewhere in the literature. Another example of this mark is found on the wheel case, not the rack, of a cranequin in Munich.[2] Perhaps also related to this group is a winder with a somewhat similar mark, dated 1551 on the rack, in Leipzig; the mark is also inlaid in copper alloy but it shows the purse only, without initials, and, as on the Munich example, it is struck on the lid of the closed wheel case, not on the rack.[3]

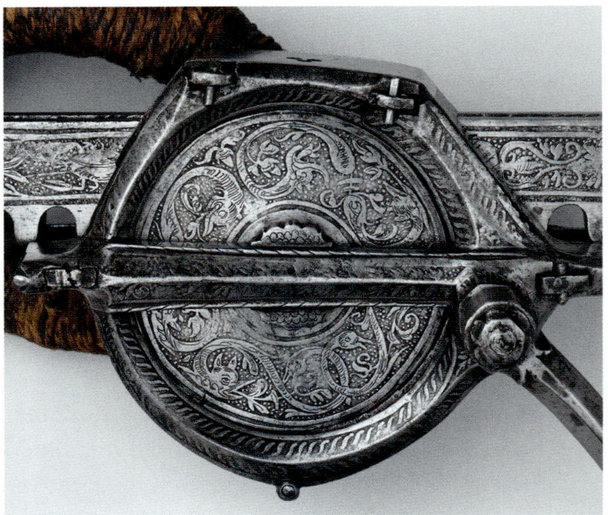

Figure 5.8

35. Cranequin

Central Europe (possibly Germany), ca. 1575–1600
Steel, wood (walnut), hemp
L. 14 in. (35.5 cm); W. 4⅛ in. (10.4 cm); Wt. 5 lb. 3 oz.
(2,341 g)
Bashford Dean Memorial Collection, Funds from various
donors, 1929 (29.158.650b)

Ex coll.: Bashford Dean, Riverdale, New York

Reference: Grancsay 1933a, pp. 241–45, no. 197

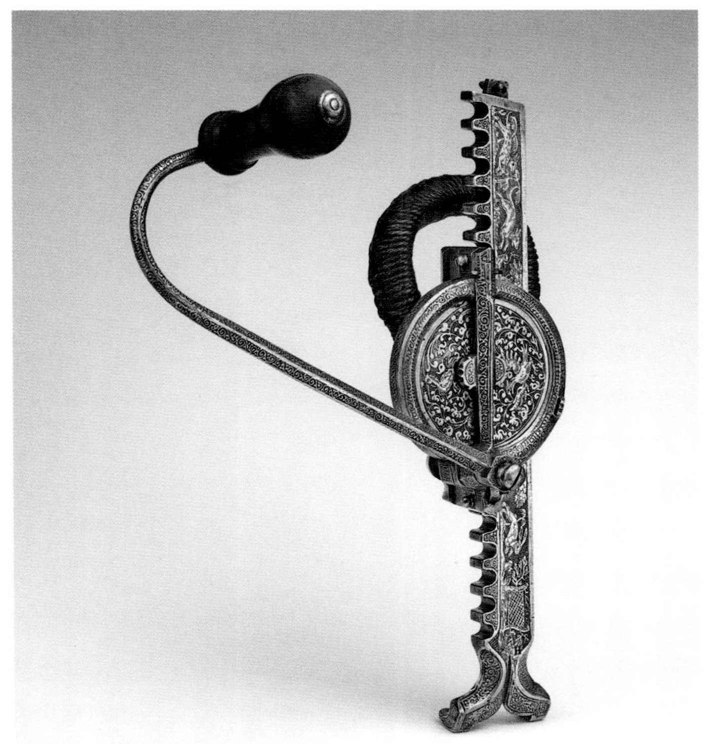

Although it displays a typical rack and stepped circular wheel case with its handle, this cranequin—like catalogue 34—is distinguished by its extensive etched decoration and relatively good condition, except for the missing belt hook and indicator. The rack is made with twenty teeth on the right and has a horizontal channel on the left, an elegantly shaped grapple in the front, and a bilobed belt-hook extension at the back. The wheel case, of the open type, has a detachable lid, and two right side plates—a rim cover for the cogwheel and one for its axis—each of which can be taken off by removing two screws. The cogwheel is pierced with a number of decorative openings, visible only through the lower rim cover, since the top of the wheel is covered by an additional disk. The handle's straight arm, of lozenged section, curves toward the end at almost a right angle and changes to a round section. The turned walnut grip and the hemp cord loop are original.

Just behind the grapple, the rack is incised with two crude letters, z h (or possibly 2 h or n h), probably an inventory mark or the initials of a former owner, rather than those of the winder's maker.

The top of the rack, its grapple, the disk above the cogwheel, the wheel-case lid, both side plates, and the entire handle arm are covered with etched decoration. The smaller surfaces show stylized floral scrolls and guilloche patterns, while on the cogwheel disk the etching on the larger surfaces displays two birds (possibly a stork and a hoopoe) and two dolphin-like grotesques among floral vines; along the rack, two hounds chase a fox, and two hares bound toward a catching net (fig. 5.9). On the underside, the rear side flanges and the bifurcation of the grapple are bordered by a deeply etched line terminating in a central tulip-like finial.

With its typical construction, the Museum's winder may have been made anywhere from the 1530s to the end of the sixteenth century, though the somewhat long side flanges and extended bifurcation of the grapple might indicate a date of manufacture before the mid-sixteenth century. The two large

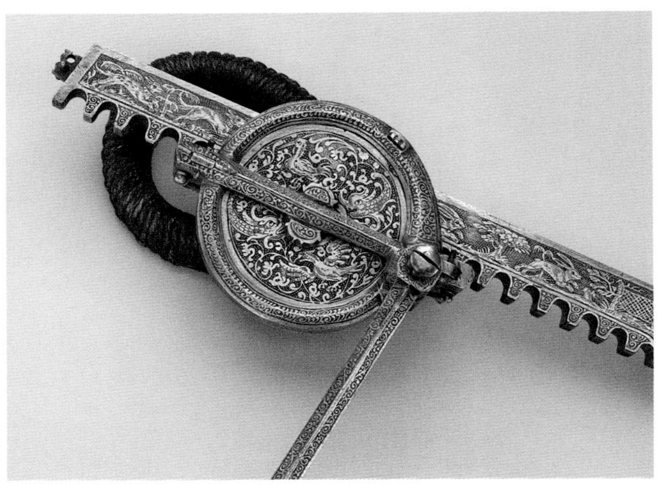

Figure 5.9

36. Cranequin for a Member of the Ayrer Family

Germany (Nuremberg), ca. 1570–90
Steel, wood (possibly ebony or plum), hemp, textile (silk or linen?)
L. 14 in. (35.6 cm); W. 3 15⁄16 in. (10 cm); Wt. 4 lb. 14 oz. (2,198 g)
Gift of William H. Riggs, 1913 (14.25.1572b)

EX COLL.: William H. Riggs, Paris

REFERENCES: Stone 1934 (1961 ed.), p. 12; Grancsay 1964, p. 35, no. 44; Nickel 1974, p. 229; Stevens 1978, p. 9

MARK:

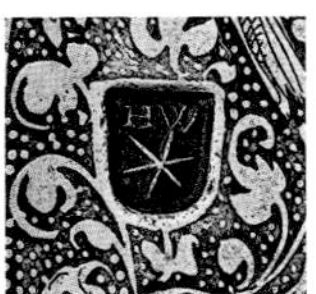

etched surfaces are also generic, but of a style that places them in the decades after 1550. The hunting scene is close to prints of the same subject from the second half of the sixteenth century, especially those by Virgil Solis (1514 [?]–1562) and Jost Amman (before 1539–1591).[1] However, details such as the ornamented belt-hook extension and the screw securing the handle arm, as well as the etching on the teeth and the embellishment of the grapple's underside, suggest that this winder was neither made nor decorated before the last quarter of the sixteenth century.

Cranequins with cord loops were interchangeable and often decorated, though their ornament rarely matched the embellishment of the weapon or weapons they accompanied, either in extent or in their iconography. And, while crossbows not infrequently bear coats of arms, names, monograms, or initials identifying their owners, such individualization on winders is rare.

This winder is composed of a plain rack and a near-circular wheel case with a long handle and cord loop; the belt hook and an indicator are missing. The decoration is restricted to the wheel case. Its lid and right side are covered with etched decoration consisting mainly of floral vines inhabited by various birds, including a parrot, on a dotted and blackened ground. Most prominent among the etched ornament are a heraldic shield on the lid and, on the right side, the figure of a nude female stabbing herself, possibly

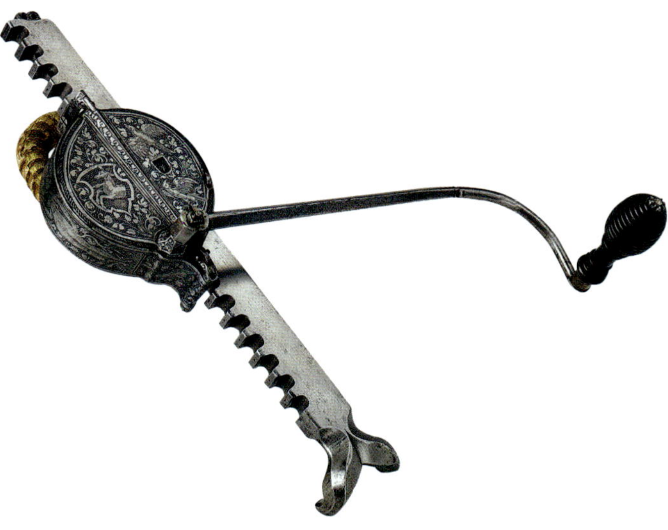

the Roman matron Lucretia. In her left hand she holds what appears to be a snake, perhaps identifying the figure also as a personification of the virtue of prudence. The wheel-case lid is struck with a maker's mark, the initials HW above a six-pointed star.[1]

More than twenty cranequins with this mark survive, making it one of the largest groups of winders by the same maker recorded to date. Several examples show the year of manufacture, which ranges from 1579 to 1589.[2] Some are plain, while the racks and wheel cases of others are profusely etched and sometimes gilded.[3] On a few examples, the decoration includes heraldry indicating that cranequins by this maker were used at the courts of King Frederick II of Denmark (r. 1559–88);[4] Duke Augustus, elector of Saxony (r. 1553–86);[5] and Count Palatine Johann I, duke of Zweibrücken (r. 1569–1604).[6] In one instance, the decoration even includes an inscription—instead of heraldry—naming not only the original owner, Hanns Kempff, "electoral Saxon master of arms," but also the place and year of the winder's manufacture: "made in Nuremberg in 1580."[7] Yet despite all this information, it has so far been impossible to identify this undoubtedly prominent master *Windenmacher* from Nuremberg.

The arms on the Museum's cranequin are those of the Ayrer family: in a red field, the upper half of a hind in natural colors, with a red tongue and a golden arrow with silver feathers embedded in its breast (fig. 5.10).[8] Originally from Swabia, the family belonged to the upper strata of Nuremberg society, as attested by the regular occurrence of the Ayrer arms in books or rolls of Nuremberg heraldry, and members of the family had been personally ennobled, or had their nobility confirmed, by several Holy Roman Emperors (fig. 5.11).

The attribution of ownership to a particular family member at first seems difficult, since a number of members of this extended family enjoyed considerable prominence in both Nuremberg and Dresden during the second half of the sixteenth century and well into the seventeenth. In Nuremberg, for example, Dr. Melchior Ayrer (1520–1579) was a noted physician,

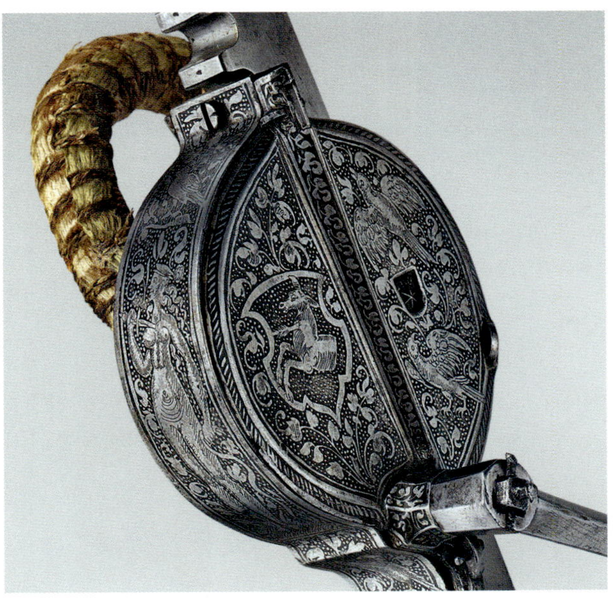

Figure 5.10

chemist, and mathematician who owned a remarkable collection of curiosities and art, while Jakob Ayrer (1543–1605) was a lawyer and notary who achieved some fame as a published poet and playwright.[9] However, the most likely original owner of the Museum's cranequin was a certain Michael Ayrer (1539–1582), born in Nuremberg but who later relocated to Dresden, where he was employed as master of arms by Prince-Elector Augustus of Saxony.[10] Michael Ayrer thus worked at the same court from which several winders struck with the HW mark survive—including that of Ayrer's colleague Hanns Kempff.[11] In addition, an Ayrer family chronicle describes Michael as a proficient crossbowman who enjoyed such trust from Augustus that his employer intended to put him in charge of the ducal silver chamber, a prestigious position that carried immense representative, administrative, and fiscal importance.[12] The actual appointment, however, was thwarted by Ayrer's murder.[13]

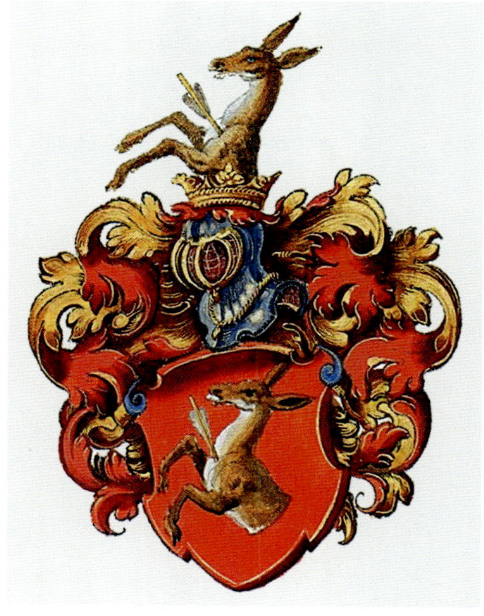

Figure 5.11 Arms of the Ayrer family, detail of a roll of arms of important Nuremberg families. German, ca. 1550. Pen and ink and watercolor on paper. Staatsarchiv, Nuremberg (Rep. 52, Rst Nbg Handschr. Nr. 219, fol. 26)

37. Large Cranequin

Germany (possibly Saxony), ca. 1575–1650
Steel, wood (probably plum), copper alloy, gold, hemp, textile (linen?)
L. 18⁹⁄₁₆ in. (47.1 cm); W. 5¾ in. (14.7 cm); Wt. 12 lb. 14 oz. (5,838 g)
Gift of William H. Riggs, 1913 (14.25.1576b)

Ex coll.: William H. Riggs, Paris

References: Unpublished

Cranequins of this size and weight were necessary to span the extremely powerful steel bows of the larger weapons known in German as *ganze Rüstungen* (cat. 11). Since these large crossbows were expensive, and their use appears to have been restricted to German-speaking areas, *ganze Rüstungen* and especially their winders are rare. One of only a few extant examples, this winder is noteworthy for its decoration.

Like its cousin of standard size, this cranequin has a plain rack with a broad grapple and belt hook, and a circular wheel case of open type with a cord loop and long handle arm; the grapple has probably been altered or repaired. The rack differs from most smaller examples only in the absence of a groove opposite the teeth. Neither the rack nor the wheel case is either marked or dated. The winder's decoration consists of gilding, mainly on the wheel case, where it contrasts brilliantly with the blued steel disk atop the cogwheel. Further embellishment includes sparse chiseled and gilded ornament on the side of the wheel case, the handle arm, and the belt hook; on a cranequin of this size and weight, the belt hook was presumably intended for suspension from a storage rack rather than from a belt.

Fewer than a dozen surviving examples of large winders are recorded. They include examples in Altena,[1] Bad Urach,[2] Berlin,[3] Dresden,[4] Grandson,[5] Prague,[6] and Skokloster,[7] and on Guernsey.[8] Among these, only the Museum's winder and the large cranequin in the Jenkinson collection show any significant decoration; that on the latter is the most extensive. The cranequins in Altena, Bad Urach, Berlin, and Grandson bear the mark of Adam Bauer of Urach (today Bad Urach), who worked for the dukes of Württemberg and between 1574 and 1624 made numerous deliveries of arms to the court, including crossbow winders;[9] the tentative suggestion that the Museum's winder is also by Bauer—the mark would have been lost because of the modification of the claw—can at present not be verified.[10]

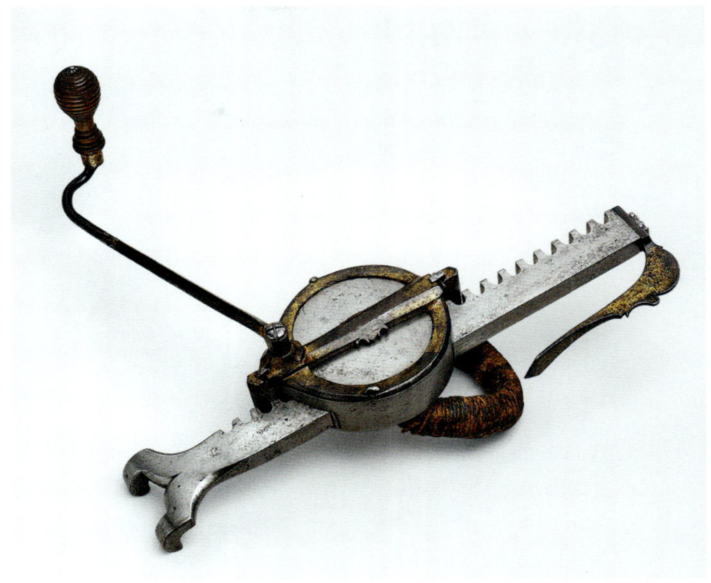

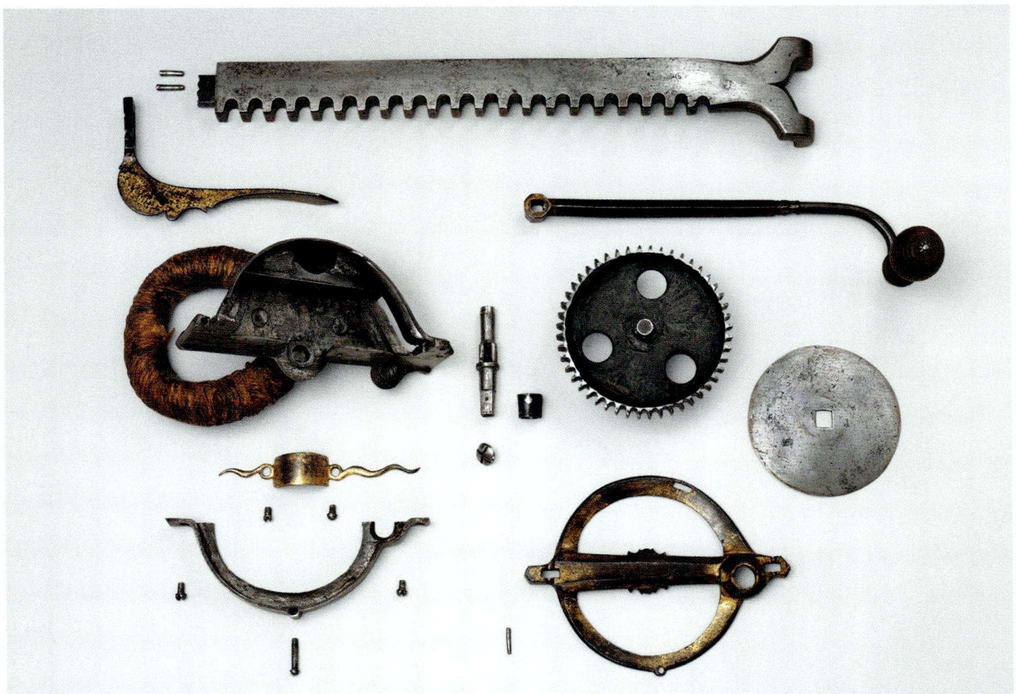

Figure 5.12
Catalogue 37, disassembled

38. Cranequin

Southern Germany (probably Nuremberg), dated 1727
Steel, horn (bovine), copper alloy, gold, hemp, leather
L. 14¾ in. (37.5 cm); W. 4½ in. (11.5 cm); Wt. 6 lb. 8 oz.
(2,942 g)
Rogers Fund, 1986 (1986.205)

Ex coll.: Frank E. Bivens Jr., West Los Angeles;
[Brian Powers, Los Angeles]

References: Fischer sale 1974, lot 125, pl. 9; Fischer sale
1975, lot 68, pl. 13; Fischer sale 1985, lot 110, pl. 1

A late example of its kind, this winder is remarkable
for the quality of both its workmanship and decoration. It comprises a rack with a grapple and belt
hook and a circular wheel case of open type, with a
hemp and leather loop and a long handle arm; typically of late cranequins, the removable parts are
secured by screws, rather than pegs or rivets. The
winder's principal embellishment consists of two
pairs of iron disks set into recesses on the top and
underside of the cogwheel. Each pair presents an
upper disk—cut, pierced, engraved with figural
ornament, and gilded—that would originally have
displayed a colorful contrast to the solid disk beneath;
these bottom disks still show traces of overall bluing.
The cut-and-pierced plate visible on the upper side
of the wheel case features personifications of the Seven
Planets, while the one visible on the underside shows
three double-tailed mermaids (fig. 5.13).

In addition, there are scrolling floral motifs,
etched on the rack but engraved into the surfaces of
the wheel case, and baluster-shaped ornament on the
upper reinforce of the wheel case, handle arm, and
lower part of the handle axis. Most of the outer surfaces of the wheel case also retain traces of gilding.
The etched decoration on the rack, just behind the
grapple, includes a mirror monogram consisting of
the letters clr below a crown (fig. 5.14) and, in correspondence on the underside, the year 1727 (rendered as A˙1727; fig. 5.15).

As a motif in the decorative arts, circular arrange-
ments of personifications of the Seven Planets date
back to at least the mid-sixteenth century; an early
instance is the design for a clockface,[1] made in 1547
by the Augsburg goldsmith and sculptor Vitus/Veit
Kels (rec. 1537–94/95), that apparently served as a
model for other works of art, including a clock, a
medal, and a bowl. From at least the early seventeenth century the design is also found on cranequins: an example in the collections of Erbach Castle
shows the seven figures delicately cut, pierced, and
engraved within an architectural framework; the
rack is dated 1622.[2]

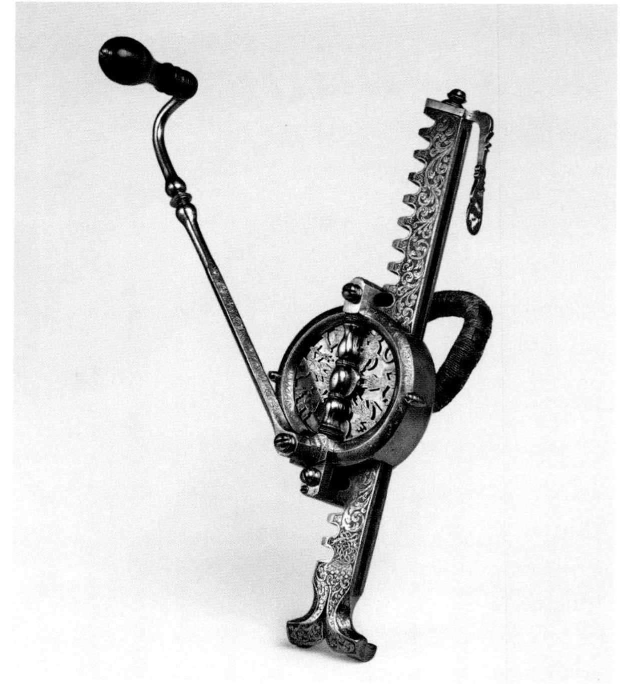

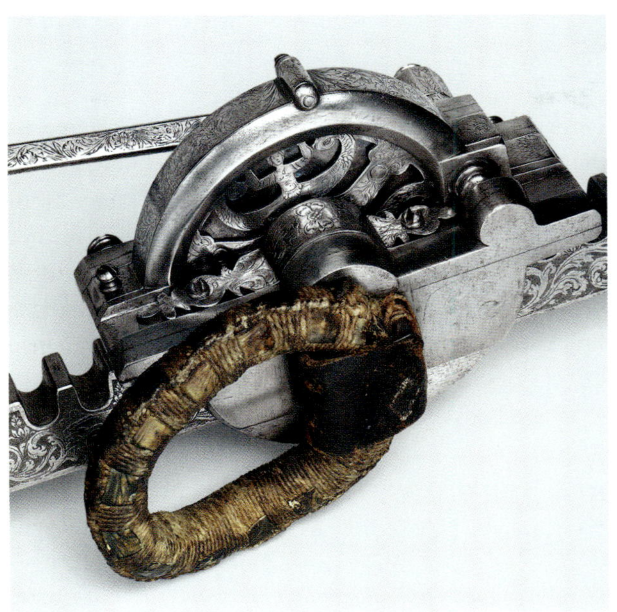

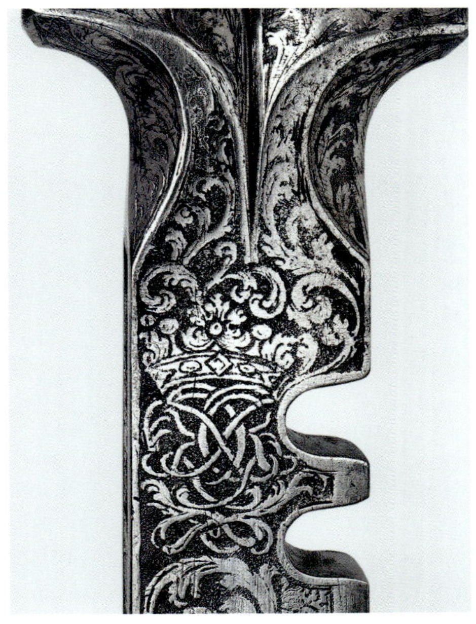

The Metropolitan Museum's winder belongs to a group with similar wheel cases and grapple forms. They include examples in London,[3] Karlsruhe,[4] Munich,[5] and Leeds.[6] Among these, the Leeds winder represents the latest example with the highest quality of decoration: a shell-like shield within the etched ornament contains the monogram L.N. above the year, 1747. The wheel cases of all the examples resemble the small-scale depiction of a winder found on a church-stall plaque donated in 1718 by the Nuremberg guild of locksmiths and crank, clock, and gunlock makers.[7] It is therefore quite probable that these cranequins were made in southern Germany, perhaps in Nuremberg itself.

The identification of the owner of the Metropolitan Museum's winder has to date proven impossible. Although the letters of the monogram have been identified as CLR, their mirrored rendition makes it difficult to establish the order in which they were meant to be read. Moreover, the letters may refer either to an individual or to a person and his or her title; alternatively, they may be the monogram of two people, usually husband and wife. The simple crown is equally unhelpful. It is of a type known in Germany as a "nobility" or "leaf" crown, normally signifying that its bearer was a member of the lower nobility. Yet, crowns like it can occasionally be found above the monograms of higher-ranking members of the nobility, such as dukes. Accordingly, the list of people to whom the initials CLR might refer is at present too long to even hazard an attribution.

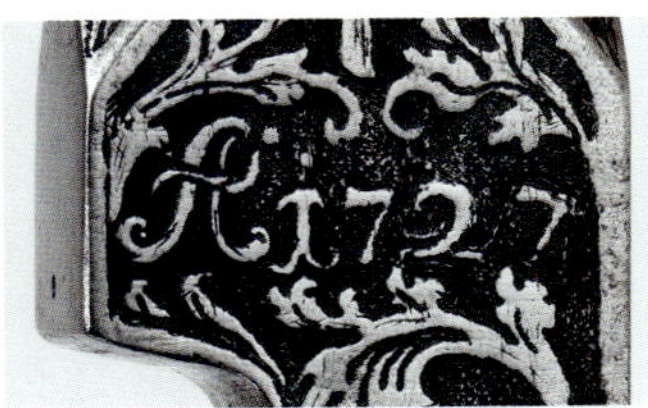

39. Pricker (Cocking Pin)

Central Europe (probably Germany), late 16th–19th century
Steel, ivory (probably hippopotamus), copper alloy
L. 6⁹⁄₁₆ in. (16.7 cm); Diam. of pommel 1⁵⁄₁₆ in. (3.4 cm);
Wt. 1.9 oz. (53 g)
Gift of William H. Riggs, 1913 (14.25.1576i)

Ex coll.: William H. Riggs, Paris

References: Unpublished

As the release mechanisms of crossbows evolved and became more sophisticated, some locks had to be prepared in order to be released. Beginning in the late fifteenth century, internal tumblers were usually pulled into place by a piece of string (cats. 4, 5). After the mid-sixteenth century, the mechanisms were readied by inserting a pin, today known as a pricker, or cocking pin, to push the internal component or components into place (cats. 8, 10–12). This pricker consists of a steel rod of circular section with a turned ivory knob at the top, fitted with a copper-alloy collar. The top of the rod is decorated simply, with a step and a stylized baluster shape.

The use of an expensive material such as ivory indicates that this pricker probably accompanied a crossbow of superior quality; the rod is of a thickness that indicates use with a large crossbow, and the pin does, indeed, fit the respective openings on the *ganze Rüstung* of Baron von Rechenberg (cat. 11), with which it has been associated at least since the

nineteenth century. Dating an accessory outside its context is difficult, but given its association with the Rechenberg weapon this cocking pin may be of seventeenth-century manufacture. However, a later date is certainly possible, since release mechanisms requiring prickers continued to be produced throughout the eighteenth and nineteenth centuries. Two other prickers survive in Dresden.[1]

40. Spanning Lever (Gaffle or "Goat's-Foot" Lever)

Western Europe (probably Spain), late 15th or first half of
the 16th century
Steel
L., extended 19⁵⁄₈ in. (49.8 cm); W. 2¹³⁄₁₆ in. (7.2 cm);
Wt. 25 oz. (713 g)
Gift of William H. Riggs, 1913 (14.25.1609)

Ex coll.: William H. Riggs, Paris

References: Unpublished

During the fifteenth century, a type of spanning lever was developed in Spain and Portugal that eventually spread to Italy, other western and northern European areas—France, the Netherlands, the British Isles, and Scandinavia—and ultimately Africa and the New World. Most surviving levers of this type are utilitarian, made entirely of steel and left plain (cat. 41). The majority comprise a lever arm, a forked part with two arms that permitted the lever to be temporarily secured to the crossbow, and a double claw that engaged the bowstring. The arm and fork are hinged together, allowing the lever to be folded up when not in use (fig. 5.16). On this example, the arm is fitted on top with a hinged and pivoting plate that serves as a handle. Other versions have plain

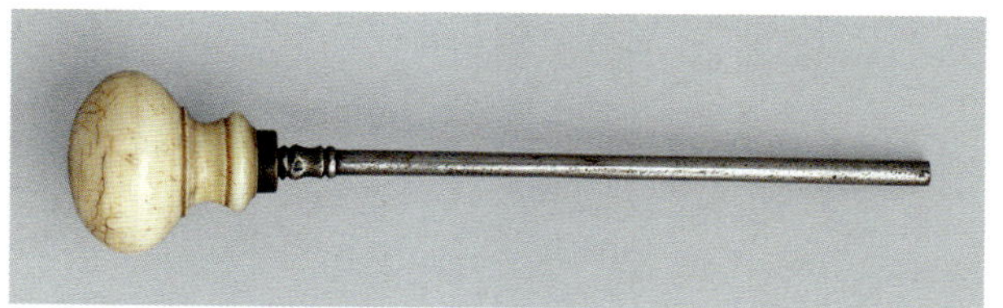

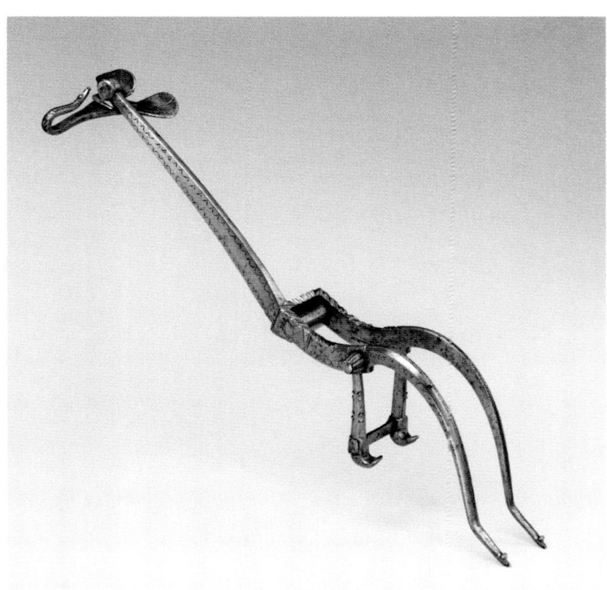

decoration, including a belt hook shaped and embossed like a pilgrim's scallop shell.[1] However, the close resemblance of the chiseled decoration of the fork—especially the animal heads at the ends—suggests that both levers come from the same region, possibly even the same workshop. Because of the type's wide dissemination, the date and place of origin of individual examples are difficult to establish, but these two levers were probably made in the Iberian Peninsula, while the extent of their chiseled decoration would indicate a date before the mid-sixteenth century.

handles and often display extensions in the form of belt hooks; such a belt-hook plate also doubled as a safety catch, preventing a folded lever from extending accidentally when suspended from a belt.

This lever is noteworthy for its subtle decoration. The shoulder and grapple are chiseled in a manner reminiscent of Gothic tracery, while the ends of the fork extensions and of the belt hook are in the shape of animal heads, possibly dragons. The surfaces of the lever arm, fork extensions, and belt-hook plate are stamped with a pattern of semicircles and dots, while the edges are filed diagonally to suggest a rope motif. The small rosette struck three times into the upper side of the belt-hook plate is probably a decorative element rather than a maker's mark.

There is a similar lever in Florence, which is struck with an unidentified maker's mark on the lever arm and features somewhat more extensive

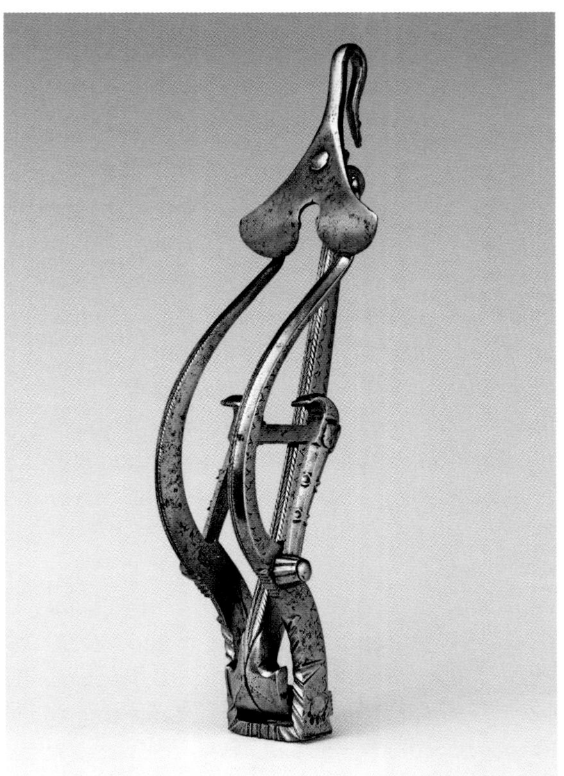

Figure 5.16 Catalogue 40, folded for suspension and transport

41. Spanning Lever (Gaffle or "Goat's-Foot" Lever)

Probably Spain (possibly Madrid), ca. 1525–75
Steel
L., extended 18⅜ in. (46.6 cm); W. 2⅝ in. (6.7 cm);
Wt. 1 lb. 3 oz. (548 g)
Gift of Archer M. Huntington, 1927 (27.160.19b)

Ex coll.: Guillermo Casanova, marqués de Dos Aguas,
Valencia

References: Unpublished

Mark:

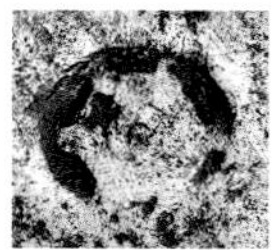

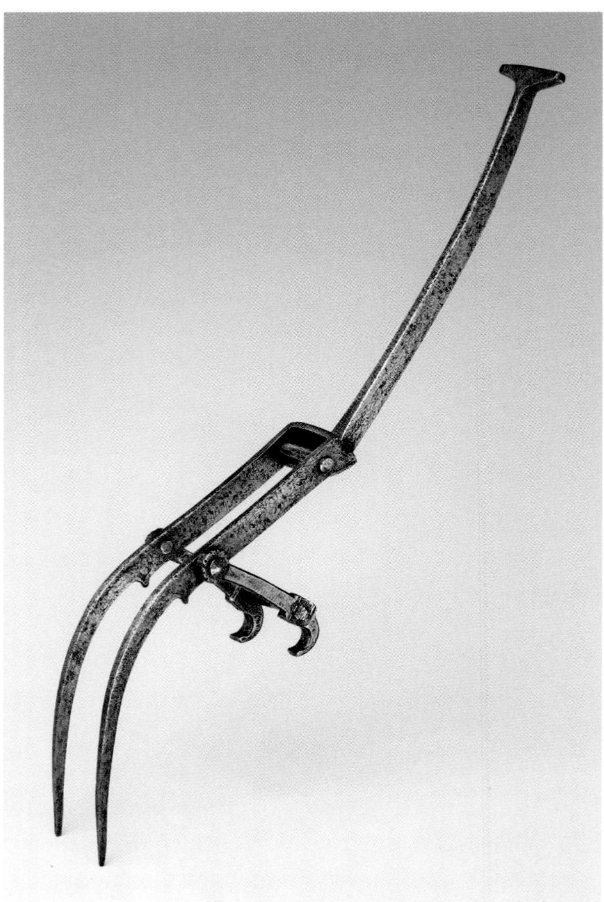

This lever is typical of the plain, utilitarian spanning
devices in use from the fifteenth to the early seventeenth century, particularly in western Europe and
throughout the Mediterranean. Made entirely of steel,
it has a slightly curved arm terminating in a short
T-bar grip at the top and a strong but slender fork
with a pivoting grapple. The top face of the arm's
hinge plate is struck with a circular mark of three con-
centric circles; because the outermost circle displays
six points or teeth, the mark probably represents
Saint Catherine's wheel. Except for the mark and a
few ornamental notches on the fork, this lever is
undecorated.

Circular makers' marks generally similar to
that on the Museum's lever are found on the steel
bows of more than a dozen Spanish crossbows in
Madrid, most of which are attributable to crossbow
makers active in that city in about the mid-sixteenth
century (cat. 6a).[1] A similar lever of somewhat superior quality was formerly in the Howard M. Curtis

collection, Hollywood (present whereabouts unknown),[2] which came from the collection of Richard
Zschille, Grossenhain, where it was associated with
a mid-sixteenth-century Spanish crossbow.[3] The
Zschille-Curtis lever's rectangular hinge plate is also
struck with a round mark: the letter *S* within a circle,
flanked by the words AVE / MARIA. The similarity
between the latter mark and the one on the present
lever, together with the Zschille-Curtis lever's former
association with a Spanish crossbow and the Spanish
provenance of the Museum's lever, further supports
the identification of these spanning devices as being
of mid-sixteenth-century Spanish manufacture.

Attributed to Juan Hernández
Spain (Madrid), recorded 1551–77

42. Spanning Lever (Gaffle or "Goat's-Foot" Lever)

Spain (Madrid), probably third quarter of the 16th century
Steel, gold, silver
L., extended 20¼ in. (51.4 cm); W. 2⅜ in. (6 cm);
Wt. 1 lb. 6 oz. (618 g)
Gift of William H. Riggs, 1913 (14.25.1608)

Ex coll.: William H. Riggs, Paris

References: Unpublished

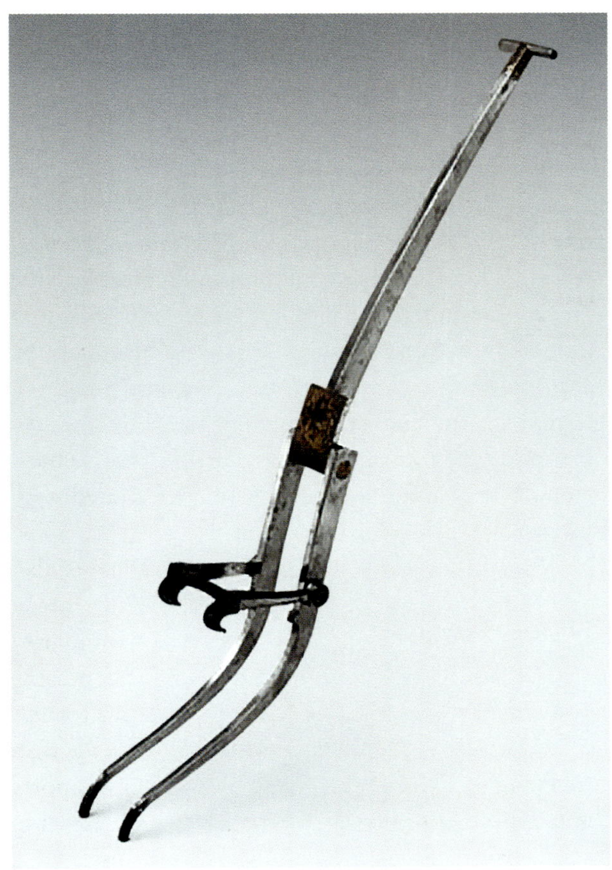

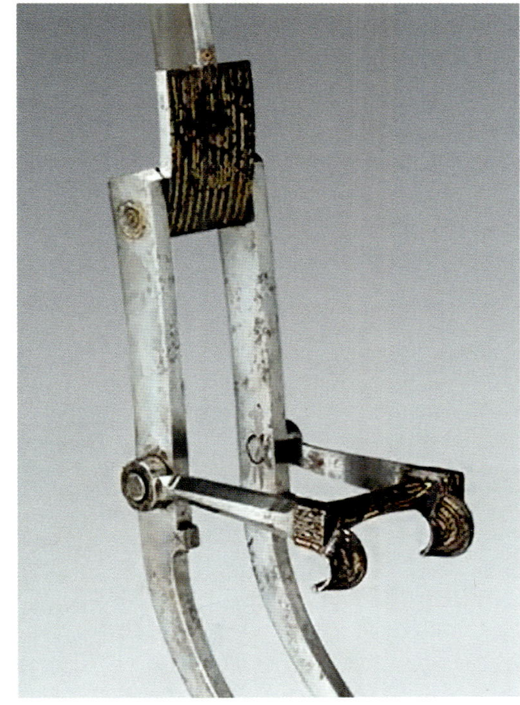

Figure 5.17

Distinguished by the quality of its construction and its elegant decoration, this steel lever consists of a slightly curved arm with a short T-bar grip at the top and a slightly downward-curving rectangular plate at the bottom. Forming a hinge, this plate connects the arm to the slender fork, which is fitted with a sturdy pivoting grapple.

Most of the lever's main surfaces are smooth and today polished bright, although faint traces suggest that they may once have been blued. The top of the hinge plate is covered entirely with parallel bands of a small, angular guilloche pattern damascened in gold and silver against a darkened ground (fig. 5.17). Similar decoration on a smaller scale embellishes both ends of the T-bar grip, the top of the arm, the outer faces of the hinge axis, and the tips of the fork's extensions, as well as the pivot section, cross bar, and each claw.

The Museum's lever is very similar to a number of examples, all of which may have been produced by the same maker. Several are in Madrid,[1] while another example is in Vitoria-Gasteiz.[2] One of the levers in Madrid is inscribed IO HRZ, which has been identified as the signature of Juan Hernández

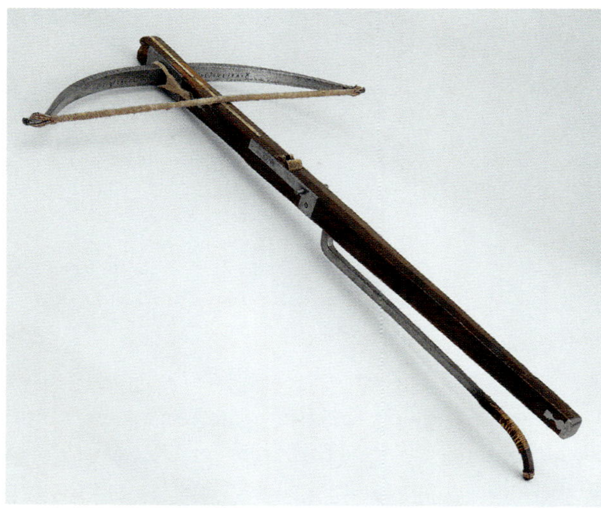

Figure 5.18 Crossbow made for the Holy Roman Emperor Charles V. Spanish, ca. 1540–50. Bow by Juan de la Fuente; trigger signed by Juan Hernández. Patrimonio Nacional/Real Armería, Madrid (J.18)

(rec. 1551–77), an accomplished crossbow maker working in that city.[3] Although the Metropolitan Museum's lever bears no maker's mark, date, or signature, its similarity to the examples in Madrid indicate that it, too, was almost certainly made by Hernández.

At least three of the levers in Madrid are associated with crossbows whose tillers are signed by Hernández but which are fitted with bows made by other Madrid crossbow makers, all of whom worked for the Habsburg court. One crossbow, made for the Holy Roman Emperor Charles V (r. 1520–56), is fitted with a trigger bearing Hernández's signature, while the bow is signed by Juan de la Fuente (fig. 5.18).[4]

A lever with the characteristically flat, rectangular hinge plate, but fitted with a heart-shaped handle and belt hook instead of a T-bar grip, is depicted in the *Inventario Iluminado*, an illustrated inventory of Charles V's armory compiled between about 1544 and 1558.[5] The collaboration with other eminent artisans—in at least one case, on a weapon for the emperor—establishes Hernández's elevated position among Madrid crossbow makers. And although the Metropolitan's lever can only be attributed to Hernández, the quality of its workmanship and decoration is at least a strong indication that it once belonged to a superior crossbow made for an illustrious owner.

43. Spanning Lever (Gaffle or "Goat's-Foot" Lever) for a Pellet Crossbow

Western Europe (probably Spain), probably first half of the
16th century
Steel
L., extended 22½ in. (57.1 cm); W. 2¼ in. (5.8 cm);
Wt. 1 lb. 6 oz. (632 g)
Gift of Archer M. Huntington, 1927 (27.160.18b)

Ex coll.: Guillermo Casanova, marqués de Dos Aguas,
Valencia

References: Unpublished

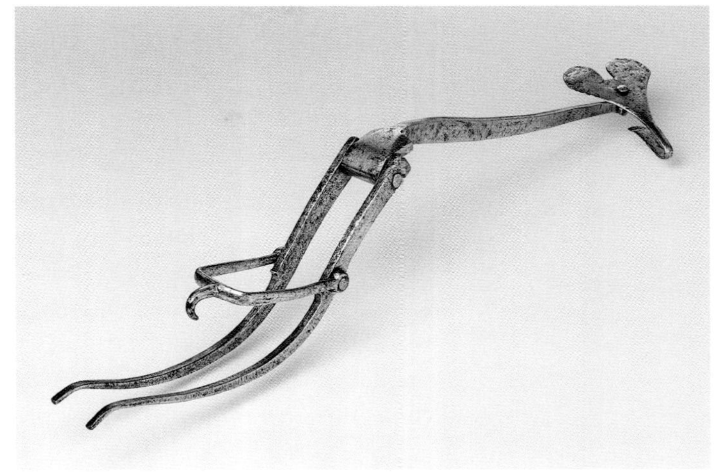

This lever is unusual in having a grapple with only a single claw, or hook, in its center, intended to span a pellet crossbow (see Section 3, "Pellet Crossbows"). Made entirely of steel, the lever has an almost straight handle arm with a heart-shaped belt-hook plate at the top, and a slender fork with curved extensions; the latter are fitted with a pivoting U-shaped bar with a central hook, or claw.

Levers constructed this way were intended primarily for crossbows with bowstrings fitted with a small central pouch that shot stones, clay balls, or pellets, used to hunt birds or small game like rabbits. Although pellet bows and pellet crossbows are already mentioned in documents of the fourteenth and fifteenth centuries,[1] they did not become common until the sixteenth century. During the second half of that century the stone crossbow developed into two predominant types, the Italian version (see, for example, cats. 19–21), which could be spanned by hand, and the German and English types, which had a spanning lever built into the tiller (cats. 23, 24). Accordingly, levers for stone crossbows quickly became obsolete, and surviving examples and contemporary illustrations are both exceedingly rare.

An early depiction—the only known detailed representation of this kind of lever—is found in the *Inventario Iluminado*, an illustrated inventory of the armory of the Holy Roman Emperor Charles V, compiled between about 1544 and 1558 (fig. 3.3).[2] That specimen differs slightly from the Metropolitan's example in the hinge connecting the grip and belt-hook plate. Two extant levers of this particular type are recorded, one in Sluderno,[3] the other—like the Metropolitan Museum's example from the Dos Aguas collection—in Chicago.[4] The Chicago lever represents yet another variety, being fitted with an indicator and a central anchoring plate (instead of a fork), similar to those found on fifteenth-century cranequins and pulley systems (cat. 29).

6 | Projectiles and Their Storage

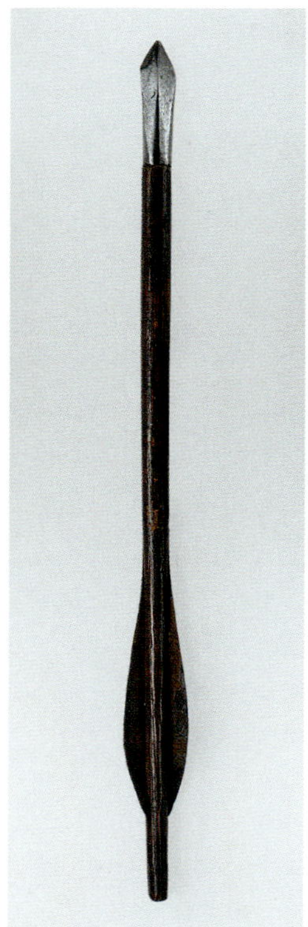

Figure 6.1 Crossbow bolt. Central Europe (perhaps Switzerland), probably 15th or 16th century. Steel, wood (oak), leather, L. 17 3/16 in. (43.7 cm); L. head 2 5/8 in. (6.6 cm); W. head 3/4 in. (1.9 cm); Wt. 2.6 oz. (74 g). The Metropolitan Museum of Art, New York, Gift of William H. Riggs, 1913 (14.25.1591j). With its steel head and leather flights, this bolt, of relatively high quality, could have been used in both war and the hunt. Note the slight swelling toward the front, and the butt, which is flattened to fit between the fingers of the nut.

Crossbow projectiles varied according to the type of weapon and its intended purpose.[1] The majority of crossbows shot bolts, also known as "quarrels" (fig. 6.1). These projectiles consist of a head, usually of metal, and a wooden shaft, the latter often fitted with small flights at the rear intended to stabilize the projectile in flight. In order to secure the head to the shaft, most western and central European heads were made with a socket; a pointed rear extension, or tang, was more common in the East (cat. 1). Bolts differ from arrows—used primarily with self-bows—in a number of ways: the arrow shaft is longer and thinner, with a nock at the rear to accommodate the bowstring; in general, an arrow is also well balanced. Because the bows fitted on most crossbows are more powerful than self-bows, a bolt shaft is shorter and stouter, sometimes with a swelling toward the front. This swelling shifts the center of gravity forward, while presumably also increasing the weight, raising part of the shaft off the chase to reduce friction, and preventing overly deep penetration. Because of the crossbow's thicker bowstring, a bolt shaft does not have a nock; it may be flattened at the rear in order to fit into the central notch, or fingers, of the nut or it may remain circular in section, when made to be shot from weapons with snap locks. In addition, most arrows have three flights, usually made of feathers, but most bolts have only two, made of parchment, leather, or wood, or occasionally of copper alloy or feathers—or none at all.

During the early Middle Ages the arrows for self-bows and those for crossbows appear to have differed little, if at all, and in some cases may have been interchangeable (cat. 1). As crossbows became more varied in terms of overall dimensions, mass, and draw weight, it became increasingly important that the weight of the bolts especially be appropriate for the weapon with which they were to be used: light bolts fly faster than heavier ones, but have significantly less power, or "effect," when reaching the target.

Bolts intended for use in war were utilitiarian in design, produced in large quantities, and hence, for the most part, of relatively mediocre quality, that is, they were made cheaply and usually had unfinished surfaces. Only those intended for more specialized purposes were better made, such as bolts with armor-piercing heads or those with barbs, the hook-like extensions that made the projectile difficult to remove; incendiary projectiles; or the large missiles discharged from enormous siege crossbows (cat. 44d). Inventories also indicate that lesser-quality warheads were made of iron, while those of better quality were made of steel, which is significantly harder.

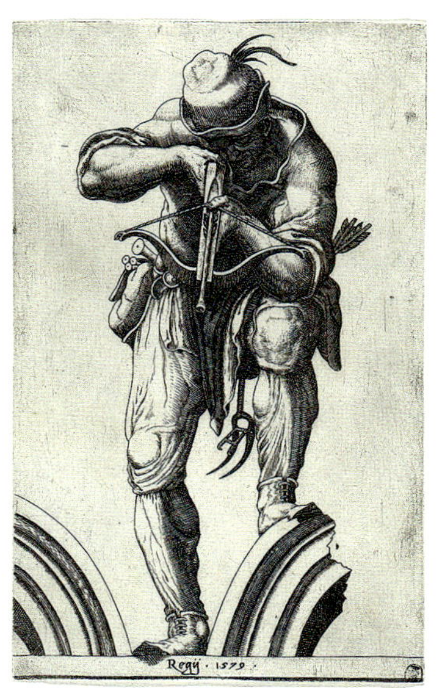

Although simple bolts intended for warfare could be, and probably often were, also used for hunting, some evidence suggests that bolts made specifically for the hunt were of higher quality, probably because they were easier to retrieve than those on a battlefield. The shafts and heads of surviving projectiles made for the hunt are better made, displaying greater care taken in their manufacture and in the finish of their surfaces, and the heads are sometimes struck with a maker's mark. Hunting bolts were also fitted with differently shaped heads, depending on the potential prey; several variations are noteworthy: the stun bolts (fig. 6.2), already represented in early fourteenth-century art, which were blunt so as not to destroy birds or other small animals completely or damage a valuable pelt, and those fitted with heads that were barbed, forked, or chisel-like, intended to cause serious, incapacitating wounds by cutting through muscle tissue and sinews in order to bring down large game quickly and effectively (cat. 45).

Of better quality still are the bolts made especially for competitive crossbow shooting. As mentioned above, during earlier periods, crossbowmen probably employed the same bolts for war, the hunt, and in competitions. However, bolts intended exclusively for this last purpose had been developed by the fifteenth century (cat. 46). One variety was derived from the blunt hunting type; comparatively large, extremely top-heavy, and fitted with coronel-shaped heads, but often lacking flights, these projectiles were used for shooting up at the popinjay. Other, pointed examples were used exclusively for target shooting. Accordingly, beginning in the fifteenth century, documents—especially personal inventories—refer to them as "target bolts," but pictorial evidence and identifiable specimens survive only from the late sixteenth century on.

Finally, mention must be made of the projectiles shot from pellet crossbows. Exclusively used for hunting, these pellets were either simple stones or small balls made of clay, marble, or lead. During the sixteenth century, they evidently were the size of a large cherry, approximately an inch, or 2.5 cm, in diameter; a rare depiction of what are probably clay pellets is found in the portrait of an Italian crossbow maker (fig. 3.1). The pellets used in the nineteenth century appear to have been somewhat smaller.

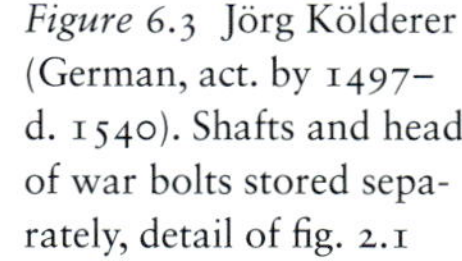

Figure 6.2 Attributed to Cherubino Alberti (Italian, 1553–1615). *An Archer Shooting a Crossbow*, 1579. Engraving on laid paper, sheet (cut inside platemark) 8¹¹⁄₁₆ × 5½ in. (22.1 × 14 cm). After Lelio Orsi. National Gallery of Art, Washington, D.C., Alisa Mellon Bruce Fund (2005.131.1). Note the lever spanner and blunt hunting bolts.

Figure 6.3 Jörg Kölderer (German, act. by 1497– d. 1540). Shafts and heads of war bolts stored separately, detail of fig. 2.1

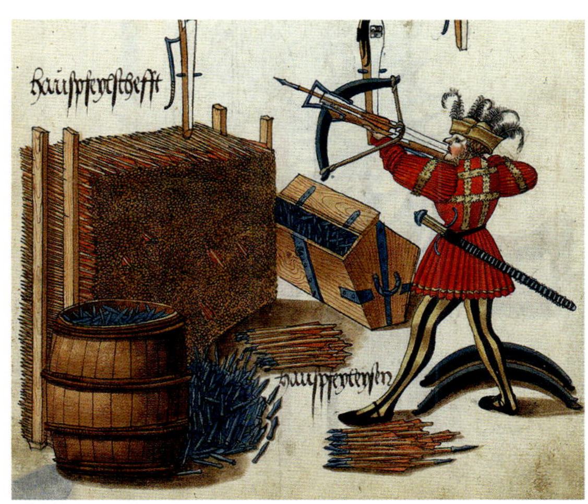

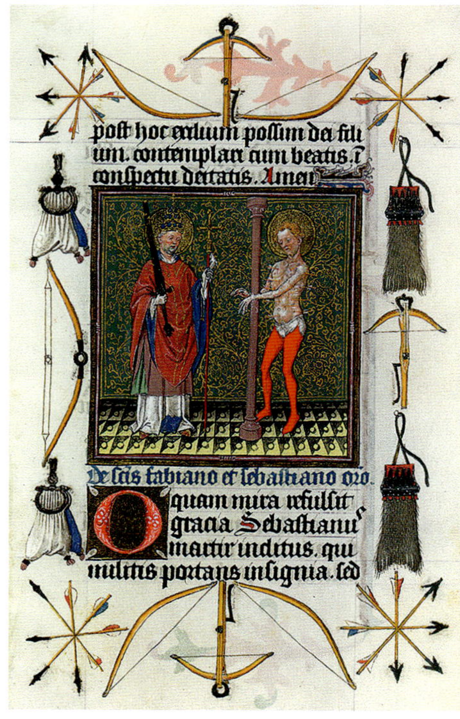

On the whole, projectiles were unembellished; only in rare examples was better quality expressed through the use of expensive materials and superior craftsmanship. It appears that the shafts of target bolts were occasionally painted, or fitted with sleeves of staghorn or metal behind the head and/or with small butt plates, which were most often of polished staghorn. Extensive ornament is found only on ceremonial bolt heads, few of which survive (cat. 47).

Munition-quality bolts, which had to be stored and transported in large quantities, were kept in wooden barrels or chests, and sometimes driven to the battlefield in special carts that held several thousand projectiles. Interestingly, war bolts seem to have been frequently stored in parts—the heads and shafts kept separately—to be assembled only as needed (fig. 6.3). Crossbowmen, whether in war or hunting, carried their personal supplies of bolts in a quiver, worn suspended from either a belt or a shoulder strap.[2] Most quivers consisted of a wooden core covered with leather or fur, and fitted with a leather lid (cat. 48); the bolts inside were invariably stored with their heads pointing up. As utilitarian objects, few quivers appear to have been extensively decorated, but some pictorial sources show examples adorned with figuratively embossed leather or openwork appliqués, presumably of polished staghorn. The balls and bullets for pellet crossbows were carried in small "pellet bags," similar to civilian belt purses or the small bags worn by falconers; if this analogy is correct, some examples were probably just as elaborately embellished (fig. 6.4).

In central Europe, from at least the late fifteenth century, bolts to be shot in competitions were kept in purpose-made bolt boxes.[3] The box proper was almost always made of wood, and early examples probably contained only projectiles, but the outside might be painted or decorated with carved ornament or inlay (cat. 49). Later boxes contained not only bolts but also other necessary tools and accessories, and until the late seventeenth century they sometimes still had richly adorned exteriors. The majority of surviving eighteenth-century bolt boxes are from Saxony, where their decoration followed current fashions in furniture and was chiefly confined to an elegant shape and overall veneer (cat. 50). Only in rare instances were such late examples lavishly embellished, mostly with inlay, as, for example, the two made for Prince-Elector Augustus "the Strong" and for his son, the future Augustus III.[4]

44. Bolts for Use in War

a. Bolt
Central Europe, probably late 15th or 16th century
Steel, wood (shaft: oak; flights: possibly birch)
L. 14½ in. (36.8 cm); L. head 2¹⁵⁄₁₆ in. (7.5 cm);
W. head ¹¹⁄₁₆ in. (1.8 cm); Wt. 2.4 oz. (68 g)
Bashford Dean Memorial Collection, Funds from various
donors, 1929 (29.158.646f)

b. Bolt
Central Europe (perhaps Switzerland), probably 15th or 16th
century
Steel, wood (oak), leather
L. 17³⁄₁₆ in. (43.7 cm); L. head 2⅝ in. (6.6 cm); W. head ¾ in.
(1.9 cm); Wt. 2.6 oz. (74 g)
Gift of William H. Riggs, 1913 (14.25.1591j)

c. Barbed bolt head
Western or central Europe, probably 14th or 15th century
Steel, wood (oak)
L. overall 15⅞ in. (40.3 cm); L. head 3 in. (7.6 cm); W. head
2¼ in. (5.8 cm); Wt. total 2.7 oz. (75 g)
Bashford Dean Memorial Collection, Funds from various
donors, 1929 (29.158.646k)

d. Large bolt head
Central Europe, probably 15th century
Steel, wood (possibly pear or birch)
L. 15³⁄₁₆ in. (38.5 cm); L. head 4⅞ in. (12.4 cm); W. head 1 in.
(2.5 cm); Wt. incl. shaft 6.2 oz. (177 g)
Gift of William H. Riggs, 1913 (14.25.1592)

Ex coll.: (44a, c) Bashford Dean, Riverdale, New York; (44b, d)
William H. Riggs, Paris

References: Unpublished, except possibly 44a: Stone 1934
(1961 ed.), p. 125, fig. 164

Bolts intended for use in war were mass-produced
and stored in great numbers in city arsenals and
castle armories. Most of these projectiles consisted
of a relatively crude head of iron or steel, and a
rough wooden shaft fitted with two flights that were
usually made of wood or parchment.

Catalogues 44a and 44b are typical of the most
common variety of bolts: the rhomboid head with a
short socket is forged from a single piece of iron
alloy, and the shaft, carved from a single piece of
wood—in this case, oak—is straight in outline and
circular in section, except for the rear, which is flattened to fit between the fingers of the nut. Catalogue
44a displays a head with surfaces left rough from the
hammer and a shaft with slightly curved flights made
of wood, possibly birch; catalogue 44b has an iron-
alloy or steel head with polished surfaces, indicating
superior quality, and a shaft fitted with leather flights.
Unmarked and entirely undecorated, such bolts were
sometimes acquired far from the places of later storage and use, so that it is today nearly impossible to
determine where they were manufactured. Nonetheless, catalogue 44b may have been made in Switzerland: more than two dozen examples with similar

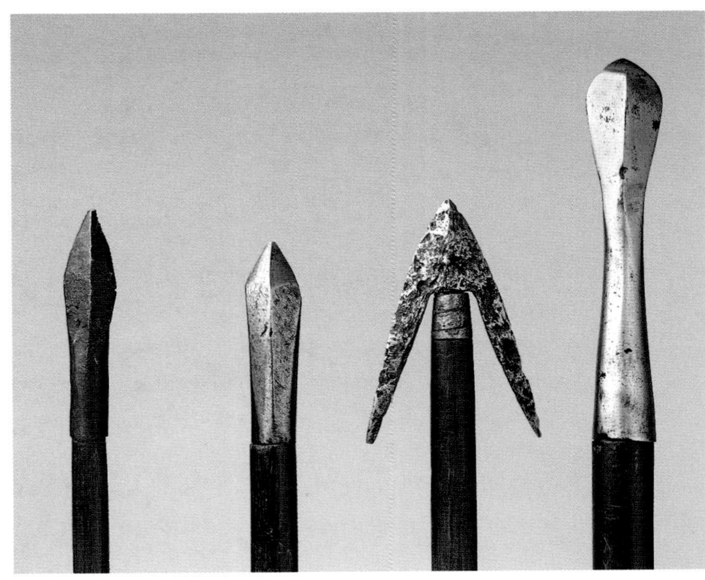

heads were found in Habsburg Castle, near Brugg, concealed within a ceiling dating from before 1559,[1] and a large number of bolts with leather flights are preserved in Zurich.[2]

Catalogue 44c, with long extensions, or barbs, may have come from an arrow or a bolt made for either war or hunting large game. This example is unusual because it was secured to the shaft by means of a pointed extension, or tang, at the back rather than by a socket. Arrows with barbed heads are recorded since late antiquity, throughout the early Middle Ages, and after, but they do not seem to have been fitted to crossbow bolts before the twelfth century. It has been suggested that heads of this type were rarely used after the early medieval period, but abundant pictorial evidence shows variations of the type employed well into the sixteenth century.[3] The shaft is modern.

Catalogue 44d is remarkable for its size and weight. These unusually large examples were shot from great crossbows or from springalds, crossbow-like, torsion-powered weapons that were stationary, much larger, and more powerful than their handheld cousins. Used in antiquity, this type of artillery was reintroduced in Europe after a long hiatus with the reappearance of siege warfare during the early Middle Ages.[4] Besieging forces and defenders alike employed great crossbows and springalds with devastating effect, until they were eventually superseded by heavy firearms, cannon, and mortars in the early sixteenth century. The projectiles for great crossbows and springalds can be divided into two distinct groups, one (the majority) about twice as heavy as ordinary heads, and a rare variety of extraordinary dimensions, examples of which are about triple the weight and length of an ordinary bolt head.[5] The Museum's head appears to belong to the latter group. The shaft is modern.

45. Bolts for Use in Hunting

a. Bolt for war or hunting
Central Europe (Germany or Austria), probably late 15th or early 16th century
Steel, wood (coniferous, probably pine)
L. 17⅜ in. (44.1 cm); W. head ²³⁄₃₂ in. (1.7 cm);
Wt. 3.1 oz. (87 g)
Gift of William H. Riggs, 1913 (14.25.1603)

b. Barbed projectile head
Europe (possibly Germany), probably 16th century
Steel, wood (probably chestnut), staghorn
L. 13¾ in. (34.8 cm); L. head 2⁹⁄₁₆ in. (6.5 cm);
W. head 2¹⁄₃₂ in. (5.2 cm); Wt. 2.1 oz (59 g)
Gift of William H. Riggs, 1913 (14.25.1599)

c. Bolt with forked head
Europe (possibly Germany), probably 16th century
Steel, wood (probably chestnut)
L. 15⁷⁄₃₂ in. (38.6 cm); W. head 1¹⁷⁄₃₂ in. (3.9 cm);
Wt. 2.4 oz. (69 g)
Gift of William H. Riggs, 1913 (14.25.1600)

d. Bolt with chisel head
Europe (possibly Germany), probably 16th or 17th century
Steel, wood (probably maple), staghorn, leather
L. 13 in. (33 cm); W. head 1²¹⁄₃₂ in. (4.2 cm);
Wt. 2.3 oz. (65 g)
Gift of William H. Riggs, 1913 (14.25.1595)

e. Bolt with chisel head
Europe (Germany?), probably late 16th or 17th century
Steel, wood (oak)
L. 17¼ in. (43.8 cm); W. head 1¹³⁄₁₆ in. (4.6 cm);
Wt. 2.6 oz. (73 g)
Gift of William H. Riggs, 1913 (14.25.1597)

Ex coll.: William H. Riggs, Paris

References: Unpublished

It can be difficult to tell heads for arrows from those for bolts, and even more complicated to distinguish those intended for war from those made for the hunt. As a general rule, however, the better-quality bolts—which occasionally display what are probably makers' marks—and certain types of specially shaped heads were primarily meant for hunting.

Catalogue 45a has a steel head with a blunt-pyramidal point of square section that changes to an elongated socket of octagonal section. The head is struck once with a mark, a five-pointed star.[1] Made of coniferous wood, the plain shaft is roughly carved and, as it lacks any cut grooves, does not appear to have been fitted with flights. Since the head and shaft are not a good fit, they were probably joined at a later date. The head is of a type that can be dated to the fifteenth or early sixteenth century, based on archaeological finds and a group of bolts with similar heads in Lucerne and Zurich.[2] A detailed depiction of a bolt fitted with such a head—the socket of which is either gilded or overlaid with or entirely made of a decoratively chiseled or chased copper alloy—is part of a hunting trophy in one of the earliest European still lifes, by Jacopo de' Barbari (act. by 1497–d. by 1516) and dated 1504.[3]

Barbed projectile heads were used in both war and the hunt to cause maximum damage and thus incapacitate the target quickly. Catalogue 45b is secured to the shaft by means of a tang, not a socket. On one side the head is struck with a single mark, perhaps a bishop's miter with a cross. The plain shaft (probably of chestnut) retains traces of two wooden flights; it is fitted with a collar of polished staghorn at the joint of head and shaft. A bolt struck with a similar mark is in Grandson Castle.[4]

Forked heads, predominantly used to hunt large game, especially deer (fig. 10), were intended to either hamstring the animal or inflict a wound causing significant blood loss, thus preventing the animal from escaping. The steel tines of catalogue 45c are slightly

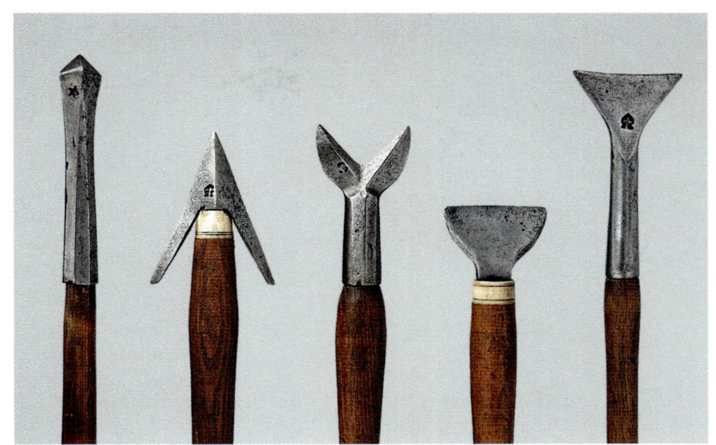

flattened, forming a concave cutting edge, while at the base the head changes into a socket of rounded hexagonal section. On one side, the head bears a mark, possibly a three-petaled flower. The shaft (probably of chestnut) may be associated; of good workmanship, it shows a distinct swelling toward the front and two incisions for flights at the back.

Chisel heads, with their wide, straight cutting edge, were used for hunting large game in the same way as the forked versions. However, catalogues 45d and 45e differ from each other in several ways. The steel head of catalogue 45d, of crescent shape with curved sides, is secured to the shaft by means of a tang. On one side of the head, traces of a mark are visible, possibly the same three-petaled flower as on catalogue 45c, the forked head. The undecorated shaft (probably of maple) lacks flights, but the joint of head and shaft is fitted with a collar of polished staghorn. Catalogue 45e has a steel head of inverted triangular shape that changes to a long socket of circular section, by which it is mounted to an oak shaft that displays a slight swelling toward the front but lacks flights. The head is deeply struck on one side with a mark, perhaps a bishop's miter with a cross, the same mark as on catalogue 45b.

46. Bolts for Shooting at Targets and the Popinjay

a. Target bolt
Germany (probably Saxony), ca. 1575–1650
Steel, copper alloy, wood (oak)
L. 13 15/16 in. (35.3 cm); Diam. head 17/32 in. (1.4 cm); Wt. 2 oz. (56 g)
Gift of William H. Riggs, 1913 (14.25.1596)

b. Target bolt
Germany (probably Saxony), probably 17th century
Steel, wood (probably birch), staghorn
L. 12 15/32 in. (31.6 cm); Diam. head 23/32 in. (1.7 cm);
Wt. 1.8 oz. (52 g)
Gift of William H. Riggs, 1913 (14.25.1598a)

c. Bolt for shooting at the popinjay
Central Europe (possibly Germany), probably 17th or 18th
century
Steel, wood (fruitwood), copper alloy, staghorn
L. 12 ¾ in. (32.3 cm); Diam. head 1 7/16 in. (3.7 cm);
Wt. 6.7 oz. (190 g)
Bashford Dean Memorial Collection, Funds from various
donors, 1929 (29.158.648b)

d. Bolt for shooting at the popinjay
Central Europe (possibly Germany), probably 17th or 18th
century
Steel, wood (oak)
L. 15 5/8 in. (39.6 cm); Diam. head 7/8 in. (2.3 cm);
Wt. 7.2 oz. (204 g)
Bashford Dean Memorial Collection, Funds from various
donors, 1929 (29.158.648c)

e. Whistling bolt for shooting at the popinjay
Central Europe (possibly Germany), probably 17th or 18th
century
Steel, wood (oak), staghorn, red pigment
L. 14 ¾ in. (37.5 cm); Diam. head 1 in. (2.6 cm);
Wt. 4.9 oz. (140 g)
Gift of William H. Riggs, 1913 (14.25.1576g)

Ex coll.: (46a, b, e) William H. Riggs, Paris; (46c, d)
Bashford Dean, Riverdale, N.Y.

References: Unpublished

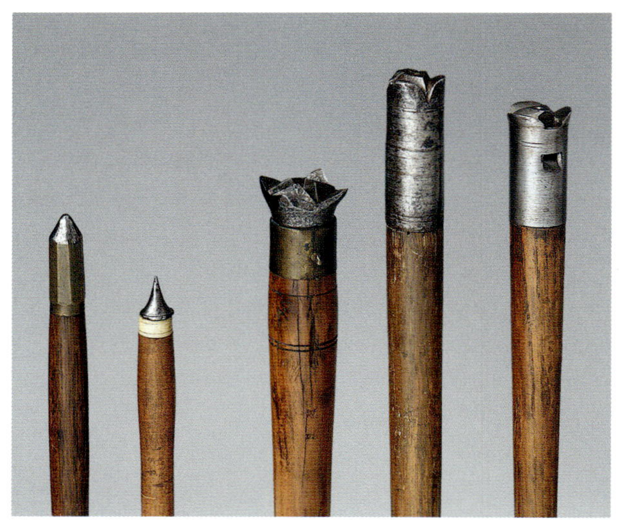

Although many depictions of crossbow competitions
have survived, few show the participants and their
equipment in sufficient detail to allow conclusions
about the projectiles that were used. It is likely that
bolts for war, the hunt, and competitions differed
little from one another, other than perhaps in quality,
until the fifteenth century. However, documentary
evidence suggests that by the second half of that century bolts specifically intended for target shooting
had come into general use, although none of these
early examples have so far been identified.

Catalogues 46a and 46b are bolts for shooting
horizontally at a target. The first has a steel head
made with a small sight, and fitted with a copper-
alloy sleeve that is octagonal in section; the plain,
unmarked oak shaft swells slightly toward the front,
is flattened at the rear, and was not fitted with flights.
The second target bolt has a short, acutely pointed
steel head, apparently made with a tang by which the
head is secured to its comparatively abbreviated
wooden shaft, probably of birch. The latter has a
slight swelling toward the front, a small staghorn collar, and no flights, and shows traces of having been
marked in ink; the fact that it is round in section

throughout, rather than having a rear shaped to fit between the fingers of a nut, indicates that it was meant to be shot from a light crossbow with a snap lock. Since bolts similar to catalogue 46a—and in at least one instance similar to catalogue 46b—are depicted in a series of individual "shooters' portraits" of members of the Saxe-Coburg court, both of the Museum's bolts likely date from the same period (fig. 6.5).

The remaining three bolts are examples of the heavy type of projectile used for shooting at the popinjay. The short steel head of catalogue 46c, probably secured by a tang, is round at the base but flares to a square at the front; its surface is quadrilaterally faceted, producing eight raised points. The thick fruitwood shaft is round in section throughout, swelling noticeably toward the front; has a staghorn butt plate and, at the front, a copper-alloy collar fitted with a sight; and is decorated with three incised lines and marked with the stamped letters RS and a now-illegible inscription in ink. Catalogue 46d, one of the longest and heaviest bolts in the Museum's collections, was probably shot from a large crossbow (cat. 11). It has a round steel head, cut deeply at the front to form a blunt central triangular point flanked on each side by a lobe, and a long socket. The oak shaft is round in section, with a slight swelling toward the front, and flattened at the rear; markings include two encircling red stripes, an incised cross, and now-illegible letters or figures in ink.[1] The steel head of catalogue 46e is of similar shape but shorter than that of catalogue 46d and it is cut and pierced on one side so as to form a whistle; the oak shaft is of nearly the same length and shape as that of catalogue 46d, but fitted at the flattened rear with a small staghorn inset. Whistling arrows and bolts have been widely employed in many periods and by numerous cultures around the world at least since antiquity. In Europe, they were occasionally used in battle during the late fourteenth and fifteenth centuries, and whistling target bolts are mentioned in an inventory of the Dresden armory as late as 1748.[2] The dating and geographical origin of catalogues 46c, 46d, and 46e are difficult to determine, but they were probably made in the German-speaking area of central Europe sometime during the seventeenth or eighteenth century.

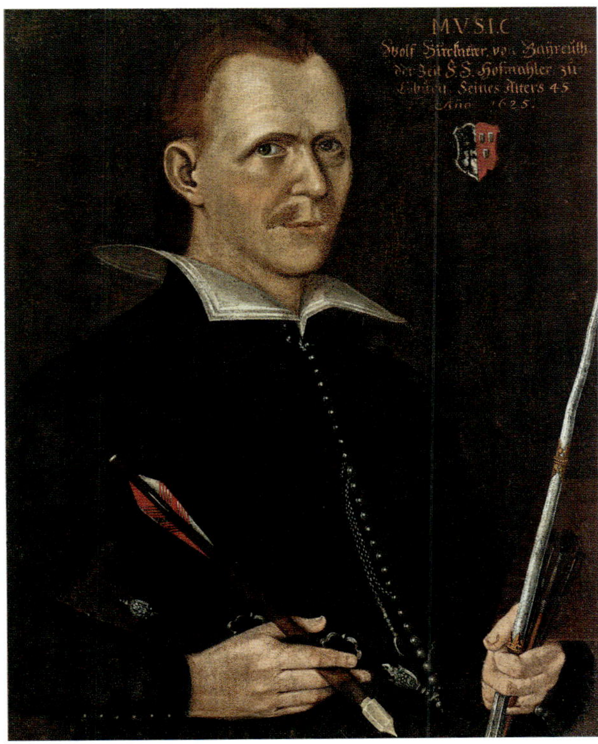

Figure 6.5 The Court Painter Wolfgang Birckner Holding a Target Bolt. German, dated 1625. Oil on panel, unframed 29 15/16 × 24 1/32 in. (76 × 61 cm). From the collection of the Coburg Shooting Society (*Schützengesellschaft*), on loan to the Kunstsammlungen der Veste Coburg (SB.073)

47. Three Ceremonial Bolt Heads

Bohemia (probably Prague), ca. 1437–39
Steel, copper alloy
a. L. 12⅛ in. (30.7 cm); W. 1¾ in. (4.4 cm); Wt. 18.2 oz.
(517 g)
Rogers Fund, 1966 (66.199)

b. L. 12⁹⁄₁₆ in. (31.9 cm); W. 2⁷⁄₁₆ in. (6.2 cm); Wt. 28.1 oz.
(797 g)
Purchase, David and Dorothy Alexander and Mrs. Ridgeley
Hunt Gifts, Bequest of Stephen V. Grancsay, by exchange, and
funds from various donors, 1984 (1984.17)

c. L. 10⅞ in. (27.5 cm); W. 1⁹⁄₁₆ in. (4 cm); Wt. 14.4 oz. (410 g)
Gift of Mr. and Mrs. Ronald S. Lauder, 1988 (1988.170)

Ex coll.: (47a) Ottoman Arsenal of Saint Irene, Constan-
tinople; A. A. Lyster, Esq. (possibly London); his estate sale,
Sotheby's London, Nov. 7, 1966, p. 29, lot 127; (47b)
Engelstein Castle, near Weitra; Archduke Eugen, Veste
Hohenwerfen, near Salzburg; his estate sale, Anderson
Galleries, New York, March 1–5, 1927, p. 134, lot 800;
Clarence H. Mackay, Roslyn, N.Y.; [Eric Vaule, Bridgewater,
Conn.]; (47c) Ottoman Arsenal of Saint Irene, Constantinople;
Sotheby's, London

References: (47a) Sotheby's sale 1966, p. 29, lot 127;
Nickel 1968; Nickel 1969; Nickel 1971a; (47b) Anderson
Galleries 1927, p. 134, lot 800; Nickel 1984; (47c) Sotheby's
1987, lot 138; Nickel 1988; (47a–c) Breiding 2005,
pp. 323–24; Breiding 2006, pp. 446–47

Since the late Middle Ages, official ceremonies occasionally featured elaborately decorated arrows and
bolts and those made from expensive materials, and
these opulent objects retained their symbolic importance until well into the sixteenth century. These
three exceptionally large ceremonial projectile
heads are the size of conventional spearheads. All
three are made of steel, their polished surfaces embellished with engraving and flush inlay of engraved
copper alloy. The points of catalogues 47a and 47b

take the characteristic form of leaf-shaped bolt
heads, rhomboid in section and widest near the tip,
but the silhouette of catalogue 47b more closely
resembles that of a spear- or arrowhead, that is, wider
toward the base. Each head is made with a conical
socket that, near the lower edge, has two opposing
rivet holes, one round, the other rectangular.

In addition to scale patterns and floral scrolls, the
dense decoration on all three heads exhibits extensive religious and political symbolism, including a
variety of emblematic monograms, and pious invo-
cations of God and the Virgin Mary in medieval
Czech, rendered in Gothic script, although the precise meaning of some motifs and inscriptions still
awaits conclusive interpretation. The only motif
common to all three is the use of the monogram AR,
which most likely stands for *Albertus rex*, that is,
Albert II (1397–1439), king of Hungary, Bohemia,
Croatia, and Germany. The presence of Albert's
monogram suggests a date of manufacture for all
three heads between December 18, 1437, when
Albert was elected king of Hungary, and October 27,
1439, the date of his death.

Catalogue 47a is inlaid with copper alloy on only
one side, so that it has an obverse and a reverse.
Moreover, it is the only head that shows the AR
monogram below a crown from which issues a single
ostrich feather, a heraldic badge extensively used in
fifteenth-century royal Bohemian iconography.[1] Also
unique to this example is the monogram AE, the letters intertwined crosswise, probably alluding to
Albert and his wife, Elisabeth of Luxembourg
(1409–1442). The inscriptions on this head are
arranged as follows:

Obverse, left flange: AR [prob. monogram for
Albertus rex]

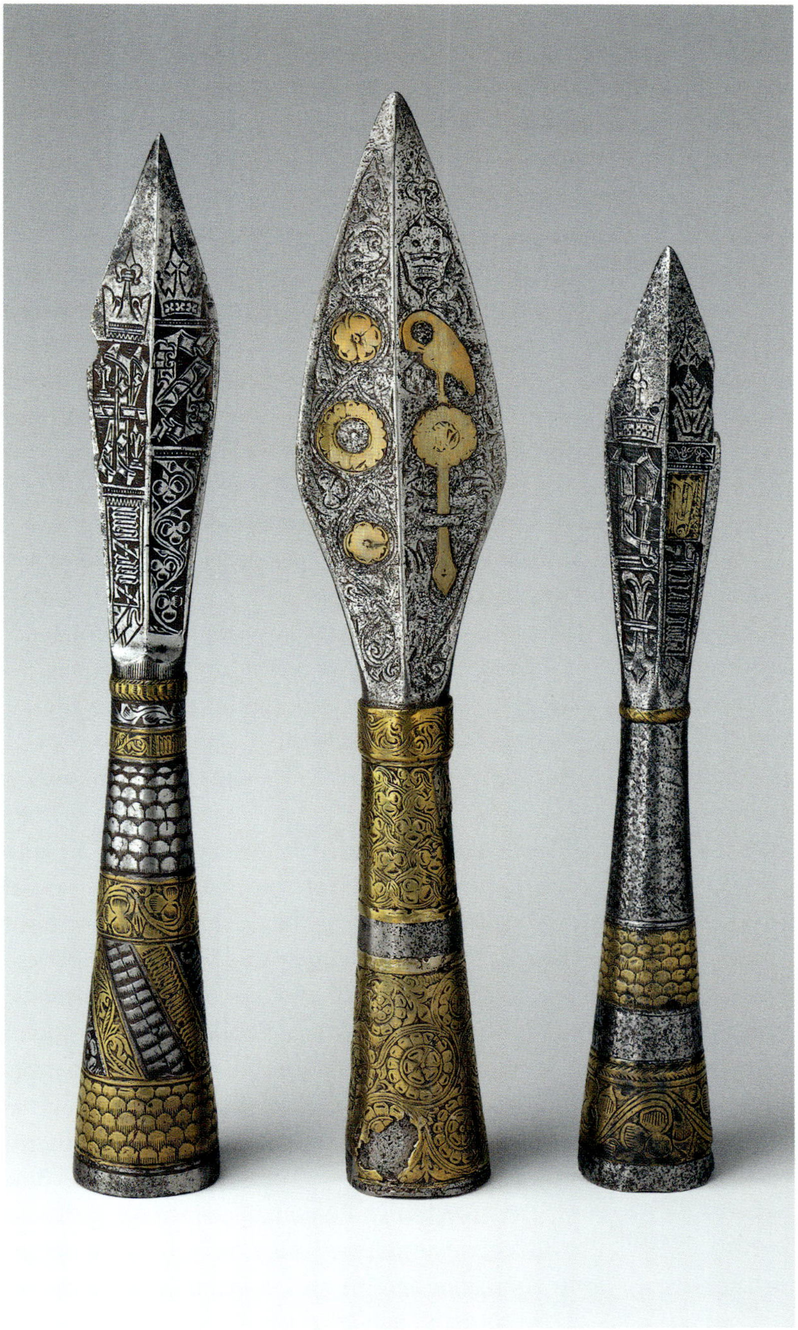

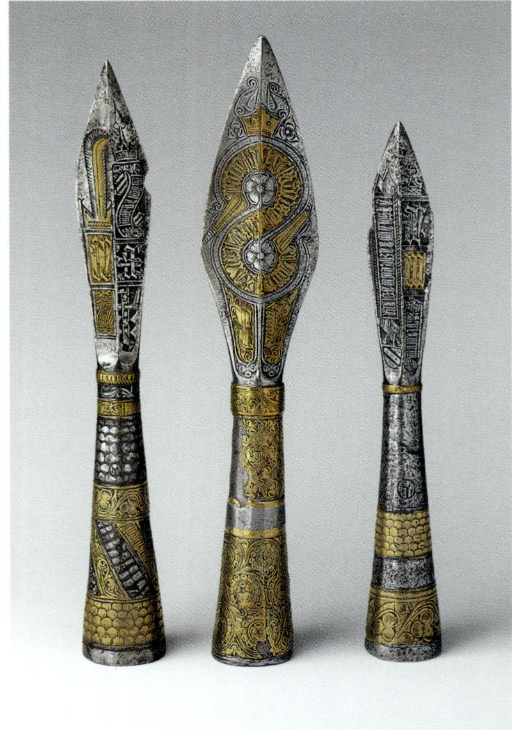

Catalogue 47 Obverse (left), reverse (below)

Obverse, right flange: AE [intertwined crosswise; prob. monogram for *Albertus Elisabeth*]; WARVY / WOKA (protect your eye); T [meaning unknown]
Reverse, left flange: X [monogram of Christ]; ZDARZ / BVO[H] (All hail, O God)
Reverse, right flange: S [meaning unknown][2]
Socket, encircling the top: MAMYLA MAMYLA (my dear [or: my love]) ([repeated twice])
Socket, on diagonal bands: MARYA / PANO / MARYA PANO (Virgin Mary) [repeated twice]; M; [monogram for *Marya* (Mary)] [repeated four times]

Catalogue 47b is unique among the group not only in shape but especially in the iconography and its arrangement.[3] The socket is almost entirely overlaid with two sheets of copper alloy, engraved with dense foliate scrolls of roses and clover leaves, respectively, perhaps allusions to Mary and the Trinity. On what appears to be the obverse of the point, engraved combined clover leaves and rose vines cover almost the entire surface of both flanges. The spare copper-alloy inlay includes a pelican below a crown—a symbol of Christ—which stands on a rosette containing the royal monogram AR. Issuing from the rosette, and threaded through the minions of a Gothic lower-case letter M, is an extension, once interpreted as the stem of the rosette, but that could also be the long end of a stylized belt. A large inverted S-shaped scroll beneath a crown dominates the reverse; it bears a partially legible inscription that is undoubtedly a pious invocation of God. The inscriptions on this head are only on the point proper and are arranged as follows:

Obverse, right flange: AR [prob. monogram for *Albertus rex*]; M [monogram for *Marya* (Mary)]
Reverse, overall: *S* reversed [prob. just scroll motif] and PANE / BOZY / SANSE[Y / . . . KLY /

RACYS (?)] / AMEN (O Lord God [indecipherable] Amen) Reverse, left flange: Y [prob. monogram for *Yesus* (Jesus)]
Reverse, right flange: R [poss. monogram for *rex*]

Catalogue 47c is somewhat plainer: its socket shows two bands of copper alloy inlay, engraved with a foliate scroll of clover leaves and scales, respectively, as well as two steel bands exhibiting traces of engraved decoration.[4] The ornament on the point includes a long pious inscription, an unidentified coat of arms (a shield displaying a bend), and two crowned monograms; the inscriptions are arranged as follows:

Obverse, left flange: VAK / SEM / NABOZRE / MYLOSTE (Go, with God's grace) / MA / MYLA (my dear [or: my love])
Obverse, right flange: AR [prob. monogram for *Albertus rex*] / M [monogram for *Marya* (Mary)]
Reverse, left flange and right flange: Y [prob. monogram for *Yesus* (Jesus)]
Reverse, right flange: PANE / MYLEY (sweet Lord)

The Museum's three heads belong to a large group, often simply referred to as "ceremonial arrowheads," more than thirty of which have been recorded. They vary in size and shape, but most are about twice the size of conventional, plain missile heads for handheld weapons. The Museum's examples and one in Istanbul are the four largest and most elaborately decorated specimens in the group.[5] While no two bolt heads in the group appear to share an identical combination of motifs in their decoration, the specifically Bohemian iconography found on all the examples—sometimes in conjunction with royal monograms and inscriptions in medieval Czech—and the similar overall style of decoration indicate that all these arrow heads and bolt heads come from Bohemia and that at least the majority of the recorded examples were made in the same workshop, possibly the royal armory at Prague. Catalogues 47a and 47c and the bolt head in Istanbul are engraved with the so-called Turkish arsenal mark (fig. 6.6), suggesting that they were taken as loot or trophies from castles or wagon trains captured by Ottoman troops during the fifteenth or sixteenth century.[6]

The precise function of these enigmatic objects remains unclear. Their size and elaborate decoration leave little doubt, however, that they served a ceremonial rather than a practical purpose. Since contemporary illustrations occasionally show men-at-arms and military commanders holding oversize arrows, the most likely explanation is that they were batons of command or other insignia of rank, perhaps for officers in the royal household serving as captains of archers or crossbowmen or holding a royal office such as master of the hunt. During the first half of the fifteenth century, probably as a direct result of the Hussite Wars (1419–34/36), Bohemian mercenaries and their commanders played prominent roles in central European feuds and warfare; not until the second half of the fifteenth century would their importance become overshadowed by the emerging German and Swiss mercenaries.[7] Against this background, it is probably no coincidence that all recorded examples of Bohemian ceremonial projectile heads appear to date from the first half of the fifteenth century.

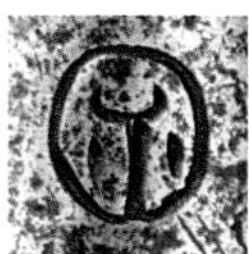

Figure 6.6

48. Quiver

Central Europe (possibly Germany), probably early 16th century
Wood (probably birch), tanned hide (possibly badger), paper, leather, iron alloy
H. 17⁹⁄₁₆ in. (44.6 cm); W. bottom 11⁷⁄₁₆ in. (29 cm); Wt. 15.8 oz. (448 g)
Bashford Dean Memorial Collection, Funds from various donors, 1929 (29.158.646a)

Ex coll.: Prince Carl of Prussia, Berlin; Bashford Dean, Riverdale, New York

Reference: Hiltl 1876–77, no. 746

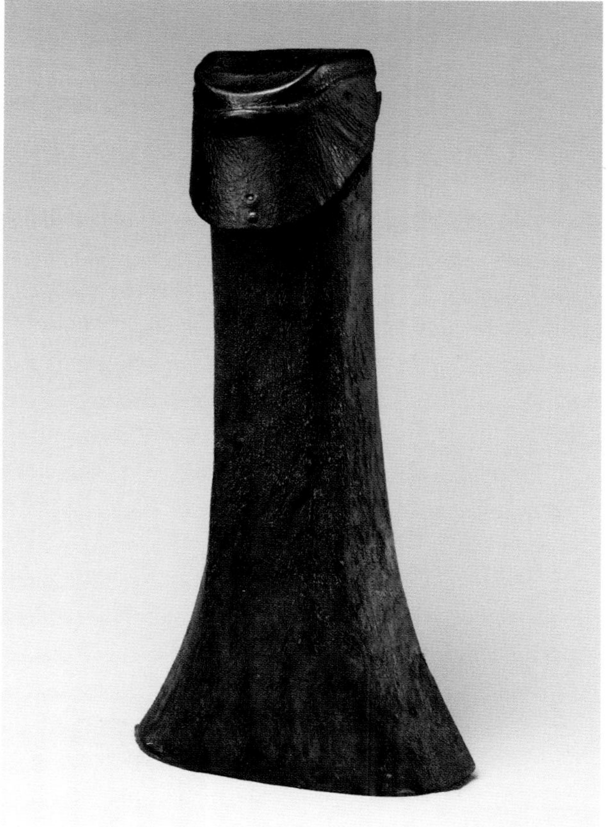

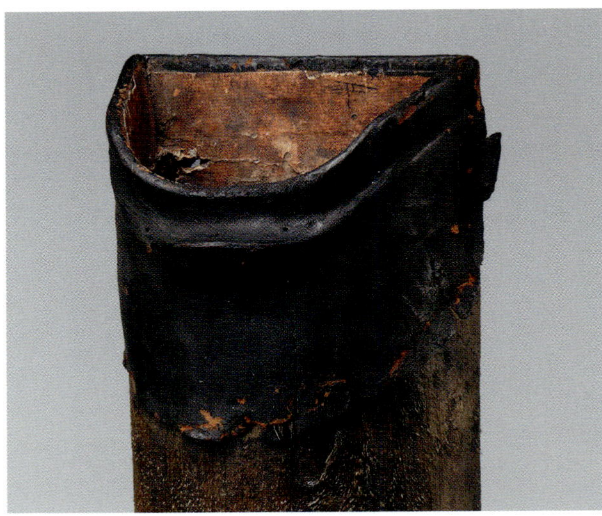

Figure 6.7

Quick access to a ready supply of projectiles was essential both in war and during the hunt. Crossbowmen on foot and on horseback usually carried their bolts in quivers, almost invariably worn at one's side, either hanging from a strap worn across the opposite shoulder or attached to a belt.

This quiver is funnel shaped, with a wide, flat bottom, curved sides, rounded front, flat back, and a small opening at the top. The body is made from thin wood, probably birch, covered on the front and sides with a single piece of hide, possibly of badger, which has apparently been glued down; the piece wraps around the rear corners but does not cover the back or bottom; only traces of hair remain. The slanted mouth, which has a pronounced lip in the front, is reinforced all around with dark leather. At the back, a lid is attached by two simple hinges formed by slits in the leather through which a leather strap is threaded; a suspension or fastening strap is missing. Most of the quiver's interior is unfinished, except for a band of about three inches at the top, which is lined with red paper (fig. 6.7).

This construction was common throughout central Europe; in addition, from the fourteenth to the first half of the sixteenth century, quivers were often covered with fur. Although visually attractive and especially appropriate for hunting equipment, the practice did not serve aesthetic purposes alone: the fur provided protection from the elements, acted as camouflage, and muffled any noise from rattling bolts. Other features are also predominantly functional: the quiver's triangular shape offered more room at the bottom for the bolts' delicate fletchings, protecting them from damage (as bolts were always stored heads up), while the red paper lining presumably provided a visual guide and masked bloodstains. One of the most detailed depictions of this type of a quiver may be seen in Holbein the Elder's famous *Martyrdom of Saint Sebastian* (fig. 5.3). Similar quivers survive in a number of collections in Dresden,[1] Munich,[2] Nuremberg,[3] Philadelphia,[4] Vienna,[5] and Worcester, Massachusetts.[6]

Quivers with a distinctly flaring bottom are often dated to the late fifteenth century. However, pictorial evidence suggests that fifteenth-century examples had predominantly straight sides, which only became noticeably curved about the turn of the sixteenth century. Accordingly, most genuine fur quivers with curved sides probably date to about 1500 or just after. What makes it problematic to establish the authenticity of surviving examples, possibly including the present one, is the fact that copies of such quivers were made in the nineteenth and twentieth centuries.[7]

Hans Wagner the Elder
Southern German (Munich), recorded 1539–56

49. Bolt Box, Probably Made for William IV, Duke of Bavaria

Germany (Munich), dated 1539
Wood (lid and front panel: fruitwood, possibly pear; bottom: walnut; inlay: possibly sycamore; later repairs: mahogany moldings and Indian rosewood veneers on sides), staghorn, iron, gold, red and white paste, paper
H. 3⅚₁₆ in. (8.4 cm); W. 16 in. (40.6 cm); D. 7³¹⁄₃₂ in. (20.2 cm)
Purchase, Bashford Dean Fund, 1969 (69.199)

Ex coll.: Frédéric Spitzer, Paris; Parke-Bernet, New York

References: Spitzer sale 1929, p. 101, lot 256; Parke-Bernet sale 1969, p. 90, lot 90; Wilson [1970], p. 320; Krempel 1970, pp. 419–21; Nickel 1971b; von Rohr 1972, p. 52; Schalkhausser 1974, p. 26

Crossbowmen carried their personal supplies of utilitarian projectiles for war and hunting in quivers (cat. 48). From the fifteenth century on, however, projectiles of superior quality, intended for shooting competitions, were often stored in bolt boxes, both for transport and safekeeping. The dimensions of this flattened, rectangular box indicate that it once served as a container for such target bolts; it is especially noteworthy for its extensive decoration.

Now comprehensively restored, this box was originally made mainly of fruitwood and walnut.[1] Instead of a single central lock that opens with a key, the box is secured and opened by means of two iron screw keys, one at each top front corner, which move internal bars that engage corresponding hooked pegs, all of iron alloy. Modern additions and repairs include the decorative mahogany moldings and the rosewood panels on the right and back sides. Likewise of a later date is the marbled paper lining.[2]

The box's principal decoration consists of flush inlay on the outside and inside of the lid and on the left side, front, and right side of the box, executed mainly in staghorn, but with some application of wood, possibly sycamore, and red and white paste. In addition, the iron-alloy hinges and hooked pegs of the lock are gilded. On the lid, divided by a baluster-shaped column, two large scenes beneath scallop-shell ornaments and pairs of festoons depict scenes from the medieval legend of Virgil and Febilla (fig. 6.8); they correspond with a similar arrangement on the lid's inner side—although beneath more modestly decorated arches—containing what may be a Fountain of Youth and Orpheus among the animals.

The last two scenes are framed by a band running along the outer edges, which contains a rhyming inscription in somewhat corrupted German:

O WEIИ DV EDLE' LAИCZMAИ • KA= // IИ PESER⁻GESELE ICH ИIE GEWĀ • DEИ ICH LIEWE' WILL PEI MIER WISSEИ • WĀ // ICH ZV MORGĒ HAB AИGEPISEИ • VD // BESCHIRM MICH VO' DE' STRAVCHEИ • WA ICH DIE STIEG HIИAW SOLT HAVCHE⁻ (O wine, you noble fellow countryman / No better companion I never won / Who I'd prefer to know by my side / When in the morning I have eaten my first bite [?] / And protect me from falling / Whenever I sneak down the stairs)

The sides and front of the box show mermen and mermaids; corresponding to the top and inside of the lid, the front panel is divided into four arcaded fields by baluster-shaped columns. A merman and mermaid on the inner fields hold scrolls inscribed M.D. XXX V IIII IAR and HANS WAGNER PIXNSC HIF TER, respectively—undoubtedly the year of the box's

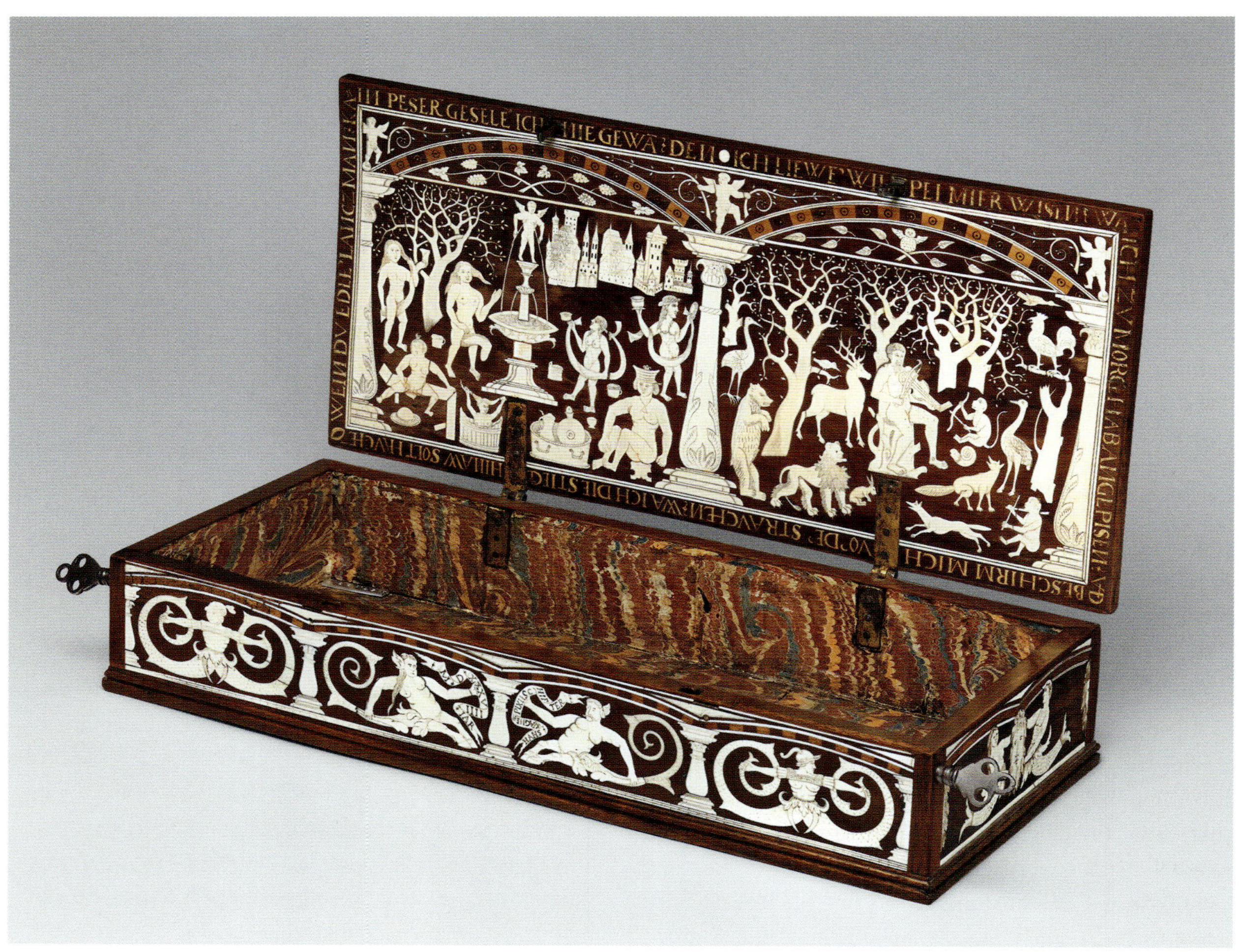

manufacture (1539) and the signature of its maker, Hans Wagner, who identifies himself as a gunstock maker (fig. 6.9).

The Museum's box is distinguished by the extensive embellishment of its main surfaces, an unusual locking mechanism, and the fact that it is signed and dated by its maker. Another box, in Munich, although unsigned and undated, is so similar in the style of decoration as to support an attribution to the same hand (fig. 6.10). The inlay on the Munich example shares the same overall arrangement of baluster-shaped columns supporting flat arches and includes fantastical animals; candelabra-shaped pedestals, one supporting a depiction of Adam and Eve; the arms of the dukes of Bavaria; and a putto holding a shield and helmet, the latter the arms of the painters' guild. Mythological figures, grotesques, and four scenes from a siege embellish the sides and front of the box. An analogous inscription consists of mottoes and monograms that, together with the ducal arms, identify the Munich box as the property of William IV of Bavaria (r. 1508–50). The presence of the arms of the painters' guild suggests that the box may have been a gift, possibly presented on the occasion of the duke's marriage to Maria Jacobäa of Baden in 1522.[3]

By contrast, the iconography of the four scenes on the Museum's box is more complex and open to interpretation. On top, the legend of Virgil and Febilla is one of passion, betrayal, and revenge (fig. 6.8). Throughout the Middle Ages and the Renaissance the Roman poet Virgil (70–19 B.C.) enjoyed great popularity. His epic poem, the *Aeneid*, was read as a standard work on Roman history and retold as a courtly romance, while his *Eclogue* 4 was read as having prophetic Christian significance. The *Aeneid* was sometimes also used for fortune-telling, and by association its author came to be regarded as a sorcerer, the protagonist of apocryphal tales. In one of these, Virgil fell in love with a beautiful Roman woman, the emperor's daughter Febilla; at first, she rejected him but at last she consented to a secret nighttime rendezvous within the well-guarded palace. Febilla hoisted Virgil up a wall in a basket, but abandoned him halfway, thereby exposing the sorcerer to public humiliation. The scorned lover took revenge with a spell that extinguished all of Rome's fires, which could only be rekindled one by one from Febilla's sex.

The right-hand scene on the lid of the bolt box shows the hapless Virgil suspended from a large, palatial structure, while in the background what appears to be a witch flies astride a pitchfork. On the left, a fully robed Febilla is surrounded by Romans (in sixteenth-century costume) holding up candles tipped with red flames. And although contemporary artists rarely missed the story's inherent opportunity to show a partially exposed female body, in this particular case, the numerous lit candles and Febilla's

frazzled hair suggest that her ordeal is almost over.[4]

This episode belongs to a tradition of cautionary tales about the wiles of women, but a connection—if indeed there is any—with the lid's interior scenes is not immediately apparent. On the inside of the lid, the scene on the right depicts Orpheus playing his lyre to the animals, while in the scene on the left bathing nude females surround a fountain topped by a figure of Eros. It has been suggested that the bathing women might be the maenads who killed Orpheus, which would imply a somber theme on the Museum's box, in contrast with the happier iconography on the presumed wedding gift in Munich.[5] However, the interior scenes can be read differently, perhaps in a more romantic vein: in the fourth book of Virgil's *Georgics*, the poet describes Orpheus as "unhappy by no fault of his. . . . Soothing his

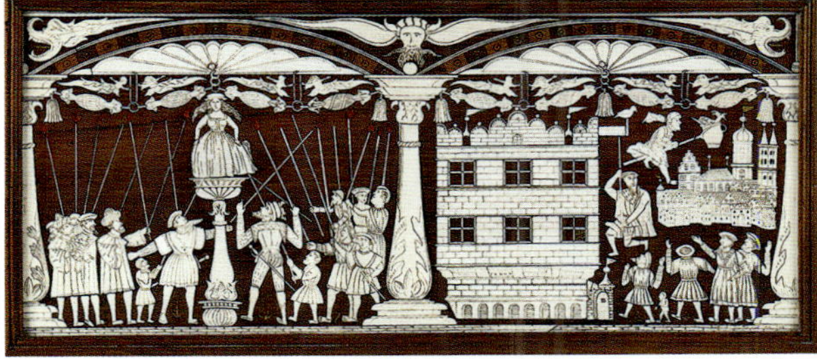

Figure 6.8

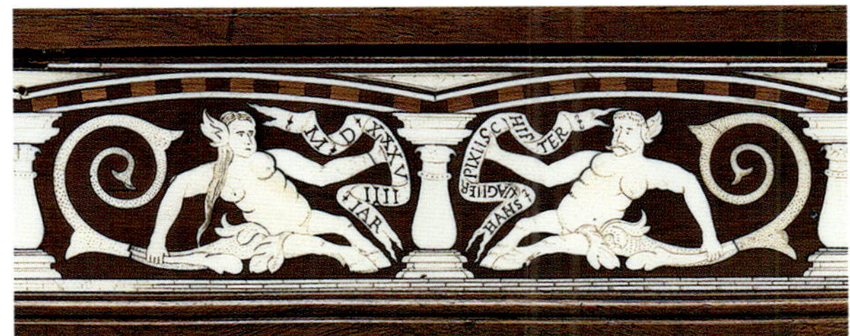

Figure 6.9

love-pain,"[6] while the bathing scene might depict a Fountain of Youth, a popular Renaissance motif that celebrated beauty but also warned against its transitoriness.[7]

Previously unidentified, the source for the inscription inside the lid of the Metropolitan's box is a German toast, or "wine-salute" (*Weingruß*), from a collection of similarly secular rhymes (*Weinsegen*) that would be recited before and after drinking. The authorship of these verses has been tentatively attributed to Hans Rosenplüt (ca. 1400–ca. 1460), a Nuremberg gun maker and poet.[8] In the early sixteenth century the rhymes were published anonymously under the title *Rebhännslein* ("Grapevine Johnny") and were soon sung to the tunes of popular drinking songs.[9] The inscription on the Metropolitan's

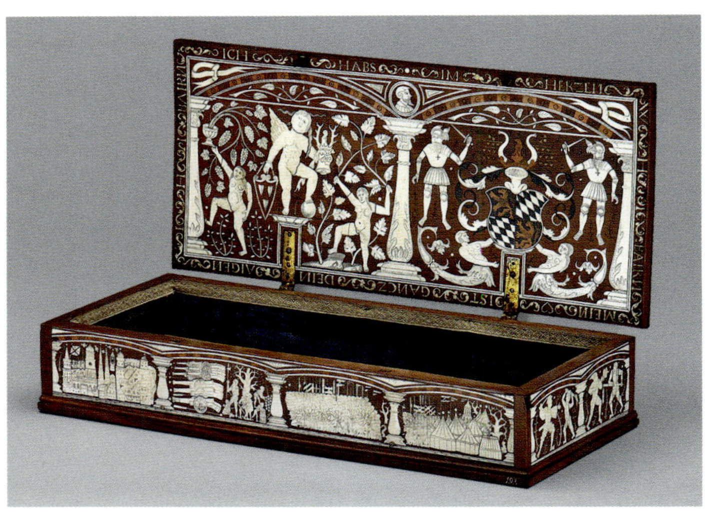

Figure 6.10 Attributed to Hans Wagner the Elder (act. ca. 1520–ca. 1550). Bolt box made for William IV, duke of Bavaria. German, after 1522. Bayerisches Nationalmuseum, Munich (R 193)

box begins with lines 1 to 4 from the collection's ninth wine-salute, but concludes with two lines that were apparently plucked at random from another stanza farther on in the salute.[10] The original verses and other drinking songs in the *Rebhännslein* echo the sentiment that he who does not appreciate wine, women, and song does not know how to live.[11] In conjunction with the celebration of female beauty and a genuinely lovesick Orpheus—the latter corresponding to Virgil's description of him— the iconography of the Metropolitan's box thus appears to be rather more nuanced than previously suggested. In particular, the juxtaposition of a scene described by the real Virgil with a depiction of the poet's apocryphal alter ego being tricked by a woman reveals a surprisingly sophisticated composition for a box made by a gunstock maker. The similarity of the boxes, especially their elaborate decoration, suggests that the Metropolitan's example was also made for, and perhaps commissioned by, Duke William.

Information about the box's maker, Hans Wagner, is scarce.[12] During the 1530s a stock maker by the name of Hanns Wagner is recorded as making shafts for firearms and staff weapons for the court of Cardinal Matthias Lang von Wellenburg (1468–1540), prince-archbishop of Salzburg.[13] Whether this is, indeed, the same artisan or a coincidence of names—*Wagner* means wheelwright or cartwright— is at present impossible to say. In Munich, the name and profession were apparently shared by a father and son: a city council record of 1556 refers to "Hans Wagner, son of the old gunstock maker," and a gunstock maker by that name was still active there in 1577.[14] Given these dates, it was most likely the elder Wagner who made the two bolt boxes, which remain his only recorded works to date.[15]

50. Bolt Box with Accessories

Germany (probably Dresden), ca. 1735–50
Purchase, Bashford Dean Gift, 1970 (1970.102.2a–k)

a. Bolt box (.2a) with removable tray (.2b–g) and key (.2h)
Wood (body and tray: poplar; veneer and moldings: walnut;
feet: plum), iron alloy
H. 4 7/16 in. (11.2 cm); W. 15 15/16 in. (40.4 cm); D. 8 3/32 in.
(20.5 cm)

b. Target bolt (.2i)
Wood (ash), copper alloy, feathers (probably goose), staghorn
L. 12 31/32 in. (32.9 cm); L. head 1 1/8 in. (2.9 cm); Diam. head
13/32 in. (1.1 cm); Wt. 1.3 oz. (37 g)

c. Target bolt (.2j)
Wood (ash), copper alloy, feathers (probably goose), staghorn
L. 13 in. (33 cm); L. head 1 1/16 in. (3 cm); Diam. head 7/16 in.
(1.2 cm); Wt. 1.3 oz. (38 g)

d. Combination tool (.2k)
Steel
L. 5 7/8 in. (14.9 cm); W. 1 17/32 in. (3.9 cm); Wt. 3.7 oz. (105 g)

Ex coll.: Armory of Frederick Augustus I "the Strong," duke
of Saxony, and, as Augustus II, king of Poland, and that of
his son Frederick Augustus II, who succeeded to both titles,
Moritzburg Castle; Royal Gun Cabinet, Dresden; Historisches
Museum, Dresden; Sotheby's 1970, p. 8, lot 38

References: Sotheby's sale 1970, p. 8, lot 38; Nickel 1970,
p. 66; Nickel 1974, p. 229

Mark:

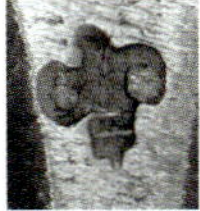

In eastern Germany, where crossbows were held
in particularly high regard, the dukes of Saxony
kept crossbows and accessories at all of their residences (cats. 13, 14). This equipment was provided
to courtiers and other guests on the occasion of

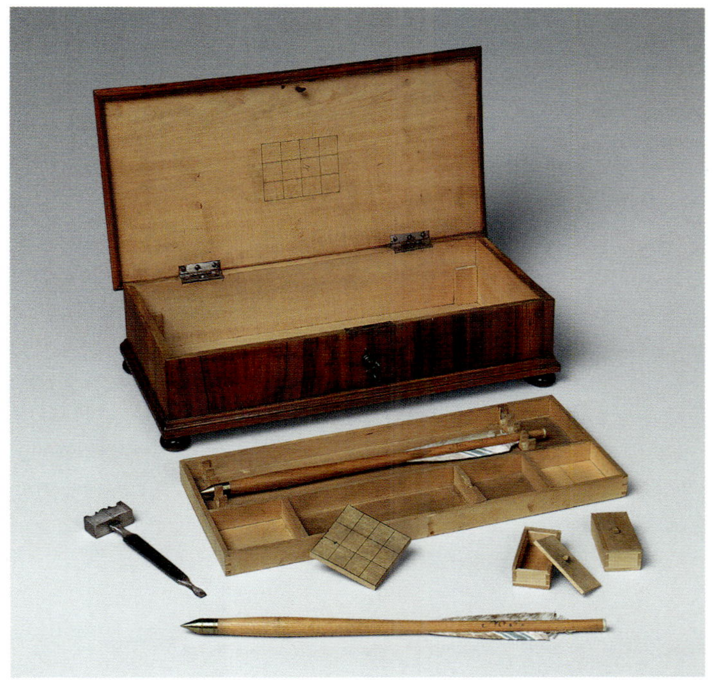

shooting competitions, a regular part of aristocratic
festivities. Crossbow accessories—that is, bolts and
tools—were often stored in bolt boxes.

This box has a lid secured by two iron hinges at
the rear and an iron lock in front, with its key, and
contains a removable tray. The latter is divided into
compartments, which include two removable containers; the bottom of the box would have held
another layer of bolts. The box came into the
Museum's collection containing two bolts, a small
removable wooden scoreboard, and a small hammer-
headed combination tool. Inside the lid, a rectangular grid of twelve fields has been drawn in black ink
and then varnished so that scores could be noted in
chalk or charcoal, and easily erased. On top, the box
is marked in black paint with the letter M (for
Moritzburg) and the number 11; the same number

appears in pencil on the underside of the tray and on the back of the removable scoreboard.

The two target bolts are almost identical in size, weight, and appearance, with heads and collars of differently colored copper alloys, and shafts of ash, capped at the back with a staghorn butt plate. Each bolt is fitted with two flights (probably goose feathers), one of which has been partially bleached and colored with a pattern of green and white stripes. The bolts are inscribed on the shaft in dark ink, one marked No 5, the other, No. 8 and 11. Both shafts display illegible traces of other markings.

The combination tool comprises a rectangular head and a flat handle. The latter has a rasping surface on one side and a filing surface on the other and terminates in a small screwdriver. Between the head and the handle, the neck is struck with a small maker's mark of unidentified shape, perhaps a stylized fleur-de-lis.

The Museum's bolt box belongs to a series of identical examples formerly stored at Moritzburg Castle, one of the foremost hunting residences of the dukes of Saxony near Dresden. The boxes were intended to accompany two series of twelve crossbows, presumably made by the court crossbow maker Johann Gottfried Hänisch and delivered to the castle in 1728 (cat. 13). Ten of the boxes survive in Dresden; none retains its complete contents, but several still include similar bolts and identical combination tools, struck with the same mark.[1] The two small containers of the tray apparently held white chalk and charcoal, respectively. An inventory of 1733 states that the original crossbow delivery of 1728 included, among other accessories, twenty-four metal canisters for storing bolts. However, it does not mention wooden bolt boxes, which means that the Moritzburg boxes must have been made, or at least delivered, slightly later.[2] An 1856 inventory confirms that the twenty-four crossbows were stored with their accessories, which now included twelve wooden bolt boxes, as well as the twenty-four metal canisters.[3]

Notes

Preface and Acknowledgments

1   For a discussion of this topic, see Monte S Turner, *The Not So Diabolical Crossbow: A Re-Examination of Innocent II's Supposed Ban of the Crossbow at the Second Lateral Council* (n.p., 2004).

EUROPEAN CROSSBOWS: AN INTRODUCTION

1   Jean Liebel, *Springalds and Great Crossbows*, trans. Juliet Vale, Royal Armouries Monograph 5 (Leeds, 1998); Peter Purton, "The Myth of the Mangonel: Torsion Artillery in the Middle Ages," *Arms and Armour* 3, no. 1 (Spring 2006), pp. 79–90; Thom Richardson, "Springald Sizes in 14th Century England," in *ICOMAM 50: Papers on Arms and Military History 1957–2007*, ed. Robert Douglas Smith (Leeds, 2007), pp. 326–31.

2   This problem is described in chapter LXXI of Yves Christe and Antoine d'Escayrac-Lauture, *Gaston Phoebus: Das Buch Der Jagd/Gaston Febus: Le livre de chasse*, 2 vols., MS. M.1044, the Pierpont Morgan Library, New York, facsimile ed. (Luzern, 2005), vol. 2, pp. 197–98.

3   http://www.oxforddictionaries.com/definition/english/popinjay

4   Egon Harmuth, *Die Armbrust: Ein Handbuch* (Graz, 1986), pp. 60–62.

5   Richard Kinseher, *Der Bogen in Kultur, Musik und Medizin, als Werkzeug und Waffe* (Norderstedt, 2005), p. 231.

1   EARLY CROSSBOWS

Introduction

1   For the study of early crossbows see C[harles] A[lexander], baron de Cosson, "The Crossbow of Ulrich V. Count of Wurtemburg [*sic*], 1460, with Remarks on Its Construction," *Archaeologia*, ser. 2, 53, part 2 (January 1893), pp. 445–64; Egon Harmuth, *Die Armbrust: Ein Handbuch* (Graz, 1986), especially pp. 20–71; Arthur G. Credland, "The Crossbow in Europe: An Historical Introduction," in William Forbes Paterson, *A Guide to the Crossbow* ([Burnham], 1990), pp. 13–24; Josef Alm, *European Crossbows: A Survey*, trans. H. Bartlett Wells, ed. G. M. Wilson (London, 1994), pp. 6–54; Valérie Serdon, *Armes du diable: Arcs et arbalètes au Moyen Âge* (Rennes, 2005); and Holger

Richter, *Die Hornbogenarmbrust: Geschichte und Technik* (Ludwigshafen, 2006).

2   One of the earliest instances is found on a weapon with a composite bow and a tiller entirely veneered in polished staghorn (Staatliche Kunstsammlungen/Rüstkammer, Dresden [U 143]); Richter, *Die Hornbogenarmbrust*, pp. 98–99.

3   Harmuth, *Die Armbrust: Ein Handbuch*, pp. 86–92, 113–20.

4   Paterson, *Guide to the Crossbow*, p. 36.

5   For the decoration of bows and tillers on early crossbows, see Harmuth, *Die Armbrust: Ein Handbuch*, pp. 93–94, 118–20, and 133–34, and individual examples in Richter, *Die Hornbogenarmbrust*, pp. 28–92.

Catalogue 1

1   The remains of Montfort Castle are located some twenty-two miles (35.6 km) north of Haifa, in the Upper Galilee region of present-day Israel; in 1926, the area was part of the British Mandate Territory of Palestine.

2   Bernd Zimmermann, *Mittelalterliche Geschossspitzen: Kulturhistorische, archäologische und archäometallurgische Untersuchungen*, Schweizer Beiträge zur Kulturgeschichte und Archäologie des Mittelalters 26 (Basel, 2000), p. 19.

3   Rockefeller Archaeological Museum, Jerusalem (37.234); Dirk Breiding, "Weapons and Armour," in *Montfort I: History, Early Research and Recent Studies*, ed. Adrian J. Boas (Leiden, forthcoming).

Catalogue 2

1   Scena Castle, near Merano. The majority of the collection of arms and armor in Scena Castle, today owned by Count Spiegelfeld, was brought there during the mid-nineteenth century, when the castle was in the possession of Archduke John of Austria (1782–1859).

2   Spišský Hrad/Spiš Castle, Slovakia (inv. no. unknown).

3   Kunsthistorisches Museum/Hofjagd- und Rüstkammer, Vienna (A 464); Bruno Thomas and Ortwin Gamber, *Katalog der Leibrüstkammer 1. Teil—Der Zeitraum von 500 bis 1530* (Vienna, 1976), p. 201. The binding and stirrup appear to be modern replacements. Beaufort-Spontin proposed in Marco Abate et al., *1500 circa: Leonardo e Paola, una coppia diseguale: De ludo globi, il gioco del mondo: alle soglie dell'impero*, exh. cat. (Milan and Innsbruck, 2000), p. 506, no. 3-2-4, that the Vienna example came from the Imperial Arsenal at Innsbruck, but unfortunately provided no reference.

4   Kremsmünster Abbey (inv. no. unknown), unpublished.

Catalogue 3

1   This discussion updates Dirk Breiding, "The Crossbow of Count Ulrich V of Württemberg," *Metropolitan Museum Journal* 44 (2009), pp. 61–87; in particular the recent identification of the inlay as staghorn, not ivory; the present hemp binding of the bow is supported by additional string between the tiller and the binding; see ibid., pp. 64–65, fig. 6. Also, for purposes of new catalog photography, the replacement nut was removed.

2   Encyclopædia Britannica Online, s.v. "Doxology," accessed May 16, 2013. http://www.britannica.com/EBchecked/topic/170553/doxology.

3   Alternatively, although this must remain speculative, the phrase may include an encrypted "signature" of Heinrich Heid; see Breiding, "Crossbow of Count Ulrich V," pp. 72–77.

4   A close connection between manuscript production and inscriptions on secular objects has recently been persuasively taken up by Radway, who pointed out that part of a different German inscription—*lach lip lach* (laugh love [or: dear] laugh)—at the end of another manuscript similarly corresponds to inscriptions found on two bone-veneered saddles that most likely date from the mid-fifteenth century. One of these saddles is also in the Metropolitan Museum's collections (fig. 1.11). Since the manuscript is a treatise on hunting, and this particular copy was commissioned for Ulrich V, it is tempting to attribute ownership of one (or both) of the saddles to the count of Württemberg; see Robyn Dora Radway, "In the Name of Saint George: Ivory Saddles from the Fifteenth Century" (honors thesis, University of Central Florida, Orlando, 2009), pp. 39–41 and 50–51. Kurt Lindner, *Von Falken, Hunden und Pferden: Deutsche Albertus-Magnus Übersetzungen aus der ersten Hälfte des 15. Jahrhunderts*, Quellen und Studien zur Geschichte der Jagd 7/8, 2 vols. (Berlin, 1962), vol. 1, pp. 75–76, identified the text as one based on the writings of Albertus Magnus (ca. 1200–1280) and Count Ulrich as the manuscript's original owner. Whether *lach lip lach* can be specifically linked to the Württemberg court or will turn out to be a phrase as widely disseminated as *hab got lieb* remains to be ascertained.

5   Josef Alm, *European Crossbows: A Survey*, trans. H. Bartlett Wells, ed. G. M. Wilson (London, 1994), p. 49.

6   The Wallace Collection, London (A 1032); James Gow Mann, *European Arms and Armour: Text with Historical Notes and Illustration*, 2 vols., Wallace Collection Catalogues (London, 1962), pp. 477–78; A. Vesey B. Norman, *European Arms and*

Armour Supplement, Wallace Collection Catalogues (London, 1986), p. 202.

7 The Royal Armouries Museum, Leeds (XI.11); Ronald Lauder collection, New York; and Royal Ontario Museum, Toronto (906.11.5a), respectively; see Tower of London Armouries, *Crossbows*, Treasures of the Tower (London, 1976), pp. 6–7; Dorchester, "The Art of the Crossbow," in *The International Arms & Armour Exposition,* (London, 1983), p. 59–60, no. 2; Stuart W. Pyhrr, "Arms and Armor," in *The Ronald S. Lauder Collection: Selections from the 3rd Century BC to the 20th Century, Germany, Austria, and France*, exh. cat. (New York, 2011), p. 201; and K. Corey Keeble, *European Crossbows in the Royal Ontario Museum, Toronto* (Bloomfield, Ont., 2008), pp. 40–42.

8 Grandson Castle, Grandson (B 132); unpublished.

9 Kunsthistorisches Museum/Hofjagd- und Rüstkammer, Vienna (A 108); Bruno Thomas and Ortwin Gamber, *Katalog der Leibrüstkammer 1. Teil—Der Zeitraum von 500 bis 1530* (Vienna, 1976), pp. 77–78.

Catalogue 4

1 Visual examination of the wood remained inconclusive, while invasive sampling was deemed too difficult.

2 The stirrup, nut, bowstring, and much of the bow's outer layers of animal sinew and protective birch-bark covering are missing. A "badly frayed bowstring" was apparently attached to the weapon when it entered the Metropolitan Museum; Bashford Dean, "A Crossbow of Matthias Corvinus, 1489," *The Metropolitan Museum of Art Bulletin* 20, no. 6 (June 1925), p. 156. The present binding is strengthened by a similar string support—like the one on cat. 3; since the two crossbows come from different collections and were acquired by the Museum at different times, the supports were most likely added in modern times, probably in the Museum's Department of Arms and Armor.

3 Johann Siebmacher, *J. Siebmacher's Grosses und allgemeines Wappenbuch*, ed. Otto Titan von Heffner et al., 82 vols. (Nuremberg, 1856–1938), vol. 7 (1921), p. 97.

4 Ibid., p. 97.

5 Ibid., p. 97.

6 Alternatively, it is conceivable that the arms might refer to Matthias's only, but illegitimate, son, János Corvinus (1473–1504). Matthias had aggressively promoted János as heir to the Hungarian throne, since Matthias's marriage to Beatrice of Aragon (1457–1508) had remained without issue. However, there is no record of János ever having used the royal coat of arms; his private and official seals, dating from 1490 to 1503, show only the ring-bearing raven, which also adorned the pommel of his sword, as depicted in a portrait

of the young prince in the Bayerische Staatsgemäldesammlung, Munich (12441); for the question of succession, see Enikö Spekner, " . . . to be judged worthy of your illustrious father and to rule over the Hungarians . . . ": Matthias' Struggle for John Corvinus' Succession," in *Matthias Corvinus, the King: Tradition and Renewal in the Hungarian Court 1458–1490*, ed. Péter Farbaky et al., exh. cat. (Budapest, 2008), pp. 513–23; for the portrait, see Péter Farbaky and Erika Kiss, "Portrait of John Corvinus," in *Matthias Corvinus, the King*, pp. 516–17.

7 Wladyslaw Kuzdral-Kicki, *Der Drachenorden: Genese, Gründung und Entartung* (Munich, 1978), p. 91.

8 The symbol of the order was a winged dragon in a curled position, with the end of its tail wrapped around its neck, and with a cross, or sometimes two, depicted on its back.

9 The Wallace Collection, London (A 1032); James Gow Mann, *European Arms and Armour: Text with Historical Notes and Illustration*, 2 vols., Wallace Collection Catalogues (London, 1962), pp. 477–78, and A. Vesey B. Norman, *European Arms and Armour Supplement*, Wallace Collection Catalogues (London, 1986), p. 202.

10 Royal Armouries Museum, Leeds (XI.11); see Tower of London Armouries, *Crossbows*, Treasures of the Tower, (London, 1976), pp. 6–7.

11 Ronald Lauder collection, New York; Stuart W. Pyhrr, "Arms and Armor," in *The Ronald S. Lauder Collection: Selections from the 3rd Century BC to the 20th Century, Germany, Austria, and France* (New York, 2011), p. 201, fig. 69. This crossbow was formerly in the Zschille Collection, Grossenheim, Saxony; Zschille sale, Christie, Manson & Woods, London, January 25–February 1, 1897, p. 109, lot 627.

12 Royal Ontario Museum, Toronto (906.11.5a); K. Corey Keeble, *European Crossbows in the Royal Ontario Museum, Toronto* (Bloomfield, Ont., 2008), pp. 40–42.

13 See, for example, a small box for game pieces in the Metropolitan Museum (54.135) decorated with scenes of courtly love on the lid and hunting scenes around the sides.

14 Most recently, Eric Ramirez-Weaver, "Saddle, Possibly of Wenceslas IV," in *Prague: The Crown of Bohemia 1347–1437*, ed. Barbara Drake Boehm and Jiří Fajt, exh. cat. (New York, 2005); Maria Verö, "Bemerkungen zu den Beinsätteln aus der Sigismundzeit," in *Sigismundus rex et imperator: Kunst und Kultur zur Zeit Sigismunds von Luxemburg 1387–1437*, ed. Imre Takács (Mainz am Rhein, 2006), pp. 270–78; and Robyn Dora Radway, "In the Name of Saint George: Ivory Saddles from the Fifteenth Century" (honors thesis, University of Central Florida, Orlando, 2009).

15 Only two other examples are known: a relatively plain fifteenth-century weapon with a composite bow, in the collection of the Musée Cantonal d'Archéologie et d'Histoire, Lausanne (MCAHL 00736; on permanent loan to Château de Chillon), and an apparently modern example with a steel bow, sold at auction by Galerie Fischer Auktionen, Lucerne, September 9–11, 2010, p. 81, pl. 115, lot 577, labeled "of eighteenth-century manufacture."

2 Crossbows with Steel Bows

Introduction

1 For steel bows in general, see Egon Harmuth, *Die Armbrust: Ein Handbuch* (Graz, 1986), pp. 86–93, 113–18, 137–40; Holger Richter, "Die Identifizierung einer Bogenmarke," *Waffen- und Kostümkunde* 44 (2002), pp. 85–87; Jens Sensfelder, *Crossbows in the Royal Netherlands Army Museum: With a List of Names and Marks of European Crossbow Makers, Bow Smiths and Bolt Makers*, ed. Harm Stevens (Delft, 2007), p. 77; Jens Sensfelder, *Armbruste in den Kunstsammlungen der Veste Coburg* (Coburg, 2009), pp. 10, 92–99.

2 Antoine Le Roux de Lincy, "Inventaires des biens meubles et immeubles de la comtesse Mahaut d'Artois, pillés par l'armées de son neveu, en 1313," *Bibliothèque de l'École des Chartes* 13 (1852), p. 63.

3 Sensfelder, *Crossbows*, p. 77.

4 See, for example, Eduard A. Gessler, "Eine Armbrust aus der Westschweiz," *Zeitschrift für historische Waffenkunde* VIII (1920), pp. 390–91; Clement Bosson, René Géroudet, and Eugen Heer, *Armes anciennes des collections suisses*, exh. cat. (Lausanne and Geneva, 1972), p. 62, and p. 154, no. 297; and Otto Markés, *Fernwaffen im Wandel der Zeit: Waffen aus der Sammlung Otto Markés, Basel*, exh. cat. (Chur: Rätisches Museum, 1985), p. 23, fig. 7; Valérie Serdon, *Armes du diable: Arcs et arbalètes au Moyen Âge* (Rennes, 2005), figs. 116–18.

5 Harmuth, *Die Armbrust: Ein Handbuch*, pp. 84–85; superseded by Holger Richter, *Die Kunst der Armbrustmacher in Dresden* (Beucha, 2008), pp. 78–82; and Sensfelder, *Armbruste*, p. 8.

6 It must be borne in mind that, although generally helpful, the terms *Rüstung* and *Schnepper* have been used with various meanings at different times and under different circumstances in period documents, as well as interchangeably or erroneously by modern writers; for a discussion, see Richter, *Armbrustmacher in Dresden*, p. 78.

7 For a history of the development of sighting systems, see Harmuth, *Die Armbrust: Ein Handbuch*, p. 182; Egon Harmuth, "Das

Armbrust-Seitenvisier," in *Waffen- und Kostümkunde* 21 (1979), pp. 159–62; and Giannoni Bruno, "Historical Sight-Systems for Targeting: An Experience in Using the Sight-System of the Italian 'Modern' Big Crossbow," *Jahrblatt der Interessengemeinschaft Historische Armbrust* (2010), pp. 37–45.

8 For examples of weapons with painted or etched steel bows, dating from the seventeenth, eighteenth, and nineteenth centuries, see Sensfelder, *Armbruste*, pp. 24–34, 67–71; and Richter, *Armbrustmacher in Dresden*, pp. 29–31, 39–42, 59–60.

Catalogue 5

1 The wooden core could not be visually examined as it is almost entirely covered by the staghorn veneer; sample-taking was deemed too intrusive.

2 Egon Harmuth, *Die Armbrust: Ein Handbuch* (Graz, 1986), pp. 81, 99–103; and Mikael Dahlström, "Some Thoughts about Three 15th Century German Crossbows," *Jahrblatt der Interessengemeinschaft Historische Armbrust* (2011), pp. 77–81.

3 A late example with a similarly slender silhouette and overall bone veneer but engraved with motifs in a different style is an unpublished crossbow dated 1567 in the Musée d'Armes, Liège (HE.16).

4 Engraved hunting scenes very similar to those on the present crossbow form part of the elaborate decoration of an entirely veneered stock of a composite wheel-lock gun in the Museum's collection (32.75.117); unpublished. While the gun's barrel and lock appear to be authentic, albeit associated, the stock is an elaborate fake.

5 I am grateful to Franz A. Bornschlegel and Ellen Bosniak, both of the Epigraphisches Forschungs- und Dokumentationszentrum at the Ludwig-Maximilians-Universität in Munich, for their assessment of the initials and the tiny inscription. Both agree that neither the letters nor the inscription is likely to date from before the eighteenth century (email communications of May and June 2010).

6 Another instance of fake decoration was identified as early as 1862: crude monograms of Albrecht Dürer and Charles V, together with one of the latter's mottoes and the year 1521, were added to the original decoration of an early seventeenth-century crossbow in the imperial collections at Ambras Castle, near Innsbruck (inv. no. unknown); Eduard von Sacken, *Die vorzüglichsten Rüstungen und Waffen der K. K. Ambraser Sammlung, in Original-Photographien* (Vienna, 1859–62), pl. LX, vol. 2, p. 48, pl. XL; Eduard von Sacken, *Werke von Albrecht Dürer in der K. K. Ambraser Sammlung* (Vienna,1863), p. 131.

Catalogue 6

1 Claude Blair, "A Royal Swordsmith and Damascener: Diego de Çaias," *Metropolitan Museum Journal* 3 (1970), p. 149, n. 3.

2 Art Institute of Chicago (1982.3071, 1982.3073); unpublished.

3 The Dos Aguas collection, acquired jointly by the Metropolitan Museum, Archer M. Huntington, and George F. Harding in 1927, included at least six crossbows of this type (curatorial files, Department of Arms and Armor). Listed as part of the shipment to New York, upon arrival two came into the possession of Huntington, who immediately presented them to the Museum; another two were part of a group of objects destined for Harding's collection; and the remaining two were acquired by Bashford Dean (present whereabouts unknown). Harding's collection of arms and armor, including the crossbows, was eventually acquired by the Art Institute of Chicago (see n. 2 above); the pellet crossbow bears inscriptions similar to those on cat. 6b (ihs / maria / arma / orla) and is struck twice with the previously unrecorded mark of a helmet in profile.

4 At least five in the Real Armería, Madrid (J.18, J.28, J.29, J.37, J.38); Valencia de Don Juan, Conde de [Juan Bautista Crooke y Navarrot], *Catálogo histórico-descriptivo de la Real Armería de Madrid* (Madrid, 1898), pp. 281–85, figs. 239, 241, 246. Another is in the Instituto Valencia de Don Juan, Madrid (177); see José María Florit y Arizcun and Francisco Javier Sánchez Cantón, *Catálogo de las armas del Instituto de Valencia de Don Juan* (Madrid, 1927), pp. 132–33.

5 Armory of the Knights of Saint John, Valletta; for an image and brief description of one (PA 1713) among several examples, see Musée de l'Armée and Palace Armoury, *Entre le glaive et la croix: Chefs-d'œuvre de l'armurerie de Malte / Between the Battlesword and the Cross: Masterpieces from the Armoury of Malta*, exh. cat. (Paris and Valletta, 2008), pp. 304–5.

6 Armeria Reale, Turin (L.4–6); Claudio Bertolotto and Franco Mazzini, *L'Armeria Reale di Torino*, Arte e Tecnica (Busto Arsizio, 1982), p. 380. Crossbow L.6 is particularly interesting as it is signed IVAN RO/DRIGUEZ/FEHA/EN MILAN, a maker who may be identical with a certain Juan Rodriguez originally (?) from Seville; Valencia de Don Juan, *Catálogo histórico-descriptivo*, p. 291 (J.101).

7 Churburg Castle, Sluderno (CH S 322); Mario Scalini and Oswald Graf Trapp, *L'armeria Trapp di Castel Coira/Die Churburger Rüstkammer/The Armoury of the Castle of Churburg*, trans. Rudolf Wackernagel and Ian Eaves (Udine, 1996), vol. 2, p. 380. The crossbow is signed by a

certain Pedro de Olarte and dated by Scalini to ca. 1500–1510.

8 Albuquerque Museum of Art and History (1982.144.1); Walter J. Karcheski, *Arms and Armor of the Conquistador, 1492–1600: A Catalogue of Arms and Armor from the Exhibit "First Encounters: Spanish Explorations of the Caribbean and the United States, 1492–1570,"* exh. cat. (Gainesville, Fla., 1990), no. 12b.

9 The bow is signed Puebla en Madrid; Florit y Arizcun and Sánchez Cantón, *Catálogo de las armas*, p. 132.

10 J.32, J.33, J. 89, and J.91, and J.90, respectively; Valencia de Don Juan, *Catálogo histórico-descriptivo*, pp. 285, 290.

11 A good example of a successful period conversion may be seen on a slightly later English crossbow now in the Royal Armouries Museum, Leeds (XI.295); Graeme Rimer, "A Decorated 17th Century English Stonebow," in *The Twentieth Anniversary London Park Lane Arms Fair* (London, 2003), pp. 45–48.

Catalogue 7

1 Musée de l'Armée, Paris (L.66); see L. Robert, ed., *Catalogue des collections composant le Musée d'Artillerie en 1889*, vol. 3 (Paris, 1891), p. 387.

2 Deutsches Historisches Museum, Berlin (W1132); Heinrich Müller, *Gewehre, Pistolen, Revolver: Hand- und Faustfeuerwaffen vom 14.–19. Jahrhundert* (Leipzig, 1979), p. 91; and Gerhard Quaas, ed., *Hofjagd: Aus den Sammlungen des Deutschen Historischen Museums,* texts by Hans-Jörg Czech et al., exh. cat. (Berlin and Wolfratshausen, 2002), p. 78, no. 41. Another crossbow in the same collection (W1129), similar in iconography but not in technique or quality, presents a later development of this type of decoration; see Quaas, *Hofjagd*, p. 78, no. 42.

3 Royal Armouries Museum, Leeds (XI.10); Tower of London Armouries, *Crossbows, Treasures of the Tower* (London, 1976), p. 9, and Dorchester, "The Art of the Crossbow," in *The International Arms & Armour Exposition* (London, 1983), p. 59, no. 1. The bow is struck with the mark of a quartered circle crowned by five rays (see cat. 10). For the example in the Národni Muzeum, Prague (inv. no. unknown), see Dirk H. Breiding, "Die Armbrust-Ausstellung 'Arma Diaboli' in Prag," *Jahrblatt der Interessengemeinschaft historische Armbrust* (2012), pp. 81–82.

4 Historisches Museum, Basel (1888.99); Eugen Heer, "Notes on the Crossbow in Switzerland," *Arms and Armour Annual* 1 (1973), pp. 57, 64. Another crossbow, in the Kulturhistorisches Museum, Görlitz (204-1959), and previously unpublished, is probably related to this group, although its

decoration is rather inferior in quality to the weapons cited above. The museum's files suggest that this crossbow came from the Saxon city of Zittau.

5   Gerhard Quaas, *Jagdwaffen: Aus der Sammlung des Deutschen Historischen Museums,* Deutsches Historisches Museum Magazin 19 (Berlin, 1997) p. 33, cat. 30.

6   For the mark, see Eugen Heer, ed., *Der neue Støckel: Internationales Lexikon der Büchsenmacher, Feuerwaffenfabrikanten und Armbrustmacher von 1400–1900* (Schwäbisch Hall, 1979), vol. 2, p. 1483 (5039, 8494, 8495); and Jens Sensfelder, *Crossbows in the Royal Netherlands Army Museum: With a List of Names and Marks of European Crossbow Makers, Bow Smiths and Bolt Makers,* ed. Harm Stevens (Delft, 2007), p. 346 (with further examples). The two crossbows are in the Legermuseum, Delft (15774, 15772); see Sensfelder, *Crossbows,* pp. 104–7 (no. 4), 122–25 (no. 9).

7   Sensfelder, *Crossbows,* pp. 104–7 (no. 4), 122–25 (no. 9).

8   Compare, for example, the arms of the town of Freihan in Lower Silesia (modern-day Cieszków/Frejno in Poland), recorded as early as 1554, Johann Siebmacher, *Wappen der Städte und Märkte in Deutschland und den angrenzenden Ländern,* vol. 6, repr. ed. (Neustadt an der Aisch, 1974), p. 74, or the arms of the God or Good family of Unterwalden, see Erwin Poeschel, *Die Stadt St. Gallen, Die Kunstdenkmäler des Kantons St. Gallen 2* (Basel, 1957), pp. 102, 132.

Catalogue 8

1   In sixteenth-century Germany, *Affe* (monkey) is recorded as a nickname; such a sobriquet might become part of a person's formal name.

Catalogue 9

1   For the use of crossbows in the British Isles, see Arthur Credland, "The Hunting Crossbow in England," *Journal of the Society of Archer-Antiquaries* 30 (1987), pp. 44–53; and Arthur Credland, "The Crossbow in England," *Royal Armouries Yearbook* 6 (2001), pp. 81–82.

2   For the identification of the birds as ravens, see Dorchester, "The Art of the Crossbow," in *The International Arms & Armour Exposition* (London, 1983), pp. 61, 68.

3   Real Armería, Madrid (J.107, J.109, J.111); William Reid, "The Present of Spain, a Seventeenth-Century Royal Gift," *The Connoisseur* 146 (September 1960), pp. 21–26; James D. Lavin, "The Gift of James I to Felipe III of Spain," *Journal of the Arms and Armour Society* 14, no. 2 (September 1992), pp. 64–88.

4   Royal Armouries Museum, Leeds (XI 295); Graeme Rimer, "A Decorated 17th Century English Stonebow," in *The Twentieth*

Anniversary London Park Lane Arms Fair (London, 2003), pp. 46–47.

5   Dorchester, "Art of the Crossbow," pp. 68–69.

6   See, for example, a French wheel-lock pistol in the Metropolitan Museum's collection (14.25.1423), unpublished. The Alsatian artist Jean Conrad Tornier (*Monsteur d'harquebisses*), active in Masseveaux (Massmünster) during the second quarter of the seventeenth century, apparently decorated both gun stocks and crossbow tillers, as well as furniture; Hans Schedelmann, "Jean Conrad Tornier, an Alsatian Gunstock-Maker," *Journal of the Arms & Armour Society* 2, no. 12 (December 1958), pp. 261–64, 269–70; and James Gow Mann, *European Arms and Armour: Text with Historical Notes and Illustration,* 2 vols., Wallace Collection Catalogues (London, 1962), vol. 2, pp. 626–27, pl. 208. For further examples of Anglo-Dutch firearms with this type of decoration, see Ye. A. Yablonskaya, *Ognestrelnoe oruzie Anglii XVII–načala XIX veka/English Firearms of the XVII–the Early XIX Centuries,* Catalogue of the Collection of the State Historical-Cultural Museum-Preserve "The Moscow Kremlin" (Moscow, 2006), pp. 41–45, 54–59, 63–64, 67–68, 70–73.

7   Howard L. Blackmore, "Muskets for the City Companies," in *The Twelfth Park Lane Arms Fair* (London, 1995), pp. 12–17.

8   The cut-and-pierced features on the Metropolitan Museum's crossbow are similar to those on the belt clip of one of the examples from the 1604 shipment (Real Armería, Madrid [J.109]) and to those on the lever trigger on the so-called Alba crossbow (Real Armería, Madrid [J.111]), which originally formed part of the 1614 gift; Lavin, "Gift of James I," pp. 74–75, figs. 3 and 7, respectively.

Catalogue 10

1   The same mark is found on the bow of cat. 16.

2   For examples of this mark, see Eugen Heer, ed., *Der neue Støckel: Internationales Lexikon der Büchsenmacher, Feuerwaffenfabrikanten und Armbrustmacher von 1400–1900* (Schwäbisch Hall, 1979), vol. 2, p. 1473; and Jens Sensfelder, *Crossbows in the Royal Netherlands Army Museum: With a List of Names and Marks of European Crossbow Makers, Bow Smiths and Bolt Makers,* ed. Harm Stevens (Delft, 2007), p. 345; for what are probably variations of this mark, see pp. 337, 338, 343, 344.

3   Inspired by models from classical antiquity, the festoon motif appeared in the decorative arts before 1600, but it became especially popular, through prints of ornamental patterns published in the Netherlands, during the first half of the seventeenth century. The prints served as inspiration for the embellishment of architecture, furniture, and—last but not least—arms.

4   Musée d'Art et d'Industrie, Saint-Étienne (2003.18.336); Musée d'Art et d'Industrie, *Armes de chasse de la mèche à la percussion sur capsules: Collection du Musée d'Art et d'Industrie de Saint-Étienne* (Paris and Saint-Étienne, 2005), pp. 58–59. Here, the overall appearance of the inlay is similar, although less dense and with smaller motifs, and instead of the dragon-like grotesques the cheek bears a large depiction of a river god, modeled after an engraving by Adrian Collaert (see Rudolf Berliner, *Ornamentale Vorlagenblätter des 15. bis 18. Jahrhunderts,* 3 vols. [Leipzig, 1925–26], vol. 1, pl. 217, no. 3, vol. 3, pp. 59–60). Two similar curly-tailed dragons are engraved on the heel of the sliding-pan cover of the lock.

5   Museo Nacional de Arte Decorativo, Buenos Aires (inv. no. unknown); unpublished.

6   Hessisches Landesmuseum/Friedrichstein Castle, Bad Wildungen (B XIV 247 and B XIV 255); unpublished.

7   Musée d'Art et d'Histoire, Geneva (inv. no. unknown); unpublished.

8   Staatliche Kunstsammlungen/Rüstkammer, Dresden (U 130); see Holger Richter, *Die Hornbogenarmbrust: Geschichte und Technik* (Ludwigshafen, 2006), pp. 70–73. The tiller shows a generally similar decoration, but it is dated 1573 and has been fitted with a composite bow. It probably presents an early example of this type of decoration, but the bow—if original to this weapon—is either the latest known example of its kind or—more likely—a later replacement.

Catalogue 11

1   The core wood of the tiller could not be examined since it does not show, and any analysis other than a visual one would have been invasive.

2   See Johann Siebmacher, *J. Siebmacher's Grosses und allgemeines Wappenbuch,* ed. Otto Titan von Heffner et al., 82 vols. (Nuremberg, 1856–1938), vol. 33 (1857), p. 59, pl. 57, vol. 59 (1885), pp. 62–63, pl. 34; the crests, omitted on the crossbow, can be described as follows: upon two barred and crowned helms, two rampant black half rams, with golden horns and red tongues, positioned back to back and wearing crowns from which three ostrich feathers alternately silver/white, black, and red, the proper right (dexter) crest mantled black and gold/yellow, the proper left (sinister) crest mantled red and silver/white.

3   The one in Dresden, Staatliche Kunstsammlungen/Rüstkammer (U 147), is dated 1582 on the tumbler but was evidently refurbished in 1834; see Holger Richter, *Die Kunst der Armbrustmacher in Dresden* (Beucha, 2008), pp. 50–53; the examples in Skokloster, dated 1592 (6554) and 1593 (6551), are unpublished.

4 Philadelphia Museum of Art (1977-67-1002); see Carl Otto Kretzschmar von Kienbusch, *The Kretzschmar von Kienbusch Collection of Armor and Arms* (Princeton, 1963), p. 281, no. 628; and Jens Sensfelder, "Zur Konstruktion europäischer Armbrustschlosse (Teil 1)," in *Jahrblatt der Interessengemeinschaft Historische Armbrust* (2012), p. 42, fig. 8.

5 For the example of about 1600 in Grandson Castle (inv. no. unknown), see Jens Sensfelder, *Crossbows in the Royal Netherlands Army Museum: With a List of Names and Marks of European Crossbow Makers, Bow Smiths and Bolt Makers*, ed. Harm Stevens (Delft, 2007), p. 29; for two seventeenth-century *Rüstungen* in the Kunstsammlungen der Veste Coburg (IV A 13 and IV A 9), see Jens Sensfelder, *Armbruste in den Kunstsammlungen der Veste Coburg* (Coburg, 2009), pp. 24–42; for those in the Kurpfälzisches Museum in Heidelberg (unnumbered), dated 1716, and the Wielpolskie Muzeum Wojskowe in Poznan (inv. no. unknown), dated 1778, see Jens Sensfelder, "Über 'Zwillinge' und 'Drillinge'—ähnliche Armbruste vom 16. bis ins 18. Jahrhundert," in *Jahrblatt der Interessengemeinschaft Historische Armbrust* (2004), pp. 30–33; and for the two nineteenth-century ones in Dresden, dated 1872 (U 140) and 1878 (U 138), see Richter, *Armbrustmacher in Dresden*, pp. 64–65 and 74–75.

6 These include the extraordinary all-metal crossbow made by Franz Kaphan for Duke August (r. 1548–86), prince-elector of Saxony, in the Staatliche Kunstsammlungen/Rüstkammer, Dresden (U 267), see Erich Haenel, "Bolzenkasten und Armbrust des Kurfürsten August im Historischen Museum zu Dresden," in *Mitteilungen aus den sächsischen Kunstsammlungen* 1 (1910), pp. 52–65; a crossbow with a tiller veneered with polished staghorn and ebony, and inlaid with mother-of-pearl, probably of late sixteenth-century date, in the collections of the Hessisches Landesmuseum Kassel (B XIV 246; currently on display in Friedrichstein Castle, Bad Wildungen), unpublished; and a weapon formerly in Erbach Castle and today in a private collection, see Peter Finer, "A Fine German Sporting Crossbow, dated 1612," in *Peter Finer Catalogue*, no. 26 (Shipston-on-Stour, Warwickshire, 1997).

7 Staatliche Kunstsammlungen/Rüstkammer, Dresden; see Max von Ehrenthal, *Führer durch die königliche Gewehr-Galerie zu Dresden* (Dresden, 1900), pp. 20–21, 117. In some instances, the initials are found conjoined (G 193, G 198, G 203, G 204, G 306, G 423), in others, separate (G 189, G 191, G 192), as on the Metropolitan's example. Among the latter group, the initials that most resemble those on the Metropolitan's weapon are on a wheel-lock gun made about 1660 in Dresden by Balthasar Herold (G 189).

8 Carl von Metzsch-Reichenbach, *Die interessantesten alten Schlösser, Burgen und Ruinen Sachsens* (Dresden, 1902), p. 86.

9 This creation was in fact something of a formality, a confirmation of the barony that his ancestors had been granted in the mid-sixteenth century.

10 Files kept in the archives of the Department of Arms and Armor.

Catalogue 12

1 Staatliche Kunstsammlungen/Rüstkammer, Dresden (U129); see Holger Richter, *Die Kunst der Armbrustmacher in Dresden* (Beucha, 2008), pp. 29–31.

2 Ibid., p. 31.

3 The crossbowmaker's son, Johann Gottfried Hänisch the Younger, was not born until 1728 (he died in 1757); ibid., p. 25.

4 National Museum/Czartorysky Collection, Cracow (XIV-606); see Zdzislaw Żygulski, *Stara broń w polskich zbiorach* (Warsaw, 1982), p. 166, no. 169.

5 Staatliche Kunstsammlungen/Rüstkammer, Dresden (U289); it accompanies the *Schnepper* (U012); both are unpublished.

Catalogue 13

1 The numbers 105, punched into the underside of the butt, and 08, inscribed in pencil on the inner face of the cheek, are later inventory or location numbers.

2 The numbers 76, 74, and 92, written in pencil, and the stamped figure 06 or 90 are probably also later inventory numbers.

3 Holger Richter, *Die Kunst der Armbrustmacher in Dresden* (Beucha, 2008), p. 89.

4 Staatliche Kunstsammlungen/Rüstkammer, Dresden (U007, U076 [No. 2], U074 [No. 3], U049 [No. 4], U053 [No. 5], U028 [No. 7], U031 [No. 9], U255 [No. 10], U266 [No. 11], U047 [No. 12], U052 [No. 13], U093 [No. 14], U275 [No. 16], U075 [No. 17], U019 [No. 18], U045 [No. 20], U040 [No. 22], U096 [No. 24]; two further examples were sold at auction, the first (marked no. 1) at the Sotheby's sale, London, March 23, 1970, lot 1, and again Hermann Historica sale, Munich, May 4–5, 2004, lot 1778, and the second (marked no. 19) at Sotheby's sale, London, July 20–21 and 24, 1922, lot 285 (ex coll. Philip de Paniagua); the present whereabouts of both weapons are unknown. Another crossbow, marked no. 23 and dated 1728, is today in the Royal Netherlandish Army Museum, Delft (15768); Jens Sensfelder, *Crossbows in the Royal Netherlands Army Museum: With a List of Names and Marks of European Crossbow Makers, Bow Smiths and Bolt Makers*, ed. Harm Stevens (Delft, 2007), p. 199.

5 Dated weapons, in addition to the Delft example, include Dresden (U 275 [No. 16], U 18 [No. 18], U 40 [No. 22]); the acorn mark is found on two bows in the Staatliche Kunstsammlungen/Rüstkammer, Dresden (U 275, U 40), and on the Delft example.

Catalogue 14

1 As on cat. 13, the numbers 38, stamped into the tiller's underside, and 13, written in pencil on the inner side of the cheek, are later inventory or location numbers.

2 See Cordula Bischoff, *Goldener Drache, Weisser Adler: Kunst im Dienste der Macht am Kaiserhof von China und am sächsisch-polnischen Hof (1644–1795)*, exh. cat. (Dresden and Munich, 2008), p. 403.

3 Holger Richter, *Die Kunst der Armbrustmacher in Dresden* (Beucha, 2008), p. 89.

4 Staatliche Kunstsammlungen/Rüstkammer, Dresden (U065 [No. 1], U001 [No. 2], U072 [No. 5], U041 [No. 7], U051 [No. 9], U050 [No. 10], U132 [No. 11], U030 [No. 12], U018 [No. 18]; another example, listed as "No. 4," was sold at the Lepke sale, Berlin, Oct. 7–8, 1919, p. 55, pl. 48, lot 720.

Catalogue 16

1 The wooden core could not be visually examined as it is almost entirely covered by the staghorn veneer; sample taking was deemed too intrusive.

2 The rear sight and metal bolt clip, the latter now broken and missing its front half, are probably later replacements: other examples of this type of crossbow are fitted with bolt clips made from horn and do not have rear sights (see below, n. 5).

3 This feature appears to be unique; to date it has not been recorded on any of the comparatives in Dresden (see below, n. 5) or on any other crossbow.

4 See the brief discussion of this mark under cat. 10.

5 Staatliche Kunstsammlungen/Rüstkammer, Dresden: U116, dated 1736 and numbered 13; U117, U125, U119, dated 1740 and numbered 100, 101, and 103, respectively; U273, U124, U114, U123, dated 1741 and numbered 105, 107, 108, and 109, respectively. For some of these, see Max von Ehrenthal, *Führer durch die königliche Gewehr-Galerie zu Dresden* (Dresden, 1900), pp. 20–21; Johannes Schöbel, *Jagdwaffen und Jagdgerät des Historischen Museums zu Dresden* (Berlin, 1976), pp. 58, 70, 87, 90; and especially Holger Richter, *Die Kunst der Armbrustmacher in Dresden* (Beucha, 2008), pp. 32–34, 36–38, as well as the frontispiece, an old photograph of the gun room, showing a stand with what appear to be ten crossbows belonging to this group.

6 Staatliche Kunstsammlungen/Rüstkammer, Dresden: U263 (dated 1737 and unnumbered) U106 (undated , and numbered 102).

7 Museo de Armería y Heráldica Alavesa, Vitoria-Gasteiz (inv. no. unknown); see Museo

de Bellas Artes de Álava, *Museo Provincial de Álava: Armería* (Vitoria-Gasteiz, 1967), unnumbered figure; Felix Alfaro Fournier and Juan Vidal-Abarca, *Museos de Armería y Heráldica Alavesa* (Vitoria-Gasteiz, 1983), p. 66.

8 Peter Finer, "A Fine and Important German Sporting Crossbow, Saxon, by Johann Gottfried Haenisch, circa 1740," *Peter Finer Catalogue* (n.p.: Raithby, Lawrence & Co., [2005]), no. 32. The weapon's butt plate, which may once have carried Hänisch's initials and a number, is missing; although this example is undated and fitted with a steel bow by a different maker, Finer suggests that it and the Museum's crossbow could have formed a pair (this suggestion is based on obvious similarities between the two weapons, but does not take into account other examples in Dresden).

9 Richter, *Armbrustmacher in Dresden,* pp. 32–34.

Catalogue 17

1 Eugen Heer, ed., *Der neue Støckel: Internationales Lexikon der Büchsenmacher, Feuerwaffenfabrikanten und Armbrustmacher von 1400–1900* (Schwäbisch Hall, 1979), vol. 2, p. 1481, no. 6466; Jens Sensfelder, *Crossbows in the Royal Netherlands Army Museum: With a List of Names and Marks of European Crossbow Makers, Bow Smiths and Bolt Makers,* ed. Harm Stevens (Delft, 2007), pp. 337–38.

2 This mark appears to be previously unrecorded.

3 The Metropolitan Museum of Art, New York (14.25.1571a); Helmut Nickel, *Ullstein-Waffenbuch: Eine kulturhistorische Waffenkunde mit Markenverzeichnis* (Berlin, 1974), p. 230; and William Forbes Paterson, *A Guide to the Crossbow* ([Burnham?], 1990), p. 84, fig. 17.

4 For the example in the Royal Netherlandish Army Museum, Delft (15778), see Sensfelder, *Crossbows,* pp. 110–13. The year is accompanied by the initials P.B.MF.S. For the example in the Historisches Museum, Bern (1791), see Rudolf Wegeli, *Fernwaffen,* vol. 4 of *Inventar der Waffensammlung des Bernischen Historischen Museums in Bern* (Bern, 1948), p. 31. For more examples of the bull's-head mark, see Sensfelder, *Crossbows,* p. 113.

Catalogue 18

1 The Metropolitan Museum of Art, New York (14.25.1571a, b); Helmut Nickel, *Ullstein-Waffenbuch: Eine kulturhistorische Waffenkunde mit Markenverzeichnis* (Berlin, 1974), p. 230; and William Forbes Paterson, *A Guide to the Crossbow* ([Burnham?], 1990), p. 84, fig. 17; or an example in the Royal Netherlands Army Museum, Delft (15775), Jens Sensfelder, *Crossbows in the Royal*

Netherlands Army Museum: With a List of Names and Marks of European Crossbow Makers, Bow Smiths and Bolt Makers, ed. Harm Stevens (Delft, 2007), pp. 114–17.

2 Royal Netherlandish Army Museum, Delft (15764); Sensfelder, *Crossbows,* pp. 148–49.

3 See, for example, *The Return from War: Mars Disarmed by Venus,* painted ca. 1610–12 by Peter Paul Rubens (1577–1640) and Jan Brueghel the Elder (1568–1625), today in the J. Paul Getty Museum, Los Angeles (2000.68).

4 Royal Netherlandish Army Museum (14431); Sensfelder, *Crossbows,* pp. 140–41.

3 PELLET CROSSBOWS

Introduction

1 For a definition of the term "prodd" see the Oxford English Dictionary Online (www.oed.com), s.v. "prodd," accessed June 4, 2013; for a discussion of the origin of "prod" as a misreading and misinterpretation of the term "rod" found in one of the inventories of Henry VIII, see William Forbes Paterson, *A Guide to the Crossbow* ([Burnham?], 1990), p. 28; and David Starkey, ed., *The Inventory of King Henry VIII: Society of Antiquaries MS 129 and British Library MS Harley 1419,* vol. 1, *The Transcript,* Reports of the Research Committee of the Society of Antiquaries of London, no. 56 (London, 1998), p. 120, no. 5098.

2 At least one depiction of a pellet self-bow, or "stone bow," exists from the mid-fifteenth century (see fig. 6.4).

Catalogue 19

1 Robert Held, *Una rassegna di 162 armi antiche ed oggetti attinenti . . . in italiano ed inglese /A Review of 162 Antique Arms and Pertinent Objects . . . in English and Italian* (Lugano, 1976), pp. 20–21; Alessio Cenni, "La lunga vita dell'arco pallottaio," in *Arco* 3 (2003). Accessed September 30, 2013 www.arcosophia.net/database/ARCO/ Anno_2003/Arco_n3_2003/Articolo_Cenni/ cenni3-03.htm

2 Kunsthistorisches Museum/Hofjagd- und Rüstkammer, Vienna (D 466); unpublished.

Catalogue 20

1 A pellet crossbow with equally extensive decoration is in the Geoffrey Jenkinson collection, Guernsey; unpublished. A partial guilloche motif, similar to that found on the Metropolitan Museum's weapon, is found on the fore-end of a pellet crossbow in the Stadtmuseum, Cologne (KSM 1996/412); see Lothar Altringer, Guido von Büren, and Georg Mölich, *Renaissance am Rhein,* exh. cat. (Ostfildern, 2010), p. 412, no. 283.

2 Kunsthistorisches Museum/Hofjagd- und Rüstkammer, Vienna (D 212); Ortwin Gamber and Christian Beaufort-Spontin, *Curiositäten und Inventionen aus Kunst- und Rüstkammer* (Vienna, 1978), p. 67, pl. 9.

3 Pitt Rivers Museum, Oxford (1907.10.62); unpublished.

4 Unfortunately, it was not possible to take the weapon apart in order to examine how exactly the front and rear are joined together or how quickly the tiller can be taken apart.

Catalogue 21

1 In the present publication, see cats. 8, 21, 23, 27, and the knee of the iron trigger guard, chiseled in the shape of a sea monster, on cat. 11.

2 Victoria and Albert Museum, London (M.162-1921); unpublished. The bow is smaller than the Metropolitan's weapon, measuring only 141/8 in. (35.8 cm) wide. There is, however, some doubt concerning the authenticity of the V&A's example (cat. 25).

3 Musée de l'Armée, Paris (L.115); see L. Robert, ed., *Catalogue des collections composant le Musée d'Artillerie en 1889,* vol. 3 (Paris, 1891), p. 392.

Catalogue 23

1 Visual examination of the wood remained inconclusive, while invasive sampling was deemed too difficult.

2 Eugen Heer, ed., *Der neue Støckel: Internationales Lexikon der Büchsenmacher, Feuerwaffenfabrikanten und Armbrustmacher von 1400–1900* (Schwäbisch Hall, 1979), vol. 2, p. 1259, no. 6365; Jens Sensfelder, *Crossbows in the Royal Netherlands Army Museum: With a List of Names and Marks of European Crossbow Makers, Bow Smiths and Bolt Makers,* ed. Harm Stevens (Delft, 2007), p. 347.

3 Victoria and Albert Museum, London (M146-1921); unpublished.

4 Hallwylska Museet, Stockholm (X.3); Hallwylska Museet, *Vapen-Europa, Orienten,* Group 34–35, *Hallwylska Samlingen: Beskrifvande förteckning* (Stockholm, 1926), pp. 213–14, and Hallwylska Museet, *Catalogue of the Collection of Arms and Armour at Hallwyl House, Stockholm* (Stockholm, 1928), pp. 54–55. Livrustkammaren, Stockholm (6796); mentioned in the 1926 description of the Hallwylska Museet example.

5 Germanisches Nationalmuseum, Nuremberg (W758); Sensfelder, *Crossbows,* p. 347.

6 Historisches Museum, Frankfurt am Main (X0925); unpublished.

7 Hessisches Landesmuseum, Darmstadt (W60/2); Sensfelder, *Crossbows,* p. 347.

8 National Museum, Prague (inv. no. unknown); Dirk H. Breiding, "Die Armbrust-Ausstellung 'Arma Diaboli' in Prag," *Jahrblatt der*

Interessengemeinschaft historische Armbrust (2012), p. 78.

9 Museum Czartoryskich, Cracow (XIV-93); Zdzisław Żygulski, *Dzieje zbiorów Puławskich: Swiątynia Sybilli i Dom Gotycki* (Cracow, 2009), p. 164.

10 Musée de l'Armée, Paris (L.124); L. Robert, ed., *Catalogue des collections composant le Musée d'Artillerie en 1889*, vol. 3 (Paris, 1891), p. 393.

11 Arms and armor collections of Wartburg Castle, Eisenach (4591); Alfons Diener-Schönberg, *Die Waffen der Wartburg: Beschreibendes Verzeichnis der Waffen-Sammlung S. K. H. des Grossherzogs Wilhelm Ernst von Sachsen-Weimar-Eisenach* (Berlin, 1912), pp. 130, 181, pl. 64, no. 493, and mark no. 50.

12 Thomas Moritz, ed., *Ein Feste Burg, die Plesse: Begleitband zur Ausstellung,* exh. cat. (Braunschweig, 2002), p. 94; perhaps related to, or identical with, Peter Seng, recorded in Württemberg in 1580/81, see Heer, *Der neue Støckel,* vol. 2, p. 1154.

Catalogue 24

1 Eugen Heer, ed., *Der neue Støckel: Internationales Lexikon der Büchsenmacher, Feuerwaffenfabrikanten und Armbrustmacher von 1400–1900* (Schwäbisch Hall, 1979), vol. 2, p. 1256, nos. 4041, 6416, and 8341; Jens Sensfelder, *Crossbows in the Royal Netherlands Army Museums: With a List of Names and Marks of European Crossbow Makers, Bow Smiths and Bolt Makers,* ed. Harm Stevens (Delft, 2007), pp. 329, 341.

2 Royal Armouries Museum, Leeds (XI.17); Charles J. ffoulkes, *Inventory and Survey of the Armouries of the Tower of London* (London, 1916), vol. 2, p. 327; Tower of London Armouries, *Crossbows,* Treasures of the Tower (London, 1976), p. 15.

3 Musée de l'Armée, Paris (L.125); L. Robert, ed., *Catalogue des collections composant le Musée d'Artillerie en 1889*, vol. 3 (Paris, 1891), p. 393.

4 Collection of Geoffrey Jenkinson, Guernsey; Christie's sale, London, Dec. 20, 1978, lot 201; and Dorchester, "The Art of the Crossbow," in *The International Arms & Armour Exposition* (London, 1983), p. 62, no. 11; and Sensfelder, *Crossbows,* p. 62, fig. 27.

5 Tower of London Armouries, *Exhibition of Arms, Armour and Militaria Lent by H. R. H. the Duke of Brunswick and Lüneburg at the Armouries of the Tower of London,* ed. J. G. Mann, exh. cat. (London, 1952) p. 34, no. 123 (present whereabouts unknown).

6 For example, in the Legermuseum, Delft (12799), Sensfelder, *Crossbows,* pp. 224–27; the Jagd- und Fischereimuseum, Munich (W 57 306), Karl Sälzle, *Deutsches Jagdmuseum München* (Munich, 1966), pp. 69–70 (according to Sensfelder, *Crossbows,* p. 341, the initials on the Munich example are found below the squirrel); and the Thüringer Landesmuseum Heidecksburg, Rudolstadt (843, 844); Carl Anton Ossbahr, *Das fürstliche Zeughaus* (Rudolstadt, 1895), p. 57. Ossbahr notes that the two marks vary slightly in the placement of the initials; see also Sensfelder, *Crossbows,* p. 341. According to Jens Henkel of the Thüringer Landesmuseum Heidecksburg, one of these (844) has been missing since 1940 (personal communication, January 2011).

7 For example, one in the Historisches Museum, Bern (1802); Rudolf Wegeli, *Fernwaffen,* vol. 4 of *Inventar der Waffensammlung des Bernischen Historischen Museums in Bern* (Bern, 1948), p. 33 (here incorrectly identified as 2002); or another in the collection of Geoffrey Jenkinson, Guernsey; see Clement Bosson, René Géroudet, and Eugen Heer, *Armes anciennes des collections suisses,* exh. cat. (Lausanne, 1972), pp. 65, no. 319.

8 It was suggested in the Dorchester catalogue (see n. 4 above) that the two words may be an abbreviation of Moritz(burg) and Sam(mlung), and that pellet crossbows thus marked came from Moritzburg, one of the hunting residences of the dukes of Saxony (see cats. 13, 50); however, this hypothesis is not supported by any evidence.

4 SPECIAL TYPES OF CROSSBOWS

Introduction

1 For rare and special types of crossbows, see Egon Harmuth, *Die Armbrust: Ein Handbuch* (Graz, 1986), pp. 182–86.

2 These include four examples in the Palazzo Ducale, Venice (Q1, Q2, Q3, Q4); and one each in the collections of the Bayerisches Nationalmuseum, Munich (W1498); The Metropolitan Museum of Art (14.25.1573; cat. 26); the Kunsthistorisches Museum/Hofjagd- und Rüstkammer, Vienna (D200); the Victoria and Albert Museum, London (M.618 1929); and the Royal Armouries Museum, Leeds (XIV.22); and one formerly in the Henk Visser collection. For all of these, see W. E. Flewett, "European Combination Weapons (Crossbow-Firearms)," *Journal of the Society of Archer-Antiquaries* 36 (1993), pp. 51–70.

3 Bodleian Library, Oxford (Ms. Huntington 264, fol. 102); see Rudolf Sellheim, *Materialien zur arabischen Literaturgeschichte,* 2 vols. (Wiesbaden, 1976–87), vol. 1, p. 274. Attributed to the author Murda ibn 'Ali al-Tarsusi, the manuscript's title can be translated as "Explanations from the masters on the methods of strategic manœuvring in battle for utmost protection and extended instructions relating to equipment and devices for use in encounters with the enemy."

4 In addition to Flewett, "European Combination Weapons," pp. 52–54, see Claude Blair, "Further Notes on the Origins of the Wheellock," *Arms and Armour Annual* 1 (1973), pp. 28–47, esp. pp. 39–42; and Claude Blair, "Nuovi documenti sulla storia dell'arma a ruota primitiva in Italia," *Armi antiche* (1996), pp. 13–44, esp. pp. 17, 30–35.

5 The 1578 inventory of Brunoro II Zampeschi (1540–1578), an Italian nobleman from Forlì, lists a "little crossbow [combined] with a [little?] arquebuse" ("balestrino con un archebusoto"); Umberto Santini, "Il Comune di Forlimpopoli," *Atti e memorie della Regia deputazione di storia patria per le provincie di Romagna,* ser. 3, 21 (1903), p. 415.

6 Museo Nazionale di Castel Sant'Angelo, Rome (inv. no. unknown); see Heribert Seitz, *Blankwaffen,* 2 vols. (Braunschweig, 1965–68), vol. 2, p. 253–55, fig. 256.

7 Bayerisches Nationalmuseum, Munich (W1498); see Erwin Schalkhausser, *Handfeuerwaffen Jagdgewehre, Scheibenbüchsen, Pistolen,* Kataloge des Bayerischen Nationalmuseums München 19 (Munich, 1988), pp. 22–23, no. 10.

8 Churburg Castle, Sluderno (CH S 332); Mario Scalini and Oswald Graf Trapp, *L'armeria Trapp di Castel Coira/Die Churburger Rüstkammer/The Armoury of the Castle of Churburg,* trans. Rudolf Wackernagel and Ian Eaves (Udine, 1966), vol. 2, pp. 201, 206, 212, 383.

9 Tower of London Armouries, *Crossbows,* Treasures of the Tower (London, 1976), p. 21, illustrates an eighteenth-century example, today in the Royal Armouries Museum, Leeds (inv. no. unknown); see also Harmuth, *Die Armbrust: Ein Handbuch,* pp. 149, 152.

10 For Frédéric Spitzer, see cat. 25.

11 For *balestrini* in general, see Charles Buttin, "Les Armes prohibées en Savoie," *Revue savoisienne* 37 (1896), pp. 111–29, esp. 115–19; D[ouglas] Elmy and N. Allen, "An Assassin's Crossbow," *Journal of the Society of Archer-Antiquaries* 15 (1972), pp. 37–39; Egon Harmuth, "Ein Balestrino," *Waffen- und Kostümkunde,* n.s., 14, no. 1 (1972), pp. 31–34; D[ouglas] Elmy and W. E. Flewett, "The Assassin's Crossbow," *Journal of the Society of Archer-Antiquaries* 17 (1974), pp. 27–34; Egon Harmuth, *Die Armbrust* (Graz, 1975), p. 122; Lionello Boccia, "Balestrino," in *Palazzo Vecchio, committenza e collezionismo medicei,* exh. cat., Firenze e la Toscana dei Medici nell'Europa del Cinquecento (Florence, 1980), pp. 135–36; Harmuth, *Die Armbrust: Ein Handbuch,* p. 184; Jean-Pierre Reverseau, *Armes insolites du XVIe au XVIIIe siècle,* exh. cat. (Paris, [1990]), pp. 76–77; and W. E. Flewett, "The 'Assassin's Crossbow'?: A Reassessment,"

Journal of the Society of Archer-Antiquaries 39 (1996), pp. 78–93.

12 See, for example, Buttin, "Les Armes prohibées," pp. 111–29, esp. pp. 115–19; Elmy and Allen, "An Assassin's Crossbow," pp. 37–39; Harmuth, "Ein Balestrino," pp. 31–34; Elmy and Flewett, "The Assassin's Crossbow," pp. 27–34; Boccia, "Balestrino"; Reverseau, *Armes insolites*, p. 76; and Flewett, "The 'Assassin's Crossbow'?," pp. 78–93.

13 Guichard Déageant, *Mémoires particuliers pour servir à l'histoire de France sous les règnes de Henri III, de Henri IV, sous la régence de Marie des Médicis, & sous Louis XIII*, vol. 3 (Paris, 1756), p. 101; I am grateful to my colleague Pierre Terjanian for correcting my translation of this passage.

14 See, for example, one in the Metropolitan Museum (36.25.2495a–j); George M. Stevens, *Crossbows: From Thirty-Five Years with the Weapon* (n.p.: G. M. Stevens, 1978), p. 9. For the type, see Sir Ralph Payne-Gallwey, *The Crossbow: Medieval and Modern, Military and Sporting: Its Construction, History and Management* (London, 1903), p. 337; Harmuth, *Die Armbrust: Ein Handbuch*, pp. 217–19; and William Forbes Paterson, *A Guide to the Crossbow* ([Burnham?], 1990), pp. 110–11.

15 See Antoine Le Roux de Lincy, "Inventaires des biens meubles et immeubles de la comtesse Mahaut d'Artois, pillés par l'armées de son neveu, en 1313," in *Bibliothèque de l'École des Chartes* 13 (1852), p. 63; Payne-Gallwey, *The Crossbow*, pp. 129–30; and Kenneth R. Andrews, ed., *The Last Voyage of Drake and Hawkins* (Cambridge, 1972), p. 73, respectively.

Catalogue 26

1 Kunsthistorisches Museum/Hofjagd- und Rüstkammer, Vienna (D 200); see Alois Primisser, *Die kaiserlich-königliche Ambraser-Sammlung* (Vienna, 1819), p. 75; Wendelin Boeheim, "Über einige Jagdwaffen und Jagdgeräthe (Fortsetzung)," *Jahrbuch der Kunsthistorischen Sammlungen* 4 (1886), pp. 63–65; Wendelin Boeheim, *Handbuch der Waffenkunde: Das Waffenwesen in seiner historischen Entwickelung vom Beginn des Mittelalters bis zum Ende des 18. Jahrhunderts* (Leipzig, 1890), figs. 501, 502; Hans Schedelmann, *Die grossen Büchsenmacher: Leben, Werke, Marken vom 15. bis 19. Jahrhundert* (Braunschweig, 1972), p. 68; Ortwin Gamber and Christian Beaufort-Spontin, *Curiositäten und Inventionen aus Kunst- und Rüstkammer* (Vienna, 1978), p. 67, pl. 9.

2 The only other recorded instance of this mark (or a very similar one) known to the author is on a bow closely resembling the one on the Vienna weapon and mounted on what appears

to be a mid-sixteenth-century Spanish crossbow, formerly in the collection of the duke de Osuna and Infantado at Beauraing Palace, suggesting that the mark belonged to a Spanish crossbow maker; Osuna sale, J. M. Heberle, Cologne, November 24–December 2, 1890, p. 25, lot 328.

3 F. W. H. Hollstein, *The New Hollstein: Dutch & Flemish Etchings, Engravings and Woodcuts*, 24 vols. (Roosendaal, 1993–), vol. 7, *The Muller Dynasty* (1999), part 1, p. 227, no. 122; vol. 6, *Karel van Mander* (1999), p. 256, nos. 46–58; and vol. 11, *Jacob Matham* (2007–8), p. 2, nos. 42–54. A set of these engravings is in the collection of the Metropolitan Museum's Department of Drawings and Prints (48.13.4[31–43]).

4 F. W. H. Hollstein, *Dutch and Flemish Etchings, Engravings, and Woodcuts, ca. 1450–1700*, vol. 47, *Vredeman De Vries*, part 1, *1555–1571* (Amsterdam, 1997), pp. 206–14, nos. 223–39 (no. 230, first figure); The Metropolitan Museum's Department of Drawings and Prints owns a set of these engravings (66.545.4.1–17).

5 Compare, for example, a wheel-lock *Doppelbüchse* (double-barreled gun), probably made in southern Germany about 1570, and another wheel-lock gun, made in Ansbach in the last quarter of the sixteenth century, both in the Kunsthistorisches Museum/Hofjagd- und Rüstkammer, Vienna (D 136, D 58); Hans Schedelmann, *Die Grossen Büchsenmacher* (Braunschweig, 1972), p. 21, fig. 37, and p. 48, fig. 89, respectively.

Catalogue 27

1 Divided into four fields; in 1 and 4, the dukedom of Saxony (a shield parted into three fields by two concave lines; on the right, in red, a rampant silver stallion turned to the left; on the left, ten alternating stripes of black and gold, diagonally overlaid with a green wreath of rue; in the triangular field, in silver, three red water-lily pads arranged in a triangle); in 2 the province of Chablais (in silver, strewn with black rectangles, a black rampant lion, with red claws and tongue); in 3 the province of Aosta (in black a rampant silver lion, with red claws and tongue); overall in the center, a small shield with the arms of Savoy (in red, a silver cross).

2 In addition to the Museum's crossbow and the one described and illustrated in fig. 4.2, only one other example of the type could be identi-fied: a rather plain pellet and bolt crossbow, more similar in appearance to cat. 19 and fitted with a sturdy bolt-bridge, currently also in another private collection in the United States.

3 Victor Rolland, *Planches de l'Armorial général de J.-B. Rietstap*, vol. 5 (La Haye, 1921), pl. CCXLVIII.

4 Spitzer sale, Galerie Georges Petit, Paris, June 10–14, 1895, lot 292.

Catalogue 28

1 See, for example, D[ouglas] Elmy and W. E. Flewett, "The Assassin's Crossbow," *Journal of the Society of Archer-Antiquaries* 17 (1974), pp. 27–34; W. E. Flewett, "The 'Assassin's Crossbow'?: A Reassessment," *Journal of the Society of Archer-Antiquaries* 39 (1996), pp. 78–93; and Bonhams sale, London, April 18, 2012, lot 103.

2 In addition to the references cited in n. 1, see Charles Buttin, "Les Armes prohibées en Savoie," *Revue savoisienne* 37 (1896), pp. 111–29, esp. pp. 115–19; D[ouglas] Elmy and N. Allen, "An Assassin's Crossbow," *Journal of the Society of Archer-Antiquaries* 15 (1972), pp. 37–39; Egon Harmuth, "Ein Balestrino," *Waffen- und Kostümkunde*, n.s., 14, no. 1 (1972), pp. 31–34; Elmy and Flewett, "The Assassin's Crossbow," pp. 27–34; Egon Harmuth, *Die Armbrust* (Graz, 1975), p. 122; Lionello Boccia, "Balestrino," in *Palazzo Vecchio, committenza e collezionismo medicei*, exh. cat., Firenze e la Toscana dei Medici nell'Europa del Cinquecento (Florence, 1980), pp. 135–36; Jean-Pierre Reverseau, *Armes insolites du XVIe au XVIIIe siècle* (Paris, [1990]), pp. 76–77. The feminine form, *balestrina*, appears to be acceptable as well; Marco Morin, "Una Balestrina del Secolo XVI," *Diana armi* 6, no. 9 (June, 1977), pp. 32–36; and Reverseau, *Armes insolites*, p. 76.

3 For example, the *balestrino* sold at Bonhams (cited in n. 1) was catalogued as "19th century or earlier."

4 At least two examples are in the Museo Nazionale del Bargello, Florence (M1371, N1789); Harmuth, "Ein Balestrino," pp. 31–34; Boccia, "Balestrino," pp. 135–36; and Flewett, "The 'Assassin's Crossbow'?," pp. 80 and 84–86, respectively.

5 Armeria Reale, Turin (L10); Franco Mazzini and Claudio Bertolotto, *L'armeria reale di Torino* (Busto Arsizio, [1982]), p. 381, no. 268; and Flewett, "The 'Assassin's Crossbow'?," p. 82.

6 Palazzo Ducale, Venice (F9); Umberto Franzoi, *L'armeria del Palazzo Ducale a Venezia* (Dosson (Treviso), [1990]), p. 120, no. 376. At least one other is in the Museo Correr, Venice (inventory no. unknown); unpublished.

7 Museo e Gallerie Nazionali di Capodimonte, Naples (OA 1907, 3642); Museo e Gallerie Nazionali di Capodimonte, *Le arti decorative*, vol. 3 of *La Collezione Farnese* (Naples, 1996), p. 334.

8 Flewett, "The 'Assassin's Crossbow'?," pp. 78–93.

9 Museo Nazionale del Bargello, Florence (N1789); see Flewett, "The 'Assassin's Crossbow'?," pp. 84–86; and Geoffrey Jenkinson collection, Guernsey; ibid., p. 81.

5 Spanning Devices

Introduction

1 For spanning methods in general see Sir Ralph Payne-Gallwey, *The Crossbow, Medieval and Modern, Military and Sporting: Its Construction, History and Management, with a Treatise on the Balista and Catapult of the Ancients* (London, 1903), pp. 73–92, 120–25, 131–44, and 161–68; Egon Harmuth, *Die Armbrust: Ein Handbuch* (Graz, 1986), pp. 125–30, 154–72; William Forbes Paterson, *A Guide to the Crossbow* ([Burnham?], 1990), pp. 38–52; and Claude Blair, "Cranequins, Crankets, Cricks, Racks, Goats' Feet, Gaffles and Benders," *Journal of the Society of Archer-Antiquaries* 45 (2002), pp. 5–13.

2 See Guy Wilson, "What's in a Name? One-foot and Two-Foot Crossbows," in *ICOMAM 50: Papers on Arms and Military History 1957–2007*, ed. Robert D. Smith (Leeds, 2007), pp. 300–325.

3 See J[ohn] D[erek] Latham and William F[orbes] Paterson, *Saracen Archery: An English Version and Exposition of a Mameluke Work on Archery (ca. A.D. 1368)* (London, 1970), pp. 85–86; and Paterson, *Guide to the Crossbow*, p. 43.

4 The earliest examples appear to have been based on the mechanisms found in stationary great crossbows; what is probably a hand-held variation is depicted in Roberto Valturio's *De Re Militari*, written between 1460 and 1472; see Roberto Valturio, *De re militari: Umanesimo e arte della guerra tra Medioevo e Rinascimento*, 2 vols., ed. Paola Delbianco and Agostino Contò (Rimini and Milan, 2006), see *Saggi critici*, p. 98.

Catalogue 29

1 Livrustkammaren, Stockholm (inv. no. unknown).

2 Suomen Kansallismuseo (National Museum), Helsinki (inv. no. unknown); see Torsten Lenk, "Medeltidens Skjutvapen," in *Vaaben*, ed. Bengt Thordemann, Nordisk Kultur 12, B (Stockholm, 1943), p. 140, fig. 12.

3 A number of examples are illustrated in Josef Alm, *European Crossbows: A Survey,* trans. H. Bartlett Wells, ed. G. M. Wilson (London, 1994), p. 85, fig. 58.

4 A somewhat similar anchor plate was formerly in the Rullier Collection; Rullier sale, Fraysse & associés, Paris, March 10, 2010, p. 126, lot 147.

5 Departmental archives (original object accession card), Department of Arms and Armor.

Catalogue 30

1 Kunsthistorisches Museum/Hofjagd- und Rüstkammer, Vienna (A 389); Bruno Thomas and Ortwin Gamber, *Katalog der Leibrüstkammer 1. Teil—Der Zeitraum von 500 bis 1530* (Vienna, 1976), p. 207.

2 Real Armería, Madrid (J.11); Valencia de Don Juan, Conde de [Juan Bautista Crooke y Navarrot], *Catálogo histórico-descriptivo de la Real Armería de Madrid* (Madrid, 1898), p. 281.

3 Musée de la guerre au Moyen Âge, Château de Castelnaud, Vézac (inv. no. unknown); unpublished.

4 Museo de Armería y Heráldica Alavesa, Vitoria-Gasteiz; Museo de Bellas Artes de Álava, *Museo Provincial de Álava: Armería* (Vitoria-Gasteiz, 1967), unnumbered figure; Felix Fournier and Juan Vidal-Abarca, *Museos de Armería y Heráldica Alavesa* (Vitoria-Gasteiz, 1983), p. 66.

5 Simon Archery Collection, Manchester (UK) (SA 77); unpublished.

Catalogue 31

1 A small L-shaped plate, formerly attached to the end of the rack to prevent over-extension and still present in 1934, has since been lost; Grafenegg sale, Galerie Fischer Auktionen, Zurich, May 2, 1934, p. 20.

2 Bruno Thomas and Ortwin Gamber, *Katalog der Leibrüstkammer 1. Teil—Der Zeitraum von 500 bis 1530* (Vienna, 1976), p. 207.

3 Kunsthistorisches Museum/Hofjagd- und Rüstkammer, Vienna (A 389); Thomas and Gamber, *Katalog der Leibrüstkammer,* p. 207.

4 Real Armería, Madrid (J.13).

5 Real Armería, Madrid (J.11); the Roman numeral VII next to the winder indicates that Charles' armory, which included that of his father, Philip I, and of his grandfather Maximilian I, then contained seven of these cranequins. Since the grip depicted in the *Inventario Iluminado* is almost identical to those on all three examples, the one on the Vienna winder is unlikely to be a later sixteenth-century replacement, as stated in Thomas and Gamber, *Katalog der Leibrüstkammer*, p. 207.

6 For these crossbows in the Kunsthistorisches Museum/Hofjagd- und Rüstkammer, Vienna (D 18, D 16, D 3), and the attribution of the Vienna winder as belonging to D 18 and the Museum's example to D 3, see ibid., pp. 205–7.

Catalogue 32

1 Historisches Museum, Bern (524); Rudolf Wegeli, *Fernwaffen*, Inventar der Waffensammlung des Bernischen Historischen Museums in Bern (Bern, 1948), vol. 4, p. 38.

2 Armeria Reale, Turin (L17); Claudio Bertoletto and Franco Mazzini, eds., *L'Armeria reale di Torino, Arte e tecnica* (Busto Arsizio, 1982), p. 381 (ill.); for reasons not stated by Mazzini et al. the Turin example is dated to the beginning of the seventeenth century.

3 Hessisches Landesmuseum, Darmstadt (inv. no. unknown); see Jens Sensfelder, "The 'Naked' Cranequin: An Example of Artistic and Technical Skill in the 16th Century," *Journal of the Society of Archer-Antiquaries* 48 (2005), pp. 23–26.

4 Musée d'Armes, Liège (10363); unpublished.

Catalogue 33

1 Johan F. Støckel, *Haandskydevaabens Bedømmelse*, vol. 2 (Copenhagen, 1943), p. 856, nos. 4956, 4957; Eugen Heer, ed., *Der neue Støckel: Internationales Lexikon der Büchsenmacher, Feuerwaffenfabrikanten und Armbrustmacher von 1400–1900*, vol. 1 (Schwäbisch Hall, 1978), p. 501, no. 7572.

2 Several, but not all, are listed in James Gow Mann, *European Arms and Armour: Text with Historical Notes and Illustration*, 2 vols., Wallace Collection Catalogues (London, 1962), p. 488, and in the references in n. 1, above.

3 According to Mann, ibid., a cranequin, allegedly with this mark and dated 1527, was included in an anonymous Sotheby's sale in London on June 6, 1935. However, the sale catalogue gives the year as 1537 and no description of the mark; Sotheby's, London, sale cat., June 6, 1935, p. 17, lot 133.

4 Kurpfälzisches Museum, Heidelberg (inv. no. unknown); unpublished.

5 Deutsches Historisches Museum, Berlin (inv. no. unknown); unpublished.

6 Visser sale, Sotheby's, London, June 3, 1991, lot 24.

7 The State Hermitage Museum, Saint Petersburg (O.53), dated 1533; Eduard Lenz, *Imperatorskij Ermitaz: Ukazatel Otdelenija Srednih Vekov i Epohi Vozrozdenija*, pt. 1, *Sobranie Oruzija* [The Imperial Hermitage: Guide to the Medieval and Renaissance Section, pt. 1, the Collection of Arms and Armor] (Saint Petersburg, 1908), p. 221. The Wallace Collection, London (A 1054), dated 1545; Mann, *European Arms and Armour*, vol. 2, p. 488; and A. Vesey B. Norman, *European Arms and Armour Supplement*, Wallace Collection Catalogues (London, 1986), p. 205; The Baumann Collection, Reichsstadtmuseum, Rothenburg ob der Tauber, (980825/315), dated 1567; Wilfried Baumann, *Historische Waffen und Rüstungen: Sammlung Hermann Baumann/Antique Arms and Armour: The Hermann Baumann Collection* (Rothenburg, 2010), pp. 30–31; and Historisches Museum, Bern (523), dated 1575; Rudolf Wegeli, *Fernwaffen*, Inventar der Waffensammlung des Bernischen Historischen Museums in Bern (Bern, 1948), vol. 4, pp. 36–37. In every case, except for the Rothenburg example, at least some of the

decoration appears to have been added at a later date.

8 According to Hugo Schneider, *Schweizer Waffenschmiede vom 15. bis 20. Jahrhundert* (Zurich, 1976), p. 135, a Hartmann Windenmacher (winder maker) is recorded in Zurich in 1541–43; however, Heer quotes the Schneider 1976 entry but notes the absence of any documentary reference in support of the citation (Heer, *Der neue Støckel*, vol. 1, p. 501).

9 Mann, *European Arms and Armour*, vol. 2, p. 488. The suggestion is probably based on the fact that Suhl, a well-known center of arms manufacture, especially firearms, was held by the counts of Henneberg. That crank and cranequin makers were active in Suhl in the mid-sixteenth century is attested by the statutes of a guild of lock makers, gun makers, spur makers, and cranequin makers, granted in 1563. Since the Henneberg coat of arms shows a hen, and a simplified version was used as a proofmark for firearms made in Suhl, it is conceivable that the present rooster mark may have been a variation of the Suhl proofmark specifically used for crossbow winders. However, since gun makers and cranequin makers in Suhl belonged to the same guild—at least since 1563—the use of separate proofmarks seems unlikely. For a concise history of Suhl arms manufacture, see Heer, *Der neue Støckel*, vol. 3 (1982), pp. 1703–7.

Catalogue 34

1 This mark does not appear in Johan F. Støckel, *Haandskydevaabens Bedømmelse*, 2 vols. (Copenhagen, 1938–43); Hugo Schneider, *Schweizer Waffenschmiede vom 15. bis 20. Jahrhundert* (Zurich, 1976); or Eugen Heer, ed., *Der neue Støckel: Internationales Lexikon der Büchsenmacher, Feuerwaffenfabrikanten und Armbrustmacher von 1400–1900*, vol. 1 (Schwäbisch Hall, 1978).

2 Bayerisches Nationalmuseum, Munich (W 560); unpublished.

3 Stadtmuseum, Leipzig (MI 300-2003); unpublished.

Catalogue 35

1 Compare especially the central plant with drooping branches to similar trees in prints of hunting scenes; Ilse O'Dell-Franke, *Kupferstiche und Radierungen aus der Werkstatt des Virgil Solis* (Wiesbaden, 1977), pls. 72 (G9), 75 (G26).

Catalogue 36

1 Johan F. Støckel, *Haandskydevaabens Bedømmelse*, vol. 2 (Copenhagen, 1943), p. 649, nos. 3157, 3158; Eugen Heer, ed., *Der neue Støckel: Internationales Lexikon der Büchsenmacher, Feuerwaffenfabrikanten und*

Armbrustmacher von 1400–1900, vol. 2 (Schwäbisch Hall, 1978), p. 1417, no. 3157. The mark is also found on another winder in the Metropolitan Museum's collection (14.25.1605).

2 *Der neue Støckel* (see n. 1) gives a date range of 1572 to 1579, though none of the five examples given displays the year 1572.

3 For example, a winder in the Museum Altes Zeughaus, Solothurn (625), is plain (Rudolf Wegeli, *Katalog der Waffen-Sammlung im Zeughause zu Solothurn* [Solothurn, 1905], p. 67), while another, in The Wallace Collection, London (A 1056), shows extensive etching, some of which is gilded (James Gow Mann, *European Arms and Armour: Text with Historical Notes and Illustration*, 2 vols., Wallace Collection Catalogues [London, 1962], pp. 488–89; A. Vesey B. Norman, *European Arms and Armour Supplement*, [London, 1986], p. 205).

4 Worshipful Company of Armourers and Brasiers in the City of London (W120); Worshipful Company of Armourers and Brasiers in the City of London, *Armour and Weapons in Armourers' Hall* (London, 1993), p. 15.

5 Formerly in the private collection of Hans Lukas von Cranach (1855–1929), then exhibited at Wartburg Castle; Alfons Diener-Schönberg, *Die Waffen der Wartburg: Beschreibendes Verzeichnis der Waffen-Sammlung S. K. H. des Grossherzogs Wilhelm Ernst von Sachsen-Weimar-Eisenach* (Berlin, 1912), p. 131 (in the literature often erroneously listed as part of the Wartburg collection). The Wartburg collection was confiscated by the Russian government in 1947 and removed from the castle; portions of the collection have resurfaced in the Artillery Museum in Saint Petersburg, but the whereabouts of the Wartburg winder are presently unknown.

6 Visser sale, Sotheby's, London, July 3, 1990, p. 30, lot 29.

7 State Hermitage Museum, Saint Petersburg (O.23); Eduard Lenz, *Imperatorskij Ermitaz: Ukazatel Otdelenija Srednih Vekov i Epohi Vozrozdenija*, pt. 1, *Sobranie Oruzija* [The Imperial Hermitage: Guide to the Medieval and Renaissance Section, pt. 1, the Collection of Arms and Armor] (Saint Petersburg, 1908), p. 221; for Hanns (= Johann) Kempff, see Gustav Sommerfeldt, "Biographisches über die Rüstmeister in Dresden, Johann von Schukowski und Johann Kempff, 2. H. 16. Jh," *Zeitschrift für historische Waffenkunde* 8 (1918–20), pp. 350–52, and Gustav Sommerfeldt, "Zur Geschichte des technischen Kunstbetriebs in Dresden, c. 1550–1590," *Zeitschrift für historische Waffenkunde* 8 (1918–20), pp. 256–57. The inscription reads: "Hanns Kempff Churf Sächsischer Rustmeister geacht / wardt diese Winden zu Nurmbergk vor In gemachtt 1580."

8 Hanns Jaeger-Sunstenau, *General-Index zu den Siebmacher'schen Wappenbüchern 1605–1961* (Graz, 1964), BayA1, p. 29, pl. 24; ibid., Bg1, p. 5, pl. 1; ibid., BayA3, p. 180, pl. 127; and Ernst Kroker, "Der Stammbaum der Familie Ayrer," *Mitteilungen des Vereins für Geschichte der Stadt Nürnberg* 14 (1901), p. 203.

9 Kroker, "Familie Ayrer," pp. 171–72.

10 A portrait of Michael Ayrer was recently discovered in a private collection; Matthias Weiss, "Die Ayrersche Wappenscheibe aus der alten Frauenkirche zu Dresden. Schweizer Glaskunst in Kursachsen," in *Die Dresdner Frauenkirche*, Jahrbuch zu ihrer Geschichte und zu ihrem archäologischen Wiederaufbau 8 (Weimar, 2002), p. 92, n. 36.

11 Erich Haenel, "Bolzenkasten und Armbrust des Kurfürsten August im historischen Museum zu Dresden," *Mitteilungen aus den sächsischen Kunstsammlungen* 1 (1910), p. 55; Sommerfeldt, "Rüstmeister in Dresden," pp. 350–52, and Sommerfeldt "Kunstbetrieb in Dresden," pp. 256–57, make no mention of Michael Ayrer, but see also Holger Richter, *Die Kunst der Armbrustmacher in Dresden* (Beucha, 2008), p. 85.

12 Kroker, "Familie Ayrer," p. 173.

13 It is possible, though less likely, that the etched decoration was added by a subsequent owner, for example, Michael Ayrer's son, also named Michael (1579–1635), who was a successful jeweler and council member in Dresden; Weiss, "Die Ayrersche Wappenscheibe," pp. 82–109.

Catalogue 37

1 Museum der Grafschaft Mark, Burg Altena, near Hagen (N2191b); unpublished.

2 Dated 1586; Stadtmuseum, Bad Urach, near Reutlingen (MU 167); Walter Röhm, *Stadtmuseum Klostermühle Bad Urach* (Bad Urach, 1990), p. 70.

3 Of the two examples in the Deutsches Historisches Museum, Berlin, one (W1114) is dated 1594, the other (W1119), 1595; unpublished.

4 There are two examples (U 144; U 147) in the Staatliche Kunstsammlungen/Rüstkammer, Dresden; U 147 is dated 1554; for U 144, see Dirk H. Breiding, "Die Armbrust-Ausstellung 'Arma Diaboli' in Prag," *Jahrblatt der Interessengemeinschaft historische Armbrust* (2012), p. 86, n. 15; for U 147, see Holger Richter, *Die Kunst der Armbrustmacher in Dresden* (Beucha, 2008), pp. 53–54.

5 Grandson Castle (C64); unpublished.

6 Národni Muzeum, Prague (inv. no. unknown); see Breiding, "Die Armbrust-Ausstellung," p. 82.

7 Skokloster Castle, near Sigtuna (6365 and 6369); for the first, signed STENCZEL HANTKE CZV BRESLA, see ibid., p. 86, n. 15.

8 Geoffrey Jenkinson collection, Guernsey; unpublished.

9 Röhm, *Stadtmuseum Klostermühle*, p. 70.

10 Personal communication, Jens Sensfelder, June and August 2011.

Catalogue 38

1 Today in the Museum für Kunst und Gewerbe, Hamburg (1975,84); Alfred Schädler, "Modell zum Zifferblatt einer Planetenuhr, 1547," in *Welt im Umbruch: Augsburg zwischen Renaissance und Barock*, vol. 2, exh. cat. (Augsburg, 1980), p. 190.

2 Erbach Castle (part of the Hessisches Landesmuseum), near Darmstadt (inv. no. unknown); unpublished. A similar example, probably also of seventeenth-century date and showing the Seven Planets on top and the signs of the zodiac on the underside, was formerly in the collections of Bayons Manor, Lincolnshire; see Julia sale, Fairfield, Maine, October 1–2, 2012, lot 2303 (present whereabouts unknown).

3 Victoria and Albert Museum, London (M225-1919); unpublished.

4 Badisches Landesmuseum, Karlsruhe (G275a); unpublished.

5 Bayerisches Nationalmuseum, Munich (inv. no. unknown); unpublished.

6 Royal Armouries Museum, Leeds (XI.24); Tower of London Armouries, *Crossbows, Treasures of the Tower* (London, 1976), p. 27.

7 See Manfred Welker, "Die Reichsstadt Nürnberg, ein Zentrum des Schmiedeeisen verarbeitenden Handwerks," in Hermann Maué et al., *Quasi Centrum Europae: Europa kauft in Nürnberg 1400–1800*, exh. cat. (Nuremberg, 2002), p. 118, fig 17.

Catalogue 39

1 Staatliche Kunstsammlungen/Rüstkammer, Dresden (belonging with crossbow U 137) and an unnumbered example; for the former, see Holger Richter, *Die Kunst der Armbrustmacher in Dresden* (Beucha, 2008), p. 36.

Catalogue 40

1 Museo Nazionale del Bargello, Florence (R.156); unpublished.

Catalogue 41

1 Examples in the Real Armería, Madrid, include J.8, J.14, J.16, J.21, J.32, J.33, J.37, J.62, J.64, J.66, J.68, J.70, J.72, J.73, J.75, J.77, J.89, J.91, J.93, J.103; see Valencia de Don Juan, Conde de [Juan Bautista Crooke y Navarrot], *Catálogo histórico-descriptivo de la Real Armería de Madrid* (Madrid, 1898),

pp. 280–91. Note especially J.89 (a crossbow) and J.90 (a pull lever), both struck with the same mark, a lion within a circle, not unlike that on the bow of cat. 6a.

2 Curtis sale, Christie, Manson & Woods, London, October 31, 1984, pp. 80–81, lot 243. The grapple is struck on either side with the letter A; other levers of the type and especially the arguments provided here suggest that the seventeenth-century date assigned to this lever in the sale catalogue appears to be too late.

3 Robert Forrer, *Die Waffensammlung des Herrn Stadtrath Rich. Zschille in Grossenhain (Sachsen)* (Berlin, n.d.), vol. 2, p. 27, nos. 1030 and 1031, pl. CCVIII.

Catalogue 42

1 Real Armería, Madrid (inv. no. unknown). Instituto de Valencia de San Juan, Madrid (178, 179); José Maria Florit y Arizcun and Francisco Javier Sánchez Cantón, *Catálogo de las armas del Instituto de Valencia de Don Juan* (Madrid, 1927), p. 134.

2 Museo de Armería de Álava, Vitoria-Gasteiz (inv. no. unknown); Museo de Bellas Artes de Álava, *Museo Provincial de Álava: Armería* (Vitoria-Gasteiz, 1967), [unnumbered figure]; and Felix Fournier and Juan Vidal-Abarca, *Museos de Armería y Heráldica Alavesa* (Vitoria-Gasteiz, 1983), p. 66.

3 Instituto de Valencia de Don Juan (177); Florit y Arizcun and Sánchez Cantón, *Catálogo de las armas*, pp. 133–34.

4 Other examples of crossbow parts signed by Hernández are found on weapons fitted with bows made by Juan Blanco (J.72) and bows signed Puebla en Madrid (J.83, J.84); Valencia de Don Juan, Conde de [Juan Bautista Crooke y Navarrot], *Catálogo histórico-descriptivo de la Real Armería de Madrid* (Madrid, 1898), pp. 281–82, 288–89.

5 Real Armería de Madrid (N.18); ibid., p. 392.

Catalogue 43

1 Arthur G. Credland, "The Pellet Bow in Europe and the East," *Journal of the Society of Archer-Antiquaries* 18 (1975), p. 13.

2 Valencia de Don Juan, Conde de [Juan Bautista Crooke y Navarrot], *Catálogo histórico-descriptivo de la Real Armería de Madrid* (Madrid, 1898), p. 392.

3 Churburg Castle, Sluderno (CH S 333); Mario Scalini and Oswald Graf Trapp, *L'armeria Trapp di Castel Coira/Die Churburger Rüstkammer/The Armoury of the Castle of Churburg* (Udine, 1996), vol. 2, p. 374. Scalini dates the Churburg lever to the late fifteenth century.

4 Art Institute of Chicago/Harding Collection (1982.3076); unpublished.

6 PROJECTILES AND THEIR STORAGE

Introduction

1 For crossbow projectiles in general, see Ralph Payne-Gallwey, *The Crossbow, Medieval and Modern, Military and Sporting: Its Construction, History and Management, with a Treatise on the Balista and Catapult of the Ancients* (London, 1903), pp. 16–19; Egon Harmuth, *Die Armbrust: Ein Handbuch* (Graz, 1986), pp. 172–78; Bernd Zimmermann, *Mittelalterliche Geschossspitzen: Kulturhistorische, archäologische und archäometallurgische Untersuchungen*, Schweizer Beiträge zur Kulturgeschichte und Archäologie des Mittelalters 26 (Basel, 2000); Valérie Serdon, *Armes du diable: Arcs et arbalètes au Moyen Âge* (Rennes, 2005), pp. 87–145.

2 Harmuth, *Die Armbrust*, pp. 179–81.

3 Ibid., p. 181.

4 Holger Richter, *Die Kunst der Armbrustmacher in Dresden* (Beucha, 2008), pp. 23–24, 43–44.

Catalogue 44

1 Museum Aargau; see Bernd Zimmermann, *Mittelalterliche Geschossspitzen: Kulturhistorische, archäologische und archäometallurgische Untersuchungen*, Schweizer Beiträge zur Kulturgeschichte und Archäologie des Mittelalters 26 (Basel, 2000), pp. 53–55 (type 2-6), 81–82.

2 Swiss National Museum, Zurich; Holger Richter, *Die Hornbogenarmbrust: Geschichte und Technik* (Ludwigshafen, 2006), p. 108, fig. 81; see also Rudolf Ritter von Haidinger, *Beitrag zur Kenntnis der Bolzen und Pfeilformen vom Beginn der Historischen Zeit bis zur Mitte des XVI. Jahrhundert* (Vienna, 1879), p. 18.

3 See the discussion of this shape (Type 5-8) in Zimmermann, *Mittelalterliche Geschossspitzen*, pp. 64–65, with a summary of the relevant literature.

4 For a detailed study of these weapons, see Jean Liebel, *Springalds and Great Crossbows*, trans. Juliet Vale, Royal Armouries Monograph 5 (Leeds, 1998).

5 Zimmermann, *Mittelalterliche Geschossspitzen*, pp. 46–48 (Type 1-5s), pp. 51–53 (Type 2-5s).

Catalogue 45

1 This mark appears to be previously unrecorded.

2 Historisches Museum, Lucerne; Swiss National Museum, Zurich; for the examples in both collections, see Bernd Zimmermann, *Mittelalterliche Geschossspitzen: Kulturhistorische, archäologische und archäometallurgische Untersuchungen*, Schweizer Beiträge zur

Kulturgeschichte und Archäologie des
Mittelalters 26 (Basel, 2000), pp. 39–40
(Type T 1-2).
3 Today in the Alte Pinakothek, Munich (5066).
4 Personal communication from Jens Sensfelder,
August 2011.

Catalogue 46

1 Three very similar bolts, marked with the
same red stripes and one "inscribed in ink
'Joseph Killell (?),'" were formerly in the
collection of Henk Visser, but their present
whereabouts are unknown; see Bonhams,
London, sale cat., November 28, 2007, p. 59,
lot 141, and Bonhams, London, sale cat., April
23, 2008, pp. 54–55, lot 206.
2 See Sven Ekdahl, "Die Armbrust im
Deutschordensland Preussen zu Beginn des 15.
Jahrhunderts," in *Fasciculi Archaeologiae
Historicae* 5 (1992), pp. 17–48, esp. pp. 18
and 29; Egon Harmuth, *Die Armbrust: Ein
Handbuch* (Graz, 1986), p. 175; and, for the
Dresden inventory, see Holger Richter, *Die
Kunst der Armbrustmacher in Dresden*
(Beucha, 2008), p. 82.

Catalogue 47

1 Helmut Nickel, "Addenda to 'Ceremonial
Arrowheads from Bohemia,'" *Metropolitan
Museum Journal* 4 (1971), p. 180.
2 The meaning of the monogram s, found on
catalogue 47a, and perhaps in reverse on 47b,
is more difficult to determine, at least when
associated with the monogram *ar*. Kalmár has
suggested a reference to Saint Sebastian, the
patron saint of archers (Johann von Kalmár,
"Pfeilspitzen als Würdezeichen," *Zeitschrift für
historische Waffen- und Kostümkunden* 15
[1939], pp. 220–21), but this is unlikely, since
Sebastian enjoyed far greater popularity
among archers in western Europe than in
Bohemia (Helmut Nickel, "Ceremonial
Arrowheads from Bohemia," *Metropolitan
Museum Journal* 1 [1968], p. 75). Similarly
improbable is a reference here to the Holy
Roman Emperor Sigismund (1368–1437),
since the monogram *ar* indicates the earliest
possible date of manufacture as December 18,
1437, nine days after Sigismund's death, when
Albert was elected king of Hungary.
3 Helmut Nickel, "Notable Acquisitions
1983–1984," *Metropolitan Museum of Art
Bulletin* (1984), pp. 20–21.
4 Helmut Nickel, "Recent Acquisitions: A
Selection 1987–1988," *Metropolitan Museum
of Art Bulletin* (1988), p. 23.
5 Military Museum, Istanbul (1597).

6 Nickel, "Recent Acquisitions: A Selection
1987–1988," p. 23.
7 Nickel, "Addenda to 'Ceremonial Arrowheads
from Bohemia,'" p. 179; and Uwe Tresp,
*Söldner aus Böhmen. Im Dienst deutscher
Fürsten: Kriegsgeschäft und Heeresorganisa-
tion im 15. Jahrhundert. Krieg in der
Geschichte 19.* (Paderborn, 2004), esp.
pp. 123–57.

Catalogue 48

1 Staatliche Kunstsammlungen/Rüstkammer,
Dresden (inv. no. unknown); unpublished.
2 Jagd- und Fischereimuseum, Munich (inv. no.
unknown); unpublished.
3 Germanisches Nationalmuseum, Nuremberg
(W2442); unpublished.
4 Philadelphia Museum of Art (1977-167-
1009); see Carl Otto Kretzschmar von
Kienbusch, *The Kretzschmar von Kienbusch
Collection of Armor and Arms* (Princeton,
1963), p. 283, no. 631.
5 Kunsthistorisches Museum/Hofjagd- und
Rüstkammer, Vienna (A134); see Bruno
Thomas and Ortwin Gamber, *Katalog der
Leibrüstkammer I. Teil. Der Zeitraum von 500
bis 1530* (Vienna, 1976), p. 202.
6 Higgins Armory Museum, Worcester, Mass.
(2006.05.1); unpublished.
7 Kunstgewerbliche Werkstätten Ernst Schmidt,
*Arms and Armor from the Atelier of Ernst
Schmidt, Munich,* ed. E. Andrew Mowbray
(Providence, 1967), pls. 18, 19, 48, and 52.

Catalogue 49

1 After its acquisition in 1969, minor repairs
were made by Robert Carroll, the late armorer
of the Arms and Armor Department; Helmut
Nickel, "Der Bolzenkasten des Hans Wagner,
Pixnschifter, 1539," *Waffen- und Kostümkunde* 13 (1971), p. 28 and n. 4. Accordingly,
most of the repairs and replacements,
including the awkwardly executed inlay on the
side panels, must have been undertaken earlier.
2 Ibid.
3 Bayerisches Nationalmuseum, Munich (R 193);
Nickel, "Der Bolzenkasten," pp. 27–28.
4 For other representations of this subject, see
ibid., pp. 30–32 (with further references), and,
in the Metropolitan Museum's collection, a
Venetian wineglass or sweetmeat cup,
ca. 1475–1500, (17.190.730a, b); Andrea
Bayer, ed., *Art and Love in Renaissance Italy*
(New York, 2008), pp. 93–94.
5 Nickel, "Der Bolzenkasten," p. 31.
6 *The Georgics of Virgil,* trans. James Rhoades
(London, 1891), p. 116.

7 Gerald J. Gruman, *A History of Ideas about
the Prolongation of Life* (New York, 2003),
pp. 35–40.
8 Jörn Reichel, *Der Spruchdichter Hans
Rosenplüt: Literatur und Leben im
Spätmittelalterlichen Nürnberg* (Stuttgart,
1998).
9 Norbert Haas, *Trinklieder des deutschen
Spätmittelalters: Philologische Studien an
Hand ausgewählter Beispiele* (Göppingen,
1991), p. 75; Hans Folz, *Die Reimpaar-
sprüche,* ed. Hanns Fischer (Munich, 1961),
[n.p.].
10 Moritz Haupt and Heinrich Hoffmann,
Altdeutsche Blätter, 2 vols. (Leipzig, 1836),
vol. 1, p. 407.
11 Eugen Heer, ed., *Der neue Støckel: Internationales Lexikon der Büchsenmacher, Feuerwaffenfabrikanten und Armbrustmacher von
1400–1900,* vol. 2 (Schwäbisch Hall, 1979),
p. 1342; Nickel, "Der Bolzenkasten," p. 33;
Erwin Schalkhausser, "Peter Peck, ein
Münchner Büchsenmacher des 16. Jahrhunderts," *Waffen- und Kostümkunde* 17, no. 1
(1974), p. 26.
12 Heinz Dopsch and Hans Spatzenegger, eds.,
Geschichte Salzburgs: Stadt und Land, 2 vols.
in 8 parts (Salzburg, 1981–91), vol. 2, part 1,
p. 1417.
13 Schalkhausser, "Peter Peck," p. 26.
14 The stock of a wheel-lock gun made in 1553
by the Munich gun maker Peter Peck has been
attributed to Hans Wagner; Nickel "Der
Bolzenkasten," p. 34. However, this stock has
since been shown to bear the monogram of
another, as yet unidentified stock maker. The
gun is today in the Bayerisches Nationalmuseum, Munich (W 1445); Schalkhausser,
"Peter Peck," p. 26, and Erwin Schalkhausser,
*Handfeuerwaffen: Jagdgewehre, Scheiben-
büchsen, Pistolen,* Kataloge des Bayerischen
Nationalmuseums München 19 (Munich,
1988), pp. 14–16.

Catalogue 50

1 Staatliche Kunstsammlungen/Rüstkammer,
Dresden (U216 [M1], U211 [M3], U205 [M4],
(inv. no. unknown) [M5], U210 [M6], U214
[M7], U206 [M8], U207 [M9], U212 [M10],
U208 [M12]); unpublished. Another
Moritzburg bolt box, with incomplete
contents and inscribed M2, is in the
Philadelphia Museum of Art (1977-167-
1011); Sotheby's sale 1970, lot 3.
2 Staatliche Kunstsammlungen/Rüstkammer,
Dresden (Lieber nos. 150, 151); Holger
Richter, *Die Kunst der Armbrustmacher in
Dresden* (Beucha, 2008), p. 89.
3 Ibid.

Suggested Reading

Josef Alm, *European Crossbows: A Survey*, trans. H. Bartlett Wells, ed. G. M. Wilson, Royal Armouries Monograph 3 (London, 1994).

Howard Blackmore, *Hunting Weapons* (London, 1972).

Claude Blair, *European and American Arms, c. 1110–1805* (New York, 1962).

Arthur G. Credland, "The Crossbow in Europe: An Historical Introduction," in W. F. Paterson, *A Guide to the Crossbow* ([Burnham], 1990), pp. 13–24.

Egon Harmuth, *Die Armbrust: Ein Handbuch* (Graz, 1986).

K. Corey Keeble, *European Crossbows in the Royal Ontario Museum, Toronto* (Bloomfield, Ont., 2008).

Guy Francis Laking, *A Record of European Armour and Arms through Seven Centuries*, intro. by Baron de Cosson, 5 vols. (London 1920–22). Repr. with new intro. by Claude Blair, 6 vols. (Cambridge, UK, 2000).

Jean Liebel, *Springalds and Great Crossbows*, trans. from the French by Juliet Vale, Royal Armouries Monograph 5 (Leeds, 1998).

William Forbes Paterson, *A Guide to the Crossbow* ([Burnham], 1990).

Ralph Payne-Gallwey, *The Crossbow, Medieval and Modern, Military and Sporting: Its Construction, History and Management, with a Treatise on the Balista and Catapult of the Ancients* (London, 1903).

Holger Richter, *Die Hornbogenarmbrust: Geschichte und Technik* (Ludwigshafen, 2006).

———, *Die Kunst der Armbrustmacher in Dresden* (Beucha, 2008).

Robert Roth, *Histoire de l'Archerie: Arc et Arbalète* (Montpellier, 1992).

Jens Sensfelder, *Crossbows in the Royal Netherlands Army Museum; with a List of Names and Marks of European Crossbow Makers, Bow Smiths and Bolt Makers/Armbruste im königlichen niederländischen Armeemuseum; mit Namens- und Markenliste europäischer Armbruster, Bogenschmiede und Bolzenmacher/Kruisbogen in het Koninklijk Nederlands Legermuseum; met een lijst van namen en merken van Europese kruisboogsmeden, boogsmeden en boutmakers*, ed. Harm Stevens (Delft, 2007).

———, *Armbruste in den Kunstsammlungen der Veste Coburg* (Coburg, 2009). Rev. repr. of an article originally published in *Jahrbuch der Coburger Landesstiftung* 48 (2003).

Valérie Serdon, *Armes du diable: Arcs et arbalètes au Moyen Âge* (Rennes, 2005).

Tower of London Armouries, *Crossbows*, Treasures of the Tower (London, 1976).

Monte S Turner, *The Not So Diabolical Crossbow: A Re-Examination of Innocent II's Supposed Ban of the Crossbow at the Second Lateran Council* (n.p., 2004).

C. Martin Wilbur, "The History of the Crossbow, Illustrated from Specimens in the United States National Museum," *The Smithsonian Institution Annual Report* 1936 (1937), pp. 429–38.

Bernd Zimmermann, *Mittelalterliche Geschossspitzen: Kulturhistorische, archäologische und archäometallurgische Untersuchungen*, Schweizer Beiträge zur Kulturgeschichte und Archäologie des Mittelalters 26 (Basel, 2000).

More specialized information may also be found in the following serial publications:

Jahrblatt der Interessengemeinschaft Historische Armbrust

Journal of the Arms and Armour Society

Journal of the Society of Archer-Antiquaries

Quaderni della Balestra

Waffen- und Kostümkunde (formerly *Zeitschrift für historische Waffenkunde, Zeitschrift für historische Waffen- und Kostümkunde*)

Catalogue References

Anderson Galleries sale 1927. *The Great Historical Collection of Arms & Armour . . . Inherited and Augmented by H. I. & R. H. Archduke Eugen, F. M.* Sale cat. Anderson Galleries, New York, March 1–5, 1927.

Blair 1962. Claude Blair, *European and American Arms, c. 1110–1805* (New York, 1962).

Boas 1999. Adrian J. Boas, *Crusader Archaeology: The Material Culture of the Latin East* (London, 1999).

Breiding 2005. Dirk H. Breiding, "Heads of Ceremonial Crossbow Bolts," in *Prague: The Crown of Bohemia, 1347–1437*, ed. Barbara Drake Boehm and Jiří Fajt, exh. cat. (New York, 2005), pp. 323–24, no. 156.

Breiding 2006. Dirk H. Breiding, "Prunkpfeilspitzen," in *Sigismundus rex et imperator: Kunst und Kultur zur Zeit Sigismunds von Luxemburg 1387–1437*, ed. Imre Takács, exh. cat. (Mainz am Rhein, 2006), pp. 446–47.

Breiding 2007. Dirk Breiding, "Eine Armbrust Graf Ulrichs des Vielgeliebten," in *Landschaft, Land und Leute: Politische Partizipation in Württemberg 1457 bis 2007*, ed. Peter Rückert, exh. cat. (Stuttgart, 2007), pp. 104–5.

Breiding 2009. Dirk Breiding, "The Crossbow of Count Ulrich V of Württemberg," *Metropolitan Museum Journal* 44 (2009), pp. 61–87.

Breiding forthcoming. Dirk Breiding, "Weapons and Armour," in *Montfort I: History, Early Research and Recent Studies*, ed. Adrian J. Boas (Leiden, forthcoming).

Christie's sale 1977. *Fine Antique Arms and Armour.* Sale cat. Christie, Manson & Woods, London, June 15, 1977.

de Cosson 1893. C[harles] A[lexander], baron de Cosson, "The Crossbow of Ulrich V. Count of Wurtemberg [*sic*], 1460, with Remarks on Its Construction," *Archaeologia*, ser. 2, 53, part 2 (January 1893), pp. 445–64.

de Cosson 1901. C[harles] A[lexander], baron de Cosson, *Le Cabinet d'armes de Maurice de Talleyrand-Périgord, duc de Dino* (Paris, 1901).

Dahlström 2011. Mikael Dahlström, "Some Thoughts about Three 15th Century German Crossbows," *Jahrblatt der Interessengemeinschaft Historische Armbrust* (2011), pp. 77–81.

Dean 1905. Bashford Dean, *Catalogue of European Arms and Armor*, Metropolitan Museum of Art Handbook 15 (New York, 1905).

Dean 1907. Bashford Dean, "Recent Accessions: Objects from the William Cruger Pell Collection," *Bulletin of the Metropolitan Museum of Art* 2, no. 3 (March 1907), p. 48.

Dean 1925. Bashford Dean, "A Crossbow of Matthias Corvinus, 1489," *The Metropolitan Museum of Art Bulletin* 20, no. 6 (June 1925), pp. 154–57.

Dean 1927. Bashford Dean, "The Exploration of a Crusader's Fortress (Montfort) in Palestine," *The Metropolitan Museum of Art Bulletin* 22, no. 9 (September 1927), pp. 5–46.

Fau sale 1884. *Objets d'art et de haute curiosité de la Renaissance et des temps modernes . . . composant l'importante collection de feu M. Joseph Fau.* Sale cat. Hôtel Drouot, Paris, March 3–8, 1884.

Finer 2005. "A Fine and Important German Sporting Crossbow, Saxon, by Johann Gottfried

Haenisch, circa 1740," *Peter Finer Catalogue* ([n.p.], 2005), no. 32.

Fischer sale 1974. *Waffenauktion.* Sale cat. Galerie Fischer, Lucerne, November 20, 1974.

Fischer sale 1975. *Waffenauktion.* Sale cat. Galerie Fischer, Lucerne, June 25, 1975.

Fischer sale 1985. *Waffenauktion.* Sale cat. Galerie Fischer, Lucerne, May 28, 1985.

Flewett 1993. W. E. Flewett, "European Combination Weapons (Crossbow-Firearms)," *Journal of the Society of Archer-Antiquaries* 36 (1993), pp. 51–70.

Flint Institute 1967. *The Art of the Armorer,* contributions by G. Stuart Hodge and Stephen V. Grancsay, exh. cat. (Flint, Mich., [1967]).

Forrer [1894]. Robert Forrer, *Die Waffensammlung des Herrn Stadtrath Rich. Zschille in Grossenhain (Sachsen),* 2 vols. (Berlin, [1894]).

Frakes 2004. Jerold C. Frakes, ed. *Early Yiddish Texts, 1100–1750: With Introduction and Commentary* (Oxford, UK, 2004).

Gay 1887–1928. Victor Gay, *Glossaire archéologique du Moyen Âge et de la Renaissance,* 2 vols. (Paris, 1887–1928). Reprint (Nendeln, Liechtenstein, 1971–74).

Grafenegg sale 1934. *Waffensaal des Schlosses Grafenegg, Herzog Viktor von Ratibor, II. Teil.* Sale cat. Galerie Fischer Auktionen, Zurich, May 2, 1934.

Grancsay 1931. Stephen V. Grancsay, *Loan Exhibition of European Arms and Armor,* exh. cat. (New York, 1931).

Grancsay 1933a. Stephen V. Grancsay, *The Bashford Dean Collection of Arms and Armor in the Metropolitan Museum of Art,* intro. by Carl Otto v. Kienbusch (Portland, Maine, 1933).

Grancsay 1933b. Stephen V. Grancsay, *Loan Exhibition of European Arms and Armor,* exh. cat. (Brooklyn, 1933).

Grancsay 1935. Stephen V. Grancsay, *Historical Arms and Armor: Twenty Plates* (New York, 1935).

Grancsay 1953. Stephen V. Grancsay, *Loan Exhibition of Medieval and Renaissance Arms and Armor from the Metropolitan Museum of Art,* exh. cat. (Los Angeles, 1953).

Grancsay 1955. Stephen V. Grancsay, *Loan Exhibition of Medieval and Renaissance Arms and Armor from the Metropolitan Museum of Art,* exh. cat. (Haggerstown, Md., 1955).

Grancsay 1964. Stephen V. Grancsay, *Arms and Armor: A Loan Exhibition from the Collection of Stephen V. Grancsay, with Important

Contributions by the Metropolitan Museum of Art, New York, and the John Woodman Higgins Armory, Worcester, Massachusetts, exh. cat. (Allentown, Pa., 1964).

Heath 1972. Ernest Gerald Heath, *The Grey Goose Wing* (Greenwich, Conn., 1972).

Helbing sale 1902. *Kunstauktions-Katalog von Hugo Helbing der vorzüglichen Sammlungen Hofrat Dr. G. J. von R. in K., Gustav Bader, Mühlhausen i.E.* Sale cat. Galerie Hugo Helbing, Munich, April 28–30, 1902.

Helbing sale 1919. *Waffen aus süddeutschem Schlossbesitz.* Sale cat. Galerie Hugo Helbing, Munich, October 20, 1919.

Hiltl 1876–77. Georg Hiltl, *Die Waffensammlung Sr. königlichen Hoheit des Prinzen Carl von Preussen,* 2 vols. (Berlin, 1876–77). Reprint (Fridingen, 1981).

Imperial Institute 1896. Imperial Institute (Great Britain), *Catalogue of Ancient Armour and Equipments of the Richard Zschille Collection,* exh. cat. (London, 1896).

Kalmár 1971. János Kalmár, *Régi magyar fegyverek* (Budapest, 1971).

Keasbey sale 1924. *Important Collection of European Arms and Armor from XI to XVIII Century: Formed by and Belonging to Henry Griffith Keasbey.* Sale cat. American Art Association, New York, December 5–6, 1924.

Krempel 1970. Ulla Krempel, "Works of Art Belonging to Rulers of Bavaria," *Apollo,* n.s., 92, no. 106 (1970), pp. 416–25.

Laking 1922. Sir Guy Francis Laking, *A Record of European Armour and Arms through Seven Centuries.* Introduction by Baron de Cosson, 5 vols. (London, 1920–22). Reprint, with a new introduction by Claude Blair. 6 vols. (Cambridge, UK, 2000).

Lepke sale 1920. *Porzellan: Meissen, China, Japan, Elfenbeinskulpturen, Gemälde und Waffen.* Sale cat. Rudolph Lepke, Berlin, October 12–14, 1920.

Lewerken 1989. Heinz-Werner Lewerken, *Kombinationswaffen des 15.–19. Jahrhunderts* (Berlin, 1989).

Mayer 1935. Joseph Ralph Mayer, *Notes on Arms and Armor,* Guide Bulletin: Museum Collections and Special Exhibitions 1 (Rochester, N.Y., 1935).

Metropolitan Museum of Art 1975. *The Secular Spirit: Life and Art at the End of the Middle Ages,* forward by Thomas Hoving, intro. by Timothy B. Husband and Jayne Hayward, exh. cat. (New York, 1975).

Metropolitan Museum of Art Guide 1983. *The Metropolitan Museum of Art Guide,* texts by Phillipe de Montebello et al., ed. Kathleen Howard (New York, 1983).

Nickel 1968. Helmut Nickel, "Ceremonial Arrowheads from Bohemia," *Metropolitan Museum Journal* 1 (1968), pp. 61–93.

Nickel 1969. Helmut Nickel, "Böhmische Prunkpfeilspitzen," *Sborník Národního Muzea v Praze. Řada A, Historie* 23 (1969), no. 3, pp. 101–63.

Nickel 1970. Helmut Nickel, "Reports of the Departments: Arms and Armor," *Metropolitan Museum of Art Bulletin,* n.s., 29, no. 2 (October 1970), pp. 64–66.

Nickel 1971a. Helmut Nickel, "Addenda to 'Ceremonial Arrow-heads from Bohemia,'" *Metropolitan Museum Journal* 4 (1971), pp. 179–81.

Nickel 1971b. Helmut Nickel, "Der Bolzenkasten des Hans Wagner, Pixnschifter, 1539," *Waffen- und Kostümkunde* 13 (1971), pp. 27–34.

Nickel 1974. Helmut Nickel, *Ullstein-Waffenbuch: Eine kulturhistorische Waffenkunde mit Markenverzeichnis* (Berlin, 1974).

Nickel 1984. Helmut Nickel, "Ceremonial Arrowhead," *Metropolitan Museum of Art—Notable Acquisitions 1983–84* (New York, 1984), p. 20.

Nickel 1986. Helmut Nickel, "Arms and Armor: Johann Gottfried Haenisch, Hunting Crossbow and Winder," *The Metropolitan Museum of Art, Recent Acquisitions: A Selection 1985–1986* (New York, 1986), p. 20.

Nickel 1988. Helmut Nickel, "Ceremonial Arrowhead," *The Metropolitan Museum of Art, Recent Acquisitions: A Selection 1987–88* (New York, 1988), p. 23.

Nickel 1989. Helmut Nickel, "Some Heraldic Fragments Found at Castle Montfort/Starkenberg in 1926, and the Arms of the Grand Master of the Teutonic Knights," *Metropolitan Museum Journal* 24 (1989), pp. 35–46.

Nickel 1991. Helmut Nickel, "Arms and Armor from the Permanent Collection," *The Metropolitan Museum of Art Bulletin,* n.s., 49, no. 1 (Summer 1991), pp. 1, 4, 9–64.

Nickel, Pyhrr, and Tarassuk 1982. Helmut Nickel, Stuart W. Pyhrr, and Leonid Tarassuk, *The Art of Chivalry: European Arms & Armor from the Metropolitan Museum of Art,* exh. cat. (New York, 1982).

Parke-Bernet sale 1969. *Works of Arts: The Jay C. Leff Collection of Chess Sets, Maiolica & Isnik Pottery, Gothic & Later Ivories, Italian Renaissance Sculpture, German Wood Carvings, Renaissance to 18th Century Bronzes.* Sale cat. Parke-Bernet, New York, November 14, 1969.

Paterson 1990. William Forbes Paterson, *A Guide to the Crossbow* ([Burnham], 1990).

Peterson 1962. Harold L. Peterson, *The Treasury of the Gun* (New York, 1962).

Priest 1940. Alan Priest, "Loans from the Collection of George D. Pratt," *The Metropolitan Museum of Art Bulletin* 35, no. 12 (December 1940), pp. 237–40.

Pyhrr 2012a. Stuart W. Pyhrr, "Armor for America: The Duc de Dino Collection," *Metropolitan Museum Journal* 47 (2012), pp. 183–230.

Pyhrr 2012b. Stuart W. Pyhrr, "Of Arms and Men: Arms and Armor at the Metropolitan, 1912–2012," *The Metropolitan Museum of Art Bulletin* 70, no. 1 (Summer 2012), pp. 1–48.

Radway 2009. Robyn Dora Radway, "In the Name of Saint George: Ivory Saddles from the Fifteenth Century" (Honors thesis, University of Central Florida, Orlando, 2009).

Richter 2006. Holger Richter, *Die Hornbogenarmbrust: Geschichte und Technik* (Ludwigshafen, 2006).

Richter 2008a. Holger Richter, "The Hänisch Family and the Crossbowmaker's Art in Dresden," *Journal of the Society of Archer-Antiquaries* 51 (2008), pp. 12–57.

Richter 2008b. Holger Richter, *Die Kunst der Armbrustmacher in Dresden* (Beucha, 2008).

von Rohr 1972. Alhedis von Rohr, "Kaminentwurf von 1533 für die Burg Trausnitz," *Berliner Museen* 22 (1972), pp. 51–53.

Schalkhausser 1974. Erwin Schalkhausser, "Peter Peck, ein Münchner Büchsenmacher des 16. Jahrhunderts," *Waffen- und Kostümkunde*, ser. 3, 17, no. 1 (1974), pp. 21–40.

Sensfelder 2007. Jens Sensfelder, *Crossbows in the Royal Netherlands Army Museum; with a List of Names and Marks of European Crossbow Makers, Bow Smiths and Bolt Makers/Armbruste im königlichen niederländischen Armeemuseum; mit Namens- und Markenliste europäischer Armbruster, Bogenschmiede und Bolzenmacher/ Kruisbogen in het Koninklijk Nederlands Legermuseum; met een lijst van namen en merken van Europese kruisboogsmeden, boogsmeden en boutmakers*, ed. Harm Stevens (Delft, 2007).

Sensfelder 2012. Jens Sensfelder, "Zur Konstruktion europäischer Armbrustschlosse," *Jahrblatt der Interessengemeinschaft Historische Armbrust* (2012), pp. 38–45.

Sotheby's sale 1922. *Catalogue of Old English & Irish Glass, Armour and Weapons, Antique Furniture, Porcelain and Pottery, etc.* Sale cat. Sotheby & Co., London, July 20–21 and 24, 1922.

Sotheby's sale 1923. *Catalogue of Armour and Weapons comprising . . . the Property of the late F. Seymour Lucas, Esq., R. A., F. S. A., etc.* Sale cat. Sotheby, Wilkinson & Hodge, London, December 5 and 7, 1923.

Sotheby's sale 1970. *Catalogue of Highly Important Arms from the Saxon Royal Collections.* Sale cat. Sotheby & Co., London, March 23, 1970.

Sotheby's sale 1987. *Arms, Armour and Militaria.* Sale cat. Sotheby & Co., London, October 28, 1987.

Spitzer 1890–93. Frédéric Spitzer, *La Collection Spitzer: Antiquité, Moyen-Âge, Renaissance*, 6 vols. (Paris, 1890–93).

Spitzer sale 1895. *Catalogue des armes et armures faisant partie de la collection Spitzer.* Sale cat. Galerie Georges Petit, Paris, June 10–14, 1895.

Spitzer sale 1929. *Medieval & Renaissance Art, Paintings, Sculpture, Armour and a Few Pieces of 18th Century Furniture.* Sale cat. Anderson Galleries, New York, January 9–12, 1929.

Stevens 1978. George M. Stevens, *Crossbows: From Thirty-Five Years with the Weapon* (n.p., 1978).

Stone 1934. George Cameron Stone, *A Glossary of the Construction, Decoration and Use of Arms and Armor in All Countries and in All Times, Together with Some Closely Related Objects* (Portland, Maine, 1934). Reprint (New York, 1961).

Thomas and Gamber 1976. Bruno Thomas and Ortwin Gamber, *Katalog der Leibrüstkammer 1. Teil, Der Zeitraum von 500 bis 1530.* Kunsthistorisches Museum, Vienna. Führer durch das Kunsthistorische Museum, no. 13 (Vienna, 1976).

Vaïsse sale 1885. *Objets d'art et de haute curiosité du Moyen-Âge, de la Renaissance et des temps modernes composant l'importante collection de M. E. Vaïsse de Marseille.* Sale cat. Hôtel Drouot, Paris, May 5–8, 1885.

Villers sale 1866. *Collection d'armes composant le cabinet de M. Villers.* Sale cat. Hôtel Drouot, Blois, April 16, 1866.

Wilson [1970]. *Art at Auction: The Year at Sotheby's & Parke Bernet, 1969–70*, ed. Phillip Wilson (New York, [1970]).

Zolnay 1971. László Zolnay, *Vadászatok a régi Magyarországon* (Budapest, 1971).

Zschille sale 1897. *Catalogue of the Collection of Armour and Arms and Hunting Equipments of Herr Richard Zschille.* Sale cat. Christie, Mason & Woods, London, January 25–February 1, 1897.

Zschille sale 1900. *R. Zschille'sche Waffensammlung.* Sale cat. Rudolph Lepke, Berlin, March 21–22, 1900.

This publication is made possible by The Carl Otto von Kienbusch Memorial Fund, the Grancsay Fund, STEGO Holding GmbH/STEGO, Inc., and Richard J. Gradkowski.

Published by The Metropolitan Museum of Art, New York
Mark Polizzotti, Publisher and Editor in Chief
Gwen Roginsky, Associate Publisher and General Manager of Publications
Peter Antony, Chief Production Manager
Michael Sittenfeld, Managing Editor
Robert Weisberg, Senior Project Manager

Edited by Alexandra Bonfante-Warren
Designed by Douglas Malicki
Production by Douglas Malicki, Jennifer van Dalsen, and Sally van Devanter
Image acquisitions and permissions by Crystal Dombrow

New photographs of works in the Metropolitan Museum's collection are by Peter Zeray, The Photograph Studio, The Metropolitan Museum of Art, New York, unless otherwise noted. Additional photograph credits: fig. 2: illustration by Douglas Malicki; figs. 7, 3.2: © The Trustees of the British Museum; fig. 13: © Victoria and Albert Museum, London; fig. 1.3: © Rheinisches Bildarchiv, Cologne; fig. 1.10: János Thuróczy [Johannes de Thurocz], *A magyarok krónikája*, Budapest: 1986; fig. 2.2: © Direção-Geral do Património Cultural/Arquivo de Documentação Fotográfica; fig. 2.4: © Philip Mould Ltd, London; figs. 2.6–2.8: X-rays taken in the Department of Objects Conservation, The Metropolitan Museum of Art; fig. 2.19: BPK, Berlin/Kupferstichkabinett, Staatliche Kunstsammlungen, Dresden/Art Resource, NY (photograph by Herbert Boswark); fig. 3.1: Sergio Guarino, and Patrizia Masini, *Pinacoteca Capitolina, Catalogo Generale*, Milan: 2006, p. 179; figs. 3.3, 5.18: © Patrimonio Nacional (Spain); fig. 3.5: © Royal Armouries; figs. 4.1, 6.1: © Bayerisches Nationalmuseum, Munich; fig. 5.1: Scala/Art Resource, NY; fig. 5.3: BPK, Berlin/Alte Pinakothek, Bayerische Staatsgemäldesammlungen, Munich/Art Resource, NY; fig. 5.5: Erich Lessing/ Art Resource, NY

Typeset in Sabon LT Std and Adobe Hebrew
Printed on 130 gsm Galery Art Silk
Separations by Professional Graphics, Inc., Rockford, Illinois
Printed and bound by VeronaLibri

Jacket illustration: *Crossbow* (cat. 22)
Frontispiece: *Pellet Crossbow* (cat. 2)

The Metropolitan Museum of Art endeavors to respect copyright in a manner consistent with its nonprofit educational mission. If you believe any material has been included in this publication improperly, please contact the Editorial Department.

The Metropolitan Museum of Art
1000 Fifth Avenue
New York, New York 10028
metmuseum.org

Distributed by
Yale University Press, New Haven and London
yalebooks.com/art
yalebooks.co.uk

Cataloging-in-Publication Data is available from the Library of Congress.

ISBN 978-1-58839-499-6 (The Metropolitan Museum of Art)
ISBN 978-0-300-19704-4 (Yale University Press)